Curtains of Light

THE SUNY SERIES
HORIZONS OF CINEMA

MURRAY POMERANCE | EDITOR

Curtains of Light
Theatrical Space in Film

George Toles

Cover image of El Silencio scene from *Mulholland Dr.* (Les Films Alain Sarde/ Asymmetrical, 2001). Courtesy PhotoFest New York.

Published by State University of New York Press, Albany

© 2021 State University of New York

All rights reserved

Printed in the United States of America

No part of this book may be used or reproduced in any manner whatsoever without written permission. No part of this book may be stored in a retrieval system or transmitted in any form or by any means including electronic, electrostatic, magnetic tape, mechanical, photocopying, recording, or otherwise without the prior permission in writing of the publisher.

For information, contact State University of New York Press, Albany, NY
www.sunypress.edu

Library of Congress Cataloging-in-Publication Data

Name: Toles, George, author.
Title: Curtains of light: theatrical space in film / George Toles.
Description: Albany : State University of New York Press [2021] | Includes bibliographical references and index.
Identifiers: ISBN 9781438484211 (hardcover : alk. paper) | ISBN 9781438484228 (pbk : alk. paper) | ISBN 9781438484235 (ebook)
Further information is available at the Library of Congress.
Library of Congress Control Number: 2021938492

10 9 8 7 6 5 4 3 2 1

For Sam, Rachel, and Thomas

Contents

List of Illustrations		ix
Acknowledgments		xiii
1	Introduction: Curtains of Light	1
2	Intoxicating Stagecraft: Billy Wilder's *The Lost Weekend* and the Mysteries of Theatre in Film	33
3	The Theatre of Aloneness in Film	69
4	Eloquent Objects, Housebound Theatre: William Wyler's *The Heiress*	107
5	Prospero Unbound: John Barrymore's Theatrical Transformations of Film Reality	141
6	Auditioning Betty in David Lynch's *Mulholland Dr.*	159
7	Theatres Rational and Irrational in Alfred Hitchcock's *Vertigo*	181
8	Stage Deaths in Film: The *Hamlet* Factor	215
Works Cited		275
Index		279

Illustrations

1.1 Eddy (Tyrone Power) prepares to traverse the pendular swing-set curtain that sways between him and Peter (Rex Thompson) in *The Eddy Duchin Story*. — 2

1.2 Everyone briefly brought together in service of play in *La Grande Illusion*. — 10

1.3 Kuang (Wang Leehom), Wong (Tang Wei), and others in *Lust, Caution*, face the abyss at the end of role-playing. — 17

1.4 "It's hard to tell where I leave off and you begin." The ambiguous space between duet and solo in *The Eddy Duchin Story*. — 31

2.1 Death dances among the upper class in *La Règle du Jeu*. — 37

2.2 Atop Busby Berkeley's cinematic perch, the women twirl below like concupiscent, kaleidoscopic cogs. — 39

2.3 Don (Ray Milland)—a few beats behind—parses his program while others tune in to *La Traviata* in *The Lost Weekend*. — 50

2.4 Don's delirium tremens transmutation of the *La Traviata* cast into a chorus of coats in *The Lost Weekend*. — 57

2.5 Don and Helen's (Jane Wyman) coat-mix-up meet-cute, soon sullied by Don's mounting thirst in *The Lost Weekend*. — 62

3.1 Maria (Maria Pia Casilio) nearly makes eye contact with us as she moves toward what's outside the frame in *Umberto D*. — 75

3.2 Anna (Lillian Gish) holds up her ring to Lennox Sanderson (Lowell Sherman), clinging to its material force in *Way Down East*.   84

3.3 Carrie (Jennifer Jones)—both grief-stricken and relieved—loses a part of herself to George's departure in *Carrie*.   90

3.4 Ruth Fowler (Sissy Spacek) beams at the completion of a successful choir rehearsal, moments before her husband, Matt (Tom Wilkinson) informs her that their son has been killed.   96

4.1 Catherine (Olivia de Havilland), alarmed to be simultaneously saved and trapped by Morris (Montgomery Clift), early in *The Heiress*.   122

4.2 Catherine responds to the heavy metallic pull of her white cameo brooch in *The Heiress*.   133

4.3 Lit by the humble incandescence of her lamp, Catherine ascends the stairs, fully entering—one pool of light at a time—her inherited abode of things in *The Heiress*.   140

5.1 Larry Renault (John Barrymore) takes in the reflection of his Hyde-like homecoming in *Dinner at Eight*.   153

5.2 Larry strikes a pose as he gathers himself for his final act in *Dinner at Eight*.   154

5.3 Slumped under a lonely spotlight, Larry relaxes before the curtain of death rises in *Dinner at Eight*.   156

6.1 Betty (Naomi Watts) basks in the beckoning glow of the Hollywood dream in *Mulholland Drive*.   160

6.2 Figures of the industry are introduced to Betty in a cramped studio office in *Mulholland Drive*.   163

6.3 Betty makes us believe during her audition in *Mulholland Drive*.   170

6.4 Rita (Laura Elena Harring) and Betty break down as they witness a performer's self-division onstage in *Mulholland Drive*.   179

7.1 "And it's all real." Scottie (James Stewart) directs Madeleine (Kim Novak) in *Vertigo*.   184

7.2 Scottie playfully proves to Midge (Barbara Bel Geddes)
that he's taking steps toward convalescence in *Vertigo*.   202

7.3 Scottie stares down an ever swirling, ever deepening loss
in *Vertigo*.   213

8.1 Simon (Bernard Siegel) bestows a final good night upon
Tito in *Laugh, Clown, Laugh*.   224

8.2 A group of curious, captivated children unwittingly watch the
swan song of Tito from the wings in *Laugh, Clown, Laugh*.   225

8.3 Professor Siletsky (Stanley Ridges)—midsalute—bends
toward death in *To Be or Not to Be*.   235

8.4 Eve (Jane Wyman) shows us both sides of herself in the
dressing room of Charlotte (Marlene Dietrich) in
Stage Fright.   258

Acknowledgments

I would like to express my gratitude to Murray Pomerance, editor of the exceptional Horizons of Cinema series at SUNY Press, for his long-term friendship and deeply encouraging support of my writing on film. He convinced me by his excitement during our initial conversation on the topic of "theatrical space in film" that there was a book in it, and that I must go ahead with it. Over the next two years, he continued to push me, with his special brand of insistence, to stay the course.

It is difficult for me to believe that I have been directing and acting in plays for more than a half century. In the course of this inexhaustibly exhilarating education, I have had ample opportunity to think practically and theoretically about the nature of theatre space and its diverse uses. Gilberto Perez, in his study of the rhetoric of film, *The Eloquent Screen*, provides some phrases about rhetorical "figures of arrangement" onscreen that apply equally well to our engagement with space onstage: "where it puts us, how it orients us, how it makes us feel" (xxi). He also reminds us of the importance of "spectator specifics" in any consideration of the deployment of film technique. What film form is able to do to spectators, what it enables them to experience in a narrative, is crucially dependent on what they "bring to it" (xxi). I have had a great many enlightening conversations over the years with theatre collaborators, valued colleagues at the University of Manitoba, and students who have shaped my thinking about the theatrical issues I investigate in this book. My screenwriting collaborations with director Guy Maddin and the courses I have taught in Acting for the Camera and Film Production (with the assistance of Jim Agapito) have enabled me to explore, at a very concrete level, how film and theatre space both inform each other, and how they establish separate realms. I shall name here just a small number of those whose contributions to my understanding of theatre and film interaction have been significant: Ross McMillan, Gregory Klymkiw, Steve Snyder, Cliff Eyland, Pam Perkins, Robert Smith, Chris Johnson, William Kerr, Sharon Bajer, Shereen Jerrett, Jane Burpee, Heather Roberts, Jane Walker, Kerri Woloszyn, Ivan Henwood, Stephanie Moroz, Kevin Ramberran, Christopher Read, Ray Strachan, Gordon Tanner, John Landreville, Carolyn Gray, Pamela Percy, Maria Lamont, Margaret Anne MacLeod, Peter Bailey, Mark McKinney, Sabrina Briggs, Mark West, Ryan McBride, Mariianne Mays Wiebe, Kirsty Cameron, Sherab Yalomo, Gretchen Derige, Trevor Mowchun, Dave McGregor, and Rob Gardiner. Early drafts of the chapters in *Curtains of Light* benefited immeasurably from the advice and appreciation of Charles Warren, Victor Perkins, Jeff Crouse, Edward Gallafant, Doug Pye, Steven Rybin, Joe McElhaney, Matt Sorrento, Faye McIntyre, Andrew Klevan, and Justus Nieland. Special thanks to Michael Silverblatt, legendary host of Bookworm at KCRW Los Angeles (a close friend since my undergraduate days at the University of Buffalo) and Jonah Corne, who have been willing, indeed inspiring, readers of so many of the essays on literature and film that I have written over the course of my career.

Mention should also be made here of some of those practitioners of film scholarship whose devotion to aesthetic matters and fine prose have helped fortify my belief that there is not only a high value in close reading, but a deeply discerning audience for it: Stanley Cavell, William Rothman, Jason Jacobs, Adrian Martin, James Morrison, David Greven, Carol Vernallis, Lesley Brill, Robert Pippin, Keri Walsh, Dominic Lash, Seth Barry Watter, Alex Clayton, Corey Creekmur, Donna Kornhaber, Cynthia Baron, David LaRocca, Noa Steimatsky, Susan Smith, Geoffrey O'Brien, Stephane Duckett, Elliott Logan, Jonathan Rosenbaum, and R. Barton Palmer. I am grateful to Rob Gardiner for his assistance in selecting the frame grabs for this book, and to Gretchen Derige for her meticulous work on the index. At SUNY Press, James Peltz, Eileen Nizer, and John Raymond have given me invaluable guidance in navigating the process of preparing the manuscript for publication and organizing a marketing strategy.

A number of the chapters in *Curtains of Light* have been previously published in different, somewhat abbreviated forms. I gratefully acknowledge the publishers' permission to reprint this material: "Auditioning Betty in Mulholland Dr." appeared in *Film Quarterly* 58, no. 1 (Fall 2004): 2–13; "Eloquent Objects, Mesmerizing Commodities in William Wyler's *The Heiress*" first appeared in the special Stanley Cavell issue, issue 22, edited by Jeff Crouse, of *Film International* 4, no. 4 (2006): 48–67;

"Intoxicating Stagecraft: Billy Wilder's *The Lost Weekend* and the Mysteries of Theatre in Film" appeared in issue 7 of *Movie: A Journal of Movie Criticism*, edited by Edward Gallafent and Andrew Klevan (May 2017): 40–56; "The Theatre of Aloneness in Film" was published in *Raritan* 27, no. 1 (Summer 2017): 132–155; "Prospero Unbound: John Barrymore's Theatrical Transformations of Cinema Reality" appeared as a chapter in *Hamlet Goes to Hollywood: John Barrymore and the Acting Tradition Onscreen*, edited by Steve Rybin and Murray Pomerance (Edinburgh: Edinburgh University Press, 2017), 98–108.

This book is dedicated to my three enormously gifted, beloved children, Sam, Rachel, and Thomas, who are all wise in the ways of film and larger than life theatrical personages in their own right. My wife, Melissa Steele, is my ideal first reader as well as my unfailingly judicious and unchallengeable editor, who has read everything I've written without yet saying, "Hold! Enough!" She is the light of my life, the glory of my days, possessing a creative imagination, a capacity for love, and a fierce humor that warrant the word astonishing.

1

Introduction

Curtains of Light

THE FIRST STIRRINGS OF THIS project occurred during a late night screening of George Sidney's 1956 musical biography, *The Eddy Duchin Story*. I was forcibly struck, during the film's concluding scene—in which Tyrone Power's Eddy is metaphorically, and heartbreakingly, ushered into death through a subtle elimination of his figure from a theatrical performance in progress—by the ways in which film space, and the space designated for a musical number inside it, kept confusing their boundaries and transforming into each other. The film's final resolution of its tension depends on the viewer experiencing film reality and the theatrical frame as deeply, inextricably, connected. In the film's closing shot, once Eddy has surprisingly disappeared from the film's ongoing present tense, the camera slowly pulls away from the interior space where Eddy's son, Peter (Rex Thompson), continues to play what had moments before been a duet with his father on two joined pianos, and takes us onto an outdoor patio, where we view the living room through an interior frame. Chiquita (Victoria Shaw), Eddy's wife, is also present in the room with Peter, and both seem to have moved past the point in time where Eddy has died and have arrived at an acceptance of loss. There has been no cut to separate this "later time" from the just concluded moment when Eddy was still in their midst. It is impossible, while watching this brief passage, which boldly announces its artifice with no sacrifice of the reality of the enveloping tragedy, to fix the boundary between theatre and film realms. It is equally impossible to say in which realm the emotional power and weight of the ending resides.

One of my central guiding questions throughout this study is "What counts as theatre space in film, and how are we led to recognize it?" Gilles Deleuze, discussing Jean Renoir's films, refers to the challenge of determining "where theatre leaves off, and life begins" (86). This manner of presenting the difficulty is misconceived. Theatre is not a realm apart from film life but ever in the midst of it, penetrating its borders stealthily and then often sneaking away again without having been recognized, or caught. Call it the half-light of theatre space's presence. Jacques Rivette, more discerningly, has addressed the ways in which cinema, in its various summons to theatre or its conscious attending to it, is able to "examine its own operations yet also maintain as part of its self-reflection, a certain distance" (Kouvaros, 133). Film can look at itself obliquely, in the form of an "elder brother," theatre: "If you take a subject which deals with the theatre to any extent at all, you're dealing with the truth of the cinema. . . . Because that [truth] is the subject of truth and lies, and there is no other in the cinema: it is necessarily a questioning about truth, with means that are necessarily untruthful" (Rivette, 27). Being on film

Figure 1.1. Eddy (Tyrone Power) prepares to traverse the pendular swing-set curtain that sways between him and Peter (Rex Thompson) in *The Eddy Duchin Story*.

is never far removed from being onstage, with the significant (but not decisive) removal of the "live event." The arrival of theatre consciousness at any narrative juncture in a film can, as André Bazin noted, "open a distance within its flow of representation," or provide an accessible bridge to conditions where gathering experiential pressures in a dramatic scene temporarily relax their grip (quoted in Kouvaros, 134).

Consider, for example, the memorable first appearance of Kathie Moffat (Jane Greer) in Jacques Tourneur's great film noir, *Out of the Past* (1947). It is part of a flashback sequence narrated by the erstwhile detective investigator in hiding, Jeff Markham (Robert Mitchum). Kathie appears to him, as if in a vision, as he rouses himself from a doze in an Acapulco cantina. He talks about himself in voice-over as we watch him, seated at a table in a beer-fragrant darkness, seeing her, clad in a white, low-cut dress with a matching broad-brimmed hat, "coming out of the sun." She is viewed by us at a distance as she walks toward him casually, taking no notice of Jeff (or so it seems) as he beholds her in a charged moment that is nearly out of time. There is no hint of a theatre stage in this realistic environment, but one vital component of the scene is certainly the resemblance to a theatrical entrance. Kathie will have a series of such entrances as the film proceeds, all linked with the first one and conveying the possibility that each reappearance has the dispensation of a new beginning, a will to start over, and the power to bring it off. In the second half of the film, when Jeff's vision of her is infected with skepticism and irony, he begins to duplicate Kathie's tactic of making sudden, destabilizing theatrical entrances himself, attempting to catch her in moments of exposure, unprepared. During Kathie's first entrance, as Chris Fujiwara notes in his study of director Tourneur, *The Cinema of Nightfall*, "she is surrounded by an aura of illusion, reinforced from several directions: by the sunlight that silhouettes her, by the [visible background] presence of a cinema across the street [the Cine Pico], and by the fact that Jeff has just awakened from a doze" in his regimen of waiting (145). Jeff, in fact, comments, in furtherance of the atmosphere of illusion, that it was music from the movie playing in the next door theatre that jarred him awake.

What sort of deceptiveness does the presence of a movie theatre in a movie betoken? And how are we to distinguish between those image-based appearances that aren't to be trusted from those that are? Surely the film wishes us to accept the material surroundings of the cantina, the location of Acapulco, Jeff's position at the table, and the fact of Kathie's arrival from the sun-drenched street as substantial impressions, drawn from Jeff's reliable memory. He is clearly endeavoring to tell the truth in this flashback confession to his current girlfriend, Ann (Virginia Huston). I think Fujiwara is suggesting that the "aura of illusion" is chiefly created by the sudden highlighting of a theatrical effect in Kathie's entrance, as though there is a dividing line that we are suddenly conscious of between the film reality that exists before the entrance and something conjured up in the midst of it. It is assuredly not the case that Kathie, at this stage, is orchestrating her movement in order to manipulate Jeff's perceptions. We have no indication that she has spotted him prior to sitting down at her own table. Nor is she nervously anticipating the presence of a possible pursuer. She appears to be absorbed in her own thoughts, and not conscious, despite the care with which she has dressed herself, of being watched. Finally, she is viewed from a distance. We have no close range access to her face or possible intentions until after she has seated herself. It is Jeff's way of apprehending her, and narrating the impact of this first visual encounter, that instigates our awareness of theatre. The time of Kathie's role-playing with Jeff is "not yet." But given the fact that he is telling a story of romantic betrayal and disappointment, it is unsurprising that his narration and the images accompanying it mingle erotic enchantment with the forecasting idea of theatrical equivocation. Theatre is an avenue of perception subtly introduced in *Out of the Past*, which is equal parts Jeff's projection and a need to get at some dimensions of Kathie that still, at the narrating moment, are concealed from him.

Another memorable instance of the conversion of realistic film space into theatre space occurs late in Fritz Lang's *You Only Live Once* (1937). Joan Graham (Sylvia Sidney) and her husband, Eddie Taylor (Henry Fonda), are both being pursued by the police after Eddie has killed a priest during a prison escape, and both of them have performed a string of small crimes in order to survive on the road, en route to Canada. At one point we see Joan deciding to purchase a pack of cigarettes for her husband from an outdoor vending machine at the Star Motel, where she has briefly stopped. We watch her pause to make a selection and find the necessary change in what is clearly designated as film reality: an ordinary, nocturnal setting. A sound then wakens the motel manager from sleep. His room is situated very close to the machine, and he can observe Joan through a barred window next to the chair where he is resting. At first he observes her neutrally, in much the same fashion as the film spectator in the previous shot. She is not completely in focus for him because he is not fully alert and has set aside his glasses. When he puts on his glasses and looks again, he considers her more carefully, thinking he may recognize her. After a short pause, he shifts his gaze to a wanted poster containing her photo. When his gaze returns to Joan through the cross barred window frame, the space has yielded to what he takes to be his new, incriminating knowledge of who she is. The frame acquires a theatrical dimension as her identity is suddenly caught in an immediate, fixed role: that of a wanted criminal. From the beginning of the film, Joan's husband, Eddie, has been consistently viewed by nearly everyone he encounters as, first, an ex-con and three time loser, and, after his trial for robbery and murder, as one who belongs on death row. The film leads us to understand how constricting and reductive these mechanical modes of recognition are. The motel manager's gradual ability to focus on Joan outside his window is the first time that Joan is subjected to the deadly, dehumanizing gaze that is Eddie's habitual torment. Joan, however, does not detect the motel manager's presence, and as a result of his isolated judgment, a police trap is set up that will swiftly result in the pair's violent death. The motel manager's seeing action therefore carries a significance far greater than we realize as it happens. What is striking is how Joan is lifted from involvement in ordinary, considerate behavior into a visual position where she is stripped of everything except for an impression of furtive villainy. We partake of the motel manager's gaze, and involuntarily assent to his transformation of Joan into an object of suspicion, one who inhabits the theatre of criminality, glimpsed in the nick of time. The motel manager thinks that his vision is improving steadily in the course of the scene. And, considered literally, it is. But in another sense, the more he is able to see theatrically, the less he sees of Joan as a person. Lang does not distort her previous appearance in the course of this complex sighting and emotional deforming, but the way her action is imprisoned in the window frame establishes a fittingly artificial space for her to occupy.

Theatre space can also be invoked or brought into play to magically repair damage, or to renegotiate possibilities for human connection even after performances of particular needs and intentions have failed. The dilemma of "how to act" or how to manipulate another's behavior in a chosen environment can make a viewer aware that a sudden manifestation of stage illusion or self-conscious theatrical deportment has been achieved.

I have already introduced the fact of theatre's frequent resort to surreptitious interventions and effects. There are innumerable instances in film where theatre space is not entirely concealed, but is rather half-hidden, partially recognized by characters but its potential for release, imaginative transformation of life circumstances, and the prerogatives arising from artifice not fully grasped. And this "hiding" of the theatrical space can equally involve the film's viewer. A telling example of persistent spectator blindness to the theatrical form can be found in Hitchcock's *Vertigo*. All of Madeleine's early, silent appearances to Scottie when he is pursuing her as a detective—in Ernie's, the flower shop, the art gallery, the McKittrick Hotel, Fort Point, the Golden Gate Bridge—are theatrical stagings, carefully blocked and performed for an audience of one. But a spectator of *Vertigo* might watch the film many times without thinking of Madeleine's behavior and movements in terms of the various stages that director Gavin Elster has chosen for Scottie's controlled beholding of her. Theatre is also undeniably part of Madeleine's secret preparation and is a major key to self-presentation, including her eventual disclosures through speech, but Hitchcock does not oblige us to dwell on the boundaries between the film's lifeworld and its theatrical venues. The latter are real spaces temporarily claimed and made over for theatrical use. In another Hitchcock film, *North by Northwest* (1959), Phillip Vandamm (James Mason) famously observes to Roger Thornhill (Cary Grant): "With such expert play-acting, you make this very room a theatre." Roger, at this point, does not regard himself as an actor at all, and offers his thin and unpersuasive real life credentials to his disbelieving captors. The metaphysical twist in the scene is that the room in which Thornhill is struggling to make credible claims to another identity is in fact a stage set, and his interrogators are themselves performing assumed roles as they endeavor to make Thornhill divulge his undercover activity as George Kaplan. Once again, the spectator takes the room in which the action is set at face value: it is part of the home of the adversary who is mistakenly grilling Thornhill for information that he doesn't possess. The stagecraft is concealed from the viewer until later on, and when Thornhill returns to the space in police custody and is confronted with its alien properties as he attempts to locate items that were previously there, it paradoxically acquires the attributes of a stage set in the process of revealing its true domestic character. Theatre space in cinema is frequently veiled in this way because too forceful an insistence on it throws the film world's own reality status into doubt. We should be conscious of film as representation, imitation, and illusion, but at the same time the film world should preserve its independent "thereness."

Theatre can be productively understood as a permanent adjoining room or neighboring property to film reality. It affords different kinds of escape routes from film reality's somewhat weightier, more consequential events. Theatre space, in effect, offers an escape within the escape of movie storytelling. In *The Eddy Duchin Story* scenes I will later analyze, theatre initially promises and secures a temporary bulwark against insupportable grief. Yet the theatre framework can at any point disavow its kinship with make-believe, freedom, and safe performance. Death as well as other brutal facts can suddenly tear the curtain of stage illusion and mingle with the performance in progress. Theatre space can supply a mirror to any sort of situation film narrative shows us, a mirror that can expose pretense, deflate exorbitant claims, yet just as easily supply transcendent alternatives to characters who feel themselves constricted and earthbound. It is the double-sided ministry of theatre frames to provide routes leading away from difficulty or further into it. Theatre space can extend the ground of privacy in film or rob this seeming privacy of meaningfulness. It can be a force to be fought against—as characters resist absorption into "playacting" or a too thin, artificial engagement with others—or a force to aspire to, a means of self-enlargement and a vision of life creatively heightened and intensified. It is both linked to reductive machinery and to the defeat of mechanical determinism. The energy of theatre can prove a curse to film characters as well as be an antidote to what ails them. In short, in Heideggerian terms, the separation from the film world that theatre offers is an indispensable key to our knowledge of that world.

Theatre space has been abundantly employed for political purposes throughout the history of drama. My investigations of theatre environments in film seldom take up political questions directly. The reading of Ernst Lubitsch's *To Be or Not to Be* (1942) in the final chapter and my brief commentary on the skeleton and ghost danse macabre performance in Jean Renoir's *La Règle du Jeu* (1939) are the notable exceptions. My general avoidance of scenes that make political intentions overt is not due to a fear that ideology might muddy the waters of my predominantly aesthetic approach. Quite the reverse: I worried that ideological affirmations and the commitment to decisive unmaskings and exposure of the lies at work in every narrative edifice would introduce too many presumptions of clarity, and a faith in the disentangling power of a perspective *outside* the work itself, that I do not share. Too often political readings of films regard the mesmerizing force of particulars as a blinding lure that obscures a larger, more general and solid truth, say, concerning Guy Debord's "society of the spectacle." Why focus on the interplay of character actions, images, cuts, and camera movements, to an inordinate degree, if a film's attitudes and values are typically in league with the delusions of a corrupt system? If there were a theatrical space in Elia Kazan's *On the Waterfront* (1954) that could disclose, in Brechtian fashion, the film's collusion with the defenders of informing to the House Un-American Activities Committee in the McCarthy era, then could we not disregard the distracting conflicts and depictions of ambiguous human striving in the rest of the narrative? If we know that the pods in Don Siegel's *Invasion of the Body Snatchers* (1956) are strongly related to Cold War fears about Communism's power to "brainwash" and rob us of our individuality, then why examine aspects of the story or presentation that do not align with this allegory? The political idea, which reveals what the puzzle means, cannot only rise above the workings of imagery and the mysteries of audience involvement and discovery, but also renders inconsequential the moment-to-moment experience of the film. An ideological critique, in its frequently pervasive skepticism, offers a critical vantage point seemingly uncontaminated by the narrative's own reductions and simplifications. Art's details camouflage and confound the clarity to which the politically alert spectator has access.

The space of political inquiry, like theatrical space, aspires to stand separate from a film world's reality, but unlike the theatrical space that I am concerned with, it doesn't wish to be vulnerably and disorientingly in dialogue with it. It generally aspires to have the upper hand and a well-insulated perspective. Political critique does not feel obliged to take fictional beings with full seriousness. They can be treated as simple constructs. Theatre, in contrast, is deeply implicated in the imperatives to believe, to get inside character feeling and predicaments, to imagine with intense specificity. Dominic Lash, in his recent study, *The Cinema of Disorientation: Inviting Confusion*, movingly reminds us that "ultimately, fictional beings exist by means of our *solicitude*, the care or attention we give them" (34). The translation of narrative meaning that political readings offer, though it seems related to figurative language, is in its effects quite stubbornly explicit. Paradoxically, the political critique feels licensed to extract a binding literalism from the slippery free play of image and sound storytelling. By literal I mean here political "face value," a practice that opts for standing still and establishing a firm line, rather than continued imaginative motion. Because it begins with skepticism about what narrative is (wittingly or unwittingly) constructed to disguise or conceal, the act of finding the key to the mechanism, one that frequently upholds the logic of an oppressive social system, tends to freeze the work's power of supplementary meaningful revelation. The critique is in danger of becoming a wall to stare at, rather than a generator of questions that will lead us back into the film for a fresh seeking, an amplification of the viewing experience.

The kinds of political theatre scenes that most attract me in film work in very similar ways to those that have no pronounced ideological objectives. A space is established in which clarity appears to be emerging, with considerable force, and then elements are reversed within the staged situation to unsettle the clarity, and finally eradicate it. The undoing of clarity might happen in the following ways. The film world adjacent to the stage sometimes provides a deceptive, intoxicating, and dangerous impression that the assembled theatre audience is not only absorbed but "remade" (permanently transformed) by the scene they are privileged to witness. But then old patterns swiftly assert themselves, and the apparent gains leak away. On other occasions, performers become so hypnotized by their newfound sense of command, as they dictate the terms of political reality from their onstage "elevation," that they break connection and faith with the show itself. They surrender, impetuously and single-mindedly, to a higher goal, trying to communicate something large and true, and in the process producing the opposite result. Without understanding what has happened, they end up with something small and false.

An outstanding example of this second phenomenon is depicted in Jean Renoir's *La Grande Illusion* (1937). A group of French and English soldiers held captive at Hallbach, a World War I German prisoner of war camp, have been rehearsing a musical revue, approved by the camp authorities, as a morale builder. Most of the scenes set in this camp subtly develop a theme of brotherhood. Class distinctions and nationalist prejudices, over time, are significantly reduced. Neither captors nor prisoners experience favorable conditions, and food and other creature comforts are in short supply. On the day the revue is scheduled to be performed, the French prisoners receive discouraging news about a defeat in the war world beyond the camp. Douaumont, a strategically important fort in a French village, has fallen. The prisoners do not cancel the show. Its audience includes not only French, English, and Russian soldiers, but German guards and officers as well. We see two acts of comic and musical entertainment, a delightful mingling of prepared numbers and improvisation. The French actor, Cartier (Julien Carette), at one point makes an affectionate flip of his coattails to one of the English showgirls (a chorus in drag singing "A Long Way to Tipperary") and then warmly acknowledges by name Arthur, a German guard sitting close to the stage. The theatre presentation allows for a charming regression to the effortless, giddy make-believe and dress-up of childhood (Boeldieu, an aristocratic career officer who declines to join the revels, describes the show preparations as "soldiers playing at being children"). The staged numbers are not especially well organized, and seem rough edged, open to accident and a convivial rush of improvisational energy. In spite of themselves, the soldiers lose touch with their anxiety about the capture of Douaumont. When the actor invites the mixed audience to join him in a chorus of "Marguerite" while he capers about exuberantly in his oversized evening coat with a huge fake carnation in his lapel, the barriers separating the various groups comprising the audience are conjured away. No one declines the invitation to join in.

The stage is a place that encourages a mixture of discipline and happy accident. At times we can't be sure whether a bit of business is planned or a delightful mistake (say, the sudden collapse to the floor of a large cardboard limousine as Cartier, the actor who has driven it on stage and honked its painted horn, struggles to step out of it). The atmosphere onstage welcomes interruptions of every sort and abrupt changes of plans. What it cannot so readily accommodate is the explosive announcement of war news. Marechal (Jean Gabin), a French

Figure 1.2. Everyone briefly brought together in service of play in *La Grande Illusion*.

officer who is waiting offstage to perform stagehand duties, discovers while glancing through a German newspaper that Douaumont has been recaptured. Unable to contain his excitement, he shouts "Stop the show! Stop the show!" as Cartier the actor is comically balanced in the arms of a prima donna in drag, who waves her plumed fan. Just before the actor has time to complete a pratfall, Marechal appears amid the bewildered group of performers, who come to a sudden halt in their intensely illuminated, gaudy stage space, their sequined dresses sparkling amid a messy assortment of makeshift theatrical props. Marechal replaces the show with his news about the French victory. The audience of prisoners rises en masse as one of the English soldiers, heavily made up and in a loosening gown, removes his wig and instructs the stage orchestra to shift its musical number to "La Marseillaise." The camera tracks away from this singer and seeks, in characteristic Renoir fashion, to adjust to the new performance circumstances, as though it had no foreknowledge of this interruption and must play "catch up" uncertainly as the soldiers attempt to shed their theatrical roles in favor of the military parts that preceded them. The camera attends to Marechal in particular as he crosses the stage recklessly to sing a portion of "La Marseillaise" with angry defiance to the ground level box occupied by German officers. His performed attack achieves its goal, briefly intimidating the officers into vacating the theatre. The camera continues its tentative scanning of the audience, showing us a rigid front row of soldiers standing at attention while singing in unison. The camera then circles back to the wigless English singer standing among the musicians. He has begun to smile at the achievement of solidarity. Almost immediately, as if in response to the cue of his smile, the camera reverses direction once more to arrive at a stationary view of standing rows of soldiers, solemnly completing *their* number as we observe the decorations hanging from the ceiling above them that were originally connected to the musical revue. As Alexander Sesonske has argued, the "Marseillaise" roughly replaces the comic stage pieces and singing that had "excluded no one." The French anthem brings the prisoners into impassioned, if mechanized, accord, but it also "marks the deepest penetration of war into [this] place, dividing the room into two hostile groups" (293).

Unlike a similar spontaneous eruption of "La Marseillaise" in *Casablanca*, the scene in *La Grande Illusion* does not surrender to the triumphal sentiment that Marechal pushes into being. The scene lies caught, as it were, between competing forms of theatre, and does not settle the question of which manifestation of togetherness has more substance and value. The immediate consequence of Marechal's "invasion" and conquest of the stage is that he is arrested, separated from his fellow prisoners, and punished with an agonizing stretch of solitary confinement. We soon learn that Douaumont's victory was nearly as short-lived as the singing of the anthem. The fortress is soon recaptured by the Germans, and as one of the French prisoners ruefully observes: "There can't be much left of it." Renoir does not make us choose between the impulse that leads Marechal and the soldiers to sabotage the carefree atmosphere of the revue and the impulse to briefly forget the pain of confinement and loss that the show itself promotes. The rehearsed entertainment has modest but valid claims to set against war loyalties; it fosters easy comradeship, a belief in the transforming power of imagination, and supplies vivid comic reminders of a world in which different kinds of human connection and order are available.

In the scene immediately preceding the musical revue, a group of six French soldiers—three in partial costume for the play—are standing by a window watching young German recruits below marching to drum and fife music. One of the observers is Boeldieu (Pierre Fresnay), a French officer who declares his dislike of performing in theatricals (though he will later be fatally wounded while staging one of his own). When another soldier says "you have to admit" that the theatrical ritual of the march is "stirring," Boeldieu replies after listening for a while in silence that he loathes the sound of fifes. The first soldier speaks a second time of his attraction to it: "Still, it gets to you." Marechal enters the conversation at this point, quietly contending that it is not the music that gets to you but the accompanying rhythm made by feet marching in unison. He is describing in advance the effect that will be produced by his shifting of the entertainment from musical comedy to "La Marseillaise." The way the soldiers stand at attention while proudly, combatively singing it produces a hypnotic effect akin to the offscreen sound of marching in this episode. The impresario of the revue, Cartier, is so entranced by the theatre of "men marching to music" in the window scene that he forgets that he has left a hot iron resting on a costume he has been preparing. A sudden billow of smoke arises, drawing his and the other men's attention back to the materials for their show. This interruption reverses the direction of the mood shift of Marechal's demand to "Stop the show" after discovering that Douaumont has been recaptured. In this scene the marching is at fault for breaking the group's concentration on theatre matters. But Cartier swiftly transforms his distress about the burnt costume by launching into a jubilant, comic song. As the scene ends the lighter mode of theatre prevails over the temptations of war-related kinds of exhibition.

A second example of a political theatre scene whose clarity is no sooner powerfully established than it is displaced by several stronger instances of confusion and ironic deception occurs in the early stages of Ang Lee's *Lust, Caution* (2007). In 1938, during the Japanese invasion and occupation of China, Wang Chia-Chih (Tang Wei) is persuaded to join a student theatre group in Hong Kong University (still a free city). The theatre group is committed to doing patriotic plays that will encourage audiences to resist their Japanese enemy, and not collaborate with them. The director of the company, K'uang Yu-min (Wang Leehom), tells Wang that the citizens of Hong Kong must be awakened from their "lives of leisure" with "drums and gongs." Wang has already suffered substantial personal losses. After her mother's death, her father moved to England, taking her brother with him. She has waited two years to be given a chance to join them in London, but for obscure reasons it has never happened. She receives a letter from him announcing that he has remarried, without making any commitment during the ever-intensifying war to rescue her. Wang accepts the invitation to act, though she has no previous sense of an aptitude for theatre. We are given indications of her strong desire to find fantasy escape routes from her present circumstances, and from an identity whose contours feel dim and stifled. She has a taste for sentimental American films. We see her weeping uncontrollably in a darkened movie house as she watches Ingrid Bergman and Leslie Howard conduct their adulterous affair in *Intermezzo* (1939). The darkness of the movie theatre melds with the darkness of the stage in an earlier scene. Wang is again an enraptured spectator as her director arranges a lighting cue. He becomes larger than life in the silent space he occupies, positioned halfway between reality and a saving artifice.

On the night that the play is presented to an overflowing house, Wang sits onstage in peasant clothes awaiting her first cue to action. She seems initially uncertain of her ability to take hold of the character she is playing and make her suffering real to the intimidating crowd, and perhaps to herself. She scans the space in front of her, bordered by footlights and filled with invisible audience members, as she tries to become involved with her stage prop knitting. The setting she inhabits has a primitive, amateur look. She hears a knock behind her, which releases her from her fear and orients her to the scripted crisis. The scene has to do with mistaken identity. A wounded officer, played by director K'uang, is brought into the peasant dwelling by the Village

Chief. Mother Chao, the mother of Wang's character, has been driven mad by grief, and confuses the wounded officer with her son, who has been killed in combat. It is Wang's task not to be lost in war delirium and despair and to tend to the wounded officer until he recovers. In the following scene further identity confusion is introduced. K'uang has organized this play and become active in student politics in part because his own brother died fighting the Japanese after graduation. His parents forbade him to follow his brother's lead and enlist in the army. Wang's onstage character, Little Hong, has a speech to deliver about her own dead brother, and how every time K'uang's officer kills an enemy, he will be avenging her fallen sibling. She movingly discusses the pledge she made to her brother to look after her mother rather than join the fight herself. During this oration, we are shown a crew member off-stage providing music accompaniment from an LP on a turntable; the sound is amplified through the hall by a microphone held close to the turntable. (Director Ang Lee wants us to see all the elements of the theatre apparatus before demonstrating his power to elicit our belief in the stage illusion.) Wang gives K'uang the scarf she had knitted for her dead brother. As she speaks of her deep attachment to this fallen hero, with increasingly powerful conviction, while unbidden tears run down her cheeks, she suddenly shifts focus and informs K'uang's character of how much he reminds her of her brother. At this point K'uang briefly loses his place in the fiction, overpowered by the sense that Wang is seeing his own lost brother in him, and summoning him back to life. This brother, she passionately concludes, "was our only hope." Wang then links the brother's fate to China's ongoing struggle, and need to prevail. "China will not fail," she cries out, with a burning transcendent faith, as she bows down before K'uang. K'uang is dressed in his officer's uniform, and Wang's upper garment is a sparkling red, which enhances the effect of fire in her address. As they kneel side by side, we have time to observe how much their present stage set resembles a prison. Wang looks out to the audience and makes her appeal to the generations to come. An elderly audience member is so intensely affected that he rises to his feet, raises his arm, and shouts in solidarity with Wang: "China will not fail." Other audience members are immediately galvanized to take up the cry and soon the entire audience is on its feet, with upraised fists, joined in the determination to take China back from its Japanese invaders. The noise of the crowd gives way to the sound of a whooshing blaze as we cut to an outdoor celebration where the celebrating cast are cooking noodles over high flames. After joyfully confirming each other's sense of the political importance of this theatrical production, they walk together through the rainy streets of Hong Kong, singing a patriotic hymn: "And take into our hands the fate of our land! Huge waves, huge waves, forever surging!"

Shortly afterward, we are returned to the stage in daylight, whose set now consists of a grouping of leafless trees backed by a painted stone wall and a white mountainous landscape overseen by three static clouds. Wang enters and wanders, bewildered, through the realm of illusion, as though the new props were part of a play she did not recognize. She is searching for her fellow actors, but pauses midstage and begins to hear the sound of cicadas and a light wind in the constructed landscape. Her friends have gathered for a private conference on the balcony at the rear of the theatre. It is crucial to note that they have not severed their connection with theatrical space. They are placed well above the stage and at a distance from it but the "elevation" they occupy is still intimately related to the theatre setting. The balcony's sole architectural function is to provide a clear view of what transpires below within the proscenium frame. Wang hears her name, and turns to face the group of her stage collaborators who are all watching her from behind the balcony divider. She is summoned to "come up" where they are and listen to them make plans to assassinate Mr. Yee (Tony Leung), a high-ranking Chinese collaborator with the Japanese invaders who is affiliated with a fake peace movement, and is currently hiding out in Hong Kong. In his effort to persuade the group to become part of the armed resistance, K'uang distinguishes between "shouting slogans" and "wrenching tears from an audience" and eliminating a "flesh-and-blood traitor." The group's new agenda will involve "real acting—you will [need to] change your identities and become part of Yee's group." The members of the company quickly agree to go "all in" with the dangerous scheme of deceiving the enemy about who they are, and join hands to indicate there will be no reversing course once this larger scale drama gets under way. Wang is the final person to place her hand into the circle. Before doing so, she exchanges a look with K'uang. He is still closely associated in her mind with the character he has played onstage. It is the Chinese officer that she has half fallen in love with, and Wang for him is the young woman in the drama who tearfully regarded him as the heroic fighter carrying on in the cause to which her brother was sacrificed. When her hand touches his as she pledges her readiness to join, her hand displays the shyness that comes from making first physical contact with a prospective lover.

From this point forward in *Lust, Caution*, there is no easy means of separating committed political action from theatrical performance. Every advance toward the group's goal depends on a deeper level of belief in the roles they take on, and (especially in Wang's case) a performance in which there is not a single word, look, or gesture that can break the illusion and awaken skepticism. A surrender to the part's intricate, consuming demands is literally a matter of life or death. Wang's barely formed, hopelessly confined, despair-laden "real self" is gradually displaced and swallowed up by the role of "Mai Tai-Tai," the mistress of Mr. Yee. Her final lostness in this role and the unthinkability of relinquishing it eventually leads her to betray (on an ungovernable "character" impulse) all of those she stands with in common cause on the theatre balcony. In a quarry outside Shanghai in 1942, after all of them have been arrested and brought to the edge of a pit for execution, they are lined up close to the edge. K'uang and Wang are once more kneeling, as they did in the climactic scene of their patriotic play. They exchange a final look. The headlights from trucks provide an equivalent of footlight illumination for the final dramatic encounter. As they and the others face the blackness of the quarry, the camera briefly leans forward, peering into its obscure depth vertiginously. The pit that will momentarily become their grave acquires the look and feel of the darkened, waiting audience on opening night.

In *Lust, Caution*, as in *La Grande Illusion*, the manifestations of political thought and action are so tightly intertwined with theatre issues as to render them almost indistinguishable. The political does not sit higher on the ladder of value or bring us nearer to reality. Neither does it provide a secure release from the serpentine spell-weaving of theatrical largesse. The space of theatre in film can accommodate any form of truth-telling without losing its grounding in imagination and dream.

Returning to our first example of spaces claimed for theatrical transformation in *The Eddy Duchin Story*, I am repeatedly struck by the way in which director George Sidney links theatre awareness to Eddy's increasing consciousness of rapidly approaching death. Eddy is still part of his world, but in the concluding scenes he has a persistent sense of it receding from his grasp. The elements around him have acquired the poignant deceptiveness of simulacra, stand-ins for a material environment that can no longer impose its solidity persuasively. He must stage the declaration of his "involuntary goodbye" to his son, Peter, in a manner that will not prove empty of consolation, but both the playground setting of his initial revelation and the sumptuously artificial domestic setting

Figure 1.3. Kuang (Wang Leehom), Wong (Tang Wei), and others in *Lust, Caution* face the abyss at the end of role-playing.

in which Peter's new knowledge is consolidated seem imbued with the father's accelerating sense of ghostliness. The two stages Eddy inhabits for his farewell appearances in life seem, by some feat of death magic, to have crossed to the other side, in advance of his own departure, as though already beyond living reach. Theater becomes the container of forms that are being taken away from him while Eddy still, as in a dream, lays claim to them.

Let us return to the scene in which Eddy and Peter are walking through a Central Park playground in New York. The father is seeking an appropriate setting in which to make a speech to his twelve-year-old son about the fact that he will soon die from leukemia. How can he best present this information in such a way that he might spare Peter some portion of a life-altering shock, followed by immeasurable pain? Without any overt break with the tenets of realism observed in this film's sometimes stylized world, the playground elements began to assert, very quietly, certain theatre prerogatives. The various familiar forms—monkey bars, slide, and swings—beheld through a mild, autumnal chill, soon become wedded to Eddy's solemn performance duty. Peter's initial pleasure in the remembered activities of the playground gives way to an angry repudiation of their innocent associations, once he begins to hear and misunderstand Eddy's prepared but awkwardly delivered "script." The playground forms have collaborated with Eddy in setting Peter up for betrayal. He had instinctively surrendered to the setting's reminders and assurance of safety. It is a milieu designated for imaginative escape, which revives Peter's sense of freedom and gives him an expansive sense of the person he is becoming. The child, in the ensuing reversal, must abruptly turn against the playground "deception." His manner of doing so leads him to adopt a theatrical role himself. Only dimly comprehending the import of Eddy's words, he strives to defend himself from the fear that his father, yet again, intends to abandon him. The theatre connection in this scene is further established by Peter's exclamation as they arrive at this location that this was the onetime site of Central Park Casino, where Eddy became a star performer in the 1930s. Peter alludes to the now vanished building and its implied stage. Eddy's own undisclosed illness links his imminent end to the disappearance of the building in which he first found his audience. Peter, before receiving inklings of his father's dark news, turns the playground into a make-believe casino by using the slide as an entrance to his own little stage. The base of the slide becomes a piano bench as he briefly mimes one of Eddy's performances from the old days. The bounds of the playground mark out an area for the father's mentally rehearsed revelation scene, one that, in its solid affirmation of childhood liberty and self-direction, will work to contain the dread of what Eddy must impart. The setting has its own separate voice, if you like, countering thoughts of collapse with an insistence on resilience and manageability. The film does not insist that we concentrate on the theatrical aspects of the playground space. It is possible, even likely, that the emergence of theatre space within this happened-upon segment of Central Park reality—reality under the sign of cinema—will be overlooked by the film spectator.

 Let us consider the more realistic elements of the scene more closely. The afternoon is overcast, with hints of a gathering storm, but the weather does not seem linked to Eddy's predicament, as in so many melodramas, but neutral and aloof. As Eddy and Peter move from monkey bars to slide to a row of swings in the play area, we sense an autumnal chill in the air. The damp walkways suggest a recent rain that may soon start up again. The scene will end before there is a decisive shift or release of storm elements. In the middle distance is a fountain in which several light, rising plumes of water are visible. The display seems forlornly excessive, given the absence of onlookers. When Peter speaks about the vanished Central Park casino, the fountain in the background combines with the talk to evoke, uninsistently, the transience of all human endeavor. The water and mist have usurped the space once occupied by the obliterated casino, and, of course, carry no memory of it. The playground area, as I noted earlier, is not depicted in theatrical terms, but the association with the creative imagination and the performance of children's games is unavoidably intimated.

Peter feels a trifle old for the slide, swings, and bars and seems to be wondering, briefly and with a measure of surprise, if he has outgrown them. We see this in his attitude toward play. He says nothing about his distance from once immediate, unselfconscious pleasures but there is a hint of effort in his "entering in." He seizes the bars instinctively when he comes near them, and conjures up a fantasy as he climbs the slide. But the fantasy is part of his now real life as an aspiring musician. When he mimes playing the piano after using the slide, he is imagining how his father felt playing on the casino stage when it still existed. Since we understand what Eddy's son will learn at any moment, we feel that his cheerful miming of piano playing as he sits at the base of the slide marks his last carefree experience of "transition" in the landscape of childhood before being banished from it. Eddy has been separated from Peter, intentionally, for nearly all of the boy's life. (For years he blamed him for Peter's beloved mother's death, which happened shortly after he was born. Band tours and extended military service in the Second World War have kept father and son steadily apart. Until very recently they have been strangers, and the fragility of their recently established bond persists.) As the two commence discussion of another impending paternal absence while they sit on adjoining benches, it strikes Peter that Eddy is planning to abandon him once more. When he concludes that his father is about to embark on another very long trip, of Eddy's own choosing, he rises and walks away from him, getting as far as the row of park swings. Clumsily, and with barely restrained anguish, Peter attempts to play the part of one who doesn't care about his father's decisions, seeking to revive the protective guise of his former genuine estrangement from him. As Eddy begs his son to listen to him, Peter—his back turned to his parent—moves along the line of swings, thrusting them all in motion as he exclaims "No! No! No!" With this gesture, Peter breaks the cover of his insulation, and sets the whole world of childhood into a protesting jangle. The swings that measure the literal distance between Eddy and Peter also remind us here of the swinging child's dream of total freedom, loosening the ties of earth and gravity, and lifting one up toward a beckoning sky.

An audible wind has arisen as Peter moves past the gauntlet of swings, and the trees in the distance sway in submission to the wind's gathering force. Instead of swing freedom, the gusty air communicates desolation and defeat. Everything of value in Peter's small domain, all hopes of stability and deliverance, seem, from the boy's pared down perspective, about to be swept away. His father calls out that he is leaving Peter this time against his will. Peter looks back at his father through the turbulent stir of empty, moving swings and shouts that what he is saying is not true: "There's no one who can tell you what to do." Eddy's response is to approach his son through the ever-more ghostly succession of swings, which seem intent on striking him as he closes the gap, as though in protest against his right to assert his love. Eddy takes possession of the final, motionless swing, seating himself there and at last referring directly to his terminal illness as the reason he can't be with Peter much longer. Eddy asks Peter, whose back is again turned to him as he audibly begins to weep, whether he understands now. The question is immeasurable, since it encompasses not only the fact of impending death, and the irreversible resumption of separation, but the unfathomable reasons why this looming tragedy must be so. "Why," he might as well be asking, "is this ghastly, ironic turn of events ours to share?" Peter faces his father and says, with wholly warranted hesitation, "Yes, I think I understand." Then Peter returns to his father, who remains on the swing, and the two embrace, as Peter helplessly repeats the word "Daddy," that he has so recently come to terms with and accepted. Peter surrenders whatever is left of a protected childhood in this scorching recognition. The play structures and their benevolent assurance of imaginative escape become tied, through a negating transformation of theatre elements, to the implacable fixity of death.

It is worth noting that as the playground theatre episode draws to a close, the viewer is able to observe, behind the embracing father and son, several swings near the one Eddy is seated on that are still in motion. The scene that follows, and will conclude the film, attempts, by means of overt and hidden theatrical devices, to build upon this "swing potential" for the resuscitation of life energy, in a setting "gripped" by the awareness of inescapable death. In certain respects, the narrative solution of how to reduce the impression of senseless horror in Eddy's passing is a simple one. Peter, like Eddy, is a musician—an unusually gifted pianist who has absorbed his father's musical standards and his style of playing. If the scene depicts father and son performing a duet together, the viewer can quite easily be led to feel that the father's spirit will be kept alive by the legacy of "shared music," which Peter already carries within him and will be able to demonstrate visually onscreen. However, the scene that we are given, while containing these anticipated elements, carries us ultimately into much stranger territory. The advance and retreat of an ever more intricate theatrical awareness enlarges the scene's emotional power and its entanglement with undispelled death consciousness. Allowing the action to put unusual pressure on the values (continuity, preservation) that the film wishes to uphold, and to make theatre as inescapable as death, moves the scene well beyond the reach of familiar genre conventions.

As Eddy and Peter return home from the park, the scene transition places us inside the large foyer of the Duchin home. Our point of view has shifted to Chiquita, Eddy's second wife and the longtime nanny/teacher/surrogate mother for Peter. She emerges—as if summoned by the father and son's hopeless, tearful embrace on the swing—through a doorway overhung by a theatrical curtain. We are given time to notice framed paintings on the wall, from Eddy's extensive art collection. We may briefly dwell on Eddy's connoisseurship, and how his residence bears even in its hallway and alcoves the forceful imprint of his artistic taste—his desire to fill every space with beauty, pattern, a sense of harmony. Chiquita's dress is split between elegant formal attire on the upper half of her body and a plain rumpled white apron below it, which gives clear reference to dinner preparation, and more important, ongoing ordinary life. The camera begins to move with her as she passes in front of an ornate curving staircase leading upstairs, which lightly echoes the fantasy of ascent in the just finished encounter with children's swings. She halts in a long hallway connected to a series of doors. We watch with her as she attends, with seeming foreknowledge of their return, to the opening of the front door. We hear the door open before it is shown to us. Then we observe Eddy and Peter enter from a distance that emphasizes their mutual smallness in relation to Chiquita. There is no cut to divide us from Chiquita's clairvoyant waiting presence and perspective. We may discern the prominent shadow of Chiquita projected on the wall pointing in the direction of the returning pair as she pauses near the staircase. The shadow theatrically divides the living wife from the part of her that, at this moment of her loved ones' return, is acutely mindful of mortality: Eddy's certainly, and perhaps her own as well. Eddy has come through the distant front entrance first, and his arrival is staged as a disappearing act. He is little more than a gray blur moving out of frame as we gaze with Chiquita at Peter, who halts in the doorway. Eddy reappears to place his hand on Peter's shoulder (still observed from Chiquita's vantage point), urging him forward as, in a gesture of quiet import, he closes the door behind them, then removes his hat.

Peter runs through the hallway to embrace Chiquita, and the first cut of the scene provides us with a medium two shot of their hug from which Eddy, through a subtle reframing, is pointedly excluded. A brief, silent acknowledgment that Eddy has told Peter of his sickness during their walk is conveyed through Chiquita's look toward Eddy and her expression. Peter's head is pressed against Chiquita, prolonging their hug as Chiquita, without Peter's awareness, searches out Eddy's face for this revelation. The first, full view of Eddy in the scene is from his wife's point of view as he nods to her, while standing at another windowed door threshold, with one hand in his pocket. A pattern is established early in the scene of figures eerily appearing and then vanishing from view—metaphysical hide-and-seek, with alternating privileged vantage points. Placed beside Chiquita is an ornate foyer mirror, which notably does not reflect anything but a bare alcove wall. In a few moments Eddy will peer into this mirror himself. Without director Sidney underscoring the absence of reflection, the effect of the "empty mirror' will delicately persist. As Chiquita mentions how she is "filling in for the cook's day off," she touches Peter's face and comments as she leaves him that he knows what that means. Much attention is given here, as in the park episode, to what Peter is now ready to understand and voluntarily accept as the burden of grown-up knowledge. Chiquita's walking out of the frame toward the kitchen as she talks about "knowing" conveys to Peter that she is aware of what Eddy has told him. Her self-conscious way of leaving the room appears, to him, and to us, as both an ordinary, familiar activity and one replete with difficult new sensations.

Once she has gone, the camera settles on Peter watching his father, who has again disappeared from camera view. The boy struggles to find words that confirm something that he now freshly realizes: "I'll take care of her, Dad." When we cut to Eddy, his back is initially turned away. He has just completed his look into the mirror, which reflects curtains arranged as if for a presentation, as well as unlit candles on a table. As I previously noted, the mirror image carries no trace of Eddy, who gazes at Peter as he hears him speak of the future, a time after Eddy is gone. Eddy seems momentarily shaken by the reminder of his own tenuous hold on life in this perfectly ordered home, and distressed at the thought of the load that his son already feels obliged to take on. After a lengthy pause, his solution to his own bafflement is to propose a "little double piano," which means playing with Peter across from him at a separate keyboard in a living room version of theatre space. Eddy's suggestion has several overlapping implications. Like Chiquita making dinner preparations,

Eddy reminds Peter of a pleasurable daily ritual, a routine available to both of them at once, that is still in place. Eddy's designated role in the performance is one he continues to fill, with comfortable proficiency. Eddy thinks that the piano duet will also lighten the present strain and uncertainty of communicating for both of them. "Playing together" may supply a temporary escape route from dark thoughts.

Another lengthy shot commences with the camera stationed inside the living room, anticipating the pair's movement through it. Eddy extends his arm to Peter, beckoning him forward as the two still occupy the foyer. The ascending stairway is included in the background of the shot, another barely stressed allusion to Eddy's impending departure from this "grounded" setting. Father and son make an almost formal theatrical entrance through a large interior frame, with latticed folding doors. Eddy's hand rests on Peter's shoulder as he leads him toward the piano. The theatre space defined by the two back-to-back grand pianos is not yet disclosed by the moving camera. Enough of a piano frame appears, however, for us to assume that Peter is standing next to the player's bench. Let us note here a marked division between spaces belonging to film reality and theatre reality that will prove of paramount importance not only in the rest of this closing scene, but in my study of theatre in film as a whole. Film reality composes a world for us in which the lives of the characters unfold. Eddy and Peter are as bound to the appearances, laws, and given circumstances of this film world as viewers are bound to the world they occupy beyond the cinematic frame.

Theatre space, as I have previously noted, offers a dispensation or temporary release from the space understood as film reality, in the same way that film reality is an abridgment, simplification, and imaginative alternative to the reality we experience outside the movie. Theatre space is seemingly less weighty, less burdened with consequence and enduring commitment than the film space adjacent to it. It is a space designed, like a conjurer's testing ground, for illusion, swift rearrangements, playfulness, games, provisional attachments, rehearsal, hiding, volatile unmasking, and of course performances. These performances are calculated for the pleasure and sometimes disquieting enlightenment of spectators, both within the film and "on the other side." What sort of protection does the overt quality of performance confer? Theatre allows ordinarily for more control than is possible in the messy contingencies striving beyond its borders. Theatre often knows its future, the final, agreed upon shape of things to come. When theatre action is in progress, film reality enters a kind of suspension. It waits to resume, off to one side, as it were. Theatre, in its parallel workings, often gains additional credence for the imperatives of film reality, while simultaneously retaining the prerogative of calling film's reality claims into question.

In the segments of *The Eddy Duchin Story* we have examined so far, theatrical space and performance have not yet been fully declared, but they have unobtrusively insinuated themselves into the Central Park playground and the slippery, evanescent materials specified as the interior of the Duchin home. The camera halts midway through its revelation of the double piano stage in Eddy's living room so that we can casually examine the attributes of this spacious chamber in their literal functions as a film environment, before the theatrical usurpation of the room causes its affiliations with hard facts and settled conditions to melt away. Eddy stands behind his son as they arrive at the glimpsed piano frame. In answer to Peter's uncertainty about what to do next, Eddy clasps his shoulders. In line with Eddy's determination to give as much of himself to his son as possible in the waning time left to them, he presents Peter with a ring he is wearing. Eddy's attention is drawn to the ring when his hand stiffens in an illness-related spasm. The father removes the ring from his own hand, then wordlessly attaches it to Peter's wedding ring finger. The open lid of the grand piano creates a dark triangle filling the right side of the frame and the keyboard area adds a long wedge of darkness that extends across the entire base of the image. Eddy and Peter are briefly enclosed within this dark outline, as though the instrument itself were helplessly allied with encroaching death. The portion of the room visible beyond the pair is showily opulent, in a manner that seems self-sufficient and disconnected from the living occupants. Paintings line the wall, and we also observe framed family photos, a massive, thriving leafy plant, and a pair of matching yellow chairs that all by themselves declare a readiness for evening parties and glittering company. The living room overall feels immured in a separate existence, one that is social and perhaps proudly artificial, proclaiming interests quite removed from the acutely vulnerable father and son in their midst.

As Peter contemplates the ring on his finger, he sits down on his piano bench and the no longer paused camera movement in the shot resumes, following Eddy as he crosses to the mirroring piano adjoining Peter's. The tracking shot also opens up the living room space further, disclosing its full expanse and, more significantly, its previously concealed resemblance to a stage set. In the background another open doorway comes into view, affording the viewer partial access to the dining room, which will soon figure prominently, with Chiquita's reappearance in the scene. The camera completes its reframing when Eddy is seated at his own piano. He begins to play a Duchin arrangement of Chopin's well-known Nocturne in E flat major. We are granted close-ups here of Eddy gazing across the piano divide at his son, appearing anxious that Peter pick up his cue, thereby exchanging the role of mournful spectator for that of a fellow performer. Peter does not meet his father's look in the subsequent POV shot from Eddy's perspective. His face is momentarily hidden from us. He is possibly still thinking about the gift of the ring and what it signifies. Or he may be staring uncertainly at the keyboard, immobilized by a fresh attack of grief. The close-ups in this brief back-and-forth are both boxed in by the raised piano lids, which supply a subtle additional emotional weight and pressure. The lids are propped up, and thus open, for now, but they could so easily be lowered. On the third close-up, Eddy facially performs a willed ebullience as he announces "Music by Duchin." The next shot restores our feeling of the stage set, framing both performers from a moderately high angle as Peter joins Eddy in his pursuit of the Chopin melody and mood. At this point Peter offers no more than a simple bass line accompaniment to his father's more demanding presentation.

I will insist once again on the powerful suggestiveness of the conversion of this living room into a theatre space. Theatrical modes of perception and involvement, with their own associations and conventions, begin to displace our sense of film reality, dwelling just past the borders of this performing area. We are aware that the two pianists are performing a familiar piece for each other, one they have worked out together on previous occasions. For both of them, initially at least, there is no larger, implied audience. But the camera placement calls another audience into being for the film spectator, one that the spectator imagines herself joined to. It does not need a direct acknowledgment or any supplementary character recognition to be convincingly established. The implied viewers for the Chopin performance, as the piece gets under way, are linked to all the live theatre events we have witnessed in Eddy's nightclubs and ballrooms throughout the narrative. Our "way of seeing" incorporates past full houses, which hover invisibly. We also maintain a consciousness of the intimacy of the duet and its removal from the collective gaze. We balance the two perspectives of audience support system (the movie audience) and poignant isolation from it.

A second audience area is then created on the other side of the pianos with Chiquita's re-entrance through the dining room, galvanizing the background within this magically expansive chamber. Without the camera abandoning its theatre space vantage point, it signals her presence in the distance, carrying a tray of food and setting it on the dining table. Once she has set the serving tray down, it seems that she becomes alert to the music for the first time. The impact of this dawning attentiveness would be much reduced if she were not a small figure in the background. Chiquita, oddly, removes her apron and places it on the back of one of the dining room chairs. It is as if, by so doing, she has completed "dressing up" in formal attire for the special concert taking place that evening. Her floral print skirt echoes and amplifies the painting of flowers and the floral arrangement that dominate the dining room setting, as we discover in the next shot, with the camera positioned in front of the dining room doorway. The abundance of flowers is linked to the first time in the narrative that Duchin plays the Chopin Nocturne. He is practicing it by himself while Marjorie Oelrichs (Kim Novak), his eventual first wife, hears him while adjusting a floral arrangement on a table prepared for dinner guests. The music captures her attention and she walks over to Eddy, and engages him in conversation about the piece, which he identifies for her as he continues to work on it. His love story with Marjorie commences at this moment of shared appreciation. Marjorie, like Eddy, dies young, in her case shortly after giving birth to Peter. It is crucial for the full effect of the scene that we see Chiquita linking up in ghostly fashion with Marjorie and the two of them sharing the role of listener-spectator. Chiquita's approach to Eddy is a recapitulation of Marjorie's. As we near the end of Eddy's "story," we are returned, musically, to his beginning. The all-important audience member, Chiquita, is singled out as she draws near to the interior stage from the other side of the screen than that occupied by the movie audience. The film spectator views this "mirroring" spectator presence through the looking glass of the theatre frame, a frame quietly suffused with ghostliness. Chiquita's gaze is fixed unwaveringly on her husband, but she remains alone in the composition for some time. The music, which continues to play, affords us access to Eddy's presence, where her look is pointed. The music becomes a stand-in or surrogate version of Eddy. And Chiquita's spectatorial work includes holding the reality of the film world together. She is both within the performance space and outside of it, monitoring the progress of the piano duet, and initiating the slow conversion of the physical person, Eddy, into an image—a movie image that is also theatre image, and a theatre image that is becoming a memory of him playing for his son. The memory, in turn, becomes the music that is an enduring "live" presence and force, not to be lost.

After Chiquita's nine-second approach to her offscreen husband, and concentrated scrutiny of him, Eddy at last reappears. He is once again placed in the penned-in piano frame, which director Sidney employed in the previous close-up shots of Eddy urging Peter to join him in the duet. Eddy does not interrupt the flow of the Chopin melody as he sends Chiquita a brief glance, conveying the message "All here is as it was before. We have found our place." Chiquita's eyes then shift forward, almost as though she were taking account of us, the theatre spectators on the other side of the pianos. Then, with the theatre space perspective restored and the performance continuing, Chiquita changes direction and moves to Peter's side of the frame, silently seating herself behind him on the arm of a chair. Her selection of the arm as her resting place makes her position as audience member feel tentative and unresolved. As she sits, Eddy completes his statement of the melody, and with no clear signal passes the task of restatement and elaboration to his son, who seems freed momentarily of a sense of his father's crisis as well as his own. He is caught up instead in Chopin's demands. The Duchin version of the Nocturne simplifies and "sweetens" it, but Peter's playing holds the sentiment of the main theme in check, allowing Chopin's requirement of a certain detachment from the melancholy to emerge, and an acceptance of whatever suggestion of loss the music inescapably carries. A curious additional ghostly element arises at this point in the dining room background. The theatre space perspective of the shot continues but our survey of the scene catches on the white apron Chiquita earlier left on the back of a chair. One of its dangling white ties has begun to move all by itself as a kind of metronome. It also calls to mind the motion of the swing in the previous park scene.

Eddy has stopped playing temporarily and rises to join Chiquita at Peter's end of the stage. The apron tie functions most expressively as an apparitional replacement for Eddy's vacated spot at the keyboard. Its silent, back and forth movement on the red chair in the depth of the frame continues as Eddy crosses to observe Peter's playing at close range. His final destination in this walk is Chiquita. He stands behind her, pressing her arms tightly as both of them watch Peter. At this point the stage once again disappears from view. What displaces it is a shot of the two privileged audience members, Eddy and Chiquita—commemorated, for a few moments, as reactors. They are equally committed to finding each other and allowing the music to connect both of them to their son, who (because he is out of view) becomes wholly fused with his playing. The performance rescues him from aloneness. Eddy and Chiquita are given their own desired seclusion and privacy for a close-up kiss, while Peter's music flows forward as an undersong. His concentration on playing (while offscreen) frees the parent listeners to concentrate on their persistence—for the time being—as a loving couple.

As the music builds, Eddy's awareness is refocused on Peter at the keyboard. He sits beside him as Peter continues to climb to the daunting peak of the Nocturne. Even while Eddy speaks ("You're getting awfully good, son. It's hard to tell where I leave off and you begin."), kisses his cheek, and strokes his hair, Peter presses on with his performance. Eddy's words—the last he will speak in the film—are worth examining for their muted, double-edged significance. Construed benignly, as the father surely intends them to be, Peter is being told that he already possesses the skill to keep Eddy present in his musical performances for others. The implication is that "I have nothing more to teach you. When you play in my manner, I will be with you. My accompaniment is embedded in your own phrasing, rhythm, and way of expressing yourself." But his praise also addresses, in a faint whisper, the curse of imitation. "No one, if you continue in this fashion, will be able to discern the difference between us. You will be the shadow performer preserving my legacy. To the extent that you break away from my example, the collective memory of the Eddy Duchin style will be diminished."

The fact that the piece being played in the scene is Duchin's "soft" romantic revision of Chopin encourages us to think about imitation both as benefit and hindrance. One of the ways in which theatre space exerts its own logic and imperious demands in this closing scene is in the felt pressure that Peter not lose his resolve—and finish the Chopin Nocturne for the implied audience that the movie spectator becomes part of. It is as though the presence of the film's spectators in the Duchin living room theatre is being inwardly acknowledged by Peter as he continues to play, reassuring us with his capacity to bear the challenge of performing in the midst of grief and to see the Chopin through to the end. When Eddy has finished offering his verbal approval, he rises and once more disappears from the frame. A disquieting two shot marks his new absence. Peter watches him in close-up as Eddy presumably widens the physical distance separating them. To the right of Peter an immobile Chiquita torso appears, with her head out of frame. The body seems to metamorphose for the duration of the shot into Peter's birth mother, Marjorie. The more forceful suggested presence of Marjorie completes the idea that was initiated with the revelation of Chiquita's floral print skirt and its associations with Marjorie hearing Eddy playing the Nocturne for the first time. At this juncture perhaps Peter fully absorbs the realization that his father's death is a repetition of an earlier huge, unfathomably senseless deprivation. He interrupts his performance, and lowers his head, undoubtedly paralyzed by sorrow. Eddy suddenly appears in the boxed piano wedge at his end of the stage, alert to the silence and the attendant despair it betokens. He glances in Chiquita's direction. In a linked point-of-view close-up, her tearstained face returns his gaze, momentarily helpless before the new stasis and predicament, where Peter's wounds are freshly exposed. Chiquita's face makes her physically present once more, but her tears encompass the fact of Marjorie's absence here.

Eddy appears as powerless as Chiquita to intervene and solve the riddle of his dying. Then his out of view hands, seeming to summon a will of their own, demand Peter's response with sharp, petitioning chords. "We are in the midst of a performance. It is not finished," Eddy signals musically to his child. "We have an obligation to complete it. The audience's needs take precedence over either of us." By theatre logic, we are made to feel that this unseen audience is yet again within the room, asserting its desires for resolution, satisfying closure, in spite of Eddy and Peter's impaired focus and interfering emotion. Once Eddy has made a strong bid to move from anxious suspension to the relief of Chopin's melody, Peter's own sense of performing mandate is restored as well. They exchange looks of conspiratorial reassurance through the piano frame tunnel that divides them, and together turn the Chopin Nocturne, through an excess of spirit, into a declaration of triumph. The reserve and "held in check" mournfulness of the piece are nearly swept away through their joint exertion. Behind Eddy, when director Sidney opts for a longer view from Peter's vantage point, we notice theatre style curtains that are not fully drawn shut. An open window space leading the eye out to the patio supplies another interior frame between the curtains. The next shot is a decisive, jarring break with all previous perspectives on the scene. We are granted an overhead view of Eddy's hands and arms confidently completing further phrases until one of the hands is stricken with pain. Eddy lifts it from the keys, then the other, and both are suddenly frozen in midair. In a further extension of psychic attunement, Chiquita's face erupts into view at the instant Eddy's hands recoil from the keyboard, as though the shock has been transmitted to her nervous system and consciousness directly. She lowers her head. Yet again we watch a spectator surrogate losing the ability to maintain viewing connection to a performance.

Peter's music continues through this break, as though he is not yet mindful of his father's "departure" from the duet. We return to the overview shot of Eddy's hands. One of them closes into a fist, then both retreat from the frame. Although we do not know it, the withdrawal of Eddy's hands here marks his final disappearance from the film's world. The hands' realization that they must "give way" before the concert is concluded covertly functions as Eddy's theatrical moment of death. When the hands—and, by subtle metonymic implication, Eddy—have made their discreet exit, the camera, with no cutting, continues to move, as if in personalized response to the music. It also accomplishes a second feat of converting space into a softly accelerated flow of time. As the camera rises up, we behold Peter over the vista of Eddy's now vacated piano, still intent on bringing the Nocturne to a close. He performs as though his father remained present within the room. Nothing in his manner suggests an awareness on his part that a disruption has taken place. Chiquita, now seated behind him, has regained her spectator composure, and concentrates without internal division on her son's playing. She rises, moves close to him, and places one hand on his shoulder, repeating unconsciously a gesture that Eddy has employed earlier in the scene. The touch appears to remind Peter that he has an appreciative listener. It does not lead him back to memory echoes and regret. His attitude seems to be: "Ah, Chiquita is here. I hadn't noticed. I am not performing to an empty house." He looks up at her briefly—the camera still at a distance, including our prior view of the father's piano—and casually acknowledges her before returning his performer's attention to the keyboard. Chiquita turns away from him, then elects to stay in the room, crossing behind an empty blue chair. She is visibly caught up in the Chopin, meditatively so, and the piano has now acquired an orchestral accompaniment. Neither Chiquita nor Peter express any direct awareness of the just established visual fact of Eddy's absence, from the room and from their lives. Time has somehow passed to such a point that grief has stabilized. It is an element of existence for the pair, to be sure, but the space they inhabit feels large enough for other things than the shock of death, and its accompanying emptiness. They appear to us finally in a kind of calm, mysterious trance of well-being.

From the moment that Eddy's hands withdrew from the frame, the camera movement has been continuous. After the camera lifts to locate Peter and then Chiquita in a sphere that is at once theatrical and domestically restored, it slowly retreats from the living room. Its final vantage point on the interior scene is from outside the house on the rear patio flanked by a profusion of Marjorie-related flowers. Eddy has made a theatrical "sleight of hand" exit from the performing space and then the camera has fused with him, becoming simultaneously his watchful,

Figure 1.4. "It's hard to tell where I leave off and you begin." The ambiguous space between duet and solo in *The Eddy Duchin Story*.

presiding spirit, the sudden disquieting chill of his abrupt vanishing, and a shared perspective with the viewing audience. We keep Peter in our sights as long as possible. Then we, like Eddy, must take our leave. The film's theatrical end clandestinely takes on the hard facts of Eddy's dying, and allows us painfully, tearfully to absorb it without any break of the stage performance in progress, and the surrounding artifice. Theatre ends the film as a stronger version of what we have previously regarded as film reality.

2

Intoxicating Stagecraft

Billy Wilder's *The Lost Weekend* and the Mysteries of Theatre in Film

SIEGFRIED KRACAUER HAS famously argued, in *Theory of Film: The Redemption of Physical Reality*, that the theatrical story, whose prototype is the theatrical play, presents a continual threat to film's highest mandate: to let material reality enter the film frame in its own right, that is, open-endedly. Theatre's "contrived intrigues" (223), evident in even the most extraordinary dramas, represent a "crude abbreviation" (219) of camera-life potential, proceeding conceptually by way of "long shots" that align themselves automatically with the stage proscenium. "The stage universe is a shadowy replica of the world we live in" (218), and thus exerts, when imitated, a "restrictive effect on film." Camera life, as opposed to theatre life, favors the wonderful indeterminacy of "physical existence." The types of narrative that cinema should develop are those that honor the camera's search for unresolved, contingent details from a reality that is not subjected to "false theatrical unity." Such narratives will deliberately leave "gaps into which environmental life may stream" (255–256). The predetermined design of theatre-based thinking and representation stand in the way of film's power to engage an unregulated sensory experience that productively blurs the boundaries of space and time. Kracauer would agree with Franz Kafka's disparagement of the film medium aping theatre's "containment of vision." Kafka "pulls away from cinema as surface continuity of images, urg[ing] an excess in seeing, a more-visual of vision" (Stephen Heath, "Cinema and Psychoanalysis: Parallel Histories," 31; cited in Trahair, 237).

Kracauer, as Miriam Hansen has stressed in her account of his obsession with film's "photographic nature," conceived the ideal film spectator as one not constrained by narrative conventions or character behavior or story directives. The psychic disposition that the camera promotes is one that advances "identification with all kinds of objects": it makes the individual lose himself in the incidental configurations of his environment, absorbing them with a disinterested intensity no longer determined by his previous preferences" (17, xxv). Kracauer advocates a spectator mind that meanders, plays with danger, and makes its own arbitrary connections en route to revelation, rather than following theatre's preordained narrative path.

Kracauer, like Rudolf Arnheim, perhaps never wholly recovered from cinema's too hasty abandonment of a silent film aesthetic. The difficult transition period from silent to "early talkie" film could easily be read as a repudiation of the medium's birthright, and a regression to a slavish imitation of theatre practice. Screen time in movies was obliged for several years (1928–31) to move much closer to stage time, with a resulting sacrifice of film rhythm and pace. And stagebound compositions seemed to paralyze the camera's quest for living fragments, what Béla Balázs once praised in an American silent film as "a thin hail of small moments . . . of material life" that an environment releases to a genuinely exploratory camera eye (Kracauer, 225). Kracauer saw theatre space in film as a permanent barrier to a "photographic approach" to the real. The cinematic spirit must defy the convention-bound ways of perceiving that theatre, with its mania for narrative order, cause-and-effect dynamics, and lucid character intention, has implanted in us. Theatre can creep into the filmmaking process anywhere—as Robert Bresson later contended, in his own Kracauer-like polemics against stage influence—and its effect is usually a contamination, a thinning out of reality's mystery.

These old arguments seem to have lost much of their manifesto urgency and point in a world where theatre's status has so radically diminished. Whatever power theatre once possessed to challenge film's new dispensation and different kinship with material phenomena has become invisible—and largely irrelevant—to contemporary filmgoers. Theatre's territory appears to have been completely assimilated by cinema and other media. It has no distinct domain—apart from the still valued possibilities of the live event—to declare as its inherent attribute and continuing advantage in the struggle for aesthetic sovereignty. Theatre has become, of course, an eager, creative host for elements from other art forms, including film and television, and it is worth noting that the version of theatre that film theorists and practitioners were most eager to discredit had to do with the proscenium arch tradition, with its elaborate sets, heavy dependence on speech, and dogmatic conception of realism.

I began with Kracauer's anxiety about theatre's insidious undermining of true film space (and time) to reanimate a once widespread debate about theatre's deficient attachment to the visible world, which it is film's mission to reveal and rescue. According to Kracauer, Bresson, Arnheim, and others, theatre is "excessively" aligned, by its very nature, with artifice, with the imaginary, with the unnatural, with fixed categories, with seductive surfaces, with condensation, with appearances wedded to deception and displacement. It is, in short, a negative force, which is dangerous precisely because it can skillfully manipulate film reality for its own purposes. It can confuse the eye of the beholder, as well as the eye of the camera, so that they settle for less than the depth and weight of the real—that is to say, settling for façades and synthetic (as opposed to organic) arrangements.

I think there is a much more fruitful way to approach the problem of theatre space in film. I shall begin by discussing a number of attempts in the early sound era to fuse theatre and film technique so that what Kracauer terms authentic camera-life is discovered at the very heart of theatricality. I shall go on to provide a close reading of a relatively obscure theatrical set piece in Billy Wilder's purportedly realist film, *The Lost Weekend* (1945). This immensely popular and critically acclaimed movie appeared at the watershed moment when Hollywood began to question whether actual locations were aesthetically preferable to "theatrical" studio settings, in keeping with a renewed postwar quest for the unadorned documentation of ordinary lives. Wilder's narrative offers a remarkable example of how the presence of theatre lends a vital indeterminacy, flexibility of tone, and open-endedness to an otherwise too schematic and mechanized naturalism.

Let me begin my response to Kracauer's many-pronged attack on the theatrical by pointing out how invincibly metaphoric his employment of stage rhetoric is. "Theatre space," as I understand the concept, becomes visible and viable as soon as it is named or pointed to or recognized as a frame that stands somewhat apart from the rest of a film's world. If, for example, characters encounter a theatre setting in the course of their narrative activities, and witness a performance there, we have an instant division of the film world into a stage realm and a realm outside it, whose reality (however stylized in its own right) asks to be thought about in somewhat different terms. Life as it unfolds cinematically on studio streets or "real" urban neighborhoods, in an authentic barbershop or bar or constructed simulations of these settings, poses certain claims and demands for acceptance that a declared theatre episode is not obliged to take on. Theatre space may, of course, comment on the dramatic circumstances beyond its frame, and indeed, in countless ingenious ways, expose the seams and rifts in the outside narrative's hitherto taken for granted solidity. But theatre still is recognizably separate from the film reality beyond its borders.

In Jean Renoir's *La Règle du Jeu* (1939), to cite a very famous instance, we are allowed to watch Berthelin (Antoine Corteggiani), in a designated backstage area, as he dons a skeleton costume for an impromptu stage performance, set to the music of Camille Saint-Saëns's "Danse Macabre." There is a full acknowledgment of artifice here. The participants in this piece seem to be self-conscious, at first, and to be hampered by a lack of rehearsal. Three figures in addition to Berthelin's skeleton arrive on a narrow, makeshift stage, costumed in white bedsheets with crudely drawn eye sockets. They are meant to be ghosts, and initially carry skeletal umbrellas shorn of covering fabric. As a player piano performs the Danse in its own ghostly fashion, we observe as something close to a child's version of Grand Guignol acquires steadily more eeriness and disturbing power. As the skeleton continues to caper about onstage, presiding as a kind of diabolic ringmaster, his ghostly cohorts, now holding paraffin lamps, move from the pasteboard stage graveyard out into the audience gathered to watch their antics.

The seated chateau guests at first seem to react with mock consternation to the spectral invasion. But with no lessening of the sense of theatrical make-believe, something more than a stage boundary has been crossed. We suddenly feel the presence of death itself accosting the increasingly uncertain crowd of spectators. The ghosts swinging of the censer-like lamps, the shimmering white of the phantoms moving about in the half-light, strikingly alter our perception of the entertainment. In a trice, we are led to feel that the lives of this elegantly dressed group of watching guests are more fragile, and exposed. Their proximity to these silent attackers render them desolate, unaware of what transpires, momentarily bereft of social identity and purpose. The disguised actors shed their affiliations with an amusing spook show, and become harbingers of a destruction that they themselves are not cognizant of. The

Figure 2.1. Death dances among the upper class in *La Règle du Jeu*.

reality that erupts from their pantomime seems to release the horrors of the coming war into this drawing room. The theatre elements, in other words, achieve a camera-truth that vastly exceeds the collective social appearances and arrangements around them. Paradoxically, pure dramatic artifice releases "the thin hail of moments . . . of material life," which Kracauer contends can be attained in film only when theatrical perception is overcome. In spite of our precise sense of the stage frame at all times, and our awareness of the player piano churning out the anxious rippling chords of the dance accompaniment, the sequence is imbued with one of Kracauer's most prized cinema goals: the loose, disorganized experiential flow that "dissociates rather than integrates the spectatorial self" (xxviii).

Film representation generally aspires to make us forget that what is treated as real and natural in a screened world is in fact a waking dream. We give ourselves up for the time being to viewing conditions that seem "more natural than reality." Perhaps we don't completely lose sight of the fantasy dimension of a film, but it is not difficult to lighten our tenuous reality grounding, because so much of our perceptions and how we partake of them is, in Stanley Cavell's phrase, "already drawn by fantasy" (*World Viewed*, 102). A film fantasy can be a welcome relief from the burdens of those fantasies that so readily structure our lives outside the movie theatre. Film fantasy is also a waking replenishment of the language of dreams, which nightly override the monitoring consciousness. Kracauer overestimates our hunger for a reality in film unhindered by fantasies of connection, or by the freedom of viewer invisibility, or by the pleasure of owning what we view, without the claims of other persons challenging our sense of sole and sovereign possession.

I would argue that theatre's interruption of a movie narrative's version of the real is a salutary reminder, to borrow Wendell Berry's frame of reference, that a film is "an ecosystem full of dependencies, and nothing in it knows what it is dependent on" (*What Are People For?*, 87). Theatre effects a temporary viewer estrangement from a movie's confidence in its own grounding. Theatre is an organized dream that suddenly faces off with the larger dream that encloses it, thereby calling film's own taken for granted phenomena (continuity, stable appearances, unmediated experience, angle of vision, and so forth) into question. Theatre's often unanticipated division of film reality into two territories obliges the territory assigned to film to confront the assumptions that permit its representations to count more fully than theatre's as "lived experience." The result of such splitting is a bout of metaphysical viewer dizziness, in which the underpinnings of film reality loosen. It is akin to the interval of morning dream uncertainty (when we are still only half awake), before we have quite restored our faith in the solidity of our everyday surroundings. Our conscious life is not instantly secure: we feel off-balance. Film's dependency on hidden theatrical components in its ecosystem is something that is frequently suppressed. When theatre declares its presence it is not imposing elements on film that are alien to it, or even separate from it. Theatre is inherently, inescapably part of cinema's identity.

The stage can, of course, easily be conceptualized as a distinct, confined domain, a set of attitudes and imaginary circumstances more static and posed than those of film, the entire entity lying in wait, as it were, behind a curtain. But such an idea is false. Suppose the curtain in question is on a stage containing a Busby Berkeley production number. At first we think we know where we are. The familiar stage-audience boundaries and orientation are firmly established. The number begins to unfold on what feels like an appropriate, constructed setting, a place more stylized, diaphanous, and hermetically sealed than the space the audience occupies. The spectators appear to have entered the auditorium from a world outside. But as the musical number proceeds, space continues to expand with a dreamlike largesse, and the perspectives we are granted on the ever-deepening spectacle seem more prodigiously mobile and untrammeled than anything presented in the film's grounded lifeworld. The stage picture in its exorbitant, near-limitless reach dwarfs the counterclaims of the film's prior, convention-suffused reality.

Kracauer's ideal of identification with all manner of unlikely objects, and the productive "losing oneself" immersion in the "incidental, contingent details of a physical environment" is achieved by Berkeley's flamboyant cinematizing of stage illusion. Berkeley spectacles pass through a forcefully delineated theatrical mode of seeing to what I will term purely cinematic vision, without leaving the raw materials of staged artifice behind. Berkeley (a name he shares with a wonderfully compatible philosopher, Bishop Berkeley) conceives of a grand film synthesis. It is attained by a bold superimposition of two large interrelated planes: one, manifestly theatrical, and the other, from a higher angle, cinematic. Berkeley sees

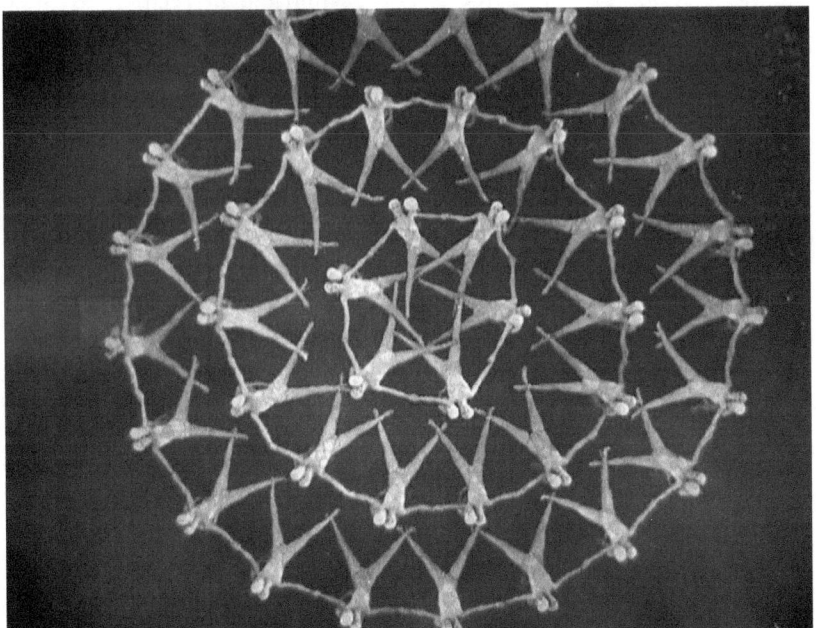

Figure 2.2. Atop Busby Berkeley's cinematic perch, the women twirl below like concupiscent, kaleidoscopic cogs.

no point in denying film's intimate ties with theatre, ties that reach back to cinema's origins. As soon as the film frame was deemed suitable for storytelling of any sort, the theatrical tradition, vast and diverse in its relation to framing action for spectators, was naturally, inexorably brought into play. For Berkeley, cinema's most enticing route to expressive freedom lay in feats of transcendent theatricality.

Theatre's restrictions can be most fully surmounted by a frank disclosure of film's elective affinities with stage territory. The camera eye merges with theatrical perception, then takes flight from this perch to something beyond the bounds of stage rhythm, stage distance, stage hearing, and visual perspectives. Kracauer might offer some objection to the machine-like character of Berkeley spectacle—female bodies as the living cogs of mechanized stage confections—as well as his mania for order and rigorously deployed symmetry. But machine analogies hardly constitute a disavowal of cinema's foundational properties. Rather, Berkeley's heavenly human contraptions pointedly acknowledge the camera and projector as mechanical instruments, which somehow engender séances, resurrecting dead time, with its glistening light and bustling spaces, for our delectation. The spectator is also reanimated in relation to these dream environments, as David Trotter phrases it, "thanks to the surrogacy of a machine's eye view" (Trotter, 21), but Berkeley extravaganzas do not settle for mechanical perception as their end point. Machine energy and dynamism combine with an intimate camera address that wavers excitingly between fugitive personal glimpses and a nearly uniform sense of the mass. Interconnectedness as a necessary component of the (usually) blonde chorine ensemble leads both to a suppression of the individual, in favor of a Soviet-style glamour collective, and to vagrant, unforeseeable eruptions of startling human presence. (We move at a leisurely pace down a magical assembly line through a stream of images of greeting, each performer gazing into the camera and smiling as a close-up finds her. The effect of these volatile moments of release are not so different from Dziga Vertov's mad pursuit of contingency in *Man with a Movie Camera*, where a vast montage harmony is the putative goal.)

Berkeley treats us to a dizzying multiplication of vantage points on his unbounded stage pictures, breaking up our sense of the whole at unpredictable intervals, then reinstating it with an equally arbitrary montage rhythm. In the course of the number's layered unfolding, there is a slipping away of interpretive grids. The song lyric, which was our initial guide to understanding the number's theme and progression, seems to give way to increasingly unanchored dream embellishments. We are neither sure of what we are looking at nor how to process it correctly. This wandering away from a rational frame of reference is comparable to Kracauer's desire for a cinema perception that feels nonprescriptive and uncodified. Berkeley's transcendent theatre is a machinery of the irrational, whose orderly elements become agents of wildness, and a giddy chaos of vision. Because the meaning of this destabilizing profusion eludes familiar categories, we are at liberty to read the extravagant details paraded before us playfully, salaciously, or—better still—with a mixture of awe and delirium. But theatre is the catalyst for all transformations. We pass through the theatrical medium in the way that Alice passes through the looking glass. Cinematic freedom depends on the arrangement of objects set up on the other side of the mirror, in the adjoining room, as it were. On the cinema side of the mirror, we contemplate the overdetermined building blocks of each production number: a cascade of Ruby Keeler eyes; swirling white pianos or glowing, electric violins; waterfalls; human coins; a face transforming into a city skyline, which then opens up for us, yielding, as we descend inward, a multitude of city dwellers racing through their everyday work schedule so they can wind up at a massive nightclub, performing a frenzied dance of fate. It is as if we are dreaming our way back to a kindergarten of perception, where any image, devoutly attended to, can be a potential world unto itself.

The time inside a Berkeley number is visionary time, which seems unconcerned about endings. It does not feel accountable to the labored tick of a clock notching off the seconds. It is the time of rabbit holes and brief spells of nodding off to a surrealist elsewhere. When Berkeley has spent a sufficient amount of dream time synthesizing order and chaos, the machine and the ecstatic garden of earthly delights, he invariably returns to theatre's normal scale and more homemade artifice. We recover the proscenium frame, a shallow stage, and a seated audience whose viewing, presumably, has been confined throughout to a single angle and distance. Whatever these spectators have witnessed, they have not been endowed with our heightened, intimate, and mobile form of imaginative perception. The return to the film's version of actuality feels like a sharp diminishing of sensory possibilities, a circumscribing of ordinary experience rather than a reengagement with life on more refined terms. The camera seems abruptly shorn of its wings, and the politely clapping audience within the film manifests no further need for "breaking bounds": propitious violations of common (perhaps too common) sense. These spectators have "gotten their money's worth," and dutifully resume contact with normative reality conventions. The everyday comes back into focus as a realm untouched by the exotic abundance that has been poured out unstintingly on the magic cinema stage. The audience members are almost relieved to bid farewell to dreamy unsettledness—an instant unlearning—as though the wonders they beheld had not amplified or enriched them.

Instead of the uncontrolled life of the drives, with its murky, licentious ambiguity, the spectators seek surface coherence and the anchor of familiarity. They shrug off the luminous flow of transcendent theatre. Where do we, as spectators of the same-but-different events, position ourselves? We are not encouraged to attach ourselves to the mindset of the confined audience within the movie. Berkeley has untwisted the chains that tie us to a movie life where everything is "at hand," subject to the control and calculation of our habitual designs. The gaps that the enigmatic spectacle has rashly opened up supply a critique of the rules of "reality" participation on the other side of the footlights. The production numbers are almost invariably the climax of the often dime store narratives in which they have so disproportionately lodged themselves. Almost no narrative time is allocated to the final acknowledgment of the characters' situation within the offstage world. What has previously counted as the realm of the real, and the arena of human conflict, is swiftly vanquished by the "antifield" of make-believe, whose fullness, aliveness, and freedom from regulation grant it more truth-telling power. Cinema as a medium of untrammeled expression and disarray is unleashed in a Berkeley number only when the stage is set before us and the houselights begin to dim. For Berkeley, as I noted earlier, theatre is the necessary portal to film's visionary power.

In the early years of the sound era, when so many ideas about talking pictures and the qualities they should aspire to were drawn from the stage, the more gifted filmmakers regarded theatre's prior, and perhaps higher, cultural status as more of an albatross than a horn of plenty. The conversational rhythms suitable for theatrical productions and the weight of the static frame were a displacement not only of silent film's visual tempo, but of the fluidity of film environments, and the swift, easy, back and forth passage from one to another. Interior and exterior spaces, in silent films, were in constant, unstrained communion. The expectation of dynamic film terrain was natural among movie spectators, in whatever location the dramatic action was set. Any environment designed for film inspection contains a variety of expressive vantage points that allow social performance and private reaction to it to intermingle and separate, at the director's discretion.

The stage world and the camera frame had not seemed irreconcilable in the silent era, but the subtraction of audible speech from the visual scheme allowed for a marked disparity in the delineation of character action. Sound's arrival and rapid entrenchment intensified the border wars between cinematic and theatrical space. The new centrality of utterance seemed to call for overtly theatrical personages, who brought with them an elaborate repertoire of gestures, verbal styles, and physicalization strategies that differed from silent film performance but retained (very often) their distance from what we might now term conventions of naturalness. Stage performers prided themselves on a combination of precision, subtlety, and a heroic scale of behavior, the latter demanding larger than life presence and vitality. Film took possession of what the studio heads regarded as efficacious theatrical staging techniques, with the accompanying conventions of dialogue exchange, stage business, and the "unfolding" of character through revelations in speech. In spite of the rather quick recovery of silent cinema resourcefulness in camera movement, montage, lighting, and compositional variety (and the addition of experiments in scoring and sound editing), filmmakers and the public at large preserved a large respect, bordering on reverence, for theatrical tradition and the mystique of theatre.

It was by no means Berkeley alone, in the early sound era, who explored the possibilities of transcendent theatricality. The most talented directors of the 1930s nearly all found ways to use the theatrical milieu, theatre metaphors, and conspicuous stage devices as a means of extending film reality, as well as wittily interrogating its own procedures. Rouben Mamoulian's extraordinary *Love Me Tonight* (1932), for example, opens with four Eugène Atget–influenced compositions of an actual contemporary Paris in the light of dawn, each of them silent except for the intermittent sound of a tolling cathedral bell, rousing the dormant city to life. When the real Paris is seamlessly matched with a studio version of a Paris neighborhood (convincing enough to be employed as an authentic urban landscape in a studio drama), Mamoulian views from a height the operations of a solitary street-repair worker, trundling a wheelbarrow that holds his tools onto the avenue, and pausing to commence work. As the laborer begins to empty his wheelbarrow, we hear the rattling sounds of items hitting the cobblestone pavement. We are then permitted to view the man at closer, ground level range as he wields his pickaxe. Mamoulian makes the sound of the pickaxe striking against cobblestone the primary shot emphasis, which sets up a logic in which the diverse street sounds begin to disengage from their visual sources and create rhythmic, synchronized patterns. The sound of the pickaxe is answered in the very next shot by the sound of a snoring tramp who is curled up beside two massive barrels. Pickaxe and snore become alternating instruments, joined in the next shot by the sound and sight of a woman plying her audibly whisking broom in front of her doorway.

The camera then races upward to take notice of rooftop chimneys releasing early morning smoke rhythmically, accompanied by metal tapping, as other sounds find their place in the ever-complicating tempo. We shift with remarkable montage speed between high and low perspectives. Shutters open in upper stories; a baby's cry is heard; a knifegrinder audibly sharpens his blade on a frame in the courtyard; cobblers hammer nails in front of their business; the metal curtains covering the display window and door of a grocery are raised; a woman flaps towels near a clothesline in an upper story; another woman in a separate window beats a rug; a cart is wheeled out of a doorway as a sudden stream of pedestrians add a volume of their own to the syncopated tumult of the district. The synchronized sound rhythms and their manner of sequential revelation lend a decisive theatrical overlay to all our visual impressions. The convincing urban setting is unmasked to exhibit a theatre setting sharing the same ground. The theatre elements emerge through the massive, artful integration of percussive effects. The uncanny reality of an inclusive, steadily enlarging stage works its way into every nook and cranny of a richly textured, atmospheric movie environment. Yet while there is no attempt to reduce the conspicuousness of theatrical devices once they have been brought into play, a stunning defamiliarization effect that seems emphatically cinematic emerges in the midst of all the overt playful contrivance.

The sound display sharpens our sight, as it were, making us apprehend more fully the beauty of work gestures and commonplace urban activities. Mamoulian reveals a festive dimension in the world of repetitive daily routines that outshines their drudgery dimension. Instead of monotony and confining tasks we observe a network of small, meaningful events that mysteriously compose a credible living environment. Material existence is redeemed, in Kracauer's sense of the word, by objects being lifted from the shadows to which distracted seeing and hearing have consigned them. In a manner not unlike that of Vittorio De Sica's *Miracle in Milan* (1951), or even his *Bicycle Thieves* (1947), the bits and pieces of observed phenomena that the camera serendipitously fastens on are "lit up from within," to use a famous phrase of André Bazin's, by the rapt delicacy of the visual treatment and the love the director feels for them (*What Is Cinema?*, volume 2, 62). We are not obliged to "escape theatre" to achieve the impact of the reality effect. Theatrical hearing and the "musical" editing rhythm are precisely the catalyst by which our hunger for marginal details is activated. A theatrical perspective enables us to penetrate more deeply the "overlooked" ephemera of the agreeably dense, tactile surroundings. The overwhelming excess of visual and auditory stimuli, akin to that confronting us in any real street environment becomes, in Mamoulian's visionary transcription, a fresh spur to imaginative engagement with the world beyond the frame.

So there is indeed no telling, no way of knowing in advance what becomes of theatre when it is inserted into film. Theatre can align itself with film's deepest efforts to mirror choice fragments of "reality" and equally with its deepest doubts about any such enterprise. (One thinks of Bazin's suggestive formulation about De Sica, "realism is more a reaction than a truth," in *What Is Cinema?*, volume 2, 64.) Theatre can serve as a safe refuge from trying life circumstances outside the stage's orbit, or a realm where experience and understanding become more perilous and painful. Theatre can enshrine artifice or be the most efficacious instrument for breaking it down. It can legitimate the kinds of role-playing that transpire throughout a film narrative or expose their evasions and fraudulence. It can mingle happily with cinema's other modes of representation or be forcefully confined to one clearly demarcated domain. The boundaries, when insisted upon, may exist for the purpose of elevating or denigrating the stage's gifts of flight and transformation. A film setting can be reclaimed at any point as a stage setting, a film character as one who is temporarily or permanently dwelling in theatrical space. Theatre can seek out the extravagant fullness of spectacle or divulge an extreme of bareness, a ground zero space where all material accoutrements and delusive appearances have been removed. One thinks of Samuel Beckett's stage or the "empty stage" so brilliantly theorized by Peter Brook. Theatre can seek out the shimmering, but also diamond-hard, opulence of a Max Ophüls opera house, or the strangely poignant simple machinery scrolling drawn landscapes of foreign lands behind the windows of a fairground railway compartment in Ophüls's *Letter from an Unknown Woman* (1948). (The acknowledgment of the artifice in the latter scene offers no impediment to our belief in a romantic journey of large consequence.) Theatre can blossom in a cramped fortune teller's tent at a carnival or claim a vast outdoor vista, as when the circus wagons depart on a dusty dawn at the end of Charlie Chaplin's *The Circus* (1928). In the Chaplin scene, the tramp sits in a vanished big top ring, holding a torn paper decoration inscribed with a star. The star is associated both with his lost love and all the melted away illusion and pageantry of the circus life. Chaplin crumples the star wistfully and kicks it away behind him with a dancer's aplomb. He does not look back before wandering off across the wide, abandoned field. Is the tramp in search of another theatrical space to replace the circus ring, or does he seek a freedom beyond theatre's reach? The film leaves the question open, as does the mingled stage-film medium Chaplin self-consciously probes. His perspective is fittingly that of one always somewhat outside and at variance with whatever theatre-inflected realm he stumbles into, yet whose dream, by turns fearful and yearning, is to be taken inside and made whole.

The rest of this chapter will present an extensive analysis of the *La Traviata* theatre sequence in Billy Wilder's *The Lost Weekend*. I've selected this episode in part because it has received almost no critical attention as a theatre-in-film set piece. It is the only sustained section of the narrative in which Don Birnam's (Ray Milland) alcoholic predicament is viewed from a somewhat distanced comic perspective. This flashback interlude almost breaks the established form of the film in the course of altering its relentlessly somber tone. Don's brief stay at the opera performance introduces a rush of surrealist mischief and libation-fueled stage harmony in a stark, step-by-poisoned step chronicle of Don Birnam's disintegration during a five day bender. The theatre segment also coincides with Don's decision to tell the story of his unwritten novel to his bartender, Nat (Howard da Silva). Don uses his arrival at the opera house as his memory portal, which opens up an alternative beginning to his narrative, one that interrupts the determinist flow of his weekend, and gives him some room to maneuver as a fantasist, playing with serendipitous chances.

The *La Traviata* sequence, and Don's follow-up enforced wait in the theatre lobby after he flees from the performance in progress, creates an atmosphere of expectation that makes possible the magically theatrical first meeting of Don and Helen St. James (Jane Wyman). Helen materializes as a kind of apparition, a protective spirit drawn to the aspects of Don that are worth loving, and who believes he can be saved. We have already been introduced to Helen earlier in the film proper, as someone nervously appraising Don's performance of unperturbed self-possession, as she debates whether she can leave him for a short while on his own. Every move of his she has contemplated thus far—in *Lost Weekend*'s present tense—has been part of a complicated masquerade, Don's desperation transmuted by a feat of actor bravado into seeming ease.

By 1945, the meeting points between stage and film could be arranged in movie narratives without the same air of competitive challenge so pronounced in the early 1930s. As I've argued, in the beginning of the sound era much experimentation was lavished on the ways in which theatre and film could be explosively fused. The sense of stage reality was often that of a testing or proving ground for a film reality claiming its own nature through the fantastic metamorphosis of theatrical elements. By the mid-1940s, the stage seldom provoked so intensively film's efforts to disclose its own ground of being, its visionary and materialist prerogatives. But by 1945, we find another significant threshold moment, as the hermetic studio worlds of Hollywood scenarios begin to mix more freely with actual locations. There was a new reality hunger at the end of the war, driven in part by the "documentary feel" of the first Italian neorealist films, which seemed like a natural continuation and extension of the documentary still photograph tradition of the American Depression. The studio-built settings not only in run-of-the-mill features but in high-budgeted films revealed, unwittingly, a more troubling connection to fabrication, and the sequestered-from-life frivolity of mere playacting. Prior to the end-of-war enticements of more authentic-seeming urban images, the atmosphere of reality in film was achieved without a strong audience awareness of what was, by design, omitted. There was not a felt division for regular moviegoers between "actuality" as a possible starting point for film storytelling and the cunningly engineered environments of the studio-made counterfeits. Perhaps the vast number of war films that attempted to create visually persuasive renderings of "fresh from the headlines" American military campaigns in Europe and Asia generated a demand for greater external verisimilitude in other kinds of film drama. One must also factor in the collective civilian response in the United States to the spectacular range and depth of war carnage—cities turned to ruins from carpet bombing, concentration camps, inconceivable death tolls, the loss of any sense of civilized order and proportion. The world suddenly needed to be apprehended at closer range, with a kind of amazement at the sheer fact of surviving presence: the raw, intimate texture of a place's thereness, or, more aptly, still-thereness. As found rather than built locales became a new Hollywood convention, previously "good enough" representations of crowded thoroughfares and rented apartments, urban parks, offices, and taverns became suspect, as though a re-creation bore the stigma of fantasy. If real places were sought out rather than cleverly approximated through stage-like facsimiles, spectator belief and full emotional engagement with movie stories—maintaining at least intermittent contact with the real—would be enhanced. James Agee's film criticism of the period is filled with exhortations to filmmakers to locate shards of "uninvented" or "unaltered" reality in their work, and Agee was profusely grateful for every image in touch with "the cruel radiance of what is." In summary, glossy representations of the pseudo-real became the new index of objectionable theatricality, a limiting connection with fanciful, too overt "imitations" of life.

The Lost Weekend, as part of this new wave of gritty, urban investigations, promoted its unusually extensive employment of New York locations to certify the seriousness of its attempt to move beyond Hollywood tricks and softening (Sikov, 220–221). It would strive to depict an alcoholic's milieu without the stratagems so customary in false environments. The stage metaphor in 1945 might readily be invoked to explain a thinning out of perceptual challenge, a preference for selective, shallow focusing rather than the tumultuous brouhaha of the urban wilderness. "Setting in depth," not merely a technique but an ideal, comprehensive vantage point, permits movies to uncover areas of their subject matter that backdrops, landscapes smelling of paint, and tidy arrangements of action on one or two planes would stylize or suppress. The look of film noir, as opposed to social problem realism, was, of course, theatrically stylized, but the expressionist dimension seemed a fitting metaphysical wardrobe for the haunted, dislocated scavengers of lost memory moving through noir's dreamlike, chiaroscuro mazes.

The *La Traviata* drinking scene in *The Lost Weekend* is not merely a stage interlude (opera no less) in an ambitious urban melodrama, but a distillation of everything that theatre signifies in 1945 as a sanctuary from the real, and a bulwark set against the search for a new vocabulary of photographic expression. The theatre is under pressure to reveal all the ways in which it is blind to (and utterly remote from) the perceptual exigencies and anxiety of Don Birnam's plight. Intriguingly, however, theatre also serves as a means of replenishment for a range of human attitudes and values that the doom-laden scenario that briefly intersects with it feels cut off from.

The sequence begins at Nat's Bar around noon, when Don, already inebriated, is flirting with Gloria (Doris Dowling), a call girl, and teasing her with the possibility of a theatre date that evening. He mentions a production of the uncut *Hamlet* that is currently running nearby (the five acts of the tragedy subtly linked to the five days of his epic debauch), and suggests that it might be a lark to see it together. He invites Gloria to speculate on Hamlet's character, perhaps mindful of the parallels with his own abiding weaknesses: a paralyzed will, and an incapacity to be forthright with the women who are drawn to him. When Gloria leaves the bar, elated that sophisticated Don has agreed to have a "dress up" evening out with her, Nat—the bar's owner—reacts angrily, accusing Don of treating Gloria and his more serious "high class" love interest, Helen, with deceit and contempt. He toys with the possibility of expelling Don from the tavern. To reingratiate himself, Don decides to share with Nat some unsavory, self-flagellating highlights from his still unwritten autobiographical novel, *The Bottle*. Its plot will presumably supply answers to the questions Nat has raised. Why is Don's relationship with the admirable Helen so vexed and punishing, and why is he unable to stop drinking? He promises Nat that it will be a horror story, and, as if to make good on his claim, commences his flashback telling at a point three years ago when his alcoholic identity is already well established. He announces "Chapter One," but it is not a hopeful narrative beginning, suggesting that he cannot retrieve a separate meaning or alternative path for his character from a time before the onset of his addiction.

The tale starts in medias res, with the fateful decisions already made, and Don's prospects already dim. We discover Don, in the visual staging of the transition to flashback time, as part of a crowd of theatregoers, perceived first in what seems the blurry mist of what Don recalls as a "wet afternoon." As the image gains sobriety focus, we are able to pick out Don sporting a derby, an anonymous member of the pressing throng in the lobby of the Metropolitan Opera. He makes his first distinguishing gesture in the act of covertly transferring a pint of rye whiskey from his suit coat pocket to the pocket of his raincoat. Within moments, a young man has collected Don's raincoat and derby and given him a coat-check claim ticket. The sounds of *La Traviata* are already audible in the lobby. We hear the jaunty strain of the champagne song, "Libiamo ne' lieti calici" (Let's drink from the joyful chalices), as Don watches his coat and its precious contents being carried away. Wilder adroitly establishes the claim ticket as having an importance at least equivalent to the unseen opera ticket. Catching up with the opera in progress, we track forward in the next shot to locate Don's position in the theatre audience as the drinking song, still unseen, is getting under way. Don is still reading his

Figure 2.3. Don (Ray Milland)—a few beats behind—parses his program while others tune in to *La Traviata* in *The Lost Weekend*.

program while everyone around him attends to Alfredo's onstage acceptance of the invitation to sing.

Alfredo is showing off his vocal prowess in an eighteenth-century Parisian salon, a more refined version of what Nat in the tavern referred to as Don's "making with the mouth" as he holds court on his barstool, garrulously confiding to anyone willing to pay heed to his drunken rigmarole. The informal action of the barroom performance space has been cleverly transposed to the opera stage. Gloria, the good-hearted call girl enamored of Don's air of worldly charm and breeding, is analogous to Violetta, *la dame aux camélias*, in *La Traviata*, a renowned courtesan whose tragedy will in part be caused by her being lured, despite her accumulated cynicism, into a serious love relationship with Alfredo. The shapelessness of Don's unwritten "Gothic novel," which he says is "all in his mind" and will, when he finds the resolve to commit it to paper, probe the unchangeable malady that consumes him, is in marked contrast with the perfect form of Violetta's descent to death. Her narrative is driven by the twin agents of love and an equally incurable illness.

The magic lightness, cordiality, and seeming harmony of the act 1 champagne song is a powerful temporary structure of feeling that will, in the way of opera, be raised high as a musical act of faith only to be shattered into heaps by later eruptions of contingency and misunderstanding. This portion of the opera, in other words, brings a realm of perfect fellowship into being as a dazzling apparition, which the audience is encouraged to escape into, with no sense of burden. While the song lasts, we can luxuriate in forgetfulness. The future consequence of sportive revelry and tipsy elated pledges are well hidden. What we behold onstage is a beautiful picture of order, where voices join as one, and every cup is refilled as soon as it is emptied. Violetta and the chorus enjoin us to become live-for-the-moment hedonists: "Let's enjoy the wine and the singing, the beautiful night and the laughter. Let the new day find us in paradise." The opera spectator takes his strongest cue from Alfredo, still blooming with youthful idealism, who finds his full, ardent voice as he urges everyone present to "drink from the joyful chalices that beauty so truly enhances." The spectator is allowed a prolonged view of an ambrosial heaven, to which music lends solidity by transfiguring physical life.

It should be noted that the drinking song, while presenting plentiful impressions of gratifying concord, contains an undercurrent of disconnection. Alfredo and Violetta have different conceptions of pleasure and love at this point, which do not come into open conflict, but are not reconciled either. They offer opposing assumptions in a festive mood that makes them sound the same, as though the gap is being overcome. Alfredo believes that the fleeting pleasures of the bacchanalia attain value when they serve as a prelude to enduring love. Violetta argues that carnal delights are like all other "foolish pleasures." Passion's quest is but one more frivolous pursuit, which quickly runs its course. To complicate matters further, Violetta's amused detachment masks an extraordinarily deep capacity for romantic subjection. Alfredo's faith in beauty and the truth of "ecstatic feeling," in contrast, is pure, but untested. He has been in love with Violetta for months, a commitment she does not yet take seriously. Alfredo is also, however, very much ruled by social convention, and this is something that neither of them knows at this juncture. Violetta may well suspect that he is an "excitable" youthful type that she has often encountered, but love, when it takes hold of her in a final fierce contest with the hold of her illness, will make her indifferent to all her sensible early intuitions. The push for a unified vision of celebration in the drinking song is, in part, designed to move Violetta's urbane perspective closer to Alfredo's fervid, trusting utopianism. The tilt toward persuasion and harmonious convergence ironically sets the tragedy of the opera in motion. Agreement about the value of love has a price. Violetta's enviable sense of freedom and self-possession will soon be gone.

What would audiences of *The Lost Weekend* in 1945 be likely to project onto the meticulously re-created stage world of *La Traviata*? Spectators could not easily forget the recent wholesale destruction of Italian cities and the disintegration of civilized values in Europe (order certainly among them). The Italy of Verdi must have seemed irretrievable. Paris, where *La Traviata* is set, had just been liberated from four years of Nazi occupation, with a shameful shadow history of collaboration. An exuberant Alfredo, in a light suit with a flowing cravat, stands on a stage filled with candle-lit chandeliers, candles in sconces and on tables in candelabra—war's fires, moderated and contained. The banks of candle light create a protective circle of radiance for a serene assemblage of party guests to inhabit. Behind a row of tables, whose white coverings match the frilly gowns of the female salon guests, is a massive rococo painting in the style of Fragonard, and on either side of it high, double-sided windows, a lustrous fragility backed by darkness. The scene has a quality of spectral emanation from an era doubly extinguished, first by time's ordinary passage, second by the just completed catastrophe, which mocks and mourns such oblivious gaiety. By now the skeleton and ghosts from the theatricals in *La Règle du Jeu* have become massive and inescapable, and are putting the finishing touches on their dreadful, long harvest. The crowd in this ancient drawing room cannot reckon with the darkness behind their glass-paned sanctuary. They seem bewitched, held in an amnesia spell that will be kept alive by their solidarity, and by the bravura force of their choral singing. Their island is safe from the future's invasion, but the ground of *La Traviata* is less firm than it used to be. The entire apparatus is kept alive by a war-weary opera audience's willingness to animate the spectacle with an act of self-conscious, perhaps excessively taxing belief. The Verdi fantasy requires mental reinforcement and a selective blotting out of "too immediate" woes. This forgetting intriguingly mirrors that of the onstage choristers, in their elaborate wigs, frock coats, and gowns.

Don Birnam's spectator challenge is, from the outset, notably at odds with that of the audience surrounding him. In a sense, his involuntary level of assent to the "truth" being represented exceeds everyone else's. He is completely caught up in the action onstage. His connection with the stage illusion grows steadily more binding as the song proceeds. Yet he is rewriting the narrative as he watches, pointing it in a viscerally more desperate direction. Don bypasses the genial argument of the singing lovers-to-be, and in fact can scarcely attend to their central position onstage. He decomposes the official proscenium picture designed by the opera's director, and in its place conducts a private visual pursuit of overdetermined objects—champagne bottles and brimming, stemware glasses transported on trays. The stage is entirely commandeered, Hitchcock-style, by point-of-view shots from Don's (implied) perspective. His single-minded concern with drinking leads us from one upraised glass to another across the entire playing area. The singers are reduced to chalice bearers. The silent, bewigged servants in tailcoats, on the other hand, who carry the champagne in bottles or on drink-laden trays become the dominant personages, transforming inconspicuous background action into arrestingly dramatic foreground. Their back and forth movements are closely monitored because they are in control of the treasured alcohol, and determine its trajectory. Don watches Alfredo and Violetta drink (in close-up) from their glasses as they pause from singing, as though the music were a mere tease leading to the suspenseful culmination of ecstatic tasting. Behind this couple, other drinkers begin to sway in a trance-like manner, their glasses functioning like a hypnotist's twirling watch, inducing a spell in Don. As these men and women move off to the left, they create a human curtain, which parts to disclose a large ornate champagne bucket against the rear wall of the set, stocked with seven bottles thrusting outward from a bed of ice. Two more servants stand motionless on either side of the bucket, like an honor guard, holding open champagne bottles in their hands with a reverence befitting spiritual artifacts.

Alfred Hitchcock no doubt drew upon this episode for the famous Sebastian party sequence in *Notorious* (1946) the following year. Concurrent with spying activity centered on keys and a dangerous planned visit to a wine cellar, the viewer of *Notorious* is made to feel uneasy about the dwindling stock of champagne at the party itself. Hitchcock highlights trays of champagne glasses, party guests' hands eagerly taking them, and bottles on ice being opened by a servant behind a lengthy impromptu bar, as the available stock rapidly thins out. A comparison of the overt stage activity in *The Lost Weekend* with the party events in *Notorious* makes it clear that Hitchcock conceived of his charged social gathering as clandestine theatre. The stage is fully operational, but not explicitly declared. The point of view of the hostess, Alicia (Ingrid Bergman)—herself a reformed drunkard—who fears the guests will consume the champagne too plentifully, thus causing her husband to need the wine cellar key she has stolen from his key ring, transforms the entire meaning of the party into one woman's mounting anxiety: a private stage performance choreographed entirely by her fearful, roving gaze.

In Wilder's *La Traviata* sequence, the vision of liquid abundance is not (as in Hitchcock) about a hidden agenda. For the characters onstage, everything having to do with drink is out in the open, frankly declared and tenaciously indulged. The open stage world powerfully contrasts with Don's shameful alcoholic secrecy. Drinking and more drinking is the only activity that links all the choristers together. A perfect drinkers' temple temporarily comes into being before Don's swimming senses that has but one purpose: merry, harmless, in fact irreproachable, intoxication. Don is emotionally united with the staged tipsy assemblage. He is at one, he imagines, with the values being celebrated. But his intense involvement with onstage gestures and signifiers missed by the audience at large—indeed, the force of his imaginative collaboration—ironically reactivates the sense of exclusion that he experiences in all the socially normative spaces of his own life. The logic of social integration presented in the *La Traviata* scene implies that, to belong, one must have a literal drink in one's hand. The possession of one's own filled glass is what permits you to be inside rather than outside the spectacle.

The comedy of the sequence is built on the tension between an invitation to pleasure and excess, offered at increasingly close range by a subjective camera fused with Don's desired objects, and the stubborn fact of spectator distance. The feeling of "film vision" proximity is continually enhanced, in tandem with the gap of theatrical separation. Film seeing is so often predicated on our being so "incorporated" in what we are looking at that we forget that we don't actually possess it. Seeing and hearing can often weave us into a fantasy space that abolishes alienation. What we behold—once we have entered the mindset of the film's world—appears to be ours for the taking. Don's theatre perception, for that reason, is sharply at variance with normal film perception. The rules of theatre spectatorship within film is that theatre viewers generally know their place, which is to say their bodily placement, more clearly. They retain the awareness of the stage as a material medium, located at a fixed distance from their seat.

The movie spectator's sense of distance from the cinema screen is one that film is at great pains to dissolve. The stream of film images, as many theorists have noted, has much in common with the language of dream and daydream, both of which have an immense ongoing role to play in our inner life. If the boundary between screen and inner life is blurred, the spectator will receive cinematic experience in a less consciously mediated fashion, as though it were transpiring not externally but within the spectator, in a manner analogous to dream, memory, and fantasy. The seat one occupies at a movie theatre is no barrier to a more intricate sustained placement within the film frame. Theatre, though associated with "live experience" rather than manufactured simulation, maintains the consciousness of physical separation from the stage as part of its reality effect. One can become deeply involved in theatre performance without losing the awareness of viewing and hearing from a certain remove. The audience space divides us from the performed action. Cinema preserves this condition of intervening space and spectator distance when depicting stage events on film. The audience space is always dramatically in play, communing in its own theatrical manner with the events onstage.

Movie characters watching a stage are rendered more dynamic if the emotional impact and challenge of distance—a systole-diastole of distance dwindling, then being reasserted—are made an integral part of the presentation. The auditorium is a second stage space, as it were. Billy Wilder's *Love in the Afternoon* (1957) provides a brilliant demonstration of the audience as a distinct performance domain, where the fact of distance is the substance of the drama. While the Prelude to Wagner's *Tristan und Isolde* is playing in a sumptuous opera house, Ariane Chavasse (Audrey Hepburn) is seated in a high balcony, distracted and daydreaming, while her date listens enraptured to every phrase, conducting with his hands as he follows along in his own copy of the score. All at once, Ariane's attention is caught by the arrival, far below her, of Frank Flannagan (Gary Cooper), the millionaire playboy with whom she is romantically obsessed. Frank's seat is in the front row, at ground level, very close to the orchestra. Ariane seizes her date's opera glasses and tries to bring Frank into sharper focus, and nearer to her. He is seated next to his own date, with his back turned. Equally unmindful of Wagner's seductive musical force, Frank flips through his program, then rolls it up and converts it into a makeshift telescope. He randomly directs his spyglass to other sections of the audience. A visual comic love duet is superimposed on Wagner's majestically yearning, doleful overture as Ariane—in close-up—remains riveted on Flannagan's activities in the theatre's cavernous depths, while his blithe, womanizer's scan of the crowd for more engaging prospects fails to locate her.

I have stressed this issue of the spectator "playing area" and the awareness of distance from the actual stage because they figure decisively in the last phase of Don's viewing of the drinking song. As I previously observed, Don's cheated point-of-view shots move us extremely close to the opera action, though his seat is separated by many rows from the stage. His perception has the camera's freedom to magnify and hyperbolize whatever drink-related details intrigue him. The framing and cutting align with (and give full license to) Don's revision of the dramatic meaning and flow of Violetta and Alfredo's musical exchange. However, the freedom to reconstitute the operatic performance, according to his private needs, coexists with the necessity of banishment from the festivities. He is trapped in a seat at the remote outskirts of the bacchanal, where deprivation is absolute. He suffers (comically) for being utterly cut off from the filmic line of action he discerns and orchestrates. Don is, in one sense, integrated into the drinking scene in precisely the same fashion that the film viewer is. This level one union is in sync with the effortless sharing and fellowship of pleasure that is everywhere ratified onstage. But Don's literal spectator detachment from the very spectacle his imagination narrates ironically turns all the signs of onstage togetherness into repudiation. It is as though the smiling choristers with their lifted champagne glasses are conspiring to ignore him, to deny him the hospitality available to all the other guests, to render him invisible. No servant will catch his eye and either acknowledge him or carry the drink tray in his direction. So, from the position of theater viewer disenfranchisement, Don feels compelled to launch an even more subjective assault on the staged proceedings.

In a comic prefiguring of *The Lost Weekend*'s climactic, harrowing delirium tremens episode, Don suddenly converts (by hallucination) the actual swaying dancers onstage into a row of disembodied cloakroom raincoats. A chorus line of mackintoshes, extending from stage foreground to background, gently swings in time with the song's rhythm. The rhythm itself, though not audibly distorted, comes to seem more plaintively clockbound, as though passing moments were insistently marked, signaling the loss or draining away of our too brief time on earth. Don is extending the prerogatives of point-of-view camera authorship here still further, bringing the stage picture into fuller harmony with himself. He translates, by hallucinatory fiat, whatever is alien and separate in the celebration into images of belonging. One of the swaying coats teasingly discloses a bulging pocket, which Don is able to see through, as though a final manifestation of theatrical illusion were being offered for his gratification. Inside the pocket a whiskey pint materializes. The bottle, in effect, breaks the fourth wall, casting an anthropomorphic glance outward into the audience and finding Don, meeting his gaze, as the joyfully inebriated salon guests declined to do. Don's self-made cinematic environment onstage becomes a prison-house of subjectivity. He dispatches, first, the logic of the opera, then its material conditions in exchange for the dream of a coat (a means of covering up). The bottle within the coat seems to take possession of Don in the act of unveiling and sighting him. It defines him unnervingly as an appendage of itself. The bottle is hidden in this fantasy projection to every spectator but Don. Hiddenness in relation to alcohol (covering up) displaces a ghostly social world in which drinking is hypervisible, the lynchpin of all positive human connection.

Another surprising metamorphosis, which is crucial to our understanding of the *La Traviata* scene, takes place in Ray Milland, the actor. He briefly sheds his affiliation with Don's desolate estrangement, and reconnects with the romantic comedy persona familiar to film audiences from his previous ten years as both contract player and star at Paramount. The beginning of the "going to the theatre" flashback interrupts the steady downward movement of *The Lost Weekend* narrative and implies—in spite of Don's preliminary insistence that he was already a drunk then—

Figure 2.4. Don's delirium tremens transmutation of the *La Traviata* cast into a chorus of coats in *The Lost Weekend*.

that we will be granted a reprieve, as Don recalls the initial phase of his relationship with Helen. Milland's series of reaction shots to the *La Traviata* libation orgy are all keyed in to the comic notion that he has made a disastrous choice of escapist fare. The internal burden appears to lighten for Milland's character even as his desire to obtain a drink escalates. Milland does not overplay his responses, but we are meant to recognize a kinship at this point between the face of discomfiture Don displays and the faces of the many hapless characters Milland has previously played who all at once find themselves, like Don Birnam, at the "wrong" opera, in an amusing fix.

The proximity of an artificial stage milieu, in combination with the memory of Don (just before) initiating a tavern yarn that he hopes will garner some sympathy from his bartender audience, create a protective aura around the figure at the center of the story "reenactment." This nattier dressed and less hardened Don is no longer adrift in an oppressively real urban environment. He has stepped—like a fictive personage—into a stylized sanctuary where the drinks are "pretend" champagne and the performers follow a pattern of merrymaking that is securely choreographed and without any hint of strain. Milland's demeanor is free to shift over to a mode of response that invites pleasurable viewer complicity. Confronted with overtly theatrical difficulties, Milland is temporarily released from the duties of full-scale anxiety. Wilder uses Milland's other face strategically in this interlude. It provides the viewer with sudden reassuring access to the dominant convention of lighthearted intoxication scenes in Hollywood film.

The vast majority of scenes portraying drunkenness in American movies made prior to 1945 are playful and mischievous. They promote a much-valued loosening of constraint—a welcome surrender to giddiness and irresponsibility. Nick Charles (William Powell), of *The Thin Man* series, was the representative alcoholic of 1930s Hollywood cinema—usually soused, but never to the point where his wit and charm founder, and whose only drink-related problem was a bad hangover. One-night benders were sometimes viewed in a melancholy light, but the excess was seldom linked to addiction. *The Lost Weekend*'s pointed determination to oppose this convention—to overthrow the regime of droll inebriation—naturally creates a countervailing pressure to return to familiar territory. The suppression of comedy in the rendering of Don's binge heightens the desire for an acknowledgment of laughter's cleansing force. Comic freedom is a sphere of knowledge (and expectation) that lies adjacent to the newly cold and dreary nightspots of the authentic "naked city." Wilder employs theatre then as a cunning passageway back to the traditional wisdom of what spirited revelry can accomplish. Milland's mask of sodden cynicism—within the confines of the "horror story" he claims to be telling—briefly comes loose, and Milland the genial comic actor is permitted to stare hungrily at a staged version of the lost frivolous pleasures that his current role, and the imprisoning world that goes with it, have cut him off from. It is not merely a drink that Milland craves, but the cost-free brio that is one of its reliable cinematic privileges.

As the drinking song concludes and the audience within the film greets it with enthusiastic applause, Milland feels obliged to abandon his theatre seat and turn his back on the stage spectacle. Though his squirming overinvestment in the champagne utopia (a utopia itself cut off from the Violetta tragedy that has not yet found its footing) unleashes laughter of the old-fashioned, gladdening sort, the flashback episode's linkage with Milland's star persona remains precarious. The fact of Milland's lack of fit in this story, with the maze of artifice set before him, causes the actor to flee, perhaps reluctantly, back to the weightier reality Don Birnam's desperate condition has called into being. But in fact Milland cannot shake off his old persona just yet, nor can Don Birnam achieve an easy escape from the space of theatre.

With the music of Verdi still audible on the soundtrack, we watch Don move briskly down a hallway leading to the cloakroom. Don presents the attendant (Frank Orth) stationed there with a second ticket of admission—his claim check ticket—which promises to afford him more reliable, tangible entertainment than *La Traviata*. The cloakroom, however, does not stand separate from the theatre he has just vacated. It is rather a continuation of the stage realm, part of the building devoted to theatrical exhibitions. The desk where the attendant is roused by Don's early "exit" and demand for his coat forms a smaller version of the opera stage, with an equally untraversable barrier. The attendant is, in effect, a comic surrogate for the bartenders such as Nat whom Don regularly confronts, with a similar power to bestow or withhold the "relief" that Don longs for. Don's departure from the theatre is significantly delayed by a confusion over ticket and coat match-up. Instead of his own raincoat (with its secret stash of rye), Don's ticket obtains—through a mistaken identity imbroglio—a woman's leopard skin jacket. Don's coat is hidden away somewhere in the mass of other opera patrons' apparel, over which the attendant stands watch. The attendant refuses Don's demand to enter this second stage area and conduct a search for his missing coat.

As with his viewing of the opening aria of Verdi, Don's spectator position is rife with vexation and a sense of exclusion. The opera stage and cloakroom both initially promise an easy route to felicity, in one case, a musical respite from pressing worries, in the second, the retrieval of his property through a reliable social form of exchange. The opera stage presentation, after bombarding Don with taunting images of "not having," is overthrown by Don's fantasy of bobbing raincoats, one of which contains a reminder that real (not make-believe) liquid salvation lies within his reach. When Don arrives at the second, cloakroom proscenium, where the "real thing" presumably awaits him, he is presented with an exotic, faintly absurd "female" substitute for the coat he naturally expects—a theatrical prop coat, as it were.

The comic tone established in Don's emotional ambush by the Verdi drinking song is strategically extended by Wilder in the cloakroom dispute. The attendant regards himself as a theatrical personage—the Guardian of Order—and fends off Don's surly, loud protests with the sturdy aplomb of a man who has served a long apprenticeship in farce. Ray Milland's full return to the identity of "Don Birnam" is delayed by this somewhat stylized, histrionic encounter. Don's agitation is dramatically softened by a deliberately highlighted plot contrivance. The world where dispiriting accidents occur is the real world, but accidents of this sort (the timely arrival of a mysterious coat belonging, we have no doubt, to a beautiful woman and a prospective partner in love) are bright confections, infused with the airy determinism of romantic comedy. The coat offers a secure basis for "meeting cute." The more galling determinism of Don Birnam's falling again and again into the throes of his addiction is temporarily offset by the lighter fatedness of fairy tale romance. Perhaps we recall Don, at this point, in his role of barstool raconteur, concocting a fable for Nat that will make him a sympathetic ally. Moviegoers of 1945 might well be reminded of Ray Milland's early-career romantic comedy hit, *Easy Living* (1937), whose plot is set in motion by a costly woman's fur coat being tossed out of a penthouse window, and landing—oh, propitious accident—on Jean Arthur (Milland's soon-to-be love interest) as she rides atop an open air double decker bus.

While Don is forced to sit disconsolately on the opera house stairway—awaiting the end of *La Traviata* and the sorting out of the coat muddle—he settles still further into the recognizable manner of Milland's star persona. He stylishly renders his impatience. Within the context of *The Lost Weekend*, this former, less shackled version of the actor (the star the audience knows) is strongly associated with the values of theatricality and its gallant propensities, rather than the stern strictures of film realism. We hear snatches of the opera as Milland sits, bemused and frustrated, on the carpeted lower steps. The music behind the wall marches Violetta inexorably toward her doom, but on our side of the theatrical partition, comedy has bought itself some time to play out a less drastic scenario. The neighboring orchestral sounds emphasize Don's separation from grandiose moods: a reprieve from the grip of compulsion. Compulsion, of course, frequently unfolds in the language of melodrama. Don/Milland is, after all, merely waiting, resignedly wagging the umbrella (which came with the leopard jacket at the coat check counter) as though it were a conductor's baton, rather than frantically seeking a drink. Wilder creates an emotional polarization between vying forms of theatrical activity. The storm and stress of not to be deterred opera misfortune contrasts with a man holding himself in readiness for a possible shift in circumstance, a meeting that is likely to supply a different kind of rescue than he anticipates. As Milland submits to the changing demands of his theatre environment, it seems as though the film narrative itself is opening up to a new tone and fresh possibilities of development. The theatre space becomes a useful arena of indecision and tantalizing wavering for Wilder the director.

Films with a too controlling thesis, and accompanying pedagogic baggage, often face the problem of appearing overly intent and clear about what needs to be communicated. A film, especially one with polemical urges, can know too well what it's about, and make that very fullness of purpose a route to falsehood. Theatre offers a space that registers doubt about the necessity of a fixed tone, and of a too narrow conception of the reality principle. In Wilder's *Double Indemnity* (1944), one of the most important narrative responsibilities of Barton Keyes (Edward G. Robinson) is to be comic playwright-in-residence in the insurance company claims office. He keeps *Double Indemnity* from getting locked in a somber melodramatic mode by reimagining one crime after another in exuberantly comic terms. He uses the various spaces of the insurance company that he pops up in as ready-to-hand stages for his impromptu performances. He enthralls his listeners by exposing the "bad plotting" of his greedy criminal adversaries. He offers bravura reconstructions of their sordid schemes once he has seen through their defective story construction. By conceiving, with Olympian detachment, all crimes as failed theatrical ventures, Keyes creates vital counterpoint for the increasingly grim writhings of Walter Neff (Fred MacMurray) and Phyllis Dietrichson (Barbara Stanwyck) in their loveless entanglement. They achieve a greater measure of realism in their sustained conflict and double-cross because of Keyes's antic effrontery, his ceaseless theatrical testing of every character's angle. Keyes's dramatist presence gives the world of *Double Indemnity* a plurality of available tones, and its reality principle a renewable comic dynamism.

The trip to the theatre in *The Lost Weekend* does not, of course, remove or even reduce Don's resolve to obtain alcohol, but it provides a different lens for contemplating it. His drive is relaxed through a disproportionate fantasy interruption. He is stymied, here as elsewhere, by conditions blocking his gratification, but in the little drama with the amusingly stubborn master of cloakroom protocol, he is assigned a task to perform that involves another person's well-being. In place of his own pint to hold, he is given a coat, and the mere act of holding it for a length of time, however grudgingly, establishes a connection with its undisclosed owner. When Don finally discovers her—they are the last two occupants of a hallway that moments before had been teeming with patrons eager to reclaim their coats and depart—they are alone together, on a markedly silent stage. In addition to the folded coats they carry, Helen raises a comically forlorn derby as "identifier" and Don still clutches a woman's

Figure 2.5. Don and Helen's (Jane Wyman) coat-mix-up meet-cute, soon sullied by Don's mounting thirst in *The Lost Weekend*.

umbrella. In the foreground is a pillared, sand-filled, standing ashtray, in which Don has wittily stubbed out his rolled up opera program.

Once the coats have been traded and Don has made sure that that his bottle remains safely stowed in the pocket, he reveals that he has had "three long acts to work you out from that coat of yours." He has built up a picture of Helen's likely name and type from the owner's initials on a sewn tag and the Toledo location of the furrier. Prior to the commencement of articulate flirtation banter, Don roughly responds to her request for her umbrella. After snarling "catch," he tosses it haphazardly in her direction. Her retrieving gesture is mistimed, and the umbrella makes a jarring noise resembling a gunshot as it strikes the bare floor. This graceless toss and drop literally restore gravity to the proceedings. The unexpected violation of a smooth, precise stage rhythm in their opening exchange throws us back, sharply, to the dominant *Lost Weekend* tone of despondent harshness. Wilder choreographs this crucial "break" as though it were an onstage blunder during a performance. An intended action is spoiled by a performer fumbling or mistiming her response. Reality suddenly seeps into dramatic artifice through the gap created by an accident. Milland promptly recovers his grace and self-possession after Helen describes him as "the rudest person I've ever met," which is equivalent to an actor cleverly repairing the breach. The umbrella "detonation" as it hits the floor inside the opera house serves an even more important function by preparing us for a rhyming action that will come soon afterward. As Don and Helen leave the theatre and encounter a still-in-progress rainstorm, Don's whiskey bottle slips from his pocket and shatters on the sidewalk, in full view of Helen. The humiliating exposure of Don's hidden object/vice, conjoined with the bottle smashing and thus emptying its precious contents, breaks the spell of the comedy and romance interlude that the theatre sanctuary had made possible. It's noteworthy that Don and Helen's delight in sparkling give-and-take precisely coincides with their lengthy traversal of corridors and stairways as they slowly depart the theatre building. Once they arrive outside—a threshold crossing forcefully marked by the appearance of gusting rain and early evening darkness—the weight of the conversation grows notably heavier. Don reverts to calculation and subterfuge, and Helen's impulsive invitation to join her at a New York party is seized upon by Don because it affords a solution to the problem of the lost pint of rye. Alcohol counts for more than Helen's own presence in his swift decision to accept her offer.

Almost immediately Don's flashback story is replaced by an image of Don still glibly holding forth in Nat's bar as Nat cleans up. The chance of an auspicious start to a meaningful love story must be evaluated entirely by reference to the theatrical frame within which all the events we have witnessed transpired. We are led from a positive to a negative reading of theatre's implications by the jolting reminder of Don as self-pitying tale spinner. Don misrepresenting himself to Helen out in the rain, followed by his failure to make good on the initial favorable impression he has made, decisively undermines Milland's fleeting retrieval of his insouciant star persona. The theatre excursion now may strike us as a retreat from self-awareness, a journey into illusion akin to Don's bouts of drunkenness.

Surprisingly, however, as *The Lost Weekend* nears its ending and the narrative attempts to give Don a credible hope of self-reclamation, theatre is once again called upon to provide "reality" with an adjoining space of possibility. The coat mix-up so central to the theatre episode is recapitulated after Don touches bottom. That nadir point arrives with his DTs hallucination of a bat fiercely attacking a mouse that peeps out of a hole in the wall of his room. The mouse's lifeblood streaming down the wall subtly resembles the spreading stain of whiskey, and the mingled association conveys the draining away of Don's will to survive. It is intriguing that as we arrive at the culmination of the film's realist excavation of alcoholic experience, we shift to mental theatre, a fantasy of horror played out on Don's mind screen. The problem Wilder faces in his closing scenes is how to introduce the rhetoric of redemption in such a way that it does not betray the film's reality effect—its essential grounding in a starkly authentic, inhospitable urban milieu.

His Ernst Lubitsch–inspired tactic is to make the crucial moments in Don's metamorphosis play out through our engagement with objects. Wilder selects Helen's and Don's coats for further dramatic attention precisely because they are imbued with a kind of magic and power, derived from our first encounter with them in the cloakroom playlet. Don and Helen both make reference to the coats as linked to the beginning of their story, a narrative they believe is, to some degree, distinguishable from the counterstory of Don's addiction. Don and Helen's fairy tale challenge is to interpret accurately the concealed meaning of the other's "performative utterance" with Helen's coat, which, in effect, turns into Don's coat once it is stolen and pawned for a hidden object. Helen is reunited with Don in a nursing capacity at the end of his "lost weekend," though his mood remains hopeless. When she falls asleep at his place, Don steals her leopard skin jacket and takes it to a pawnbroker. Initially misconstruing his gesture as a total repudiation of their relationship, and a callous betrayal, Helen locates the pawnshop and arrives there without any coat in spite of a rainstorm, which echoes Don and Helen's first post-theatre contact with the world outside as a newly formed romantic pair.

She discovers at the pawnshop that Don has not pawned the jacket for drink money, as she feared, but has swapped it for a gun, with which he intends to kill himself. The decision to trade the coat for a gun reconstitutes the jacket as an emblem of value. Don is not contemptuous or unmindful of the coat's prior significance. Rather, because he can no longer conceive of himself as a person worthy of it, believing he can do nothing for its owner but further augment her pain, he severs their tie by choosing to give up booze and life with one stroke. He imagines that his theft of the coat will prove to Helen that he cares nothing for her, and thus set her free, when in fact it convinces her that she is the only living figure who has not emotionally dissolved for him. Helen fathoms the mystery of the theft correctly, and leaves the coat with the pawnbroker, running back to Don's apartment while getting soaked to the skin (in a manner that anticipates Shirley MacLaine's New Year's Eve run at the end of Wilder's *The Apartment* [1960], also linked to a pending threat of suicide). Helen's abandonment of any thought of protective covering for herself gives the viewer a visceral sense that she is attuned to Don's degree of "exposure," and is prepared to meet him in that spiritual place. Back at Don's apartment, his willingness to open the door and let her in, which pulls him away from his inspection of himself in the bathroom mirror, on the verge of his contemplated shooting, suggests that he has been drawn, at least for the moment, out of his trance of utter estrangement. His ability to respond to her restores a sense of otherness to his shrunken world. As he urges her to leave, he is conscious of her sopping wet state and offers her his raincoat so that her return to the streets will be less punishing.

As she stands near the doorway, Helen is granted a propitious, almost supernatural view of Don's revolver in the bathroom, through an oval mirror reflection. This sighting is meant as a corrective to the language of hallucination earlier in the narrative, including both the DTs segment and Don's opera fantasy of the dancing raincoat, when the pint of rye materializes, through a blend of stage and cinema sorcery, within the coat pocket. After spotting the gun's reflection, Helen retrieves a half-empty liquor bottle that she has concealed in an umbrella stand (and in so doing, harkens back to the umbrella from the theatre scene, in another instance of sleight-of-hand transformation). She urges Don to choose the glass of whiskey she pours for him over the gun, and offers to drink with him.

Helen's last theatrical action is to take over Don's previous role of barroom storyteller, pleading with him to conceive a new life narrative in which his drinker and writer selves are no longer regarded as separate beings, but aspects of a single person. Don gradually enters into the spirit of her reworking of his story, and demonstrates his resolve to start afresh as a writer by dropping a lit cigarette into his beckoning whiskey glass, thus converting the *Traviata* "chalice of joy" into an ashtray. This action is linked to a recurring Milland gag—highlighting his comedy persona—of him turning his cigarette around in his mouth so he doesn't try to light the filter. Usually this action is performed in Wyman's presence, and is another Lubitsch-inflected idea for releasing wit from sodden helplessness. As Don begins to retell his story of the weekend, gaining some authority over it by taking on—as the film concludes—the responsibility of film narrator, we are led back to the film's opening theatrical image of a bottle suspended by a cord outside Don's apartment window, hidden from every perspective but the one we share with the camera. The privacy of this revelation is, in Kracauer's terms, theatrical. The sighting has a preordained air, a quality of contrivance. The bottle looks back at the viewer, in much the same fashion that the fantasy pint flask on the opera stage seeks out Don and, in effect, winks at him. We discover Don once again through his window, in the same position he occupied at the beginning of the film. He stands above his bottle, with his back turned to it, but in full knowledge of its whereabouts. The bottle still dangles as a prospective outcome within Don's accompanying narration. Don, as storyteller, "writes" his ending in advance of living it, as a decisive turning away from his series of ruinous failures. But the air of the undisclosed secret knowledge, the lingering tie with his compulsion, visually persists.

The reality principle conspires with theatrical dreamwork in the concluding phase of *The Lost Weekend* to create a delicate balance. Wilder stays in touch with the obdurate city chill, present not only in the sleeting rain but in the grungy rooms of Don's apartment. The rooms, with their unrelenting subdued light, a light of metaphysical grayness, are a strong indicator of how things presently stand for Don Birnam. The resigned helplessness that these spaces steadily project is not vanquished. Yet, as I have argued, the objects that are brought into play in this drab arena are steeped in theatrical color, possessing what one might call the power of theatrical suggestion, and destabilizing the naturalist propensities of the plot. Theatre does not assume full control of the proceedings, but it manages to impart a certain elasticity to Don's character and predicament. The objects that he perceives, handles, comments on possess a transformative power of their own, established in the orbit of *La Traviata*'s stage world, and Don borrows some of their "converting" strength by association. Helen's continuing faith in Don—visualized through her coat-mediated recognition moments—depends for its persuasiveness on the mythic force of the theatrical gaze, which is anchored to her first appearance in the film. A woman appears on a bare stage, holding Don's coat and mournful, bereft derby, awaiting discovery and connection. Before Don can see himself in the finale, he must see her, shorn of more than her coat, as though for the first time, thereby closing a circle. The objects that carry forward from the fiercely festive and harmonious spectacle of *La Traviata* bloom afresh in the sodden aftermath of Don Birnam's weekend, and provide viable experiential openings for him. Theatre is the spell-weaving, Ariel emissary from another world—undefeated even by the Second World War's banquet of horrors. Ariel's world rests inside film's dream of the real, and is consecrated to shape-shifting, marvels, unlikely restitution, and a higher, more flexible causality.

3

The Theatre of Aloneness in Film

> The Actors . . . are a glass in which we see our own faces; each Spectator presently turns an Actor in the Tragedy, and plays over his own Passions, though insensible and unseen. . . . all the Fiction and Personating upon the Stage is of itself cold and insipid, and never entertains us delightfully, till it have found within our selves some Reality.
>
> —Jacques-Bénigne Bossuet, *Maxims and Reflections on Plays*

THE MOST FREQUENTLY ANALYZED narrative segment of Italian neorealist cinema may well be a tone poem of solitude in Vittorio De Sica's *Umberto D.* The scene concentrates on a maid named Maria (Maria Pia Consilio) who wakes up in the apartment house where she is employed, and unselfconsciously performs a number of activities, chiefly in the kitchen, that constitute what we assume is her daily early morning routine. The fame of this brief episode is partly due to the fact that André Bazin singled it out for extended comment in his original review of *Umberto D.* He concludes his description of it with the glowing prediction that "it will remain one of the high points of film" (*What Is Cinema?, volume 2*, 81). Bazin was struck by the fact that this essentially undramatic documentation of the maid doing ordinary chores escaped from the net of the main plot and its perhaps too strictly preordained order. For four and a half minutes of nearly continuous time in Maria's company, what is at issue is "the succession of concrete instants of life, no one of which can be said to be more important than another, for their ontological equality destroys drama as its very basis" (81). De Sica finds the visible poetry of existence through the discovery of what he might term uneventful spectacle. It is difficult, of course, for any viewer not to privilege certain moments in this lengthy interlude of "Maria by herself" over others. Viewer memory automatically creates its own hierarchy. I immediately think of Maria awakening to the sight of a cat noiselessly moving across the long, grimy, screened skylight above her; the manner in which she groggily puts on her robe as she walks through a high-ceilinged, beautiful, deserted hallway; the way her attention is caught—as the camera approaches her from the other side of the large kitchen window—by some beckoning impressions outside; her repeated attempts to light a match for the stove against a wall streaked with white markings from former bids for a flame; and, supremely, Maria making a game of trying to close the kitchen door with her outstretched bare foot while she stretches out on a chair with a coffee grinder in her lap.

Nor is the scene entirely disconnected from significant dramatic questions, as Bazin's analysis implies. At one point Maria pauses in the midst of coffee preparations to look down at her stomach, touch it, and then respond to the just revealed fact of her pregnancy. Her progression of facial attitudes begins with a look that one might hesitantly characterize as wonder mingled with apprehension. Almost immediately, we see her blinking back tears. The camera gently moves in toward her face to contemplate her uncertain mood, and the music on the soundtrack lyrically commiserates with her, with a soft, bell-chiming accompaniment that reminds me of both the mysterious cat treading on the roof and the water dripping melodically from a kitchen tap. The sadness of her plight is not passed over, but it seems absorbed promptly in resumed work activity and the serene spell cast by the morning light and the quiet room. Moments after the arrival of her tears, Maria distracts herself successfully not only with coffee grinding but also with her playful attempt to reach the unclosed door with her foot. Millicent Marcus has noted that the kitchen episode serves an "interiorizing function. This is Maria's personal space which she claims as her own through a series of small, ritualized gestures" (quoted in Klevan, *Disclosure of the Everyday*, 108). Most intriguingly, for my purposes, Marcus sees the kitchen as offering a stage for the "private re-enactment" of her innermost self (quoted in Klevan, *Disclosure of the Everyday*, 110).

In this chapter I will be considering numerous instances of characters in film who contend with a state of aloneness. Sometimes the character is literally by herself, as Maria is, at other times she experiences acute isolation in the presence of others. I shall be regarding the depiction of aloneness in film as a disguised theatrical stage. Inwardness there is revealed to the camera in a manner that strengthens the illusion of privacy. Aloneness is, of course, as fictitious as any other dimension of film narrative. It is a condition performed by an actor for a witnessing camera, and will ultimately be shared with all the spectators who behold this estranged or stricken or merely solitary figure at intimate range. The character isolated onscreen is both alone and together with us, and directors organize the staging so that we are led to engage with this solitary self-revelation in a variety of ways. Some of these involve entering it empathetically, and some encourage an increase of emotional distance. In one instance we may feel an immense desire to intervene in a character's plight and alleviate it, but at the same time feel powerless to do so. In another situation, we may be anxious to detach ourselves from identification because of the character's too exposed, harrowing circumstances. There are many occasions where we may be eager to see an ordeal prolonged or exacerbated for our pleasure. Just as often we may try to devise and project onto a character potential escape routes from a weighty, troubled mood that entraps her. Obviously, the precise degree of our affiliation or detachment is something that everything in the director's manner of framing and dramatizing the sequestered figure's actions is meant to control. The "stage," as it were, is invisible, but it is strictly supervised.

I will talk about how the theatrical spaces of aloneness in film can give the sense of privacy different modes of access to the adjacent, somehow kindred life of objects, to the forces of light and shadow, to spaces that successively open and contract, to enhanced disarray or recovered clarity, to outward showings of what goes on within. Edward Snow, in his brilliant critical study of Vermeer, links the painter's solitary figures in rooms clothed with light with a "wish-fulfillment of the artistic process itself": for consciousness to be "released from the perspective of the isolated self and reabsorbed into the field of vision" (10). Snow's consideration of "dynamic unrest" in Vermeer's rendering of poised stillness impressively extends the list of tensions that operate in cinematic depictions of aloneness: "a conflict between emergence and recession, sensations of intensification and easing, quickening and fading, clutching and letting go, labor and deliverance, suddenness and attenuation" (14).

Aloneness can, as in *Umberto D*'s scene of awakening and early morning tasks, temporarily unknot the plot's dismal quandaries, restoring not only our sense of calm but our trust in what calm can make visible and redemptive. Character isolation can also build spaces where cinema seems to be alone with its own basic properties, reflecting on what they are, and putting figures in touch with the motion picture's own lonely sense of being, a fixed past dreaming itself into a seemingly animated present tense, a recurring present whose every reach for the "here and now" is inescapably inscribed with what is finished and done, already lost.

Most of the commentary on Maria's awakening in *Umberto D* that I have read does not emphasize the release from the initial constraints of aloneness that occurs during Maria's dreamlike navigation of the apartment rooms. Maria is alone in certain obvious respects, and no doubt experiences some of the pangs of isolation. In other ways, however, her aloneness is alleviated by a number of accompaniments: the musical score; the twice-encountered cat on the roof; the objects in the kitchen and hallway; the beckoning open window; the sometimes conspicuously moving camera; and, crucially, the presence of the spectator. De Sica subtly establishes the threshold of the kitchen doorway as a boundary crossing for Maria, one that permits her burden of care and uncertainty to be briefly transfigured into a calm, centered stillness.

Her full awakening is preceded by a phone call occurring within earshot of her bed in the hallway. Umberto (Carlo Battisti), the retired, impoverished civil servant who is the film's protagonist, has phoned the hospital about a feigned illness, in order to get himself taken there by ambulance and thus halt the eviction plans of his landlady. Umberto's present woes do not immediately affect Maria, though she is fond of him and regularly shows him consideration. Umberto, his call completed, carries his agitation out of frame, and for the next five minutes we lose sight of it as well. A narrative opening is created for Maria, a peripheral figure in the film's central drama, to claim our complete attention. Her act of rousing herself from sleep is composed of different elements than Umberto's fretful scheming. Her mood answers to the morning light in a self-replenishing fashion that Umberto is not able to summon. We have just observed the old man lying in bed the night before, unsuccessfully struggling to silence his alarm clock, finally burying it (still ringing) under his covers. The views of him frantically (and not amusingly) lurching about in his bed, consumed with fear, markedly contrasts with the graceful slowness of Maria's return to wakefulness. Her eyes first come to rest on the sight of a cat, directly above her, moving with rapt delicacy on the other side of the skylight arch, exploring its rooftop realm noiselessly, without hurry. After loosening her bedcovers and placing her hands over her face as she completes a short, song-like morning prayer, Maria walks down the enchantingly spacious, quiet hallway as she dons her housecoat, picking up unconsciously something of the cat's liquid pace and integration with its surroundings.

We hear Maria's feet scuffing along the floor as she advances down the hallway in long shot, the gossamer score preserving the yearning mystery and wistfulness that were established when Maria absorbed the image of the apparitional roving cat. She opens a door that leads into the large, unoccupied kitchen and crosses into this domain that is well-known to her but unfamiliar to us. As she enters, the space encloses her with the secure, cleansing light of a Vermeer painting. Maria's movements from object to object in medium shot and especially her turn toward the window, which offers her a vista to contemplate for a short interval with a fullness of repose, remind me of the pregnant woman in Vermeer's *Woman in Blue Reading a Letter*. This equally soothing solitary figure finds momentary equilibrium, absorption, and containment as she reads the folded letter page she clasps in both hands. It is an ever-deepening moment of placid balance that all the objects within Vermeer's framed room—wall map, two chairs, a table, a book, and an open box on a tablecloth—collaborate to secure for her. Edward Snow has noted that the reading woman's pregnancy "becomes an emblem for the fullness of inner life that requires our acceptance of her as other than ourselves" (6). Visibility sharpens in relation to the painting's several assertions of hiddenness—the separate life swelling within the woman (reinforcing the secret of her own inwardness); the letter whose message we are not privy to; the open box whose contents we are not in quite the right position to see.

What is most hidden in the *Umberto D* kitchen scene is the maid's attitude toward her experience there. Maria passes through a doorway she opens and seems (from our placement) to be released into an ordinary time that feels timeless. There is a steady easing of narrative pressure as we observe Maria half-attentively engaged in her round of mundane duties. The kitchen is not entirely silent—the dripping faucet tap is especially pronounced—but the impression that builds in the kitchen is of a space enveloped in quiet and light. The atmosphere of this windowed chamber and every visible entity we observe seem hushed in response to the lyricism of the score, which treads softly around the periphery of sadness. The things Maria casually handles live somewhere between the ordinary and sacramental ritual. They are available for unreflective use but also, at a level Maria seems unconscious of, for communion. It is as though the singular facts of our surroundings have souls that reflect back our human souls, yearning to express themselves, to unveil their being. At the very least, the objects that Maria engages with loosen the grip of her solitariness.

De Sica has chosen a nonactor to play Maria—Maria Pia Consilio, a former seamstress who shares her character's first name. His hope is that her face will reveal things to the camera that are not linked to actorish intention. In this respect, De Sica's aesthetic aim resembles Robert Bresson's, who seeks "models" who are free of guile, theatrical manipulation, and prompting in the actions they are assigned to present. Maria's face is an open, enigmatic surface that does not resolve the question of how she relates to the phenomena unfolding before her. If some sort of spiritual release is occurring in the "internal drama" of her awakening, Maria must not be shown knowing it, or visibly taking it in. Maria seems to be ever on the verge of awareness, presenting a neutral face that is not quite blank, one that unwittingly absorbs impressions. There is a wonderful moment early in the kitchen scene when Maria almost looks directly into the camera, as she catches sight of the window. The camera and the spectator are placed on the other side of it, in the "outside world," and our shared view inside includes the window's crossbars. Maria accepts the camera's invitation to gaze through this enticing frame, walking closer to the window and us. It is here, if anywhere, that she is conscious of the kitchen as a kind of stage on which she is placed to disclose herself. When she looks out, she is granted her second view of the cat she had beheld in her first waking moments, the image that carried the outer world's thereness back to consciousness. This time Maria views the cat from above rather than below, and it is as though she is once again imbued with the cat's grace and sense of restful exploration.

The viewer, peering through the window, not only observes Maria, but flows into the room with the morning light. From this moment on, our union with the beatific, gentle pace of her actions intensifies. We befriend her as the cleansing light does. We enhance with our secret shadowing of Maria's movements the kitchen's power to protect her, to grant her refuge. We deepen the scene's focus on her somnolent, half-alert investment in her chores with our growing consciousness of their

Figure 3.1. Maria (Maria Pia Casilio) nearly makes eye contact with us as she moves toward what's outside the frame in *Umberto D.*

distinctive beauty, their fleetingness. The viewer's empathic bonds with Maria tighten and affirm a togetherness. It is perhaps the force of our joining with Maria that makes the perceptual transfiguration of ordinary circumstances happen. Maria's look in our direction lets us in at the window, as it were, and then she accepts, absorbs our accompanying presence as "something in the air" that reduces her isolation. The duration of our protective stance toward Maria is uncertain. When Maria blinks back tears after briefly considering her pregnancy, they do not fully expose her to privation or fear. Her face does not surrender to the feeling of possible bereftness that the tears issue from. Her impulse to weep contends with her composure, but does not dislodge it. We are transfixed by the restorative light and peacefulness of these magical surroundings, and endeavor to keep Maria open to them as well—in a self-forgetful, freeing way. She projects, in all of her appearances in the film but in the kitchen scene most of all, a striking absence of ego, even in her distress. Maybe this is why her child's game with her outstretched leg provides such a delicate climax to the segment, pulling all the perceptual threads together. The "cat stretch" of her foot reaches out to the door that minutes before had opened up for her this calm kitchen sanctuary, and now she seeks to close the door in such a fashion that the grace mysteriously at work in the atmosphere will be held in and prolonged (by dint of a child's faith in play). But Maria is called back to the normal tumult of the apartment building and to Umberto's suspended plot by a harshly ringing telephone in the hallway. When she vacates the room to answer it, her expansive aloneness and the Vermeer spell that allowed us to dwell, equally blessed, in that aloneness with her (as the companion spirit of peace) are dissolved.

Another film scene in which solitude and a character's pregnancy powerfully conjoin occurs in King Vidor's 1928 silent film, *The Crowd*. Silent film has a special affinity for wordless experiences of characters "going it alone," and often these narrative interludes include direct acknowledgments of the film apparatus, creating theatrically framed portrait spaces for the rendering of heightened private feeling. The scene from *The Crowd* that I will examine follows a bitter breakfast quarrel by a young couple in their cramped Manhattan apartment. Mary Sims (Eleanor Boardman) and her husband, John (James Murray), have been married for less than a year, and they are faced with financial woes, disapproving in-laws (in John's case), the tedium of John's barren office job, and the stultifying routine they have both fallen into. The quarrel has escalated disastrously after an initial round of breakfast table bickering. Mary announces her intention to leave John, pulls out a valise, and begins to fill it haphazardly with clothes yanked out of a cabinet near the apartment door. Instead of urging her to reconsider and reducing the flow of hostility, John declares that it's "fine" if she goes away for good, and without the slightest hesitation departs for work, slamming the door behind him. The slam, though silent, is designed to instigate a "shock cut" to Mary, clutching two stray items of clothing, as she rises up suddenly into a close-range subjective reaction shot. For the next seventy seconds, we are permitted to study her in a sustained medium shot, with no camera movement, as she processes the fact and implications of her abandonment. It is a "stream of consciousness" portrait, even though we view her from the outside. The shifts in her facial expressions, accompanied by arm and hand gestures, subtly illuminate the sinuous path of her thought and feelings. Mary's face presents no obstacle to our reading of her internal struggle, as she runs a mental gauntlet from pain, bewilderment, and apprehension to her recollected pregnancy and its claims on her, with a final letting go into unbridled terror. We are peripherally aware throughout of the sparse background elements of an open cabinet door, striped and flaking, a sizable expanse of bare wall directly above it, and to the right, behind Mary, the closed false door that stores the apartment's Murphy bed. Mary's hair is somewhat askew (her husband had criticized her neglect of it) and her housecoat is shabby and rumpled. Her face, however, seems lit from within and is charged with emotional energy. She uses her right hand, which almost instantly drops the white garment it held, to alternately cover and disclose her features, as though each hand pass wiped another shade of feeling away and drew another down to take its place. In contrast to the *Umberto D* kitchen scene, here the background elements fail to speak or lend support to Mary Sims's privacy. They recede rather than emerge, and Mary's mental tumult briefly removes her from her domestic surroundings. Solitude on camera means that one has escaped, for an interval, the mediating effect of the relay of looks from other characters, and their limiting judgments, whether favorable or antagonistic. There is certainly no "crowd" infiltration in this framing of Mary's private trepidation (as there are in most of *The Crowd*'s crises). Vidor's film is laden with crowd images and is everywhere addressing the question of how the striving multitude impinges on individual aspiration and the quest for distinction: the need to "stand out" somehow. Part of Mary's distress at the prospect of being abandoned with an infant is the rough, censorious treatment she imagines receiving from the social mass. She fears "standing out" in the wrong way, as a pathetic object lesson. As in *Umberto D*, the camera is minutely attentive to her ways of experiencing her aloneness—this time on a practically bare stage—and once again the hidden spectator is a vital component of this attending.

Mary's husband has proven unable to find any sympathetic connection to his wife in their morning dispute. Her spirit has become invisible to him. John sees her as the only available scapegoat for his accumulated frustrations and sense of entrapment. The woman who, in previous episodes, has appeared to him as the embodiment of earth's highest beauty—an ideal to venerate and try to be worthy of—as well as his impetus to succeed, now has herself turned into a weight, a stagnant image, a shame-inducing reflection of his many failures. The camera placement on Mary in the seventy-second portrait to some extent operates in tandem with John's just ended altercation with her. Its immobility and close framing hem her in. The framing does not simply witness her anguish, it works to release it by amplifying the pressures of confinement.

Her apartment world has been stiflingly small, and now it feels smaller still, unlike the hallway and kitchen spaces in the *Umberto D* sequence, which steadily opens up, renewing contact with the enticing, mysterious urban vista beyond the kitchen window. Mary has begun preparations to flee the apartment herself before John echoes her threat, and then makes good on it. Mary's threat to leave was a thinly disguised plea for John to acknowledge that she still matters to him and to turn conciliatory. She is not at all reconciled to the reality of his departure and the possibly final separation it implies. At first, in standing still shock, she can hardly believe it has happened, but she cannot instantly find the will to pursue him or call him back. Abasing herself is a humiliating move to contemplate. Nor does she know how to give him a reason to revise his bleak assessment of their relationship. Nothing will change until he remembers who she is, what she has meant to him, and how to behold her. Vidor treats the flow of Mary's mimed conflicting feelings as a magically extended moment. The unusual duration of the internal soliloquy shot is presented as the stop-time of an accelerated thought process. Mary several times in the course of her panicked, ricochet shifts in attitude covers a portion of her face with her hand as though to conceal her vulnerability from our watching. She conveys, intermittently, a sense of being exposed to onlookers.

She gradually returns from the emotional whirlabout brought on by shock to a sense of her body in its more grounded state. For a few moments, she, like Maria in *Umberto D*, places her hands on her belly. We see her become more mindful, through touch, of her pregnancy, and as her hands move to give herself a protective hug, she produces a brief, barely conscious smile. As she then further recollects her intention to share the news with John, terror returns with a more crushing realization of what his absence signifies. And it is here that her aloneness grows unendurable. She must regain contact with him immediately and somehow rekindle his awareness of a not-extinguished closeness. The soliloquy shot ends with her crying out John's name, hands to head, and then racing forward. The cut repositions us outside Mary's exceptionally large apartment window, which functions in the next short narrative segment as a literal theatre frame in which she presents herself to John, on the sidewalk directly below her. Her performance is designed to summon for him the image of the woman he remembers loving. Time has been suspended during Mary's "rush of thought." It is as though John's decision to storm off to work has been held in abeyance—arrested midstream—as Mary burrows inward on the upstairs "stage" of introspection. The apartment window makes the theatre frame more overt.

Mary raises a drawn shade to begin the scene at the window, and the visible curtains on either side of her heighten our recognition of a proscenium as she "enters" and captures the attention of her chosen audience. Until John hears her voice and looks up, he strikes us as still intent on leaving. As soon as he glances toward her, Mary adopts a forbearing, beckoning-to-the-bedroom manner, resting head and arms upon the windowsill. Her fingers delicately cajole him. The intimacy she performs is for the near-at-hand camera, and though it is a silent film, one feels that the voice she employs is a "beside one's partner's pillow" voice. She is aiming her gestures, gaze, and words at John, but he is not in an ideal viewer's position. Mary's enactment of her need for John is powerfully rendered for the camera and spectator (both in close proximity) and we instantly become collaborators in her attempt to re-create a vision of the wife that has been lost to memory's sight. Her manner of inviting John to return and find her is beautifully understated and uninsistent. Down on the sidewalk, John stands behind a barred metal fence. Since he must gaze upward to answer her, he has no alternative but to see Mary placed at an ethereal height. So often in their marriage, John acknowledges, with shame or wonder, his sense of Mary's superiority to him. As Mary continues to entreat him with a single slowly curling finger, we notice from our high window vantage point (maintained throughout the exchange) that John's fingers are also moving, although his hands remain at his side. His fingers are attuned to Mary's conciliatory motion. James Murray, who plays John, has unusually eloquent, expressive hands, and throughout *The Crowd* they keep us in touch with his so often thwarted or withheld sensitivity.

The window theatre interlude, while it bodes well for Mary's and John's peacemaking, does not end our involvement with Mary Sims's aloneness. When John agrees to come back inside and talk, Mary pulls away from the window proscenium and reenters the room where her "thinking" had been depicted as entrapment. In her brief time away from this space, the room seems to have expanded. We now view it in full shot with Mary paused before a welcoming open door. We notice a framed painting of flowers in a vase on the hallway wall just outside the door, which glows now in the light reflected from the window and entryway. The objects within the Sims's apartment have emerged from dormancy and indistinctness. The open door of the clothes cabinet rhymes with the larger main door standing open in front of it. The framed pictures above the cabinet seem to acquire eyes, momentarily, which tranquilly contemplate Mary as she apprehensively waits, holding the edges of her morning coat together, with one hand raised protectively near her neck.

Her abandoned traveling valise rests forgotten on the floor, but it too glows with the whiteness of the article of clothing spread on top of it. Mary's environment testifies once more to the solidity of her existence within it, but before John reenters she is oblivious of these reminders, and stands separate from them, casting a shadow against the wall to which she has retreated. The room as possible benefactor—a place that contains her and speaks to her sense of herself—is an impression that the viewer is granted ahead of her. Her awareness hasn't yet caught up to what we feel on her behalf.

Yet, when John is inside the room, poised uncertainly by the edge of the door opening inward, Mary does not hesitate to approach him, reaching out to grasp the brightly patterned open cabinet door in passing, then stepping to the main door, which she calmly eases shut. Mary is no longer alone, but Vidor extends for a little while longer our experience of her separateness by his method of framing her. She is shown standing against the door in profile, a few feet away from a symmetrically profiled John. She repeats her earlier gesture of the beckoning finger, and John, crisply dressed in his office suit and fedora, moves toward her until they are close enough for his hat brim to touch her hair and for her to touch his suit coat buttons. When this position of diffident, solicitous proximity has been achieved, Vidor cuts to an expressionist medium close-up of Mary. She is in an envelope of aloneness, blurred around the edges, with the background mostly of softly lit wall space. John, who has moments before been directly in front of her, has disappeared, as she confides the news of her pregnancy. She seems to maintain eye contact with him as she speaks, but we feel that Mary still dwells apart from him, in a realm that only we and the camera are allowed to penetrate—the distance of private soul from lived event. When we return to John's face, we clearly register the difference of light and space that he inhabits. He endearingly tears off his hat in a gesture that both expresses respect for Mary's revelation and emulates her bareheaded exposure.

The snarling, violent man of the prior argument scene unmasks, in effect, with the removal of his hat. His inner face is suddenly sprung from its hiding place. What we behold is the oft-returned to child-man demeanor of John, a figure deeply prone to weeping and other displays of unprotected vulnerability. As he hears that he will be a father, his features seem imbued with the dream of infant security, almost a longing for it. We are reminded that John lost his own paternal protector when still a young boy, and to a certain extent he has felt adrift ever since. The scene ends with John's efforts to restore Mary's faith in the security, value, and staying power of their living arrangements. He demonstrates to her that all of his previous failures of perception and understanding at breakfast can be revised. Breakfast begins again with his leading her to the table, watching her sit, and then pouring her coffee, as though each small show of attentiveness could be a devotional act, a matter of wonder and consequence for both of them. The connection to home space that Mary lost in her frantic thoughts of abandonment has been reanimated and, for the time being, restored to her.

The practice of using close-ups as private spaces for memory and charged introspection was developed and raised to sublimity in the silent films of D. W. Griffith. He conceived of elevated inner portraits, reserved for moments of crisis and usually featuring women. The close-up is framed with a black or haloed background, sequestering the flow of unfettered feeling or feeling ignored by another character (in what we might term aloneness time) from outer reality. James Naremore writes at length about one such instance of close-up theatre in Griffith's *True Heart Susie* (1919). After Lillian Gish's Susie accidentally witnesses the man she has loved since childhood proposing marriage to a frivolous rival, she steps away from the doorway, unobserved, and leans against a wall for support, displaying a remarkable variety of emotional responses in a sustained private presentation. Naremore argues that Gish's departure here from the seemingly simple attributes of her character type—childlike sweetness, in combination with unselfconscious naïveté and guilelessness—frequently occurs in these isolation portraits. We gain access to her strength, her superior knowledge, and her capacity for veiling her true state of mind—when she is out of range of other characters' observation. She confides the fullness of her being, its complex, hidden reserves, to the privileged viewer. We are not enjoined to identify with the feelings so much as behold them in a kind of wonder. They are searingly laid bare for the camera's sheltering gaze, and we become their secret sharer and supportive mirror. We adjust our quality of perception as Susie entrusts us with her heart, so that the delicacy of what is revealed to us is not shattered or coarsened by an indelicacy of response.

To the right of Gish's head and upper body is an area of encroaching darkness that marks the line where seeing breaks off, where face and feeling alike return to nothing, to sheer impenetrability. We naturally side with the work of illumination that the camera and Gish jointly undertake. I am always struck, viewing this scene, by Susie's faintly absurd, pie-brimmed straw hat, completely visible throughout the close-up above her face, and holding in its round, hopeful shape the clearly defined, benignly trusting persona that the face below it leaves behind. Though the hat seems to perch lightly on her hair, the face of Susie is engaged in a struggle with the reliably simple self that the hat stolidly embodies and imposes on her. The hat demands, or seems to, a lightness of attitude that Susie's countenance, buffeted by difficult feelings, cannot presently summon. Her comic headgear turns into an upraised mask as Susie's shocked laugh bursts from her lips, swiftly arrested by a spasm of grief. Susie explores her mouth at some length with a single, oblivious, wandering finger, as though in search of words that will be up to addressing the loss of her beloved, William, and allow her to regain self-possession. Then her hand strokes her face as her eyes desolately convey her continuing lostness, her inability (as yet) to pull herself together. We see her stagger past a friendly, carpeted staircase and a warmly lit hallway, hunched over and nearly deranged by disappointment, repeatedly alternating as she vacates the house between mirthless laughter and racking sighs. In less than a minute, however, she will be forced by someone who intercepts her to return to the house and the room in which she made her awful discovery, and offer congratulations to the engaged couple.

At such times within this narrative, for all our confidence that the conventions of pastoral comic romance will eventually lead to a positive resolution, we are still confronted with a persuasive private abyss, whose power of darkness is disproportionate to the genre conventions that work to stabilize it. There is another type of aloneness that Griffith experiments with in his hermetic close-up worlds. It has to do with the experience of abandonment and of being rendered emotionally invisible in a scene outwardly shared with another character. Although dialogue may continue to be exchanged and the victim of rejection may continue to be noticed and dealt with in a perfunctory fashion, the viewer's sense of the scene is of utterly separate realms, from which all trace of human connection has vanished.

An extraordinary example of the aloneness effect in the presence of another can be found in D. W. Griffith's *Way Down East* (1920), when Lillian Gish's Anna Moore learns that she is not really married to her husband, Lennox Sanderson (Lowell Sherman). He admits to her, without remorse, that the wedding had been a sham ceremony that he had staged to deceive her. The segment of the scene that I will be discussing is set in the large central room of the house they have briefly shared. They occupy two chairs that are separated by only a few feet. The spatial configuration of the room and the two figures' placement within it have been clearly established. The chairs are the obvious primary focus in the living quarters, but we feel that Gish's seat is not grounded in the way that Lowell Sherman's is. Anna seems untethered and afloat in a space that feels empty and vast. The close-ups of Gish further detach her from her physical location. She inhabits a theatrical frame that allows for the full, untrammeled exhibition of private feelings, which Sanderson take note of from his chair, but in no sense absorbs. The impression is of a willed blindness, which he successfully sustains. Part of the dramatic effect is our keen sense of his lack of access to what is so cogently on display: an incandescent spirit requesting clemency and visibility, both of which he casually refuses.

The silent film's "isolated consciousness" frame is somewhat akin to the spoken subtext spaces that Eugene O'Neill devised for his mammoth intergenerational family drama, *Strange Interlude* (1927). His characters would shift back and forth between shared dialogue passages and subtextual monologues, which almost invariably supplied an additional level of internal conflict with the partial or false revelation of their public utterance. O'Neill wished to open up an arena of verbalized thought onstage, which the audience could witness even though they were not being directly addressed. Characters were allowed to be both within scenes and separate from them simultaneously, with the subtextual zone as the realm of ferocity and (however chaotically) emotional truth. D. W. Griffith believed that cinema could visualize the movement of emotionalized thought through the luminous private chamber of the psychological close-up.

As Gish's Anna processes the meaning of Sanderson's denial that they are legally married, she first attempts to persuade herself that he's merely joking. She lifts up the wedding ring that she wears on a necklace beneath her dress and clasps it tightly in one hand, as though its material substance made the ceremony she recalls a thing with comparable reality and weight. As the camera cuts even closer to Gish's face, after an intertitle, it is as though not only Sanderson but the spectator is being pleaded with to adjudicate her claim. The viewer must make up for the manifest deficiency of Sanderson's response. Anna's lonely appeal becomes, by close-up transfer of available presence, our responsibility. Her direct communication of her need is something we cannot hide from. It is transparent and massive, and while we watch her place the ring on her finger, moving it anxiously up and down, so it becomes the emblem of every moment of trust and belief that Sanderson has extracted from her, her beseeching look places her face in our keeping. It is we who must

Figure 3.2. Anna (Lillian Gish) holds up her ring to Lennox Sanderson (Lowell Sherman), clinging to its material force in *Way Down East*.

protect it from the contamination of another's coldness or the crushing out of its inner light. Her face withholds nothing from us, and plays against our own sense of concealment in the viewing darkness of the theatre.

When Gish's look outward is replaced by a view of Sanderson, he is facing in the opposite direction from her, still seated on his chair, but entirely out of alignment with Anna's presence. He is seemingly waiting for an opportunity to conclude his unpleasant talk with her, and leave. As his eyes lift toward the ceiling, in a gesture of impatience with her excessive demonstration and unwillingness to accept the facts, we cut back to Anna, still beholding us in close-up, as though we had decided—with Sanderson—to turn away from her and repudiate her claims. In this shot Anna explodes in swiftly transitioned phases of outright anguish, disbelieving laughter, shy retreat (born of shock) into conciliatory forbearance, then a hysterical terror at the degree of his manifest estrangement, his unknownness, and of her own isolation. Sanderson's shot is backed by the furnishings of the room, Anna's by pure shadow, as though her feelings have temporarily obliterated all sense of external reality and support.

One of the gifts of silent cinema is the ease that such transitions from outer to inner conditions and back, within a shared environment, can be effected, with no suggestion of jolting discontinuity. The Griffith convention powerfully confirms the reality of separate worlds in what passes for human communication, and that the experience of aloneness can be most devastating when another person is externally very near, but fails to "take in" our behavioral and verbal expression. After another two shot, when Anna clings to Sanderson physically and even attempts kissing him to bring him back from his stupefying distance, she relents to the fact of his emotional absence and sits once more in her chair, acknowledging defeat along with the sad truth that the man she loved had never existed. Although his outward form remains seated beside her, the man in essence is nowhere to be found, and cannot reply to any feeling language she has at her disposal. Between them a third chair suddenly becomes noticeable, and we observe his folded overcoat and cane resting on it, signs of his imminent departure. These objects hasten him along in his final speech to her.

Assuming that her calmness means that she has become reasonable, Sanderson turns at last in her direction and leans toward her in a two shot. Griffith then cuts closer to him in a medium profile close-up. He is positioned at the extreme left side of the frame, emphasizing his proximity to Anna as he smilingly explains the difficulty of his situation and his good intentions, which circumstances didn't allow him to act upon. When we return to Anna's face, still backed by darkness, she has turned away from him, shaking her head slightly in disagreement with his facile reasoning, but composing herself at a distance from this speaker who ceased in her mind to be a real human entity. He does not occupy any space that enters into hers. When he rises to depart in full shot, her chair has become a glowing foreground island in a sea of sinister shadows and encroaching emptiness.

I will consider one last brief example of Griffith's sequestered close-up technique, drawn from a scene later in *Way Down East* where genuine mutual feeling is present, and a male speaker's meanings are actively understood and accepted. David Bartlett (Richard Barthelmess), the squire's son at a farm where Anna is employed, sits with her on a riverbank, and declares both his love for her and his desire to marry her. We are granted another close-up of Anna that creates a separate memory landscape for her in the present tense of her interaction with David. Her hair is arranged differently than it was in prior shots. Her expression is ruefully pensive, as she thinks back on the past circumstances that pose a seemingly insuperable obstacle to her accepting David's proposal. Her eyes are turned away from both David and the viewer. She hears what he says, and is moved by his profession of devotion, but she is simultaneously—unbeknownst to David—far away, in a space of the past that is unknown to him, and inaccessible. The past and its still oppressive burden are, however, available to us in this soft-edged memoryscape. We penetrate and see into the aloneness of Anna that David, limited to a different set of appearances, is denied access to.

William Wyler's *Carrie* (1952), adapted from Theodore Dreiser's novel *Sister Carrie*, is a film rife with painful instances of characters performing aloneness—both in solitude and in the company of others. One segment from the narrative is especially memorable for its rapid set of variations on different registers of isolation, and for delineating the power of environments to emotionally confer security and then ruthlessly pare it away. We begin with George Hurstwood (Laurence Olivier)—a once prosperous businessman who is now professionally disgraced, unemployed, and virtually penniless—being persuaded by his second, considerably younger wife, Carrie Meeber (Jennifer Jones), to reconcile with his grown-up son from his first marriage, who will be returning that day from a honeymoon abroad. Carrie, long discouraged by George's inability to reestablish himself in his profession, has begun to have some success of her own as a stage actress. George's son, with whom he was once very close, will be arriving in New York by ship, which will make a meeting between them relatively easy to arrange. Carrie is unaware that George committed an act of theft at the time that he escaped (with Carrie) from his loveless former marriage, and attributes his subsequent job failures and "bad luck" to his lack of drive and discipline. Although the money George stole was returned to his former employer, his criminal behavior has been widely publicized in the high-end restaurant world where he had previously flourished. George strikes her as a man curiously adrift, one who, for unaccountable reasons, has given up. He now feels like a millstone to her as she has acquired both ambition and a measure of recognition for her work as an actress.

Carrie has resolved to use George's chance to reunite and reconcile with his wealthy son as an occasion to leave him. His departure for the planned harbor meeting will give Carrie time to pack her clothes and flee, a turn of events that George does not remotely anticipate. In the first shot of our sequence, we see Carrie brushing his worn, sole remaining suit coat and adjusting his handkerchief in his coat pocket as he stands before her fearfully, hoping he appears sufficiently presentable to show himself to his son. George assures Carrie that nothing that transpires at the harbor will cause him to be parted from her for any length of time. "You'll be with me," he tells her, with as much firmness as he can still lay claim to. Before he passes through the doorway, Carrie, still dressed in her morning robe, requests that he kiss her. She bids him goodbye in a manner he does not recognize as final, and once he has left the apartment she calls out "Good luck" after him. Until this point in the narrative, Carrie has been generally straightforward in her dealings with George, in spite of the fact that she is by temperament a natural actress. The pattern of the relationship thus far has involved consistent deception, in large and small matters, on George's part, with Carrie gradually losing the capacity to trust his declarations to her. Most of his duplicity is motivated by his desperate devotion to her, as well as a compulsive need to protect her, both from the taint of his own disgrace and the knowledge that the ruin he rashly brought on himself, on two occasions, was entered into "for her sake." Even at this late stage in their time together, there is still crucial information about his past action that he withholds from her. He does not, however, make any excuses to her about his "shameful" failure to find his footing again.

Carrie's chief act of withholding, perhaps from the outset, is the pardonable lack of admission that her love for George Hurstwood has never risen to the level of his for her. The dynamic of deception decisively shifts on the morning of George's planned visit to see his son again. After he reads of his son's impending arrival in the newspaper, and debates how to relay this information to Carrie, we have an opportunity to observe her new physical attitude toward him (revealed not so much in speech as in the set of her indifferent face, her unkempt appearance, her slumped, listless posture, and the telling detail of her emptying the dregs of a battered coffee pot into the sink). She plainly conveys her desire to hold herself separate from him, and her involuntary repugnance at the extent of his decline. George is unmindful both of the facial evidence of her disgruntled recoil (possibly it has become habitual to her) and the rapid transformation of her attitude as he announces the possibility of reestablishing contact with his son. Carrie and George both slip into their own private worlds. Although Carrie's subsequent responses to him are supportive and markedly tender, the viewer is let in on the fact of Carrie performing her warm solicitude. Like many fine actors, she is not aware that she is now making theatre of her conduct. It is not that she is bereft of affection for her partner, but every action she enters into in this preparation for his departure is colored by her awareness that she is poised to leave herself, without any provision for return. The actress in her gives an extra measure of attentiveness and consideration to all her words, looks, and gestures, as though she is re-creating images of her past attachment to him for George to be nourished by in her absence. She does this by reflex rather than by calculation, to show herself that her decision to sever ties is not cold, or prompted purely by self-interest.

George is somewhat distracted by his apprehensiveness about the impending reunion, and his attendant fear of how his living situation with Carrie might be affected. He strives to reassure her that they cannot be separated, that he won't allow that to happen, while the final division between them unfolds for the viewer's gaze. Neither George nor Carrie is cognizant in the moments before George leaves of how alone each of them already is within the orbit of the exorbitant plans being formed. When Carrie tells him that this is a chance to get help and that he should take it, she straightens his tie and pats his lapels before repeating the phrase "take it." Although she is looking at him directly, she is addressing the advice to herself, and the viewer shares the private resolve that George fails to notice.

The camera stays on Carrie as George disappears through the door. He apparently feels no need to look back and meet her gaze when she wishes him "good luck." He might well be humiliated if he were to measure her customary gesture of encouragement against his own doubt and already wilting determination. Leaving with apparent confidence may be little more for him than a "face saving" exercise. As Carrie hears George's footsteps descending the stair, she knows she can abandon the performance she put on for him. Now she is truly by herself. As she closes the door on George and their life as a couple, the camera unobtrusively moves into position for an extreme close-up, as Carrie presses one side of her face against the door, knots one hand against the doorframe, and surrenders to an anguished fit of tears. The viewer is sole witness to this full volume engulfment, and at first it seems that Carrie has no sense of playing to an audience. But it is likely that the pain she shows herself expressing is partly a mask for the relief she keeps hidden. Carrie no doubt authentically mourns the slow wearing down of her feelings for George Hurstwood, as his loss of dignity, professional standing, and courage gradually diminished him. She is sad to have deceived him about her decision to go away, and her need to place her own interests above a continued sense of obligation to him. Her forceful rending by an uncontrollable grief is a retreat to a theatre of mercy from the alternative—clinical detachment and self-aggrandizement. It is an escape to the literal theatre world that she is contemplating, after all. As her lament proceeds, we see her draw back from it a little, as though the size of the display does not "fit" her. The close-up, in effect, is too big to be filled. She then begins to look searchingly for something she cannot pinpoint, possibly some lost portion of herself.

Wyler lap dissolves this image of Carrie's "lost" looking into the shot of a large crowd gathered at the New York harbor pier, waiting to greet returning travelers. As we catch sight of George within this group, we are granted a ghostly glimpse of Carrie pulling away from the door, in effect fleeing the sentiments that might prolong her captivity. All of the figures assembled on Pier 12 near the newly arrived passenger ship have their backs to the camera and George seems utterly anonymous and alone in their midst. The superimposition of the image of Carrie turning from the door in haste over the image of George becoming visible in a crowd reinforces our sense that his last human support has been removed. His waiting instantly acquires a different character from the imagined state of those surrounding him. He feels abjectly disconnected from the object of his quest. George hopes to be discovered and greeted without obtrusively pushing himself forward, making a show of being there, and presuming he has paternal rights. When we get our first look at George's face (in medium shot) he has apparently worked his way through the mass of onlookers until he has gained a position directly behind the entrance gate. Arriving passengers should have no difficulty obtaining a clear view of him. George then spots his son and his son's new wife as they descend a ramp. The son casts a searching glance toward the camera in long shot that momentarily suggests he has noticed George, and, by extension, us. But as he turns his attention back to his wife, we (sharing George's reaction) realize we have made a mistake in our overeagerness to be found. Two extreme close-ups of George follow, in quick succession, both immensely intimate, sending a loud, silent plea for recognition and acknowledgment. For the second time George appears to have been identified, since the son's scanning gaze makes contact with someone and he raises his hat to confirm the sighting. But the anticipated encounter is derailed by the sudden arrival, directly in the son's path, of George's ex-wife and a placid, respectably dressed gentleman we assume to be her own new husband. This pair—the actual recipients of the son's eager wave—rushes close to him and receives the unstinting warmth of the newlyweds' effusive hugs and salutations. The son directs one more (seemingly regretful) glance in what we take to be our vicinity as he—in long shot range—pats the shoulder of the surrogate father, but once more the line of his gaze does not connect with George's.

We return to George's face for a third close-up, this one resigned to isolation and an invisibility he tries to draw around himself like a cloak. He watches the reunion as if from a great, impassable distance, certain that he has not been discovered and no longer waiting for any contact. He has no will to force a connection that has not arisen naturally. He construes his presence as superfluous to the occasion: he cannot be anything but an imposition and an embarrassment. The young couple and the designated "parents" live in the present. He is fixed inexorably in the past, an impecunious ghost who foolishly imagined he had a "flesh and blood" stake in the proceedings. When the brightly animated group

Figure 3.3, Carrie (Jennifer Jones)—both grief-stricken and relieved—loses a part of herself to George's departure in *Carrie*.

passes near George, he raises his hand to his face, covering it in shame, and thus preventing his last chance of being detected. He shifts his body away from them, and then makes a full, stealthy circle, while standing in place, in order to observe his son's disappearance. He closes his eyes as a boat whistle sounds and begins to walk away, pushing against the flow of those still waiting, and alive with expectation. As this shot nears its close, we are returned by a lap dissolve to the empty apartment where we had our last private contact with Carrie.

But before we reenter the apartment, let us consider a bit further the viewer's relation to George's aloneness at the pier, and the nature of our task in sharing it. As in all the examples we have dealt with so far, it is we that the strange theatre of aloneness is aimed at. When George is still anxiously eager to be seen and reclaimed, our response to his magnified image is to amplify the need (on his behalf) and to silently "call out" in his stead. We attempt mentally to increase the visibility that is so visible to us. Here George Hurstwood stands, without defenses against possible rejection and in plain sight. Everyone—the logic of the image declares—should have eyes for loved ones who belong to them and have suffered undue hardship. When it becomes increasingly clear that he will not be discovered, our response grows more shielding. He experiences the twin terrors of invisibility and unwantedness, and feels humiliated by the "beggar" dimension of his presence. At this point we strive to mitigate his own deepening sense of estrangement and worthlessness. It is these sensations that stick to him like burrs and "single him out" in a wrong, demeaning way. He cannot find the courage or will to reduce the menacing gap that keeps him apart from his son. Given his paralysis, perhaps the viewer's manner of perceiving him (when no others can) will relieve the extreme degree of his strandedness. As he shrinks back from detection, we become the power of divination that holds him in focus. Our gaze is all that prevents him from dissolving into the crowd, an unmarked cipher.

When we reenter his small apartment with him through the same door that only a minute of screen time before Carrie has leaned against, sobbing, we are initially struck by the immaculateness of the sitting room and the friendly rectangles of daylight offered by two long windows, both covered by curtains that seem strangely diaphanous. The door catches while George clasps the knob, and he must close it twice before it securely shuts him in. As he walks across the room toward his "elderly man" rocking chair by the left side window, he appears to be conscious of the objects around him inspecting him critically. Even in the midst of these modest, mute furnishings, he must try to pass muster. They seem to hold the power to reduce him further. He picks up the newspaper lying in his rocker, sits down, and attempts to fathom a next move. Earlier that morning, we watched him sitting in this same rocker—viewed from the identical distance and angle—reading about his son's unexpected arrival in New York. The repeated rocking chair shot ironically makes a rhyme with his prior clutched-at hope, and starkly measures the decline he has suffered in just a few hours. Carrie was still part of his world then. He could call out to her in the adjoining room and she would answer and appear. She is no longer present, though he is of course not yet aware of the fact. If she is nearby, as he suspects (and fears) she might be, he has not found the resolve to face her. The immaculateness of the room suddenly begins to speak the language of empty space. Carrie has done a thorough tidying to ease the likely shock that her abandonment of him will bring. George leans forward in his rocker as he hears footsteps in the hallway. He clearly registers at this moment the fact that Carrie is probably out somewhere, and that the sound may well indicate her returning. He braces himself anxiously for her anticipated entrance and inevitable questions about his reunion. He continues to grip the newspaper and remains seated in his chair.

Wyler highlights moment-to-moment duration in this scene, in a fashion similar to De Sica. A single long shot composition has covered all of George's actions since he has returned to his apartment. The room gathers an oppressive stillness as the shot lengthens, and is coiled tight with the expectancy of George learning the full extent of his new, companionless situation. When the footsteps become audible in the outside hall, the camera reframes by moving toward the door, as if attuned to George's apprehensive inertia. Carrie will once again be confronted with his failure to achieve a reasonable goal. The camera's fresh vantage point presses more closely near the edge of George's chair and makes the closed quarters feel even more stifling. Another door in the hall squeaks open, so George has attained a bit more of a reprieve before the ordeal of Carrie's certain disappointment. Wyler ends the shot with another lap dissolve. It is unclear how much time has elapsed. George continues to sit in his rocker, the unread and forgotten newspaper still in hand, testifying to his dazed state of mind. The camera has drawn somewhat closer and is now moving in the reverse direction from its prior "attraction" to the door.

This camera movement subtly continues to trace George's thoughts as he now considers the adjoining bedroom in its silence, and the possible meaning of Carrie's now worrisome absence. He rises and passes through the bedroom doorway. We are placed inside the room just ahead of his arrival there, and have a few moments to take stock of the evidence of Carrie's escape, which we know about before George catches up with us. The camera allies itself at this point with George's point of view, moving twice in accord with his shifting gaze as he checks the bedroom for some reassuring signs we are confident he will not find. Wyler adopts a Hitchcock subjective vantage point (the first of a series) as he cuts to George's hands reaching down to the neatly made bed and picking up, first, a small drawstring purse containing some crumpled paper money. In the same composition we observe—still from George's implied point of view—a freshly ironed white shirt, on top of which rests, unmistakably, a farewell note. George slowly lifts it up to read it, and there is a cut to the dreadfully spare message, which fills the screen as we read it along with George. The words Carrie has written are surprisingly lacking in feeling, containing neither expressions of regret, lingering fondness, nor encouragement. "Good-bye George—You will be happier with your son—I was not good for you. Carrie." The size of the image disconcertingly stresses the austere brevity of Carrie's leave-taking. Wyler includes the thumb of George's right hand and a finger of his left on the note to heighten our sense that we are partaking of George's reading.

We are then given another close-up of George, still attired in the suit that Carrie had fussed over as she readied him for his momentous encounter with his son. He looks "presentable" during his slow-motion absorption of another devastating loss. His mouth opens and closes in an effort to forestall weeping, then he immediately busies himself seeking further proof that she is indeed gone. An invisible clock has begun to tick audibly. George looks back toward the other room, where he previously sat in ignorance. The entire space is at one with his emptiness, and can do nothing to lessen it. George turns around to face Carrie's clothes closet, flings open one mirrored door but finds only one piece of clothing still hanging there, the unpalatable bathrobe she had worn to see him off that morning. Gripping Carrie's crumpled note in one hand, he passes behind the stern prison bars of a bedstead and approaches a shabby dresser on which the ticking clock is revealed on a desolate stretch of cloth. The camera dollies in closer to the side drawer George yanks open. The belled alarm clock above the drawer is placed in such a manner that it appears both as a sound witness and a sight witness to his search for some meaningful trace of Carrie's lost presence. The open drawer, it turns out, is not quite empty. Tucked in one of pocket folds affixed to its inside walls, a missed item brushes against his sifting fingers.

A hairpin that Carrie has either overlooked or not needed is retrieved so delicately from its hiding place that it seems, at this instant, imbued with every aspect of the vanished woman that George cherishes. He inspects this keepsake helplessly, as the image fades to black.

The progression of George's movement in this scene is from a gradual finding out that Carrie is not "at home" now to the realization that her absence is final. We know ahead of George that she in all likelihood has opted to abandon him, but there is still suspense residing in our lack of certainty about how she has arranged her flight, the nature of the message she will offer George by way of justification, and the possibility of her "constraining" second thoughts. The usually inhospitable, grimly confining apartment has never looked more invitingly livable and in good order than during George's gradual discovery of her desertion. Carrie has made sure that the rooms have an accommodating appearance. They show signs of attention and care, which makes the terse note George picks up from his thoughtfully ironed shirt on the bed all the more startling in its chill rejection. The phrase "I was not good for you" is both an acceptance of blame and a verdict on all the couple's experiences from the very beginning. The note implies: "There is little to mourn, by either of us, in my decision to sever ties."

The most powerful extended moment in the entire narrative segment is George's chancing upon the hairpin—the smallest conceivable reminder of Carrie for him to hold onto. We progress from George finding out all that Carrie prepared for him to see and understand to finding something that was not part of her intention, a stray particular that had escaped her notice. It is an item that would contain no value for anyone except George, but the viewer participates fully in the process through which his hand and gaze join forces to emotionalize it. The apartment and its contents have been swiftly reduced to meaninglessness by Carrie's refusal to stay part of its living process, but just as this evacuation of sense has occurred, feeling pours back in through the unexpected retrieval of a hairpin. The audibly ticking clock measures the dire prospects awaiting George Hurstwood in his aloneness, the fleeting time of his actual brief relationship with Carrie, and the unfathomable memory time that the found hairpin consecrates. Near the end of *Carrie*, when George gathers his few belongings, wrapped in paper, after a night spent in a flophouse, we recognize the hairpin among them.

George Hurstwood crosses the boundary of forsakenness in *Carrie*. In Todd Field's *In the Bedroom* (2001), adapted from a story by Andre Dubus, Matt Fowler (Tom Wilkinson) and his wife, Ruth (Sissy Spacek), cross the boundary of their only child's death by murder. Frank Fowler (Nick Stahl), a college-age son still living at home, is killed by the jealous ex-husband of the young mother, Natalie (Marisa Tomei), whom he has been dating over the summer vacation. The sequence I will examine—which will conclude the chapter—is set on the day of Frank's funeral. It concentrates primarily on the father Matt's isolation and grief, and his inability to penetrate his wife's withdrawal, in which frozen rage contends with despair.

The first images (occurring immediately before the funeral scene, when Matt has not yet informed his wife of what has happened) reveal Matt walking up the stairs and down a long corridor in the school where Ruth is rehearsing with her choral group students. The group's voices can be heard as Matt advances, performing a Balkan song that, in plaintive atonality, addresses suffering in terms of river flow. Matt has just received word by phone at his office of his son's death, and, in his stunned state of shock, can only think of seeking out Ruth, and letting her know in person. The light in the section of hallway that Matt traverses is subdued, in keeping with the accompanying harsh choral sound. But further down the hallway, past the doorway to the auditorium where Matt pauses, uncertainly, we see a fuller, brighter light. Before Matt reaches the doorway, the camera has followed his heavy walk from behind. We have watched him dazedly attempting to maintain control and purpose as he advances. Once he halts near the doorway, he debates whether he should enter the performing space and interrupt the song-in-progress before it has concluded. Is the news he bears for Ruth news that cannot wait? Field frames a shot of Ruth at the opposite end of the auditorium, standing at her music lectern and facing the camera as she conducts the unseen chorus. She is expertly attuned to each dark phrase of their a cappella rendition. Her gestures seem to control the singers' mood and guide their vocal progression with the subtlest emotional awareness toward a designated final rest. Matt is visible in the far background, a suddenly small figure watching this woman who briefly dwells still in a drastically different world of knowing and feeling than that which he has just entered. Ruth's mouth is open as she conducts. She silently sings along with her students, and when they abruptly halt at her command she beams with satisfaction in their direction, praising their work with the single word "great," then raising her thumb to reinforce it.

We return for a few moments to the school corridor, where Matt stands stock-still in his brown suit, which blends with the brown of the corridor. He faces an array of small window reflections near the open

Figure 3.4. Ruth Fowler (Sissy Spacek) beams at the completion of a successful choir rehearsal, moments before her husband, Matt (Tom Wilkinson) informs her that their son has been killed.

door, but he—like the viewer—is barely conscious of what is in front of him. The image fades to black, and the blackness remains for a lengthy interval. We gradually hear, before sight is restored, what might be the sound of wind, and inside it a thin, distant voice intoning words we cannot readily make out. We are suddenly shown a cemetery setting, and what first strikes our eye as we emerge from darkness are two large matching gravestones, viewed from behind. As we cut to other stones in the cemetery and then to close-ups of faces of individual mourners, we can more clearly distinguish the words of the speaking voice that are taken from the celebrated passage on death from Kahlil Gibran's *The Prophet*. Father McCaslin (Jonathan Walsh) is reading it as a prayer before Frank's burial takes place. The voice, attempting to remain calm, establishes continuity with the chorus singing its lament in the just concluded school scene. One ritual—a music rehearsal—gives way to another—a gathering of family and friends at a gravesite, after a funeral. Gibran's text attempts to help the listener deal with the fearful trembling that death engenders. One is enjoined to see the stopped breath of dying as a "freeing" of the breath so that it may "rise and expand and seek God unencumbered." Drinking from the "river of silence," the prophet continues, is the only possible preparation for real singing. The lines of comfort are difficult for the mourners as well as the viewer to attend to. We are given the chance to survey a variety of faces and attitudes of those placed in "a river of silence." Most seem not only immobile but ravaged—so overcome by the horror of the senseless loss that they can scarcely keep in mind the voice that is droning in their midst. The priest's reading lacks the stirring authority of the choral performance. His reading feels tentative, even mechanical, though he is undeniably in touch with the grief state of his auditors. It may be no more than the simple flow of a voice issuing sounds (from the silent river) that the group can take in.

Ruth and Matt's faces, the last we are given to contemplate, are near to each other. The two parents stand side by side, but we are shown their reactions separately rather than together. They are on separate islands—Ruth's demeanor shattered, conspicuously in agony, Matt's more remote and sealed off. Both of their faces are off-center, on the left side of the frame. Between the shots recording their expressions is a jarring shot of his hand covering hers, his arm presumably having reached around her shoulder to locate it. The hands appear disconnected from their owners, in our experience of the image: insensible hands, affording no access to the tragedy as something shared. The final shot of the burial rite is of the small mourning party in high angle long shot—the flower-covered coffin at the center of a sparse human circle. The priest concludes his reading with the reassuring phrase "then shall you truly dance." No one breaks out of his or her stiff, solemn, formal poses. Silence returns, which none of the mourners know what to do with. We lose contact with Matt and Ruth, who are situated unobtrusively on the left-hand edge of the composition. They now appear anonymous and hidden within the gathering that exists chiefly to share their ordeal, in some limited, helpless fashion.

Another fade to black marks the transition back to the Fowler home following the service. In the unusually prolonged section of *In the Bedroom* devoted to the exploration of parental grieving, mounting isolation, and resentment, the blackness "divider" between episodes is consistently employed. The tactic is meant to disrupt any viewer expectation of flow, emotional release, or reengagement with "normal" living activity. We enter the Fowler home accompanying Matt who is instantly shown moving slowly behind French doors, prominently placed in the foreground of the image. We are conscious of this imprisoning glass barrier before any other details of the environment emerge. Matt tries with bewilderment to penetrate his once familiar domestic space, but it is completely alien to him. We are also adrift, since we are granted no "readable" emotional access to him.

The first example of aloneness investigated in this chapter had everything to do with integration. The servant, Maria, in *Umberto D*, discovers one unexpected opening after another in carrying out her assigned morning duties. This "entering in" assuages, albeit temporarily, her sense of hardship and her wholly warranted fear of a threatening future. The rooms, their ordinary contents, and especially the beneficent light all stealthily move closer to her for what amounts to a metaphysical embrace: being ensphered by being. The marital quarrel in *The Crowd* begins with a jarring severance from the materials that add up to home life, a potent concealment of their value and significance until the couple's reconciliation retrieves and replenishes them. In the other scenes I've analyzed, we have ventured toward ever greater extremes of aloneness and emotional destitution, where everyday world particulars (with the exception of Carrie's hairpin) are deprived of their power to offer support and consolation. Vision beyond the inward-looking turmoil of an unwieldy self is hard to achieve in these episodes, and impossible to sustain. There are certain heroic exemplars of aloneness in film—such as Charlie Chaplin's tramp, Buster Keaton's equilibrium-seeking striver, or Giulietta Masina's trustful road-waifs in *La Strada* and *Nights of Cabiria*—who astonishingly maintain a crucial insulating margin (at most times) from the paralyzing torments of loneliness. Their versions of solitude are abundantly creative. Each of them reclaims all sorts of odd, unlikely, overlooked, and throwaway material for perceptual absorption, wondrous puzzlement, and improvised engagement. Their home spaces are invariably provisional. They build meaningful alternatives to home throughout their wanderings, and the ephemeral becomes for them the basis of authentic grounding and clear-sightedness. Everything they encounter can and will transform—positively or negatively, one can rarely predict—and relinquishment is an accepted component of any experience of belonging.

Most of the scenes of aloneness I have selected for study dramatize the failure of a character's resourcefulness and resiliency in crisis circumstances. I have charted a progression to the arctic perimeter of aloneness, where the death of a child is involved. In the scenes from *In the Bedroom* I am considering, something like the dread contagion of a pair marked for inconceivable suffering is at work in our viewing. We cannot bear to think that a tragedy of this measureless scale might be reserved for us. The viewer may well crave some sort of saving distance from Matt and Ruth Fowler in their woe. We seek our own protective barrier—akin to the French door glass standing in front of Matt—from the prospect of too much empathy. Ruth and Matt's core capacity for sympathetic awareness and "getting on" may have received irreparable damage. At present, there is no likelihood for either of them to make emotional headway.

Director Field is careful to make us feel less joined with Matt as he numbly contemplates the well-meaning invaders who have "taken over" his home after the funeral than we are joined with the awkward guests, baffled and muddled in their observance of tragedy etiquette. Matt initially appears to be searching for some permissible emotional outlet—an escape from agonizing bottled-upness. For a few moments he casts an enraged look at two children—a young boy and girl—leaning against the other side of the glass partition "screening" him, and for some reason laughing. They cannot pretend to be in touch with a grief that has no direct relation to them. They exhibit without knowing it the ease, uncomplicated enjoyment, and promise of youth that the Fowlers' son, Frank, so recently possessed. All of that has been snatched senselessly away from Frank, but tauntingly persists in the form of these imposters. There can be no surviving child here whose appearance is not an accidental affront to Matt's perception, given Frank's absence-without-end. In a suddenly more constricted point-of-view shot alignment with Frank, we leave the harrowing (for Matt) sight of the amused children and move past an opaque wooden barrier, until we discover, once more through the dividing medium of glass, Father McCaslin in an adjoining room chatting inaudibly with a young man, with several other members of the mourning party nearby them also engaged in normal conversations. No one appears in a state of shock or emotional disarray. It is as though all those attending the postfuneral "reception" have already succeeded in stepping away from the Fowler calamity, and their briefly suspended personal affairs have fully revived for them.

Matt stares at them blindly, as if from an insuperable remove. His face is tightly enclosed by one of the barred rectangles of the French door. Shadows and reflections pass over the glass, which conveys the unreality, the unnerving lack of solidity of the human spectacle being so lightly enacted. After a few moments of hopeless floundering in his petrified confusion, Matt is joined on his side of the glass partition by his closest friends, Willis and Katie (William Wise and Celia Weston). Willis asks if he can get Matt anything while Katie looks on empathetically, from within her own glass rectangle. The French door continues to mediate their kind attempts to approach and offer Matt comfort. With his back to us, Matt hoarsely whispers, "Where's Ruth?," and is informed by Katie that she has already left the gathering and gone upstairs to lie down. Matt excuses himself and walks in the direction of the stairway. In the next shot, the French door is taken away as an obstructing screen between Matt and the moving shadows of his inimical home, to be immediately replaced by a large mirror set on the wall next to the stairs. The mirror supplies the frame through which we observe Matt begin to climb the stairway, one hand on the bannister for inadequate support.

Abruptly we cut to the inside of the Fowler bedroom where we have a slightly elevated full shot view of Ruth stretched out on her side of the marital bed, motionless, with her body turned away from us, facing the far wall. The black clad figure, with crumpled Kleenex on both sides of her, has a deathly fixity, which the bright light pouring through the bedroom over a colorful floral arrangement only intensifies. The light seems sequestered in its own area, and Ruth's inert body is insensible, its stern, bent blackness repudiating the cruel beauty that ineffectually gestures toward her. We hear Matt's footsteps approach the comfortless bed, and then he materializes, standing at the foot of it, looking at Ruth (his back turned from us as well), and debating whether to speak. Shall he rouse from oblivion this one credible fellow sufferer? Dim sounds from the people downstairs are still audible here, and for the rest of the scene prevent Matt's total descent into a private silence. After stepping closer to the bed, Matt decides that Ruth, awake, will have nothing to give him that could lessen either his desolation or sense of estrangement.

He leaves Ruth and walks down the hallway toward Frank's now exiled and forsaken room—his former living space. Matt pauses with trepidation by the door, considering whether he has the strength to go inside. But the door, rather than being shut, is temptingly ajar. It responds effortlessly to his reaching hand, beckoning him into a warmly lit "refuge" from insupportable life noise. It slowly swings wide open with only the slightest physical assistance from Matt. Field, as I've noted in the prior bedroom scene, has elected to accompany Matt's examination of the room's contents with murmurous reminders of life sound from downstairs. These sounds are a steady counterpoint in the ensuing visit of Frank's left behind belongings, playing against our sense of what has irremediably vanished from this now hallowed spot. Our first survey of the bedroom—from the inside—is an implied point-of-view shot, with Matt and the viewer fused, as a panning camera surveys the space as it looked when Frank last left it. It is imbued with the force of the dead son's casual "parting glance." The bed is unmade. A richly patterned blue garment drapes over the lower end of the vibrant orange-checked bedspread. Frank's shirt rests on the back of a chair, as though he had just removed it and set it there. Other clothes lie strewn over the floor in a patch of bright light. Everything the eye rests upon suggests a temporary interruption of activity and the promise of return. The chair, desk, and bed express active waiting for the person attached to them. What now commences—as a subtle continuation of the son's objects "awakening" in his room—is a close point-of-view scrutiny (with a moving camera) of Frank's architectural drawings, in black-and-white and color. They are attached to the bedroom walls above his drafting table and dresser, but are dynamic rather than static as they are revealed to us. The living thrust of the lines is amplified by the camera's slow, entranced progression across their surfaces. The imaginative vision that gave birth to them is released once more, in a manner that feels both joyful and poignant. The hand that drew these designs has been stilled, but the image in motion persuasively sets the hand going again in a splurge of free-flowing inspiration. The drawings, like the blurred voices, threaded with laughter, from below, aspire to light, energy, and continuation.

Matt is abruptly reintroduced as a bulky physical presence in a shot where his gray-coated back appears above Frank's pillow on the bed. His hand cautiously extends to touch it, then with the greatest delicacy conceivable, presses down on the center of it where Frank's head used to rest, and follows up on that pressure by lightly moving across the pillow's white surface, in a kind of caress. The next shot further extends the exploratory hand motion of this one, but in close-up. Matt runs his finger across the artificial ground surface of a scale model dwelling Frank has assembled. Though the tone of these shots of touching has a heartbreaking gravity, the emphasis on motion rather than frozenness preserves a linkage with the vitality of Frank's art. At this point we arrive at a shot that resembles George Hurstwood's recovery of the hairpin in *Carrie*. A close-up of a child's old metal tin, used for storing items related to fishing, quietly erupts into view. Matt's hands—all that we see of him (another implied point-of-view shot)—hold the box as he raises its lid to disclose two plastic, red-and-white bobbers, associated with long ago fishing trips with his son. Fishing was perhaps their foremost shared passion. The box also contains a translucent blue piece of glass with printed initials, which Frank had found somewhere and decided to keep, perhaps because its color struck a chord in him. The reason for his decision to preserve it in this box is lost now, as he is. In its brokenness and unintelligibility, this chance object outlasted him. Matt's perspective as lonely discoverer here puts me in mind of the last lines of Rilke's poem "Sunset" (Robert Bly's translation):

> leaving you (it is impossible to untangle the threads)
> your own life, timid and standing high and growing,
> so that, sometimes blocked in, sometimes reaching out,
> one moment your life is a stone in you, and the next, a star.
> (Rilke, 26)

Matt's encounter with the blue fragment reverses the order of recognition in the poem's last line. The upraised glass shines briefly as a star before descending like a stone inside him. The bobbers and the glass chunk make harsh rattling sounds in the tin as Matt first handles them. Tightening his fingers' grip on the mysterious blue glass, Matt can contain his pent-up sorrow no longer. In profile we witness his hand pressed to his mouth as he surrenders to a half-stifled fit of sobbing. He sits down at Frank's drafting table—again we are placed behind him, with access only to his turned away head and back. He picks up a sheet of paper containing markings Frank has made, tries to concentrate on it, to steady himself, then gives up, resting his head and arms on the desk, where he emits three unbearable, unearthly sighs.

Field's camera documents, without undue lingering over Matt's anguished face, the extremity of his aloneness. We are unobtrusively fastened to Matt's inward gaze, and finally sealed in with it completely during his sighs. We collaborate with him in the creation of his vision of Frank's room—the lost sanctuary. But we are granted the power to absorb, concurrently, possibilities for reconnection that Matt is in no position to recognize. The central issue that Matt contends with, inevitably, is the unyielding fact that his son is gone from this place, forever. Surreptitiously, however, the camera enables the viewer to feel the ways in which Frank is not gone. He is still present in the vigorous lines of his artwork, in the room's warm light, in the strange atmosphere of ongoingness, temporary interruption, anticipated return, and continuation. Our manner of beholding Frank's things endows them with a calm radiance, as well as the spirit of everything that transforms, even in apparent arrest, and moves forward. (This will to move, to shift is most forcibly present in the lines of Frank's restless, searching drawings. His architectural plan for an ideal home, as he once explained to his girlfriend, Natalie, left an enticing open space at the center, where all the isolated energies from the separate private rooms are irresistibly drawn to spill forth and gather together.)

It is Matt who is distanced from us, paradoxically at the same time we are fused with his perspective. He is a somnambulist whose body seems poised to crash with the impossible weight of loss that he carries. And he finally does collapse at his son's desk, in the one sobbing breakdown he permits himself in the aftermath of Frank's killing. It is Matt who is gone from a room that Frank's still tangible spirit powerfully illuminates. Both Matt and Ruth will remain stymied in their crushing bereftness: unresponsive to each other, to those in need around them, and, most disturbingly, to themselves. In the very next scene, we see that Matt has made himself into a hulking variant of Frank's memento in the tin box—let's call it a blue stone, or, in fishing parlance, a "sinker." In deathly stonelike fashion, he is unable to catch and hold the light as he goes through the motions of offering assistance to Ruth.

This scene, set at night, is composed of a single lengthy shot, with a stationary camera. In the fade to black transition into it, we hear the sound of TV talk show applause, which almost seems to be a grotesque audience acknowledgment of Matt's bent back sighing in Frank's room. When the image joins the sound, we see Ruth seated at the far end of her sofa, which is covered over with a light brown blanket. There is a near spectral effect of dimming the physical properties of the living room furniture. Ruth's head leans against the fist of her upraised arm, which is itself propped on the sofa, as she gazes in a blank trance at the television planted in front of her. A small, warmly lit lamp rests on the table beside her, but her implacable attention is grimly drawn to the pale blue light of the television screen. The TV host's empty impersonation of enthusiasm is matched by equally mechanical bursts of audience approval. Language reenters *In the Bedroom* in this utterly impoverished form, where every phrase spoken is coated with meaninglessness. It is speech operating in a time-killing vacuum.

Matt enters, with apparent resoluteness, from the hallway and quietly offers to refill Ruth's cup from the pot of tea on her side table. She nods and watches vacantly as he performs this small courtesy. Her eyes immediately go back to the TV image without her having said a word to him. Instead of joining her on the sofa, Matt seats himself in a chair set against the wall across from her. Beside him is a sailing ship model (associated with Frank). His chair is out of range of the TV screen, and his choice of seat indicates an unwillingness to join Ruth's feigned involvement with it. Gradually his position becomes as frozen in its apartness as Ruth's. He knits his hands together and waits—perhaps imagining that it is Ruth's place to initiate some conciliatory or merely human exchange. It is equally likely that he is settling into a judgment of her icy remoteness, which seems pointlessly aimed against him in his hideous cut-offness. The image fades to black on their zero degree mutual isolation, with the television soundtrack doing the duty of suggesting, however unpersuasively, that life, ease, conviviality, laughter go on normally somewhere, for other people.

Yet, our viewers' position is behind the television with its invisible screen, and we are naturally more allied in this situation with vitality and other emotional resources than the achingly uncoupled pair we contemplate. The grief they inhabit is a bottomless hole, in the words of Mary Ruefle, "the hole in sadness from which no words escape and no soul can spring, it is the calorific sadness of bombs" (38). Our place as beholders of their aloneness brings us back to the idea of theatre with which we began. The stylized close-up frames for aloneness devised by D. W. Griffith and other silent filmmakers made theatre and shared privacy a conspicuous element in film reality. One might characterize the dark background—in which expressive, suffering faces were lit like jewels for our merciful inspection—as viewer confessionals. The faces testify their heart truth to the spectator, without direct acknowledgment of the camera. No other character within the camera subject's reach possesses adequate sensitivity or discernment for the work of comprehension. It is to us—in our kindred aloneness—that the figure makes its unconscious appeal. And more often than not we, like mantled-in-shadow priests on the other side of the confessional window, grant the singled-out tormented one solace and absolution, though she can't give us signs of knowing it. The convention of a separate realm for inward revelation did not survive the silent era in its original form, but Griffith's "laying bare" of the apparatus is a powerful reminder of how necessary staging is for every private experience on film. The camera and the spectator need to disappear as legible components in the display of the lonely soul or the illusion of character isolation will be shattered. When we read a work of literature, we can gain extraordinary vibrations of both the appearance and consciousness of aloneness. But literature cannot duplicate film's magnifying glass for the physical contours, conduct, and moment-to-moment shifts of demeanor on the naked face as aloneness defines the entire world-in-the-frame.

The camera in its realist aspirations is a sociable instrument, surveying events and establishing legitimate connections with those participating in them. The camera is permitted to see the public side of things—indeed, a visitor by turns welcome and culpable in its avid prying—but it additionally claims the privilege of spiriting into the private realm, and unearthing secrets. This sort of boundary crossing heightens the potential for illegitimate trespass and prurient violation. The camera acquires its point of entry because the private is in fact a theatrical extension of the public spectacle. But theatre-as-theatre goes to great lengths to disguise or erase itself when moments of painful exposure are rendered. The spectator may well feel that film is at its most "cinematic" when authentic truths are mined from an unguarded face. Yet it could easily be insisted that the kinds of actor absorption and careful positioning and framing required for such passages have a profound linkage to theatre—even though the barrier of physical distance from the performance space has been removed.

    The figure experiencing the demands of aloneness is secured at every point for beholding and emotional accompaniment, and every detail of the physical environment is determined in its fluid capacity to support the lonely character, or to further rob her of defenses. The solicitation to the viewer to reduce the ordeal of aloneness by drawing nearer and answering the character's need for comprehension and protection is dependent on an authentic ground for privacy within the film image opening up, a place cleansed of obvious deception, which will bear the weight of our presence. At some level we know that film privacy is a theatrical mode, but we conspire in a richly intricate dance with the medium to keep the theatre frame hidden, so that the aloneness we aid and abet can be both the character's impasse and our own.

4

Eloquent Objects, Housebound Theatre

William Wyler's *The Heiress*

I hope I know an heiress when I see one.
—Theodore Dreiser, *Jennie Gerhardt*

∽

IN WILLIAM WYLER'S MOST thing-saturated film, *The Heiress* (1949), every scene is devised with objects (e.g., keys, gloves, lamps, mirrors) as a central expressive component. This collection of vivid, telling entities, which might be described as the lyrical inanimate, carries the imprint of every major character's psychology. The objects speak, in each pointed appearance, the language of motive, dream, fixation, longing, apprehension, and delusion. In their combined effect, they chart the maneuverings of fortune and fate. This chapter will offer a reading of the salient objects in Wyler's extraordinary, punitive design for the film. We will discover how objects gradually infiltrate the entire space of *The Heiress*'s lifeworld. Initially they reflect the mental operations of the characters, then gradually they seem to become the characters' minds, and finally replace them with their own immobility and imperviousness. The film is adapted from Henry James's novella, *Washington Square*, but though it adheres quite closely to the structure of James's plot, the overall mood and material weight of the film are more strongly affiliated with the work of Theodore Dreiser. Before embarking on my analysis of *The Heiress*, therefore, I will attempt to delineate the habits of thought and modes of object illumination that Wyler inherits, directly or indirectly, from Dreiser, his nearest literary counterpart.

It is not surprising that William Wyler directed a film adaptation of Dreiser's novel *Sister Carrie*, given the two artists' career-long fascination with how characters define themselves through their relationship with things. Dreiser memorably describes himself in his autobiography encountering, as a newly arrived young man of uncertain means and negligible attainments, the new department store windows of Chicago, ablaze with light. "You need me, you need me," the contents of the windows proclaim to their instantly diminished observer from the sticks. Dreiser finds himself "unmade" by the resplendent array of hitherto undreamed-of material possibilities. As Philip Fisher has noted in his reading of *Sister Carrie*, Dreiser's characters only know selfhood "in anticipation," a condition to be arrived at when the right corner is turned and certain crucial, life-enhancing objects can be counted as possessions. (Perhaps identity always contains this knowledge of incompleteness as its one inalterable feature. We can only see what we are, and take stock of it, by reference to "not yet.")

William Wyler's films are typically crammed with gleaming, self-sufficient items in settings organized like display windows, commanding the heightened attention of camera and character alike. Wyler's recurrent plot, like Dreiser's, deals with selves in anticipation, caught in the grip of the things they strive to own, or self-deceivingly imagine they can infuse with their own substance. In Wyler, as in Dreiser, matter over mind is the natural arrangement. And it is both an abiding truth and a topic of permanent interest in their narratives how clothes, and a heap of other goods, make the man (and woman).

The overt sexual charge in a Dreiser novel is most memorably ignited by the sighting and handling of objects that hold the power to clarify whether one's inner stock is full or empty. Or to put it another way, is one's individual life—relative to the imagined life of the crowd—moving up or down? Dreiser's eye, like that of a movie camera, dispassionately grants objects an interest and aura equivalent to that of the people stationed in their vicinity. Taking possession of a thing frequently involves the internalization of its associations, as though one were being possessed in turn. In advance of getting something that "out of the blue" seizes their desire, Dreiser characters imagine themselves ever more deeply in its reflected light, and in so doing become strikingly vulnerable to the force they project onto the commodity. They are also vulnerable, of course, to the meanings that others project onto these valued assets (which seem more decisive and powerful than the attention paid to a "mere person"). How commonplace and dispensable we seem without the shielding radiance of the socially admired object. It is no wonder, Dreiser tells us, again and again, that we collaborate, avidly, in the process of being mistaken for the objects in our keeping. Inwardly and outwardly we long and need to be confused with them, but then become indignant, or fearful, that we can't be found out in our "true" separateness.

In his essay on collecting, Stanley Cavell suggestively characterizes the self as itself "a collection requiring a narrative" to hold it together (46). We are always revising the museum catalogue of our self-collection. We want our inner acquisitions to be housed in as solid a dwelling as possible: a compartmented gathering place when our lives feel ordered, and a jumbled clearinghouse for things and ideas when they don't. (Things and ideas can, of course, readily blur together. Ideas, for example, in our mechanical use of them, achieve the sturdiness and neatness of mounted things.) We alternate perhaps between pictures of ourselves as static (the things composing us labeled and assembled for display) and in chaotic flux (where the labels have come off and the displays are broken up and discarded). In the flux picture, nothing at all feels settled. As Dreiser puts it in *Jennie Gerhardt*: "So shadows march in a dream" (392). Dreiser conceives his characters' life struggle as a dreaming through barriers that all bear some resemblance to the department store window. On the other side of the window divide lies a fit image of the coherent, organized psyche, brightly appareled in all the "faraway things" one has yearned and worked for. In the saving light of these indispensable possessions, one eludes capture by emptiness, or muddle. Because of Dreiser's governing intuition that objects are the most reliable means of securing placement in life, the object that is given or held under false pretenses, or rashly borrowed, is the recurring nightmare element in his best scenes. Just as we can be made into a person by staking legitimate claims to the right commodities, so these objects can be the means of our undoing, as they "disown" us. "Now she felt as though life were tentatively loaning her something, which would be taken away after a time" (*Jennie Gerhardt*, 167).

Dreiser's great novel, *An American Tragedy*, contains a memorable episode built around an exchange of objects (a pair of painfully mismatched Christmas gifts) that could have been expressly designed for a William Wyler film. Clyde Griffith pays a forlorn visit to the cramped room rented by his lover, Roberta Alden, of whom he has grown weary. He is finding it difficult to extricate himself from the relationship, in a manner that he can convince himself is at least slightly honorable. The timing, on this occasion, feels wrong. Roberta is about to depart for a brief, no doubt miserable Christmas stay at her bleak rural home. He is hesitant to give her still further immediate cause for despondency. He is also afraid to tell Roberta that he has secretly begun seeing someone else, who is socially from a much loftier station. In fact, he is already in love not only with the new young woman, but with the plush, glittering, carefree world she occupies. Roberta could make trouble for Clyde if she chooses to (the affair has until now been concealed from everyone that Clyde knows). He is hoping to secure a short holiday reprieve before making the necessary grim announcement of his decision to leave her.

Clyde has brought Roberta an extravagant Christmas present, which he imagines will make up, to some degree, for his recent neglect of her and possibly also conceal his growing indifference. Clyde's gift, and to a lesser extent the heartfelt gift he receives in return, which he must somehow pretend to rejoice in, provide the emotional fulcrum of the scene. All of Roberta's and Clyde's complicated feelings, mostly unspoken, play through the two by no means neutral articles. Clyde's present carries the full taint of the giver's sticky, perfidious intentions. Of course, at the most obvious level, the gift is a bribe masquerading as an expression of love. Its costliness reflects Clyde's current social aspirations—his sense that he is moving, in an almost predestined fashion, into a higher category that will justify his casting off of Roberta. The sumptuousness of the gift has nothing to do with any value he still sees in her. The purchase is designed to show off the casual munificence of the one who is now capable of such gestures. Clyde expects no return on his investment; he allows it to be understood, or half-understood, that the present, though lavish in Roberta's eyes, entailed no sacrifice on his part. He can let the gift go as something that has never occupied his thoughts or made a strong impression on him. In a short while, he may have difficulty recalling what the gift was, though he is likely to remember that he was generous. Clyde's main desire on behalf of his "parting of the ways" token is that it would be articulate about an affection that was once undoubtedly real, but which he can no longer summon on his own. The gift must somehow supply a compensatory heat that will reduce the "frost" and colorlessness that he fears his own "anemic" manner conveys. Let the object serve as an eloquent intermediary for the tongue-tied, reluctant suitor; let it promise something at least in its own right that Roberta will not instantly disbelieve.

Clyde's deceitful role in the scene is entirely clear to the reader from the outset, but Roberta, though her intuitions prompt her to be suspicious of Clyde's change of heart and allegiance, is so fearfully and vulnerably attached to him that she can't permit herself to exchange doubt for hard knowing. The exchange of presents thus also effortlessly stands for the possibility of passing from one state of mind (turbulent yet fluid) to another (fixed and irreversible). As Roberta unwraps Clyde's present and then begins to handle it—finding her response, as it were, through sight and touch—she feels compelled to read him through it. The dramatic logic of this episode derives from her halting effort to bring man and gift together in her mind, so they mean the same thing. If she succeeds in assigning the gift a decisive personal significance (beginning with the fact that this object is clear and definite) she might escape her agonizing, ever-fluctuating impressions of Clyde. Like the object, Clyde's image, "cradled by tempests," would resolve itself and become graspable.

How much clarity an unopened present can give hope of yielding, both for good and ill. The good of it comes from the conviction that while this mysterious item was being looked for and chosen, the recipient loomed large in the giver's thoughts. Whatever the package holds, is it not likely that it was selected with her alone in mind? The more hurtful clarity, of course, proceeds from the discovery that the gift chiefly expressed carelessness or haste. A gift can also too often seem a wounding mistaken guess about who the recipient is. Clyde urges Roberta to concentrate on what he's brought for her just before she opens it, "anxious to divert her thoughts from this desertion [a posh party he's attended] which he knew was preying on her mind." Roberta begins to "untie the ribbon that bound his gift" (338), dwelling helplessly as she does so on the possible loosening of Clyde's ties to her. Her act of removing the slight, thin "binding" material makes her a momentary collaborator in Clyde's wish for release. Before she arrives at the stabilizing object beneath the wrapping, she is beset by a flurry of half-formed thoughts about Clyde's new female friends ("her mind was riveted by the possibilities of the party he had attended"), as though she is also untying and letting loose all the anxieties stored up inside her. Dreiser informs us, by means of a close Wyler-like framing of Roberta's face striving to become a mask, that she was "attempting to conceal the true mood that was dominating her" as she attends to "removing the paper and opening the lid to the case that contained her toilet set" (338). The identity of the present is anticlimactically slipped in at the close of this sentence devoted to unwrapping.

What is the gift able to say, and further become, once it is made known as a specific commodity? Clyde has purchased Roberta a fancy toilet set, which she instantly understands is "exceptional . . . never before had she possessed anything so valuable or original" (338). In that phrasing, the toilet set is inwardly characterized in much the same language that Roberta would apply to Clyde himself, this "valuable" figure who has improbably entered into a relationship with her, and who at times she has regarded herself as "possessing." The toilet set is beautiful, she tells him, and exceeds her expectations, as Clyde himself regularly does, even by the mere act of putting in an appearance in her tiny living quarters. Roberta's next thought is of her more modest gift to him, a pen and pencil set that his "exceptional" generosity has effectively eclipsed. "My two little presents won't seem like much now" (339). Everything about Roberta's gift expresses her longing for stronger attachment. She seeks as well a visible display on Clyde's person of some sign, some small token of her existence in his life. Roberta tells him that she imagines the pen and pencil fastened to his shirt pocket at the factory where they both work, and in that place proving "useful" to him. She urges him to consider the poetic aspect of her present as well, declaring how she pictures him "always [having] them near you, next your heart, where I want them to be" (339). So she imagines these humble articles, with which he might someday commit his feelings for her (permanently) to paper. In the meantime they will be attached to his body, unobtrusively clinging to him, as near to his heart as possible.

Clyde will repeatedly disappoint her often-stated request that he write her a letter, a card, or a brief note. Once he opens the "small box" (another version of Roberta's little room) containing her present, he is prevented from seeing what she has given him genuinely. He is instantly mindful of the challenge of assuaging her and keeping his emotional defection a secret. Even while he holds the pen and pencil in his hands and exclaims over them, he is only appearing "to examine them with the utmost pleasure" (339). In truth, he can't focus on them at all while trying to find and then maintain the right tone. To demonstrate his resolve to "use them all the time," he does make a show of tucking them in his shirt pocket. At that moment, they effectively disappear from narrative sight and from Clyde's mind. He embraces Roberta to thank her, but even while she is in his arms he marvels at how all of his earlier feelings for her have disappeared, never to be revived. His arms, like his pocket, have become a burial site; they hollowly fasten themselves around Roberta's weeping form, but she does not feel held, or "near to his heart." When Roberta selected her gift for Clyde, she envisioned these objects being transformed, under the warmth of his delighted gaze, into potent heart language. The gift, in her consciousness, is softened and animated by the love that led her irresistibly to it. When Roberta watches the actual "metal" pencil and "silver ornamented fountain pen" passing from his ill-at-ease hands into his oblivious pocket, they are deprived of their earlier shimmering aura. Their fluency perishes and their commodity hardness, which Roberta had lost sight of for a time, bluntly reasserts itself. Roberta is made over into the likeness of the crude, inanimate implements absent-mindedly stuffed into an obscure cleft in Clyde's well-tailored shirt. No doubt they carry too heavy a reminder of the factory and his routine, undistinguished labor for Clyde to enjoy dwelling on. The shirt would appear to better advantage—less bulky and encumbered—without them.

What Clyde's toilet set articulates (to the extent that it gives away some hint of what he still wants from Roberta) is a vague hankering that she might magically improve herself, change her social image in the way that he, because of his accidental family connections, has managed to: "Clean the past off you, Roberta, with steady application, and keep up your grooming until no one, including me, is able to recognize you as a simple farm girl from the lumpen-place called Biltz." A toilet set requires a mirror's steady presence for effective results. Roberta in the future can hold Clyde's hairbrush and study her image in solitude, guiding the brush and its companion objects to stroke and caress her person, as Clyde once did, and smooth out imperfections as they multiply in the glass. The toilet set is also eloquent about waiting in a sealed up case, yet another cramped cubicle, waiting for an internal summons to the mirror where one can seek out all the confirming evidence of what one lacks, including the gift giver, who enjoins Roberta, by way of this keepsake, to "make herself prettier" for him, in the unlikely event of his return. The toilet set, grander than Roberta's other possessions, does not coexist with them comfortably. The gift must be assigned a shabby place in their midst, creating "displeasure," as it were, with its inadequate lodgings. The very elegance of this kit, designed to aid in bathing, cosmetics, hairdressing, and costuming, is an implied repudiation of the ordinary woman who dares to lift the fine articles from their case, as though she had a right to them. The toilet set seems borrowed from a person of higher status, to whom they might properly belong—for example, Sondra, who has already taken Roberta's place in Clyde's affection. Why would these grooming articles not recoil in derision when made to touch this no-account female supplicant that they are forced to attend to?

We do not hear any more about this gift until after Roberta has drowned in a rowboat accident, engineered by a desperate Clyde, who regards himself as trapped by her pregnancy. When the gift turns up again, as an incriminating item among Roberta's pathos-laden effects, it shifts its hardness so that Clyde is the one afflicted by it. The gift constitutes another unmistakable proof, for Clyde's accusers and jurors during his trial, of stoniness of heart and treachery. In fact, it did originally have something to do with those qualities in Clyde, but when recast as evidence in a court case the object becomes overdefinite and misleading—a ponderous exclamation point in a tabulation of villainy.

William Wyler's *The Heiress* consistently employs objects in the weighty and barbed manner that is so pronounced in the gift exchange episode in *An American Tragedy*. Like Clyde's and Roberta's Christmas gifts, most of the things that characters take in or take up in *The Heiress* have invisible claws. Their power to tear and pierce is often cumulative, revealed through recurring use and belated recognitions, or (equally damaging) misrecognitions.

The protagonist of the film, Catherine Sloper (Olivia de Havilland), is made known to us as a pliable and generous person, open to influences of many kinds and exceedingly vulnerable in her general, trusting responsiveness. The title identifies her through her status as an heiress, one who is conditionally defined in her world by a future possession of considerable wealth. She has not yet inherited the main part of her fortune, but will one day come into holdings sufficiently impressive that her value (independently of anything she is or does) will tangibly assert itself. In the transitional category she presently occupies, she is judged plain and uninteresting, though appraisers of every sort can see the material good that lies just over the rise from her conspicuous deficiencies. Wyler places Catherine in a theatrical dwelling where nearly everything is hard-edged, exactingly decorous, and cold. Wherever she turns in her father's house, she comes upon nothing that matches her soft spirit or that rewards her curiosity about who she might actually be, apart from the severely proportioned and disciplined opulence.

Catherine's house contains a secret, which its aggregation of things and the way that they are disposed against her (never permitting her to fit in, to feel like a fit occupant) seem to hint at steadily. Catherine is not good at taking their hints, or letting herself in on the knowledge that at some level she already holds in her possession. The secret of the house is that her father, Dr. Sloper (Ralph Richardson), doesn't love her. Indeed, he is incapable of allowing any feeling for Catherine to enter his heart, beyond an exaggerated sense of parental obligation to make her, somehow, presentable. Sloper's beloved wife died from complications attending Catherine's birth, and he is frozen at the threshold of what he can only think of as Catherine's accursed, poisonous coming-to-be. "Only I know what I lost when she died," he confides to his sister in an early scene, "and what I got in her place." Over the long period in which Catherine preserves her ignorance of the house's secret, she does her best to fashion herself according to its requirements. She appears to fail, however, both in her efforts to meet her father's "kindly" expectations about becoming an educated or in some way polished young woman, and in her attempts to imitate her fantasy version of her deceased mother. Catherine sometimes endeavors to please her father by appearing in a maternal guise—including a disastrous attempt to wear a red gown identical to her mother's that he particularly cherished. Catherine's stiffly self-conscious deportment and inability to "find her tongue" in the presence of others are due to her reasonable supposition that however she presents herself, in social or family settings, she is not only imitating but imitating badly. We watch Catherine move from one rigidly framed and coldly ordered domestic space after another, which oppose, with theatrical expressiveness, her out-of-place softness.

Her father, in Catherine's view, has formed a fair, considerate idea of what she might become, and is supplying her with well-meaning directives to guide her toward it. Though he is at great pains (she can feel it) to be patient and lenient with her, she knows that she hasn't begun to measure up to the absent woman on whom it seems so natural for her to pattern herself. The house supplies clues as to what sorts of appearance need to be mastered and the things she ought to try her hand at, but it also seems, as I previously noted, strangely in league against her, as though it has taken an engraved impression of her unworthiness. Catherine seeks to acquire forms of grace that will comport with so many stiff-backed, impervious household fixtures, human and inanimate. Things counsel her to divest herself of her natural gentleness, her warmth, and pliability as expeditiously as possible, and they judge her awkward in her confusion about how to go about it. Catherine tries, through her deep submission to tutoring in her father's house, to secure self-acceptance through love. She doesn't imagine her aspiration in quite these terms. She lacks the idea to explain what her emotional survival instincts dictate. When, the ironist might inquire, will the time be right for her to acknowledge the manifest absence of love, or the prevailing "house wisdom" that her birth was a tragic misfortune, and that no love can flow from it? In a sense, the house gives her whatever understanding she has of the lost mother who gracefully, and by all accounts lovingly, presided over it. Though the house, in its present workings, speaks forcefully and consistently in her father's voice, Catherine must parse this stern idiom for traces of her mother's differently pitched sound, the remnants of a countermelody.

The plot of *The Heiress* is about Catherine's gradual discovery of the emotional necessity of vacating this house if she is ever to find love, and her subsequent, more desolate, self-deceiving discovery that she must forever remain in the house, since there is no imaginable love for her elsewhere. Catherine's best chance of escaping imprisonment in her father's cold conception of her is the handsome, stylish, well-spoken suitor, Morris Townsend (Montgomery Clift), who begins to court her at the one large social gathering (an engagement party for her cousin) that she attends in the course of the narrative. Her view is widened, bracingly if perilously, as soon as she leaves the unrecognized cage of her home. Catherine's father no sooner learns of Morris's interest in her than he concludes that the young man is a fortune-hunter, from whose cunning machinations Dr. Sloper must protect his defenseless daughter. Sloper's swift diagnosis of Morris's motives turns out to be accurate, though Wyler keeps the viewer uncertain for a considerable length of time about Morris's exact designs, or his commitment to deceit.

It is crucial to Wyler's plan for documenting the objects' gradual comprehensive takeover of *The Heiress*'s lifeworld that Morris initially be associated with an inviting indefiniteness and elasticity. (The initial objects he uses to express this indefiniteness playfully are a dance card with a pencil attached by a string, which he handles in a feigned clumsy, mock-secretive manner to set Catherine at her ease. Soon after, he makes further comic use of punch glasses to express his disappointment as a "rejected suitor" when he watches her dance with an older man.) As spectators, we are not sure that we can read his feelings, but the genuine mystery of his intentions only enhances his charm. When he says goodbye to Catherine as she leaves the engagement party, Wyler's camera remains trained on him after she turns away, and his stillness and attentive expression perfectly resist our skeptical probe: he is beautifully inscrutable. Unlike Dr. Sloper, Morris seems alert, tactful, and a happy improviser when confronted with Catherine's diffident sensitivity. He may have squandered his own inheritance, as we learn early on, but Dr. Sloper has made us distrustful of hoarders, and Morris's impulsiveness initially combines in an attractive fashion with his changeableness. He is, we rightly gather, still intent on finding a direction for his life. Like Catherine, he does not strike us as fully formed. If the two appear slightly implausible as a romantic couple, they are at least united by their mutual openness to possibility.

Eventually, we are obliged to conclude that Morris's primary attraction is to the Sloper house, and the style of lax, privileged living he considers possible within it. He is willing to accept Catherine's desire to "belong" to him in exchange for being dependably warmed in an easy chair by her spacious fireplace. The film offers a number of stunning transpositions of the idea of emotional belonging (with its nebulous market value) to images of ownership—belongings that can be counted, socially prized, and held under lock and key. Morris, so driven to arrive somewhere quickly and to make a mark for himself that will mean fair exchange for his good appearance, becomes an accomplice of Sloper, his ostensible foe. He seems to agree with Sloper's basic position that everything be reduced to the fixed standards of the house. He learns to appraise himself by his degree of access to the house's comforts. Morris, by deserting Catherine after she renounces all claim to her paternal inheritance, forces her to conclude that it is only Sloper's holdings that he covets, and in fact loves. Henceforth, it is as though no alternative space to the house exists for Catherine, where her search for love—as something beyond the scope of "domestic commerce"—might be continued. The house assimilates love, as well as power, within its starkly luxurious frame.

Henry James often tells tales of consciousness navigating through the dense jungle of material trappings, ranging in kind from the beautiful and sacred to the crushingly hideous. James is keenly aware of how objects enchant the eye and mind and work their spell on even the most imaginative, capacious spirits. Yet the dross of thing worship is never sufficient in his narratives to block the rich flow of the reflecting mind. Consciousness, even under paralyzing outward circumstances, always provides fresh matter for stimulation and speculation, and thus room to maneuver. Wyler parts company from James and his novel *Washington Square* in his conviction that things cannot only erode the work of consciousness but take it over almost completely. In the by turns lulling and contentious presence of one's significant (inanimate) other, the inquiring imagination can effectively be put to sleep, and lose all appetite for resistance. One can sleepwalk in the company of one's defining objects, and gradually accept their offer to "speak" in our place: to become not our literal mouthpiece, of course, but a set of instantly intelligible orders. Responding to the orders sent out by our calmly insistent possessions takes care of so much of what we need to see, think, and say.

The progression of Catherine in *The Heiress* leads to a series of shocks that cause her to shed her inner relations with the people who at one time had meant most to her, and to replace this severed emotional connection with object surrogates. That is, she turns to a life of contemplation, contemplation of the things once attached to her renounced and irretrievable loves. The tightening circle of things invests her, and her numbed affections, with residual responsibility. She becomes a conscientious caretaker of the goods that have been left to her, in several senses. But with the tightening comes a drying up of any mental energy held in reserve for larger uses. The objects spell out, without any need for further contributions from Catherine, a self-sufficient picture of her "collected" past, her present daily round, and her "secured" future. A credible completeness is achieved by this phalanx of essential, customary things that compose Catherine's living space. The objects are not themselves divested of emotional life, but what feeling resides in them has only one register: stifled regret and bitterness masquerading as tranquil resignation. Catherine's favored possessions allow no fresh entry points for desire. No objects lying beyond the house are considered worth "adding on" to Catherine's collection, to remedy a felt lack. Catherine might allow herself the dream of putting aside certain things that have served their purpose; she could, in other words, narrow her field of action by reducing still further the items she attends to. But whatever is sacrificed will not open a space, much less an acknowledged need, for anything new.

Catherine's consciousness is not required to animate the objects that seal her in. The things rather supply a semblance of ongoing life to the owner, who cannot abide any less rigid modes of contact. If, late in the film, she resembles, while seated at her embroidery table, an antiquated child quietly at play, we can observe no freedom in the playing. She is monitored by everything that stands around her. All of the furnishings name her in the same terms, and observe and regulate (through their own changeless associations) what she can find of herself to dwell on.

To more fully demonstrate how objects achieve their conquest of the spaces originally assigned to character psychology in *The Heiress*, I shall examine two episodes from the film in considerable detail—the first occurring approximately at the midpoint of the narrative when Catherine accepts Morris's initial marriage proposal, and the other at the end of the film when Catherine, years later, locks Morris out of her father's house (and herself into it) after pretending to accept his second proposal. I shall supply, for each of the key objects in the two narrative segments, brief accounts of their shifting role throughout the film. It is important to see how an object's use at any given moment reverberates with the effects of many different moments and moods. In the first proposal segment, a cluster of noteworthy objects are mobilized by Catherine's sudden full acknowledgment of her love for Morris. The objects dramatize a lonely, forbearing nature confronting, in a dazzling rush, so many sensations and cravings that have for an entire life been trammeled up, barely recognized, inside her. The things that release Catherine's responses here not only synchronize with her radiant blossoming, but are sufficiently imbued with her newfound light that they expand her feeling outward, until it almost remakes the house in her own image. The Sloper home briefly strikes us as a place of becoming—receptive to even the most gossamer human transformation. At the very least the setting accommodates Catherine's rapturous mood—her hushed gratitude at being Morris's beloved—though it doesn't perhaps quite surrender its inveterate force of resistance. The materials Catherine consults and touches bend, as it were, in deference to her immense, unprecedented joy and noble defenselessness. (Some of these materials are imports from outside the house, attached to Morris's own person.) Yet the things of the home preserve their former allegiance to irony and constriction. They yield momentarily to an ardent pressure, but they retain the power to snap back in an instant to their usual adamant chill. If Catherine's feeling is strong enough to flow out in waves to the things of this house, we are aware through Wyler's framing of how the waves are contained, held in check. Objects throughout this episode acquire a solemn equipoise, balanced between acceptance of the reborn Catherine and a gathering will to block her.

Let's join Catherine and Morris as they prepare to leave the dining room table where they have just completed a tense evening meal with the fastidious, caustic Dr. Sloper. Sloper has left the table first, announcing that he must attend a meeting. He has privately instructed Catherine's Aunt Lavinia (Miriam Hopkins), who also lives in the house, not to forget her duties as chaperone in his absence. Lavinia Penniman is Catherine's closest female friend, in spite of their considerable age difference. She is an animated, sometimes amusing companion, but seems incapable of approaching (or imagining) any life situation in terms that are not floridly theatrical. Her speech and gestures are designed to enclose human action in artificial scenarios where real pain and strife have no access. If it were possible, she would reduce Catherine's guileless sincerity to a set of ingenue poses. Aunt Lavinia is another kind of child juxtaposed with

Catherine. In her case, however, girlishness has overstayed its welcome by many years, and has become a sterile corset for any lingering traces of spontaneity or naturalness. She has made vivacity and a too strenuous attempt at charm a consistent theatrical mode of response to Sloper's predictable ironic detachment. She also resembles Dr. Sloper in certain respects: her unyielding coquettishness stands at the same distance from expressive communication as his calculated impersonation of paternal regard. Both parental figures are relentless role players, though one form of theatre is grounded in coolly rational cleverness while the other traffics in a garish mimicry of honest sentiment. Their ways of thinking within the house and with respect to Catherine have jointly atrophied. From two directions their behavior leans toward the inanimate, as though their spirits are in league with Catherine's mother's death: everything has become formalized, a game played out at an emotional standstill. The heavy labor of preserving social forms with a hollow heart seems once more to be a matter of taking one's cues from the frozen, settled objects in the Sloper interior. Things are in command, their indifferent fixity phantasmagorically disseminated to their superficially active owners.

Just before Morris and Catherine rise from their chairs at the supper table, Lavinia theatrically feigns a headache (holding a black-bordered widow's handkerchief to her head). She lets it be known to her niece and Morris that she is playacting illness in order to make light of Sloper's demand that she keep an eye on them. Morris pretends to be taken in by Lavinia's transparent performance when he and Catherine are left alone, though he does so in such a manner as to let Catherine share the joke of her aunt's considerate maneuver. "Poor Mrs. Penniman," he declares sympathetically, then smiles at Catherine like a modest fellow conspirator. Lavinia's handkerchief is the first significant object in the scene, and its appearance is coupled with a single lit candle that is set under a casing of glass on the dining room table. When Lavinia makes her show of pain and raises the handkerchief to her forehead to verify an ache's presence there, she is framed directly behind the candle under glass. The widow's handkerchief attests to Lavinia's long history of trading on a grief she does not feel over the loss of a clergyman husband she hardly cared for. She regularly proclaims this grief as the dominant emotion in her life, and those who hear her practiced lament pretend to believe it, though no one really does. Moreover, Lavinia is not concerned whether her listeners do or not, as long as they maintain the appearance of polite concern. The widow's handkerchief (bearing witness to the copious tears it has reputedly absorbed) neatly encapsulates all the social weaponry she has employed to coerce Sloper to make a permanent place in his home for her. The flame under glass coalesces with the theatrical kerchief to reveal Aunt Lavinia in her entirety. Her animal heat (clearly visible in her strong attraction to Morris, say, and her love of dancing) is transparent, but glassed in; her grief, like her headache, are imposed as a weak social alternative to a vitality she cannot release directly. She parades a self-congratulatory artifice, and though a dammed up sexuality, not so different in kind from Catherine's own, drives her, she cannot make true emotional contact with it.

Lavinia's by now anticipated display of overt theatricality seems both harmless and laughable to the viewer, thus diverting viewer suspicion from Morris's recourse to a subtler form of theatre with Catherine. Melodramatic gestures like Lavinia's headache prove embarrassing to Catherine, because they emphasize the tactical ruses necessary to hasten Morris's courtship (with the suggestion that aunt and niece have worked things out together in advance). But Morris's act of bringing Catherine together with him in a shared acknowledgment of the aunt's good-hearted foolishness makes them suddenly a pair united in understanding that they stand for something different: a tender intimacy with no need of ostentatious inflation. Although Morris's actual degree of affection for Catherine is still indefinite, the fact that Sloper is so confident that he is a scoundrel and that Catherine is once again proving herself a fool, unable to look after herself, makes us eager for Morris to exhibit at least the potential for romantic worthiness. There is a great need in nearly everyone, after all, to believe that a child (of whatever age) can eventually be seen and valued for her best qualities. This need intensifies in a case such as this one, where a sole parent has been unable to find any way to bestow approval, much less love, on his daughter. "What if you can't love your child?" is one of life's large, terrible, seldom-examined questions. As viewers of *The Heiress*, we are compelled to have some faith in Morris's capacity to evolve in his appreciation of Catherine, for our own sake as much as for hers.

When Catherine offers, as an escape from her discomfort, to serve Morris after-dinner port in the drawing room, she is able to lead him down the hallway, seeking a return to the protection of the proprieties observed at dinner. Circumstances would appear to dictate that wooing Catherine will take precedence for Morris over sampling Dr. Sloper's port. And at this juncture that proves to be the case. Later in the narrative, the deferred port will return as perhaps the clinching evidence of Morris's venality. When Sloper takes his daughter to Europe in an effort to weaken Morris's hold on her feelings, Morris becomes a frequent visitor to the house, at Lavinia's invitation. We catch him lounging in this same drawing room, where he is happy to plunder Sloper's stock of liquor and cigars while feigning a flirtatious interest in his garrulous hostess. In this incriminating future scene, Morris is sufficiently loosened by brandy to be openly covetous in his appraisal of the doctor's plentiful creature comforts. Sloper discovers, upon his return, damning evidence of Morris's visits in the form of empty wine glasses on the mantel and a cigar band that the doctor brandishes on his finger like a schemer's wedding ring. He exclaims that the impertinent, shameless suitor has treated the Sloper residence "like his private club."

But in the earlier proposal scene, Morris derails the couple's progress to the port by initiating an embrace in the drawing room doorway. Alarmed by his swift advance in physical closeness and his composed decisiveness in taking her hand, Catherine instinctively draws back, but as she leans for support against the door behind her, it reveals itself as a pocket door that begins to slide open, causing her to lose her balance. Morris, alert to the small mishap, catches the door with his free hand

Figure 4.1. Catherine (Olivia de Havilland), alarmed to be simultaneously saved and trapped by Morris (Montgomery Clift), early in *The Heiress*.

and halts its movement, in the process pinning Catherine into the narrow space between the door frame and the adjustable span of the pocket door. It is a quintessential Morris action, perfectly balanced between timely intervention in a situation where Catherine requires aid and a subtle, nearly blameless pressing of his own advantage. The compromising position that results from Catherine being cornered—hemmed in by a too forceful admirer—is somewhat ameliorated and rendered more acceptable by the fact of the door's ease of movement. If Catherine evinces genuine fear or discomfort, the door could instantly extend itself and grant her as much freedom as she needs to relieve her distress. Morris's hand, presumably attuned to Catherine's mood, controls the "unstable" door, keeping it stationary to prevent a recurrence of the former slipping, and ready to monitor its further widening if Catherine is so inclined.

Morris's talk, while Catherine is pinned in place, interestingly concerns her willingness to disregard her father's decision, if he elects to oppose Morris's courtship. Sloper's judgments and resolutions are frequently associated with closed, sliding doors in the film: thick partitions with a guillotine edge that separate Catherine from his consultations with patients and acquaintances, as well as from his serious thinking about matters he has determined are beyond her ken. He lets her know more than once that he is conscientious about sparing her any needless worry. The pocket doors also come to embody, more than any single feature in the house except perhaps the staircase, Catherine's deeply equivocal status in her filial relationship. The door granting access to her father's person appears to Catherine, throughout her time of growing up, neither strictly open or closed. Sloper insists to her that he is approachable, that there is no formal (formidable) barrier that she must overcome to draw near to him. The without-warning rapidity with which the variable opening in the pocket doors can glide shut sends a contrary message, however: it captures precisely her sense that the way to father is always doubtful, an aperture without stable dimension. And when Sloper eventually encounters resistance from his daughter, in her vow to remain steadfast in her attachment to Morris, the pocket door dramatizes his threat to cut her off—both from his will and his favoring presence. Once Morris finally deserts Catherine on the night of their planned elopement, she resigns herself to remaining inside the house with the father she blames for it (his own poverty of feeling now completely exposed as well). She begins at this point to commandeer Sloper's sliding doors for her own purposes. She denies him the access to her that he has always taken for granted, enclosing herself silently behind them without resorting to outbursts of the sort that she released just once when she was utterly certain that Morris would not be coming for her. (Aunt Lavinia, on that occasion, sealed the pocket doors to screen Catherine's uncontrolled display from observation, and to prevent the noise from carrying.)

The pocket doors transfer entirely to Catherine's authority after Sloper realizes that his daughter is avoiding him in the dwelling they coldly share. It is now he who is unsure of his daughter's plans, as well as her state of mind and heart. He weakly passes through these doors to appeal to her when he falls seriously ill, only to discover while in her presence that the Catherine he had considered for so long irritatingly changeless and dependable is nowhere to be found. Sloper is brought to a stunned point of collapse by his realization that he cannot read her feelings or know what she will do in the future with her money or her freedom. Noting his loss of power, Catherine grimly taunts him with the fact that he will never know, since he will soon be in his grave. Wholly severed from any lingering hope of courtesy—much less forgiveness—from Catherine, he stands, stricken and aimless, then staggers to the pocket doors behind him, which he barely has the strength to slide open. Catherine watches, implacably still, as though presiding over his banishment. Through the narrow opening he secures, Sloper seems driven to make his escape. Were he to remain in the room, he is terrified that his daughter would strip him remorselessly of every thought but one: "she cannot wait to have me dead."

In the proposal scene, where Morris has control of the door, and Catherine feels obliged to break free of him, she declares, with the impressive strength of her simplicity, that she could never tell her father that his opinion on any question pertaining to her doesn't matter. Catherine then retreats to the drawing room and stands, in a frozen position that attests to an excess of emotion, with her hand resting uncertainly on the stopper of the port decanter. The state of suspension that comes from being filled to overflowing with the tumult of first love is repeatedly contrasted in *The Heiress* with forms of physical arrest born of rigidity. Morris promptly follows Catherine to her halting place at the decanter and, placing his hand on top of the hand fumbling with the stopper, releases her from her freeze-tag position. His action and words seem, on the instant, to restore her faith in her untried capacities, just as he has managed to do—with equal impressiveness and tact—in the couple's two previous courtship scenes. He tells her, in a statement that might be construed as a continuation of his pushiness in the doorway, but that somehow feels a more attractive kind of push, "you could do anything for one whom you love." This line strikes home, even though Catherine has not yet directly acknowledged her love for Morris.

Her face rises to meet his gaze, lifted by the unexpected realization that there is already a strength in her sufficient to meet the challenges that stand in the way of her love's fulfillment. It is not merely the case that a cunning Morris is hastily extracting consent to a marriage proposal from a too susceptible, naive girl. If that were our dominant impression, the predatory implications of the scene would feel too heavy-handed. In addition, the conspicuous manipulation would flatten, and coarsely ironize, Catherine's swift acquiescence. The proposal is rather about Catherine visibly becoming a larger, more daring, self-aware, and thrillingly exposed being. Her earlier identifying gesture of shrinking back in fear of what is being offered by her suitor is replaced by an aspiring, unreserved forward movement. Morris's jacket and the scent of cologne it carries become Wyler's best medium for recording Catherine's illumination by love.

Catherine's last show of disbelief in Morris's passionate avowals is her half-worded protest: "But I am, I am so . . ." One readily imagines the words "ordinary" or "unworthy" being added to complete her thought. Morris vanquishes this reflexive abasement with an impulsive, unrestrained kiss. All sense of unworthiness dissolves in the persuasive answering pressure of Morris's desire. His kiss enjoins her to silence, and for the first time in her adult life perhaps, silence becomes a place for her to be fully at home with another. The most stunning moment of self-confidence Catherine achieves in the film is her effortless, uncoerced "Yes" in reply to Morris's proposal. She requires no time at all—not even the space of a pause—to consider her response, and she is beautifully struck by the untimorous completeness of her assent. Though she may be surprised by her readiness to take this leap of faith, she does not draw back to the slightest degree once she has pledged herself. It is Morris rather who appears momentarily undone by her audacity, and for once at a loss for words. It is at this juncture that Morris's jacket becomes an energized presence—a third character, if you will, in the romantic exchange.

In close-up Catherine slowly sounds out the words "I—love—you," almost to herself, after telling Morris "Yes" for a second time when he asks her whether she loves him. Morris's face is turned away, both from Catherine and the viewer, and what she addresses herself to in his partial absence is the warm expanse of his coat. Because her face is so overcome with wonder, tenderness, and the transport of a hitherto unknown security in another person's arms, she must bury this too incandescent portion of her in the suddenly strange cloth that, amazingly, covers him. It is a kind of blotter for the things past naming that swim in her eyes and mouth and burn on her cheeks. It is also a slow motion dive into his sustaining presence to see whether the reality of him will bear up under the vast emotional weight she has just impulsively surrendered. When Morris, without disengaging from her, begins to discuss how Catherine's father might be brought around to accept the match, she touches and plays with his lapels continuously as she offers to intercede for him. (In the past, she could scarcely find words in her father's presence even when there was no trace of discord. Now she feels certain that she has a voice equal to the task of entreating and arguing with him.)

Morris then hesitantly tells her that the term "mercenary" will undoubtedly be used against him by Sloper when she makes her plea on his behalf. Catherine, in reply, asks Morris whether he is "very sure" of his choice of her. He allows her to study his expression unreservedly and at length when he asks: "Can you doubt it?" Catherine, having a lover's courage to sweep aside any lingering apprehension, elects to kiss Morris again, but in a different manner than before. Instead of a renewal of passion, with its vertiginous bewilderment, she explores his face with her lips more inquisitively, with what seems a lucid, ever so delicate curiosity. Behind the embracing couple is a dark, framed painting of a poised young woman feigning surprise as she casts a coy glance toward the painter who has dictated her pose, and the viewer who has paused to appreciate her. Catherine, meanwhile, is soon led from her face probe back to Morris's coat, which she now presses into shyly, like a child or animal, inhaling its fragrance and laying claim to it as a place of perfect repose—a home unto itself.

This action lays the foundation for a final, moving, love-induced cascade of object reveries that commences when the couple part company for the night at her front door. As she says goodbye to him she slowly and with deep reluctance presses the door closed, narrowing then extinguishing his still-as-a-statue image, which hovers like an apparition in the evening light. A judicious cut confuses us for an instant with a subtle perspective shift. The space that Morris occupied in the frame is suddenly taken over by a mirror reflection of Catherine still leaning against the large front door. She catches herself unawares staring at her own, briefly estranged likeness. It is the first time in the film that Catherine has confronted herself in a looking glass, and here it transpires by happy accident. The discovery is oddly exhilarating, as if it were an unhoped-for blessing, and a reprieve. An illuminated lamp on the table below the mirror and two sizable bolts on the door close to where Catherine rests her head are caught in the same reflection that holds Catherine's alchemized face. Though both lamp and locks will figure prominently in the closing scene of *The Heiress*, neither give a hint of their negative potential in this encounter. Everything surrenders to the astonishment of Catherine beholding herself as the one whom Morris has seen and loved and chosen.

Perhaps we recall Morris's last question, "My dearest girl, can you doubt it?," as we enter the swift moving current of Catherine's expanding subjectivity. Because she has put her complete faith in the miraculous tidings that Morris cherishes her, her face (however small the space it takes up in the mirror) seems to become a wide territory, across which countless untried thoughts and gradations of feeling are now at liberty to wander. She permits herself one smile at the power that these never praiseworthy features of hers have managed to exert over another's heart. She appears to have arrived fleetingly at a condition of ideal balance between her inward and outward looking capacities. The mirror, standing in for the just departed Morris, "sees" Catherine, and she does not draw back from its gaze, or put on an expression that will try to remedy whatever old disappointments happen to be disclosed about her. She is ready to accept the newfound person her reflected image unveils. She is lit by the same household light as always, but is now transfixed by the revelation that this Catherine, unadorned, has been found by someone whose natural inclination is to love her.

This mirror-sanctioned inward view seems to turn, as on a hinge, to create an equally spacious view outward. As her glance moves down from her reflected happiness she discovers Morris's gloves on the table. He has left them behind in the excitement of their farewell. The music that accompanies this realization on the soundtrack is "Plaisirs d'amour," the piece that Morris has introduced her to—and given to her as a present. He has become acquainted with the song during his recent tour of France, where, as he puts it, he has "enlarged" his own "capacities." The song softly, sweetly gives warning that the "joys of love last but a short time," perhaps a time almost as concentrated as the chance interval during which these gloves rest so contentedly on the table—making themselves at home there, as it were. Catherine approaches them as though there were now no more precious, significant articles in the world. She places one of her hands over the glove facing her, and attempts to match her fingers to it, smoothing out its thumb, in a lover's trance, in order to align her hand perfectly with Morris's surrogate hand. (One is reminded of the going-away present Morris will later bring to her on shipboard before her trip to Europe with her father. He modestly offers her a small, metal handwarmer. Catherine will of course be required to supply the hot coal for its hollow center, in order to make it work.) Catherine is not so audacious as to place her hand inside Morris's glove. She is content simply to stroke it, as a holy object capable of mediating between the lovers in their separate spheres.

Wyler moves us, through a dissolve, from the "realm of spirit" close-up of Catherine's hands on the gloves to Sloper's return home by way of the tranquil, gated, and lamplit night street of Washington Square. Wyler secures our concentration, after using the dark hall staircase as a preliminary interior frame, on the top hat and cane that Sloper ceremoniously hangs on the rack by the doorway. The lean sharpness of the cane and the shiny, elevated formality of the hat remind us here of Sloper's careful, mock-genial aggressiveness. However, the fact that he sheds them and then retraces with his own eyes the still warm line of Catherine's gaze leading to Morris's gloves intimates that he may be less tightly sealed off than usual. We observe that Sloper holds his own gloves while absorbing the presence of Morris's, establishing one more connection—however unacknowledged—between the two men.

Catherine is curled up asleep on an especially uncomfortable looking Victorian settee in the hallway. She has obviously attempted to wait up for her father's return so she could impart her great news immediately. Sloper no doubt takes in the unusualness of Catherine's sleeping presence here. He silently approaches her, still holding the keys to the front door, and jingles them over her lightly as though he were playing with a pet.

The keys say a number of things at once in their bright, metallically assertive way. They remind us that Sloper owns the house, and exercises final control over who enters freely and who is sent away. Part of his "teasing the kitten" posture with the keys has to do with Sloper's assessment of Morris as a sly creature of stealth who must, with even more adroit slyness, be outmaneuvered. "Ah, the man has pretended to forget his gloves so he will have a pretext for a swift, follow-up visit." Sloper mimics the other invader's clandestine behavior by his alert manner of sizing up the situation in a glance—unobserved—and then creeping up on Catherine to go to work on her. Sloper might have roused his daughter from slumber by touching her gently, a small gesture of physical closeness. Instead he allows the keys to do the work of closeness in a surrogate fashion. He shakes them gingerly, which could be construed as kindliness, but at the same time there is an element of condescension present. He cannot greet her, even when she is asleep, without some show of ironic detachment and veiled teasing. As soon as she awakens Catherine leaps up eagerly to inform her father that she has something important to communicate. Sloper extends his game with the keys by stepping backward in a manner that theatrically mocks her exuberance.

He then urges her to wait with her news until they shift location to the same drawing room where Morris earlier proposed to her. We soon learn that Sloper finds Morris's romantic gloves a strong piece of incriminating evidence against him. He is chiefly struck by how expensive they are—pure chamois. Morris selfishly purchased them and other finery, in Sloper's view, rather than give any assistance to his financially distressed widowed sister and her young children. By such a calculation, Sloper effectively douses the spiritual light by which Catherine and, by intimate extension, the viewer had previously observed the gloves (a mutual reaching out in romantic faith). He restores them peremptorily to their status as a commodity—tainted goods, by his standard of measure. As he prepares to listen to Catherine's appeal on Morris's behalf Sloper turns up the light on a lamp similar to that which stands on the table beneath the hallway mirror. At its simplest level, his action corresponds to his intention of shedding some light on the subject brought before him—or, as Sloper might wish to phrase it, "making a diagnosis.'" The diagnosis will be made in the clear light of reason, whose instrument (the lamp) Sloper judiciously regulates. He listens to his daughter "recite" her artless prepared speech on the little stage he has prepared for her. While she describes the marvel of Morris's proposal—his decision to choose her over so many other worthy, eager candidates—he is conscious of seeing into the real situation far more acutely and deeply than she can. "The poor girl prattles on blindly about this worthless suitor's affection. If only she were able to appraise his motives impartially, as I can, and assign them their true significance." What gives Sloper his calm certainty, of course, is his fixed belief that she is unlovable. She has never been able to summon any strong feeling in him but impatience and resentment. Therefore, Morris's interest could only be traceable to her money, which, as the saying goes, her father holds "in trust" for her. Sloper also can't recognize his anger at the suitor's impertinent challenge to his own decision against him at dinner earlier that night. He conveyed his refusal of Morris's courtship with a graciously diplomatic set of hints, which his guest has seen fit to disregard. Sloper's lamp of reason cannot penetrate the depth of Catherine's resolve to be faithful to Morris "no matter what comes," as she has just pledged to her beloved. What the lamp does show him, unmistakably he thinks, is a young woman in his keeping who must be saved from the workings of her imagination, and from her fantasy that she could inspire interest and affection in her own right. He is supremely confident of the outward light that he sees by. The viewer doubts and dislikes his mode of illuminating her, but it must be noted that while he is present as our human equivalent of the lamp, it is difficult to bring forth supplementary candles (gentler light) to retain our hope that she is other than naive in her expectations. We may be touched by her newborn eloquence in making her case to Sloper, but the lamp of Sloper's austere, commanding point of view diminishes her unwelcomely in our eyes, makes her seem too slight for the romantic challenge she has taken on.

After Catherine retires for the night, cheerfully unmindful of what her father's reason has made of her, he carries the lamp over to his writing desk. He commences to draft a short note, inviting Morris's sister to his home (without Catherine's knowledge). He is convinced that she will ally herself with him, if she has a conscience, supplying the proof he seeks of Morris's deficient character and shabby practices. In this illumination (the lamp that becomes a mirror) Sloper appears to have lost sight of the fact that family attachments, even outside his own home, amount to anything, emotionally. Sloper puts on a suitably grave face as he writes his note, but he is also secretly complacent about his scheme. He feigns, before his sole witness, the lamp, a reluctance to undertake so unpleasant and mortifying a duty. He takes these cruel measures solely for his daughter's sake. He can't locate a particle of his own rage (at Morris) or delight (at his own craftiness) as he sets out, as always, to do the right, austerely principled thing.

In the second episode chosen for extended commentary (which occurs at the end of the film), Catherine, just before taking her final leave of us, picks up the lamp that her father has left for her to see by, as it were, and carries it up the endless staircase into the undispellable darkness of her house. Her manner resembles that of one deeply hypnotized, acting on the suggestion that when she hears her name cried out and a knocking on the door, she must raise her lamp high and proceed upstairs. It is surely a preordained pattern we are looking at, in which the putative free agent making a choice is performing at the behest of an authority she can't recognize. Catherine is clad in an expensive, glacially white gown, and in our final sustained view of her she resembles a younger, no less aggrieved Miss Havisham, another high priestess of acrid, entombed chastity.

The scene has been interpreted by many viewers as a triumphantly executed staging of revenge. In this reading, jilted Catherine—having already repudiated her father and refused to comfort or attend him in his dying—has grown into a figure of steely, assured resourcefulness, fully capable of repaying Morris properly for his callous desertion. Considered merely in terms of its plotted action, the closing scene appears to fulfill perfectly the demands of a "tables are turned" revenge scenario. Morris is impressively hoodwinked, and is left to stand in desperate amazement outside the locked front door of the Sloper dwelling. He beats his fists against the door in a panic, as though if he does not gain admission here, there is no home in the universe that will open to him. And there can be no question that Catherine has acquired an outward self-command. She comports herself with the "dignity" that Morris ascribes to her, which he now sincerely regards as "magnificent." Her bearing and attitude are not even slightly askew, suggesting no self-consciousness about her higher status. She has a new style of utterance as well. Her voice has deepened, and her speech has taken on a crisp, dark fluency. Her vocal control has been gained, however, at the expense of her former expressiveness. That has been lost, and perhaps, by her estimate, well lost. Overall, a sense of a precise, well-run mechanism seems to unite her speech, gestures, and bodily carriage. Catherine has become a finer actor than her Aunt Lavinia, and more imposingly regal in her physical presence than her tight, forbidding father. If an increase in mastery is one's measure of maturity, there is abundant evidence that Catherine has grown impressively.

Yet if we read the concluding scenes with sufficient attention to the sharp signals and darting communications of objects, the triumph of Catherine's revenge becomes an elaborate home burial. The ending is, of course, structured most conspicuously around the door itself, drawing on its automatic associations with acceptance and access. Just as Catherine spent her young life seeking to "unlock" the doors leading to her father's person (his conscious awareness and "pleased" heart), so now Morris must seek an opening through the entranceway that his own past behavior (his ignominious flight from a wide open door) has barred against him.

At the beginning of this episode, Aunt Lavinia, trying for the last time to be a winsome go-between, brings a repentant Morris to the front steps of the house. Inside, she blithely urges Catherine to hear him out, assuring her that she will be persuaded of his honorable intentions and continuing devotion. Wyler shows Catherine fussing with a teapot when Lavinia, planted on a nearby sofa, declares: "I have seen Morris

Townsend!" Lavinia taps the sofa for emphasis as she speaks the forbidden name, and before we observe Catherine's reaction, the sharp clink of a teacup sounds in direct response to the sofa slap. When we cut to Catherine, her body briefly taut with dread, she recovers herself in the act of slowly turning away from the teapot (revealing her face to the camera, which gives additional force to the "sinking in" of the name). Setting down the teapot gives a final, capping weight to her realization.[1] As Lavinia continues her speech, Catherine seems once more to be struck motionless, except for her hand, which creeps over, seemingly of its own volition, to the sturdy teapot, as a means of reconnecting herself to the room. When Catherine responds to Lavinia, she wavers between outrage at her aunt's continued willingness to be an advocate for Morris and a visible anguish over the memory of his abrupt disappearance from her life. Wyler frames her midway between a mirrored reflection of the stairway she climbed when certain that Morris would not come for her (which she will soon climb again, after rejecting him) and the lace curtain blowing in the breeze of the open drawing room window. This window achieved prominence while open once before. On the night of her long, hopeless wait for Morris's carriage to arrive and bear her off, she had stood before the window and informed Aunt Lavinia that this would be the last time she would ever be found in her father's house, looking out upon Washington Square. The lone window is the old dream of escape revivified. Its fluttering curtains convey a not extinct yearning, though Catherine in this scene never faces the window directly. A small portal to elsewhere remains unsealed in the Sloper house, perhaps out of reach.

Catherine turns her attention to her embroidery needle as she rebukes Aunt Lavinia—making up her mind, it would seem, to close the subject of Morris for good. With no sign of her former deference she tells Lavinia to "save her breath. I will not see him." Like the teacup's reply to Morris's name being spoken, the front door chimes tinkle softly

---

1. The sound of the teacup echoes the sound from an earlier major moment of pained discovery by Dr. Sloper. When he is seated with Catherine outdoors at a London cafe that he had once visited with his wife, he begins to soften uncharacteristically into a mood of reminiscence. The gray, blustery day cannot stanch the flow of tender nostalgic yearning. Catherine, however, accidentally reveals that she is still corresponding with Morris, which instantly shatters Sloper's peace—his single lapse into an unguarded state. Sloper marks the closing off of his sympathy by two sharp taps of his coffee cup with a spoon. He caps this harsh pair of clinks with a petulant toss of a coin for the waiter on the marble table top (it rings harshly) and a nerve-scraping backward movement of his chair as he rises to depart.

on the heels of her refusal. The sound of the chimes enters Catherine like an arrow: she hasn't had time to barricade herself adequately against the emotional shock of Morris's nearness. She immediately knows that it is Morris who waits by the door, and before she has willed her way to an appropriate iciness, her expression peels away the years of facial hardening as though they were a mask. We recover for a slight interval the countenance of Catherine as it appeared before the "masters" of cruelty, as she calls them, had completed their training of her.

After Lavinia sadly goes off to deliver Catherine's unequivocal message to Morris ("I am not at home"), we hear offscreen Morris's voice in the presumably unblocked doorway. The live sound of his speech once again restores pure vulnerability to Catherine's features (well hidden, here and throughout the scene, from every view but the camera's). The camera closes in on Catherine's face, and its movement seems perfectly allied with the rustling lace curtains in the window and the voice floating toward her in memory waves. Wyler once more positions Catherine between two articulate objects. On her left is a sizable fluted white pillar,

Figure 4.2. Catherine responds to the heavy metallic pull of her white cameo brooch in *The Heiress*.

which is all fusty decorum, coaxing Catherine in her matching white gown to imitate its aloofness. On her right is a more fragile glass-chimneyed table lamp, reflecting scattered points of light but casting a pronounced shadow. Suspended from a chain on Catherine's neck is a large white cameo brooch fringed with metal. It looks like a cumbersome yoke—a congealment or crystallization of the owner's "injured heart." At first, in the lengthy close-up of Catherine, her face is drawn upward, longingly, toward the music of Morris's speech in the doorway. Then the weight of the brooch seems to draw her shoulders down, literally, restoring her facial mask and at the same time reactivating the low, metallic timbre of Catherine's mature voice. She calls out, "Come in, Morris," without a drop of warmth. The colorless brooch is a simple, eloquent sign that Catherine is no longer working from a soft center. It materializes the place where Sloper's and Morris's words have pierced, lodged, and left scars. The jagged outline of a profiled woman in white on the brooch suggests a kind of merger of Catherine's deceased mother and her daughter, the latter a minister and keeper of the flame at a private altar of the dead.

Catherine remains seated at her embroidery table, where she tries unsuccessfully to concentrate her attention. On its initial appearance in the film, the embroidery table is positively linked with Catherine's shy, unobtrusive presence in the household and her modestly creative solitary work. Its significance shifts in the major confrontation scene between Sloper and Catherine late in the narrative when he unleashes his full vituperative power against her. Sloper lets Catherine know that she has nothing whatever to offer a prospective husband beyond her wealth and her pathetically inconsequential ability to "embroider neatly." Catherine's implied perseverance with embroidery in the years following this imperious paternal dismissal does not mean that she is keeping faith with the "old" Catherine. It would be more accurate to say that the table has become a rack on which her accustomed pain can be nursed and stretched. At the conclusion of *The Heiress*, the embroidery table is presented to us in a consistently harsh light. We are mindful of the sharp, compulsive insertions of Catherine's needle and the tension of the stretched cloth, which is being impersonally ornamented with all the letters of the alphabet. The table has acquired the joyless efficiency of a factory machine that one must serve daily for a set number of hours.

Morris's first conversation with Catherine in the film had as its teasing subject the dance cards that each of them held—identically blank. Morris set Catherine at her ease by his playfully awkward way of handling the small pencil secured by a string to his card, and then astonishes her by writing her name again and again on every available space, each time saying it aloud. The embroidery writing returns all past promises, names, and phrases to the dead field of the "uncommitted" alphabet. In her verbal dealings with others, Catherine has reduced social language to a similar noncommittal embroidery. Her father would no doubt approve of her uniform, carefully managed courtesy. She makes sure that the words directed to her by servants and relatives will not touch her emotionally, and immediately rebuffs any expression of praise or admiration. When the family servant, Maria, for example, compliments Catherine's majestic white dress, Catherine reproaches her for using "false blandishments" to get the night off.

After Catherine admits Morris to her drawing room and pretends to accept both his explanation of his former conduct and his second marriage proposal, she confides to Lavinia that she is finishing her last embroidery. There will be no need for any more, she declares. At this turning point, the abandonment of the embroidery table does not represent, as Catherine supposes, "a putting away of childish things." It is more troublingly a removal of herself from any felt relation to her own history. The last embroidery is a willed termination of expectation as well as regret. Though she is determined to cut her ties with a useless, fraudulent past, she allows herself no compensating belief in the future. Catherine times the finishing strokes of her needle on the letter "Z" to coincide with Morris's nighttime return to the house. She waits to snip the last thread, with her scissors poised in the air, until she hears Maria loudly secure the bolt on the door.

Before Morris departs the Sloper house to make his preparations for the revived elopement plan, the viewer has become convinced, for all of his feeble, unconvincing words of self-serving apology, that his attitude to Catherine has decisively changed. He is now clearly dazzled by her, and has come to resemble the younger Catherine in his genuine need for love and acceptance. When he is briefly alone with Aunt Lavinia, he exclaims, "I'm home, really, truly home." He is almost tearfully glad to behold the old gleaming fixtures and fittings of the ample Sloper rooms, but apart from this ironic reunion, he speaks as one who has felt himself exiled for a very long time from anything real and sustaining. In Morris's present, actual craving for Catherine's former faith and ardor, she no longer sees herself reflected. She judges him with her father's eyes, whose way of measuring value she has internalized and come to appreciate: Morris is weak in his neediness, and contemptibly vulnerable to my manipulation. He has failed father's test: running away because he lacked firm resolution. It is curious to witness Catherine speaking respectfully to Morris about her father's wise tactics for ascertaining a suitor's true character. It is as though she must justify in retrospect the necessity of his cruel behavior to her, and make him pleased (beyond the grave) with her belated grasp of his logic.

When Catherine agrees to Morris's second proposal, she gives him the wedding gift that she purchased for him years ago, during her trip to Europe. The gift exactly expresses the process of Catherine's subsequent education and undoing. Her original plan was to surprise Morris with a seemingly plain and inauspicious set of buttons. The buttons, in fact, are inlaid with costly, sparkling rubies. Catherine had hoped that Morris would eventually see the fitness of this "transformed" small and ordinary thing he had been good enough to take a chance on. By the end of *The Heiress*, however, when he finally holds them in his hand and has his first glimpse of them, their meaning (for the viewer at least) has powerfully shifted. Catherine herself now possesses the ossified gleam of the cold gems, but the tender appeal of the underlying buttons has been vanquished—and, as it were, effaced. Morris imagines that the button girl stands before him still, magically decked out like an empress, but he is wrong to count on a constant, fluently simple nature beneath the elaborate costume.

Morris's goodbye kiss echoes Catherine's quietly devotional exploration of Morris's cheek in the first proposal scene. This time the eloquent object is Catherine's heavy earring, which matches her brooch and contains yet another image of an embossed, severe female profile. The earring intrudes visually between Morris's attempted gentle kiss (in close-up) and the strain of Catherine's recoil from physical intimacy. She appears to turn every part of herself away from him but the earring, which, as she says of the ruby buttons, "suits" him.

The jewels prepare us for the sleeping beauty curse that holds the house and its heiress in an unbreakable spell in the film's closing sequence of actions. Catherine, the sleepwalker, must ascend the staircase (after taking leave of the ghosts in her so-called waking life) and disappear into the heavy, dreamless repose, the rapt immobility of the house's other objects. The coda commences with Morris poised for takeoff in the hallway, where for once in his blighted romantic history with Catherine, he seeks a pretext to linger and—simply because he wants to—prolong his view of her. He stands in front of the hall mirror and unconsciously re-creates the stance that we saw when Catherine closed the door on him on the evening of the first proposal. This time he is positioned further away from Catherine, and appears to be sculpted in space, like a memory image. When he turns to go through the door we are able to see him leave the frame twice, first in his own person and then in mirror reflection. The mirror frame captures his entire exit from the house, including the door closing behind him. Wyler amplifies the sound of the reflected door as it shuts.

As soon as Morris leaves, Catherine moves to the large windows in the drawing room and begins unfastening the bulky drapes (whose fabric resembles that of her beautiful gown) and pulling them closed. Aunt Lavinia stands behind her, oblivious of her intention, and chatters aimlessly about the lovers' reconciliation. This contrast is meant to mark firmly the distinction between a foolish woman trapped in naïveté (as Catherine herself arguably was as a young woman) and a woman trapped in irony, disbelief, and something more that we can't yet identify. We may, in fact, legitimately wonder whether irony and skepticism can rightly be called a trap in the wake of so much deceit-spawned suffering. Catherine has begun the Poe-like process of bricking herself in—sealing off all external views and quenching the light of the larger world. When Lavinia is finally permitted to understand Catherine's plan for revenge, she asks her if she "knows what she is doing." In spite of the consistent limitations of the aunt's perspective (whether the subject is cruelty, neglect, or romance), this question is a pertinent one. Although Catherine replies "yes" without hesitation before forcing the nonplussed elderly romantic seeking a happy ending to leave her (and the narrative), the issue of what Catherine does and doesn't know about her actions continues to reverberate.

Promptly, a further darkening of the image commences. In our one glimpse of Morris's living quarters, we observe him in a rather cramped rented room, closing up the traveling bags that crowd his bed, hurriedly putting on his coat and blowing out the room's single lamp. One feels that everything of value that Morris presently owns is inside these bags, and that the room itself, in its shabby temporariness, holds nothing that makes the slightest claim on him. His way of moving conveys urgency more than confidence, as though an anxiety having to do with previous failures and a general sense of "too lateness" have begun to fracture his once elegantly composed façade. His blowing out of the lamp dissolves into a close-up of Catherine's embroidery. Her hand is visibly hastening through the few remaining stitches on the letter "Z." The sound of Morris's breath extinguishing the light is followed in the dissolve by a chiming clock, musically propelling us to the hour of nine. Haste and "too lateness" are aptly conjoined in these parallel views of the two figures in their separate locales.

The sound of Morris's carriage in the street, which Catherine had waited for with mounting apprehension, and then agony, years before, seems to be traveling through Catherine's memory ear as she sits in her drawing room, listening to her clock complete its announcement of the hour. She raises her head just before the hooves on the cobblestones become audible. It seems clear that she has never stopped waiting for this sound since the far off night of her abandonment. It joins the collection of ghostly sounds that Wyler has assembled, all of which seem more imagined and recollected than experienced directly. The past-laden force of the sounds undeniably supersedes their literal function. Catherine will not look out her draped windows to see this carriage or the man inside it. She insists on keeping them as imagined presences only. In this form they do their best to penetrate the house and sweep her, against her rigid will, back into the tumultuous flow of life. The ringing of the bell, for example, with its merrily expectant jingle, seems to blossom out of the barely vanished chime of the clock.

On Morris's side of the divide in this episode of foiled communication, we have a massive double door with a circular brass knocker and two ornate door knobs. Above the door is a fanlight, which reveals to Morris that there is activity inside the house, though it is only discernible as a mesh of dancing lights and shadow. Morris's own shadow is sharply delineated beside him on the doors, mimicking him as he successively rattles the knobs, impatiently raps the knocker, and attacks the door with his fists. Morris eventually resorts to his voice as his best instrument for gaining admission. He calls out the name "Catherine" repeatedly, at first to confirm his identity ("Don't you know who this is?"), and then with ever greater fearfulness that his identity is no longer an acceptable calling card. His behavior is that of a person who, without any warning, has been unmasked in his core weakness. He can only remove himself from this scalding exposure, it would seem, if someone will let him pass through this door. The taunting shadow cast upon the wood surface sets Morris at odds with it. Unlike the man who pleads from the outside, the shadow is already incorporated with the door, at one with its substance rather than confronting it as pure barrier. Morris, by contrast, is "a poor bare forked animal" seeking to break through something to regain a substance that feels utterly lost to him. The "eyes of the world" are all gathered in harmony behind this wall of separation. Morris passes, with alarming speed, from the appearance of someone making a polite request to that of a desperate prisoner begging to be released. All of the film's underlying dread of being judged by those with the power to erase your value "beyond repair" is suddenly permitted to erupt through the unlikely figure of this impeccably graceful, handsome suitor. Morris cries out for acknowledgment, and his despair at not being recognized and answered seems to carry the entire tragedy of this love-emptied narrative in a single image. The presentation is so coated with irony and the satisfaction of retribution, however, that the image's full meaning (appropriately) is scarcely visible.

On the other side of the door, Catherine's own burden seems curiously, but not quite attractively, lightened. After making herself into a silhouette, matching Morris's shadow outside, by putting out the lamp in the parlor, she glides apparitionally to the spot in the hall where she bid good night to Morris after they became engaged, and raises another lamp, this one still illuminated, which she needs to light her way upstairs. She lingers for several moments close to the door, as though seeking to inhale the sounds of Morris's distress like an intoxicating oral fragrance. She reminds me briefly of Bette Davis's Regina in Wyler's *The Little Foxes*, waiting in foreground close-up as her husband staggers helplessly behind her, in the throes of a fatal heart attack. The resemblance lies chiefly in the intense focusing of a woman's face that will not allow itself to be reached (unfettered, if you like) by the supplicating anguish of a man who stakes everything on remembered bonds of kinship. Regina's face threatens to break apart from the strain of stifling any impulse that might penetrate her sturdy sense of grievance. Catherine's face undergoes what one might paradoxically term a brightening into coldness. It is as though she sheds the weight of her accumulated emotional injuries, but in the process becomes a kind of burning husk.

Mere inches away from her, Morris flings himself forward like a maimed animal, protesting its pain and captivity. Catherine silently says "goodbye to all that" and luxuriates in the clean, well-lighted surfaces of the domestic interior she has now fully inherited. She has the look of someone who has been interrupted in her search for something important that has unaccountably slipped her mind. "The thing," in Alice Munro's phrase, "that was your bright treasure" ("Chance," in *Runaway*, 83). Having lost sight of it, you are randomly reminded of something else, something lying upstairs, perhaps a pair of slippers in a closet. Early in *The Heiress*, fresh from her father's reproving gaze, Catherine flinches as a fishmonger in the street casually lops off the head of her purchase with one blow of a cleaver. As Morris is bolted out, she flinches again, as though acquiescing in the thought that she is now untouchable: the age of squeamishness is at an end.

Catherine floats up the stairs, lamp in hand, in a daze that quickly ripens into a trance. The light pushes aside the crowding darkness on the stairs, but the lamp can only clear a small circle at a time from this gloom of family shades. Catherine's upward progress easily confirms the possibility of rescue, of leaving behind whatever exorbitant, animal thing would menace her from below. She lifts herself beyond the fray, but is en route to a goal immeasurably far within the house—that is to say, within the strict confines of her father's will. She seems to be further lacquered in her dream of the inanimate with every step. She communes with the too well-known things around her, as one who is irreversibly attached to them, having become their frozen equal.

Figure 4.3. Lit by the humble incandescence of her lamp, Catherine ascends the stairs, fully entering—one pool of light at a time—her inherited abode of things in *The Heiress*.

5

Prospero Unbound

John Barrymore's Theatrical Transformations of Cinema Reality

JOHN BARRYMORE IS THE SUPREME embodiment of theatre on film. No matter what roles he plays, the aura of theatre inescapably and (so often) magically defines his relation to the camera, and to his fellow performers. Far from seeking to distance himself from his legendary career onstage or from boldly theatrical effects, he makes conscious use of them onscreen. To sever the theatre tie, he suggests, would only diminish his magnetic force as an actor, pressing him needlessly toward a common lot resistant to ungovernable vitality and feats of largesse. Theatre for him offers as its greatest lure the potential to burst the boundaries of an assigned role at any moment, to annul the threat of confinement to a tediously fixed disposition. Barrymore seems always a visitor to the land of film from another country. He carries the burden of exile, though in an antic fashion. We feel his true home and deepest commitments lie elsewhere. Like his character the Baron in Edmund Goulding's *Grand Hotel* (1932), he is drawn to shadow spaces on the periphery of the designated main action. He emerges for brief intervals as a half-spirit, half-charlatan, seeking a kind of connection and fulfillment that are unattainable. One feels he prefers the elusive or impossible goal, and secretly craves to have his aims thwarted.

His roles, more often than not, seem designed to test the distinctions between film's sense of the real and theatre's. He is certainly a creature of this borderland, and many of his most famous characterizations highlight division, and the necessity of repeated transformation. Film offers the possibility of direct human revelation. The camera divines a presence separate from the demands of acting, if a performer is willing to be seen and known in his own right. (Not known fully, of course, but beheld with fewer impediments: the eyes and face are more open to intimate inspection than in most ordinary human interactions.) The camera desires to discover who the man Barrymore is, without the protections of disguise. Barrymore resists exposure of the self behind the theatre personage, yet so many of his characterizations are precisely about masks gradually torn away and a subjection to merciless social scrutiny. Perhaps the role in which Barrymore is most caught up in theatrical flummery and at the same time most painfully probed by the camera is Larry Renault in George Cukor's *Dinner at Eight* (1933), a figure who is lethally entrapped on the illusion-shredding stage of his hotel room. Interestingly, however, Barrymore's conception of this ham actor stresses that his destruction results in large part from lack of theatre conviction: insufficient belief in theatrical transformation, and theatrical means for approaching truth. Renault cannot disappear behind a mask, and as a result, with no place to hide, and no role-playing skill to draw upon, he is prey to almost everyone with whom he comes in contact. The elements of Renault's failure to believe in theatrical metamorphosis until the role of a literal dead man presents itself to him as a way out of his difficulties will be my primary focus in this chapter. But before examining the Renault performance in detail, I would like to talk briefly about the characters of Oscar Jaffe in Howard Hawks's *Twentieth Century* (1934) and François Villon in Alan Crosland's *The Beloved Rogue* (1927), and to examine them as keys to Barrymore's whole conception of acting.

One reason Oscar Jaffe is widely regarded as Barrymore's lodestar film role is because it places no limit on his transforming impulses. Jaffe is free to improvise his attitudes, needs, values, and behavioral language with reckless abandon and no fealty to coherence. His temperament contains multitudes of evanescent personages, and he can get by with no ground beneath his feet other than the license to pretend in all directions. Only the chalk-marked space of a rehearsal stage makes sense to Jaffe as a realm where things have a dependable order and intelligibility. Elsewhere he is "transcendentally homeless," and though often frantic as his masquerades and stratagems crumble, is happy to stay that way—unsettled to the core. Though Jaffe is a creature of farce, there is what Sigmund Freud beautifully terms a plaintive "afterwardness" to his contract with existence. Whatever might be real in his life has happened to him already, in an earlier, irretrievable time. All that is left to him now is a succession of gossamer incarnations, taken up as mood dictates, to deflect the exigencies of a too onerous present tense. He commits himself wholly, but briefly, to the predilections of each mask in turn. They facilitate the retrieval of precious, zestful desires that were once natural and even authentic to him.

In a letter to his second wife, Michael Strange, written during their courtship, Barrymore spoke about his intense identification with the fifteenth-century French poet François Villon, whom he regarded as an extraordinary mental escape artist, and incessant wanderer, after his own heart. Villon, in fact, might supply an approach applicable to the creation of any film character:

> He [Villon] was a creative artist, a poet, and everything happened in his head. When he is caught by Life in these movie situations, which always demand a rather asinine, heroic activity, he is frightfully up against it. Only by his amazing dexterity and imagination can he elude them, maintain a certain whimsical integrity, and prevent himself from looking like an ass, the audience being the only person he takes into his confidence. I think the picture of Villon skipping, bounding, and crawling on his stomach through a Gothic dimension of a dying chivalry and a brutal and slightly sacerdotal materialism till almost the very end, when he is forced, through the reality of suffering, his mother's death, etc., to a different attitude—always, however, flecked by a sort of pinched gaiety—is something I can have genuine fun with and accomplish something real. (Fowler, 188)

Barrymore addresses here the vexing dilemma of an actor (whether officially performing a role or not) being "caught by Life" in false situations and their attendant false attitudes. He conceives of "heroism" as a behavioral stance foisted on him by those who have no conception of what such an ideal might actually entail, by way of sacrifice and suffering, and who make it into something self-servingly "asinine." He invokes the counteragents of tart whimsy, burlesque, buffoonery, and (my favorite) "a sort of pinched gaiety" as the surest means of preserving a degree of integrity in the midst of script and director-dictated heroic posturing.

The film or stage Villon, for example, must contend with the Gothic rigmarole associated with a "dying chivalry." The actor must oppose the convention of languid gestures and a perfumed fatalism by adding exuberant outbreaks of physicality—"skipping, bounding, and crawling on [one's] stomach" through the misty poetic territory. He should release brutality in the rendering of wistfulness and a harsh materialism in his quest of the sacred.

To pursue acting on a higher, freer level than current theatrical and film conventions dictate demands a dexterous, spontaneous imagination that allows one to "elude" ready-made solutions at every turn. Barrymore sees the crucial channel of communication existing not between himself and the other characters, important as those are, but between himself and the spectator. It is so easy for those circling you on stage to impose script-sanctioned demands that drastically hem you in, with a fearful need for orderly arrangements, predictable limits. The spectator, in the hypothetical François Villon project, will be the only one that Villon will take into his full confidence. In that respect, he resembles Barrymore's two most celebrated roles, Hamlet and King Richard III. Barrymore describes the final destination of the Villon performance—the place where its truth crystallizes—as a "something real" forcibly held back until "almost the very end." The bulk of the Villon performance would be spent in outlaw evasions of those external and internal agents who strive to conscript one into false service. One exorcises various modes of inauthentic stage behavior by playing at cross-purposes with it. He will secure the right to honest sentiment, pathos, nobility, and tragedy by strenuously resisting the facile temptations that counterfeit versions of these qualities offer to him throughout the dramatic narrative. It is like an actor's pilgrim's progress, strewn with moral obstacles. It may require an entire performance to clear a space for a few real, unforeseeable moments of revelation. (I think immediately of Barrymore's brief spasm of weeping near the close of his segment of *Dinner at Eight*, immediately preceding his character's return to delusion.)

When Barrymore is on film, his association with theatre is linked with power—power from another realm that is equally tied to make-believe and the spiritual. This available power works to separate him from others in the film world, even when they also display theatrical attributes. In Barrymore's case, his apparent access to power is never far removed from his character's manifest weakness, and he often deliberately betrays the true nature of that power by using it as a mere protective shield for his weakness. A character like Svengali, for example, fears that to expose his frailty, his abject dependency on his seeming puppet, Trilby, is to ensure destruction. So much of his art-making power, then, is futilely lavished on control and concealment. Barrymore's more contemporary characters—like the Baron in *Grand Hotel*—seem socially adept and available to others, after a fashion, but the Baron's preferred mode of conduct has to do with stealth. As I noted earlier, he moves around the edges of his milieu, almost destitute (a baron in name only), alone and in shadow. He performs his relationships with a smiling verve, but his exertions—even in his love scenes with Grusinskaya (Greta Garbo)—are suffused with an unshakable melancholy. The theatrical component of his self-presentation cannot be relinquished, and the play-acting fatigues and sequesters him. His brief love affair with the ballerina is possible because they recognize each other as fellow creatures of the stage, equally imprisoned by it. The Baron's only enduring attachment is with his dog, who in a sense mirrors his own helpless dependency on those who "feed" him, but whose instincts are free and untainted, spared the ongoing demands of make-believe.

Barrymore characters often appear ready to be destroyed from the outset. Part of that readiness comes from the theatrical burden they carry. They have emptied themselves out through increasingly disconnected, brash, and heedless role-playing. There is a sense that the Barrymore character, wearily stoic after a chain of defeats, almost relishes the prospect of being stripped of his theatrical resources, even though he can't conceive of anything to replace them. A Barrymore performance typically derives enormous energy and focus from the impending threat of breakdown, of hollowing out. Circumstances plot a return to abject vulnerability. He aspires to the reality of suffering without recourse to noble poses. The gaiety that survives the Barrymore character's stripping down to bare essentials may be "pinched," flecked with gallows humor, but what inspires it is a deep relief—akin to rejoicing—from no longer having to keep up appearances of any sort. So often Barrymore is allowed to be alone with the camera in his final extremity. The ghostly audience outside the world of the film is all he has left. What he has to show to this audience is his performance failing, but its failure is his channel to truth-telling. Barrymore yearns for a tragic conclusion, marked by the laughter that comes with the surrender of his theatrical identity.

In George Cukor's 1933 film adaptation of the Edna Ferber–George Kaufman play, *Dinner at Eight*, we have a remarkable example of how every aspect of theatre and role-playing is turned against Barrymore. Theatre is made into an instrument of relentless humiliation, which conspires with other sorts of delusion to drive his character to suicide. Barrymore might at first seem to be strangely, and masochistically, cast in this film. At a time when his authority as a film star was still uncompromised, he elects to play Larry Renault, a has-been silent movie actor who is presently alcoholic, penniless, no longer handsome, prey to many delusions, and distastefully autocratic to the few underlings who can still be made to do his bidding. We are even informed that Renault's acting talent, when he was successful, had never been substantial. His reputation depended entirely on his looks and a confident bearing. His agent, Max Kane (Lee Tracy), disdainfully alludes to the "great profile" at one point, which was a crucial feature of the Barrymore stage and film persona. Edna Ferber and George Kaufman had already written a popular comedy about the Barrymore clan, *The Royal Family of Broadway* (1927), in which John Barrymore's vanity, petulance, womanizing, and heavy drinking were vividly lampooned. Though the comedy in the first play was affectionate, Ferber and Kaufman's later portrait of an actor with neither creative gifts nor survival skills was painful and ferocious. The figure of Renault begins as a small man who grows steadily smaller in the eyes of all who have dealings with him. The viewer witnesses a series of repellently deflating defeats, in which our judgment of Renault differs little from those who reject him. He is granted no quarter or effective acts of resistance during a many-sided onslaught. The Renault scenario is literally a chamber piece. Barrymore's entire performance is limited to two extended scenes, both of which take place in one room of his hotel suite, in the aptly named Hotel Versailles.

Within this tightly confined space of borrowed opulence, Renault is introduced offering a moderately convincing performance as a renowned actor with plentiful career prospects to his easily impressed current lover, nineteen-year-old Paula Jordan (Madge Evans). While pontificating tipsily to her, he receives a phone call from Paula's mother, inviting him to a formal dinner party later that same evening, an invitation he reluctantly accepts due to Paula's surprising insistence. Paula's mother, Millicent (Billie Burke), is ignorant of their affair; Paula hopes that it can soon be revealed to everyone. Renault's change of mind about the dinner in the course of the phone call—with Paula hovering near him, as coach—is the single act of calculated deception that the actor does not bungle in an ever-accelerating ordeal of unmasking. Yet even in his handling of the phone call with the foolish, superficial society woman, Barrymore emphasizes Renault's lack of ease. He projects an air of dated—almost moth-eaten—gentility, bringing a quality of waxy stiltedness to his assumption of the grand manner. His "too muchness" is reinforced by the elaborate smoking jacket he wears, which is adorned by a large, gaudy LR monogram and an embroidered coat of arms. A silk handkerchief peeps ostentatiously from the jacket's upper pocket. As Renault attempts to charm Millicent, he is revealed facing a framed photograph of himself set by a window. The window's floor-length, cord-tied drape strongly evokes a theatre curtain. Behind Renault is a folding screen, which suggests intimate concealment. Director Cukor noted in an interview that Barrymore added the phrase "dear lady" to his talk with Millicent, and did so in order to make his courtesy feel old-fashioned, a relic of another time rather than a supple display of sophistication (24).

The ensuing dialogue with Paula about the state of their relationship is played as though he can hardly summon the energy to hold on to her, to maintain even the appearance of continued romantic interest. When he accepts the dinner invitation on the phone, Paula gratefully kisses him, and he responds to her gesture with an audible sigh. He sighs again, somewhat more surprisingly, after he and Paula exchange a prolonged passionate kiss while stretched out on his hotel room sofa. He is clearly in desperate straits, but makes no attempt to hide his alcoholism from her. He is equally transparent in his display of emotional enervation and his fatigue with the rigmarole of desire, despite the fact that Paula may be the only person who remains convinced of his value.

Barrymore specializes in playing characters who can feign an affable engagement with the affairs of life, but who have in fact no continuing stake in the din and strife. The Barrymore character is frequently introduced in a condition of unearthly, becalmed detachment. Barrymore is stunningly versatile in his ways of embodying remoteness. His unconcern is sometimes joined to the tasks of winsome benefactors. But his "remoteness" can also manifest itself in pitched battles with isolation and the siren song of self-destruction. In Mitchell Leisen's *Midnight* (1939), Barrymore plays a wealthy fairy godfather, Georges Flammarian, for the radiantly covetous chorus girl, Eve Peabody (Claudette Colbert). Although fully aware of her deceit and her schemes to advance her own financial interests, he nevertheless becomes, the instant he first sets eyes on her, a secret supporter of her false identity as a baroness, and her plan to procure a wealthy husband. The film's plot supplies a quasi-rational motive for his unstinting advocacy of her ambitions. Georges is attempting to break up his wife's affair with a sophisticated, well-off ladies' man, Jacques (Francis Lederer). He imagines that Eve's "Baroness" will provide an even more bewitching romantic prospect for the charming Lothario rival to woo. But the film provides only the flimsiest evidence that Georges remains vitally attached to his wife (Mary Astor), or driven to rekindle her affection for him. He appears more persuasively entranced by Eve's belief that her world is pure theatre, through which she moves like a dancer in a gold lamé dress with matching hood. This dress and her similarly lustrous evening bag are her sole surviving possessions, but she is confident that they are sufficient to open the right doors, and get her where she wants to go. She is a kindred spirit to Georges, given her view that one can sensibly devote all one's life energy to playacting. Georges has long ago forsworn a grounded, consequential existence, one that contains serious, ache-inducing attachments. He is an untroubled, untroubling Prospero, dwelling on an island of gossamer magic and stratagems. He naturally throws in his lot with another phantom, a floater, who scarcely cares about anything that she has been in the past or presently is. Eve Peabody is mostly in touch with an enchanting "will be" for which she is continually auditioning. Her staged, delectably "made up" self is as close to the melancholy fog of reality as Georges is willing to venture. His efforts on her behalf are carried out with no hint of trepidation or solemnity. His interventions seem free of risk for him. He exhibits at all times a perfect, enviable immunity to danger or loss. Every dicey shift in the plot he oversees is greeted by him with a hilarity that stands apart from any sense of struggle. He is as outside the game he is playing as if he were already a ghost. Theatre is what remains visible to him, but it no longer offers a route to something meaningful.

In William Wyler's *Counsellor at Law* (1933), produced the same year as *Dinner at Eight*, Barrymore's character, George Simon, is much more thoroughly invested in actual life experience. He is embroiled in his clients' dilemmas, cares about his marriage, his mother's well-being, and his own reputation for integrity. Yet despite his forceful and convincing busyness in his tumultuous office world, there comes a point quite late in the narrative where it seems that his many purposeful connections to others fall abruptly away, and he is suddenly revealed lost in that familiar Barrymore region of remoteness. He appears bereft of performing resources, a creature walled up in a silence that turns all his prior enterprising brashness to dust. He sits facing his office window, contemplating a suicidal plunge. What saves him is the propitious arrival of an underling with a solution to his current disbarment crisis. This rescuer is a fellow creature of theatre, who insists on "staging" his good news in the form of a long-winded tale, comically laden with digressions. Barrymore's George Simon returns to life by becoming a theatre spectator, in thrall to another's performance.

Returning to Larry Renault's impatient love scene with Paula in *Dinner at Eight*, we are shown Barrymore alternating between several different voices in his responses to her, none of which emerges convincingly as his natural voice—the voice that identifies his true position. Each vocal register Renault takes on is steeped in feigning, often unconscious feigning. He cannot slip free of bad faith, no matter how desperately pitiful his plight becomes. Renault assumes that he can distinguish between straight talk and posturing, but in fact the voices available to him have no power to express his actual condition. Even when he is profoundly humiliated at a later point in the narrative, he cannot speak from the place where humiliation thrusts him. It is a case in *Dinner at Eight* of a bad actor having no escape route from spurious theatrical effects. Renault cannot keep his tattered personae clear or prevent them from colliding and blurring incoherently.

One of his voices is that of the petulant, intransigent drunk, who flaunts his out in the open, massive consumption of alcohol, and regards his outbursts at Paula's gentle remonstrances as daredevil valor. He declares the rebel's right to "do as I please." The second voice he employs belongs to the gruff-speaking man of the streets, the sort who can report on life's accumulated hardships with bracing honesty. Unlike Paula, he is acquainted with the "real facts," because he is engaged in an honorable fight "every second" against those who betray him and fail to give him his due. He is proudly battle-scarred from being forever "up against it." Renault uses this same harsh vocal pitch to assess the defects of the play he imagines he will soon be signing a contract to star in. He rasps out reassuring reminders of his ability to put weak material over by sheer force of personality. While he is still applauding himself for shrewd, pragmatic accommodation and describing his skill at "dominating" onstage, his nerve fails him. His hardheaded tone and stance go hollow, and his voice crumbles. His third stage voice is wrapped in romantic gauze. It strives for the mellifluous cadence of Dickens's Sydney Carton at the end of *A Tale of Two Cities*, as he evaluates his magnanimous sacrifice. When Carton climbs the steps to the guillotine, he recognizes that it is a "far, far better thing" he is doing than he has ever done.

Barrymore shifts rapidly between his petulant and man of the streets voices as he tells Paula of his three failed marriages, and of his current numbed state, which is beyond the reach of love. He weaves dizzily between a farceur's mockery of his marital misfortune and rueful resignation to his accursed luck. Then he shrilly pours forth his envy of his third wife's massive success as a film star, before finally arriving at the promised land of sweet-voiced largesse. He encourages Paula to be done with him and return to well-meaning, eligible Ernest, her fiancé. Renault comes nearest to "unstaged" utterance when he declares she knows nothing whatever about him, brushing briefly against the usually suppressed fact that her lack of such knowledge matches his own. He pauses at one point in his recitation of his woeful love history after saying "and now I'm . . ." but is at a loss for an answer. He strokes his chin, stands wreathed in stage silence, and casts a downward, audience-attentive glance at nothingness before reaching further back into the past and acknowledging his countless dalliances, "too many" for another one to count. His attempt at a large, meaningful gesture to Paula occurs as he sits on the sofa again and admits that he is "burned out," with no loving substance inside him to draw upon. However, moments later, he is converting his confession to Paula and his relinquishment of any claims upon her into a theatrical event of shimmering grandeur. He views it as a tearful theatre patron might, and appraises its value (with tender surprise) as perhaps the only decent thing he has ever done. But Paula is by no means ready to give him up, and he knows it. Her stubborn youthful ardor soon pushes him back into petulant mode, and he spoils the mood of heroic sacrifice with a weak, cranky insistence that she submit to his will—an enervated, befogged will. And in fact she resolves to have her own way. Renault must capitulate as they are interrupted by the arrival of his overtaxed, exasperated agent, Max.

Preparing for the challenge of his first major Shakespeare role, Richard III, in Arthur Hopkins's legendary 1920 production, Barrymore worked extensively with the great vocal coach Margaret Carrington to expand his limited range. Arthur Row, who acted with him in that production, recalls that in previous stage appearances, his voice had been light and his diction "atrocious . . . he had about three notes to his voice [and] as they say in theatrical argot, no legato." Row went on to observe that by opening night of *Richard III*, his intensive, fiercely disciplined vocal study had resulted in an entirely different instrument, revealing "an English as near perfection as any human being can achieve" (89). In *Dinner at Eight*, Barrymore makes the maladroit ham actor Renault into someone who flounders vocally. The sounds he makes are awkwardly unfitted to his needs and the sense he hopes to convey. His rapid shifts of vocal character imply a frantic scramble among dwindling, mechanical options. All of his impersonations feel tentative, uncommitted. His vocal skittering deprives him of centeredness and its accompanying weight. He lacks a voice that can serve as home base, on which he can stand and hold his ground after his bouts of conscious playacting. Alcohol further debilitates his focus. He exhibits the drinker's proneness to spontaneous flights of fancy, but he lacks the good actor's adeptness at reining them in, imposing any sort of control.

As I noted previously, Barrymore's performances consistently announce his license to use theatrical devices—heightened physical and vocal expressiveness and nimble mask-to-mask transitions. In *Dinner at Eight*, it is not Renault's overt theatricality that does him in, but rather his poverty of stage resources, his lack of belief in what he acts out, and hence his lack of adaptability. Laurence Olivier, discussing his initial extreme reluctance to play the drunk, hammy, miserly James Tyrone in Eugene O'Neill's *Long Day's Journey into Night*, talked about the challenge of portraying a character who is an actor, without self-protective tricks and the wrong sort of overstatement. (On another occasion, paying lavish tribute to Barrymore's Hamlet, Olivier wrote: "When he was onstage, the sun came out" [43].) No sun is allowed to emerge for Larry Renault in the single room torture chamber where his final breakdown transpires. Barrymore endows him with minimal panache, charismatic pathos, or self-awareness in his vain strutting and helpless fretting through the demeaning encounters he undergoes in the hour before his suicide. Apart from his time with Paula, Renault has no moments with any of his visitors where he rises above the indignities heaped upon him. The bellhop he sends out for alcohol, the room service waiter he asks for a meal, his agent, his prospective theatrical producer, the hotel manager and his assistant who serve notice that Renault must promptly vacate his suite—all see through his transparent maneuvers. They treat his disarray and lordly, muddled pronouncements with embarrassed distaste or open scorn. He is an unmasked individual who still mistakenly believes he has command of his audience. He flails clumsily and obtusely, without a trace of ingenuity, through every theatrical gambit, especially the act of self-possession. Renault's performing talent is such a thin "commodity" that the spectacle of his groping abasement is at all times available for inspection. He has neither vocal nor physical invention left to cover it over. An actor who has no vital artifice to transform himself, Renault stands stricken and rigid in the glare of the hideous real.

Barrymore is deeply drawn to characters who are pushed to a "poor bare forked animal" state of extremity. He revels in "dance of the seven veils" descents into quivering, shameful emotional nakedness. Renault most fascinates him when he has lost his last pathetic safeguards and defenses, and is pinned, writhing, under a collective, repudiating social gaze and then, finally, his own gaze. The latter proves so unendurable that Renault fabricates a suicide role to perform as his sole means of interrupting it. The prototypical scene of a Barrymore character held captive as all his dishonor and iniquity rush to the surface, for another's burning scrutiny, occurs in the 1920 film, John S. Robertson's *Dr. Jekyll and Mr. Hyde*, which Barrymore performed at roughly the same time he played Richard III, a similarly deformed and malignant artist of villainy. Sir George Carewe (Brandon Hurst), the father of Jekyll's fiancée, confronts the doctor in his laboratory, demanding to know the nature of his relationship with "a vile thing like Hyde." Jekyll's answer to Carewe's demand—which is accompanied by a threat to end his daughter's engagement—is an involuntary transformation into Hyde. What Barrymore emphasizes is not the terrible ignominy of Jekyll's exposure, but the ebullient triumph of Hyde's release from concealment. Yet there is enough residual fear of discovery imbibed from Jekyll that Hyde pursues Carewe into the street and clubs him to death with his walking stick. Barrymore loves to consider the ugly remnant of an actor who has forfeited his role-playing privileges, and must contend with the nullity of an evacuated self. It is a desperate homecoming, indeed—the original human shell bereft, swept clean of "saving" characters.

The Hyde ugliness has its counterpart in *Dinner at Eight* when Max Kane, Renault's agent, forces him to examine himself in a mirror. Kane taunts him with the assertion that he was never an actor: "You did have looks, but they're gone now. . . . Just look in any mirror. They don't lie. Look at those pouches under your eyes. Look at those creases. You sag like an old woman." As Kane's diatribe proceeds, Barrymore is framed in what appears to be a haunted mirror reflection. Renault can't quite manage to focus on himself in his drunken stupefaction, but the viewer can. The face swims forward from a mirrored darkness. It is a ghostly ruin, all of Barrymore's own legendary beauty fled. There are intimations of a former nobility in his features, but stronger evidence of present decay. Barrymore bravely exhibits a fifty-one-year-old face that seems considerably older, plainly disclosing the effects of Barrymore's epic intemperance. The mirror is not hospitable to the shade that peers from its illusory depth. To paraphrase Max's capping insults: "Your looks are gone, Renault. Without them, you have no acting power, no ability to enchant or persuade, either in film or onstage." If this is the case for Renault, how do we see differently the Barrymore visage here, with its disintegrating aura? Is it a face shorn of secrets, revealed with the shock of a sudden Mr. Hyde eruption, a monstrous laying bare? Or is the face saying that all showing is a complicated intermingling of being and hiddenness? Barrymore allows himself to emerge defenseless in the guise of Renault, a man who cannot rise to the challenge of assessing his own image, who cowers blindly in the act of beholding himself. What Barrymore enacts, in other words, is a coming forward (in his own person) that is also a face-saving retreat (for Renault), a withdrawal of Renault's character "I" from the camera eye. Barrymore sees what Renault dares not confront, accepts the image verdict and absorbs the wound of visibility in Renault's place.

Later, when Renault is alone and resolved to kill himself, he approaches the mirror again, this time with a firm resolve to examine his features, as an actor preparing to go onstage. Instead of emptiness this time, Renault contemplates an image of himself he can live with, fastidiously adjust to, and die with. He smooths back his hair, strokes his mustache like a stage gentleman attending a soiree, dons his fancy dressing robe once more, and makes sure it is not rumpled or carries

Figure 5.1. Larry Renault (John Barrymore) takes in the reflection of his Hyde-like homecoming in *Dinner at Eight*.

any hint of inelegance. Tie, shirtfront, and jacket must perfectly ratify the noble head that crowns them. It is not his own suicide that Renault is readying himself for, but rather a postdeath discovery scene that can be properly staged, lit, and felt. If his death pose can be foreseen and controlled by an actor who correctly gauges the theatrical impact of its presentation, then the audience response to his work will also be under his control. Spectators will have no choice but to be moved. Those who dismissed Renault as "being through" and worthy only of derision will recognize that he now rests serenely above and beyond their degrading touch. Like the manifold hero of a Shakespearean tragedy, he at last breaks free of the petty appraisals and standards of measure applied by lesser men. Deathly stillness offers a powerful reply to the chaotic storms of life.

Before Renault turns on the gas, seats himself, and assumes his striking "great profile" pose for the hereafter, he recalls the photo of Paula that might be found among his few effects and draw her needlessly into a scandal. (He had earlier attempted to pawn the frame of this photo

Figure 5.2. Larry strikes a pose as he gathers himself for his final act in *Dinner at Eight*.

for a bottle of whisky.) Renault carries the photo to his window, high above the city streets, gazes at Paula's image fondly, then tears the photo into pieces and watches as they flutter down toward the pavement. Barrymore incorporates some drunken teetering into his last inspection of the photo, as well as a magnanimous benefactor stance while he stands by the drapes, which once again resemble theatre curtains. A second pair of sheer curtains add their own soft, breeze-stirred accompaniment to Renault's chivalrous gesture. The irony of his theatrical deportment is not unduly emphasized here. We may well be moved by his ability to recall the needs of another person as he hastily completes his preparations for quitting the earth. In part we are moved by Barrymore's honesty in his approach to this moment of sentiment. Renault tries to make his act of leave-taking from Paula count for something. Barrymore suggests that it counts for less than he thinks it does. Renault's appeal to the theatrical, even here, keeps his awareness blurred. He releases the torn fragments to the night air, but they provide little ballast for the moment he strives to build. He is not, of course, the sole observer of this episode. The camera beholds him, and Barrymore treats the camera as surrogate for Renault's imagined theatre audience. His death scene, Renault is confident, will play to a larger, more real group of spectators. His only concern after his "backstage" mirror check is that the elements of the stage picture for his last appearance are right. He repositions the armchair near the opened fireplace gas jet, and makes the standing lamp behind the chair function as a spotlight. He straightens his hair one more time as he seats himself and takes his stage position. Once he has placed his arms on the chair arms and leaned back, he can relax. As he does so, his arms slip from their resting place. The stage business he executes here removes for him the necessity of taking stock or bringing things mentally to a close in his own right. Instead, he has looked after the requirements of his stage character, ignoring all else. He is fully lost in his role.

George Cukor's camera announces itself at this juncture, dollying in for a close-up of Barrymore/Renault that restores his time-ravaged countenance to a semblance of its former radiant beauty, and acknowledges his classic profile. Renault's delusions are redeemed somehow by the camera's eagerness to partake of them, and to declare "saving appearances" as cinema's highest priority. A bell chimes on the soundtrack as death quietly submits to theatrical reconfiguration.

There is a fleeting, third Renault mirror contact that we have yet to account for. It transpires just after Max has made his merciless farewell speech and departed. When Renault is alone, he staggers back to the

Figure 5.3. Slumped under a lonely spotlight, Larry relaxes before the curtain of death rises in *Dinner at Eight*.

glass Max has forced him to peer into, in order to confirm the agent's verdict for himself. Renault once more fails the self-beholding test. He is too clouded over with the effects of drink to absorb the stranger's image that unsettlingly tries to meet his gaze. The reflection appears more solid than the phantom man on the other side, and has good cause to doubt his reality. Renault collapses on the bureau beneath the mirror and struggles to formulate an intention that will give him incentive to move. He spots a crumpled telegram on the floor that Max left behind, one that describes him as a "bit player." He stumbles and collapses full length on the carpet as he endeavors to retrieve it. The fall would appear to mark the moment when Renault touches bottom. Surely there is nothing more for him to suffer by way of mortification. It is part of the brilliance of this segment of *Dinner at Eight* that Renault's downfall plays out in such a streamlined manner, with the mad tempo of farce. Since the entire debacle is compressed into two scenes of an otherwise crowded narrative, it can gain an almost unearthly momentum and sustain it. The doorbell sounds and Renault must deal in short order with the contemptuous bellhop, returning the worthless valuables he has been sent to pawn for drink, and the hotel manager and assistant who politely evict him. When he is by himself once again, he reaches for the fireplace mantel and undergoes a second head-bowing collapse, one rhyming with his prior crumpling before the looking glass. Barrymore grants Renault the release of a few piercing sobs—the only such untrammeled, despairing lament of Barrymore's film career—before he hits upon the idea of doing away with himself. It is striking that the wails arise without any accompanying insight into how this dire predicament has come to pass. It is woe made more terrifying perhaps by including an element of blankness. Renault is like an animal thrashing in a trap whose meaning he cannot penetrate. Barrymore places Renault's last hideous, piteous outcry at the threshold of a final theatrical recognition. Theatre arrives like a ministering angel to light up a clear path to an ending, an ending that makes luminous sense, if he is enough of a performer to believe in it.

6

Auditioning Betty in David Lynch's *Mulholland Dr.*

Anything that is not anonymous is all a dream.

—William Maxwell, *The Chateau*

Early on I learned to disguise myself in words, which were really clouds.

—Walter Benjamin, "Berlin Childhood around 1900"

∾

A MONG THE MANY RICHES beckoning to us, like a mirage, in the dream kingdom of David Lynch's *Mulholland Drive*—where we seem always poised between a bewitchingly full and an equally bewitching empty experience—is a master key to the mystery of star acting in movies. I know of no film that provides a more comprehensive demonstration of how a star performance works, and how it achieves its boundary-shattering control over us.

Most of the revelations about star acting are concentrated in one astonishing segment: Betty's audition scene, which occurs in the course of the long day and night in which Betty (Naomi Watts) dematerializes. On the one hand, Lynch slowly reveals to us a deluded, modestly talented, aspiring actress failing to achieve more than a stand-in status in her own life. Only in the private screening rooms of the actress's fantasy and dream life, we eventually determine, is there any hope of escape for her, but even there she can never escape the trap of performance. On the other hand, in the course of the pivotal audition scene Lynch manages to show us, just as our skepticism about "all things Hollywood" has reached fever pitch, what the power of performance can make happen: how it can swiftly confer a sense of identity and a groundedness that have sphinx-like credibility. A young woman who could barely be described as real becomes, through acting alchemy, a figure whose hold on life and on her turbulent inner forces seems stronger, more fraught with consequence than our own—at least for the length of a "try-out." We would be hard pressed to say exactly to what we are assenting, or what warrants our shift to a believer's vulnerable faith. We believe without knowing, or needing to ascertain, what it is that an irresistible performance is asking us to sanction. Moreover, we find ourselves capitulating (like moviegoers in childhood) to everything we see and hear immediately after receiving elaborate assurance, within the hideously false context of an ill-managed Hollywood audition, that there is no possible basis for belief of any kind.

Figure 6.1. Betty (Naomi Watts) basks in the beckoning glow of the Hollywood dream in *Mulholland Drive*.

Once Betty's audition ends, and she emerges from what might justly be termed a kind of possession, or performer's trance, we viewers may well experience a shrugging or shaking off of a kindred enchantment—our too deep immersion in the belief engendered by make-believe. We can rouse ourselves from a strange interlude of belief, or awaken from it, and in the slightly groggy aftermath wonder whether belief is really the right word to apply to an embarrassingly full involvement. This reflex renunciation of the credulous mood we were in a minute ago is similar to our disavowal of a curiously intense dream experience once we are restored to daylight, followed, more often than not, by a swift disintegration of the dream details in our memory. I reassure myself that an experience was "just a dream," as though that settled the question of my helpless enthrallment to its reality while the dream was still in progress. Such enthrallment is obviously sustained by a total, innocent acceptance of whatever happens as happening "for keeps," however absurd or overblown the events appear to us in retrospect.

Before Betty's audition scene, we are granted a full advance look at the script she must perform, and her confused amateur's approach to it in a dry run of the scene played with Rita (Laura Herring), her nonactress roommate. The scene Betty must try to bring to life is manifestly hollow; every line of dialogue seems unworthy of a genuine actress's commitment. The dialogue is overexplicit, repetitive, and information-clogged, denying any recourse to an inner life. As for the actress who is earnestly laboring to make the scene play in rehearsal, she seems hardly more realized or humanly credible in her own right than the character she seeks to inhabit. At this point in the film, she seems at one with her improbable name, the flimsy comic-book moniker "Betty." "Betty" is a character so entrenched in naïveté and the hokey paraphernalia of small-townness that her whole confected being is a hymn to unreality. The viewer is discouraged from imagining her life history as anything more than an amusing pastiche of stale movie conventions. She is a plastic newcomer to big city ways (like Pamela Tiffin in the embalmed 1960s remake of Rodgers and Hammerstein's *State Fair*). From Betty's first appearance, she is armored in a niceness that keeps her virtually untouched by the confounding, fearsome events taking place around her. She leads a vacantly charmed life, floating into the movie as a beaming ghostly apparition at a jitterbug contest, and continuing to float in her subsequent more substantial appearances on escalators at the L.A. airport or in her tour of her "borrowed" apartment. One quickly learns to watch Betty's responses to situations with the confidence that cheerful puzzlement and pluck will invariably be the dominant notes. On a few occasions, something darker creeps almost imperceptibly into her expression for a moment, but the viewer is not expected to catch these tiny shifts. We are held by our first, forceful impression of her: intractable sunniness.

Naomi Watts, who plays Betty, is remarkably adept at finding fresh ways to rearrange the sugar packets of Betty's concerns. Watts is sincerely (as opposed to condescendingly) engaged with her character's buoyancy and shadow-free conviviality—without needing to hide the fact that Betty is disconnected from any world larger than her movie-defined "hopes." Naomi Watts was known to film audiences prior to *Mulholland Drive*, if at all, as a competent "background player" (one whose job was to blend in rather than stand out). For that reason, Betty cannot draw extra definition and weight from our familiarity with an already established Watts persona. Lynch makes it difficult, in other words, for us to see around Betty, and thus gauge the separate reality of the actress who endows her with an appearance and a voice.

It is fair to say then that nothing in either Betty or in Naomi Watts's unselfconscious (to the point of not seeming self-aware) way of depicting her puts the character at odds with the two-dimensional audition scene apparatus she confronts when unctuous movie producer Wally (James Karen) leads her into his office. We see a nervous, smiling young woman, almost certainly out of her depth even in this emphatically shallow Hollywood setting, being introduced to an assemblage of mostly interchangeable personnel who have some connection to a low-budget movie that Betty has been invited (as a courtesy to her aunt) to read for. Although *Mulholland Drive* has challenged us with many bewildering, pathless, teasingly thorny episodes prior to the audition scene, we are encouraged to feel more securely placed and confident about what is going on at this narrative juncture than perhaps at any previous point in the film. We link the audition scene with the many previous glimpses of "insider" movie culture that Lynch has offered us, all of which share a quasi-satiric tone. The behavior of the people in the audition room as they are hastily presented to Betty increases our conviction that they have no serious claim on our attention. They are industry stereotypes, designed for service in a comedy sketch. We understand them at first glance: the Producer, dispensing dried-out blarney; the pretentious fool of a Director, sporting a dismally unflattering Errol Flynn mustache, who tries to sound knowledgeable and fails at every turn; crisp, polite, but visibly skeptical and bored Casting Agents; and a sybaritic Leading Man, who has spent too much time in the sun and in throwaway TV movies, and whose face resembles a grinning catcher's mitt. The names attached to these nondescript professionals in the fatuous round of introductions refuse somehow to stick to their putative owners. The perky unreality of Betty's name is like a virus communicating a kindred improbability to the many names exchanged (or floated) in her presence: Wally, Bob, Woody, Jack, Lynnie James, Chuck.

Our already established suspicion that the script for the intended movie is nonsensical easily leads to the judgment that the material has found just the right group of people to ensure that its mediocrity will be respected—in fact, vigilantly protected on all sides. The atmosphere is thick with satiric signals that there is no place for art in this gathering, and that if art entered by accident, it would go unrecognized. The vocabulary of fraudulence that defines—and binds together—this club of seasoned hacks is an instant corrosive to any lively intuition or flash of inspiration. If we were asked to predict the outcome of Betty's audition early in the scene, my guess is that most viewers would envision (perhaps even wish for) a disastrous comic deflation of poor Betty's hopes. There is potential for ugliness in Betty's humiliation, since she has no experience with Hollywood guile, or its familiar sidekick, casual brutality. Though Betty is strictly a B movie creation herself, both in her innocence and star-struck yearning, Lynch has alerted us (here and in his other films)

Figure 6.2. Figures of the industry are introduced to Betty in a cramped studio office in *Mulholland Drive*.

that he is able to reduce even plastic ingénues to spasms of compelling woe. For Lynch, the fact of a character's conspicuous fabrication is no safeguard against real hurt. He often reserves his greatest torments for those most deeply enfolded in artifice, as though the artificial (in its nearness to dream) were the natural seedbed for trauma.

The possibility that no one viewing this film for the first time could foresee is that the audition would be electrifying in an unsatiric, unironic manner—in other words, a legitimate triumph. Even if Betty is able to persuade the unqualified observers sleepily spread about the studio office that she has an appealing freshness or the "right look," we assume that she cannot rise above her own cleverly molded limitations to escape the flatness of Betty's emotional life. She "wants the part," to be sure, with the foursquare eagerness of many a daydreaming neophyte, but she has no resources, no audacity to bring to the task of revealing herself to the camera. Further, the role itself seems built for the express purpose of thwarting truthful exploration.

The actors—Betty and her offhandedly lecherous assigned partner, Woody (Chad Everett), who looms over her—are given almost no space in which to play the scene. They begin in the most awkward position imaginable, nearly backed against a wall. Woody holds her tight and seeks openings for permissible groping as he prepares to repeat, for the twentieth time, in a smooth, automatic fashion, the dull lines he has long since grown weary of. The director, Bob (Wayne Grace), intervenes just before the audition gets under way with some advice that is neither intelligible nor capable of being clarified. Bob cautions Betty that the audition (and the scene itself) should not be regarded as a contest. A contest, of course, is precisely what an audition is, and the only clear thing in the script pages Betty has worked on is that a power struggle (another contest) is taking place. Bob goes on to set up the characters as incommunicado monoliths: "the two of them . . . with themselves." He concludes with the injunction that they not "play it for real, until it gets real." This would imply that the roomful of listless spectators has all the time in the world for the performers to consult the temperature of their emotions "in private." Betty and Woody should hold off on interacting until they are fully convinced that reality, unvarnished and incontestable, underwrites their relationship. Woody, as confused as Betty, gallantly (as he sees it) takes up her cause, attempting to relieve her embarrassment with an old pro's directness and simplicity. He decides to "make it real" for her by playing it "nice and close," pressing her against him with the wall as backup. To compound Betty's worries, he declares his intention to duplicate the strategy he employed in an earlier, no doubt memorable audition with another actress ("the girl with black hair"). Betty, having not been present for the black-haired rival's reading, and having no clue about what made her approach intriguing, is promptly reduced to the status of body double for an absent (still vividly recalled) predecessor. Woody is dusting off a performance that once had a spark of life in the moment of playing, and enjoins Betty to revive the "ghost" of her unseen competitor so he can reenact his own good bits. Bob again intervenes, apparently delighted to be reminded of the audition in question. He urges Woody to remember "this time" not to rush the line "Before what?" as though Woody were the actor trying out and the one to whom Bob planned to pay attention. At the moment when all the hokum and degrading absurdity of the moviemaking process have been stripped bare and savagely mocked, Woody launches Betty into the scene with the courtly blandishment that they're going to play it "just like in the movies."

And into the movies we go, but, as I've already noted, not at all in the manner that we could anticipate. Betty has come to the audition space dressed in a gray suit, which is clearly meant to evoke forceful memories of the famous gray suit worn by Kim Novak in Hitchcock's *Vertigo*. In that film, Novak's initially hidden primary character, Judy Barton, wears the suit when she is impersonating the wandering, tragically innocent, lost-to-memory, and romantically possessed Madeleine Elster.[1] Betty removes her gray jacket in order to perform more freely (gray gives way to her sky-blue blouse), divesting herself, it would seem, of a layer of formality. The *Vertigo* connection cues us to be on the lookout for a second Betty identity, one somehow at variance with the first—less assured, perhaps, or less shielded from whatever trouble the situation is clearly preparing for her.

When Lynch selects a medium-shot vantage point to frame Betty's audition (one that allows actors and space, finally in proper attunement, to blend properly), he is subtly displacing "Bob" as the directorial presence.

---

1. Madeleine is Hitchcock's Eurydice, half-returned from the underworld and fated to turn back there irretrievably when her lover insists at the end on taking her literally (thus, making her literal). He demands that she not merely show herself (as a re-created vision), but declare once and for all who she is. Scottie Ferguson is given more chances to look back than Orpheus, but he sees no better and fails more tests—just as decisively. Betty is just as certainly David Lynch's Eurydice. She attempts to revoke her alter ego's death (presumably, while a bullet makes a leisurely journey through Diane Selwyn's brain). The only earthly identity that might be strong enough to undo death is that of an actress on the verge of stardom.

Until this subtle transfer of directorial authority, the whole office space had felt disproportionate and off-kilter as a cinematic setting. The room is a long rectangle, whose furnishings seem wrongly situated for comfort (much less intimacy). One is mentally driven to rearrange things, to reduce the overall clutter and sense of unnatural distance and fish-eye elongation. Even the socially maladroit spectator could come up with a more sensible seating plan: everyone in the room looks slightly out of place, either poised for quick flight or resigned to entrapment. Nothing provides a center or gathering point. The room's color scheme is arduously brown, reminding me of the insanely overdetermined burnt sienna color coordination in Gene Tierney's desert hacienda in *Leave Her to Heaven*. In the midst of so much chocolate decor, the possibly rich wood paneling acquires an air of basement rec-room flimsiness. Lynch does not place undue emphasis on these design "mistakes." Betty's nervousness and our willingness to share her mildly hallucinatory point of view, while scouting out portents unnoticed by her in this loaded milieu, seem to justify the disagreeable, tilting congestion.

Our sense of time leading into the audition is equally disjointed. The editing takes its rhythm, a bit aimlessly, from Wally's meandering, one-by-one introduction to Betty of his production team. Wally, who means no more to us than his associates, emotionally controls the time-flow in the room as he moves Betty, in a herky-jerky manner, through an incomprehensible tangle of alien points of view. There is another time shift (from torpor to urgency) once the introductions have been concluded. Wally makes it known, with hammy relish, that there's to be no more dawdling; Betty must instantly shift gears and "play the scene." Though Betty is dressed as a Hitchcock heroine, the progression of images thus far is the obvious antithesis of Hitchcock lucidity and fluent, "infallible" viewer placement within an event. We are naturally inclined to link ourselves with Betty, but we have a little difficulty maintaining contact with her. She is never hidden, but neither do we have a clear emotional channel to her. I would argue that though the time within the room unfolds subjectively, it is not necessarily her subjectivity that governs it. Not until Betty speaks her first "within the script" line ("You're still here") do film space and time, in Walter Benjamin's phrase, "come into their own [within the scene] and find each other" (42). The previously inhospitable audition room and its erratic "clock" are effortlessly adjusted to the performers' advantage.

When Betty had rehearsed her audition scene with Rita in her kitchen, her entire performing strategy depended on gradually reduced physical distance from her adversary. As her character's threats intensify and her homicidal intention crystallizes, she planned to close in on her victim. Woody destroys this possibility by insisting that Betty begin to speak while caught in his bear-hug embrace. The viewer is initially apprehensive that Betty is thrown off by this switch and loses her bearings. We have no reason to imagine that her talent or resourcefulness will enable her to deal with unforeseen developments. It seems less a question of whether she will be deprived of confidence and control than when. Since Betty has evinced barely a trace of sexual awareness in her previous scenes—even when she chances upon naked Rita in her aunt's shower stall—we no doubt feel that she is unequipped both as a person and as an actress to fend off (or take in stride) Woody's "automatic pilot" lasciviousness. However little credence we give to Betty as a fully developed character, we can't easily avoid feeling protective of her when she is so overmatched. Woody, with his massive bulk, appears to be intimidating a small, childlike woman, who is frightened but situationally constrained from saying so. We resent the actor's pushiness and his falsely paternal arrogance.

Betty appears to be forced by the unwelcome proximity of her partner to speak her first line before she is completely ready. We also imagine her consternation at the discovery that a scene she had construed as a climactic quarrel is being treated as a love scene. All her notions about her appropriate emotional relationship to her partner are abruptly taken away from her. The authentic notes that Betty is striking in the first exchange of the audition derive from our sense that Betty is not yet acting: she is merely unable to conceal her agitation at what her fellow actor is doing. She "forgets" (so we imagine) how much the audition means to her, and with an instinctive protest born of discomfort she pushes Woody away after he kisses her without warning, then holds him off with a suddenly firm, even imposing, outstretched arm. We are surprised, and impressed, by a degree of physical determination that we have not before now encountered in her. On the instant, her seeming frailty is backed by a steel will.

Betty holds her open hand against Woody as though she has every right to take command of the situation; she is flustered, but not apologetic. What is most remarkable here is the way that Lynch makes us uncertain of whether we are watching an actress or a character defending her. Because we are more or less persuaded that Betty is an unimaginative, severely restricted performer, when we witness her expressing genuine turmoil in her struggle with Woody, we are likely to conclude, at first, that it is the actress who cannot manage her feelings, and who is compelled to resist him. We arrive at this conclusion before we have had time to process the thought that the behavior we assign to the actress bears virtually no relation to the "Betty construct" we have up to now been working with. The viewer is not sure if he is watching the audition scene unravel. Betty may well be making "mistakes" as her raided innocence awakens her survival instincts.

Though we aren't permitted to observe the reactions of those watching the audition, we may naturally wonder how they are interpreting what they are looking at. "Do they see what we see?" is a reasonable phrasing of our concern. Lynch encourages us to imagine that we are one or two jumps ahead of the Hollywood dullards who are carelessly assessing Betty's performance. It is quite possible that they imagine that Betty is, so far, reacting to Woody "in character." The judges of this audition don't know Betty as well as we do; they perhaps interpret her squeamishness, her upset, and her aversion as feigned for the sake of the written scene. How long will Betty be able to extend her involuntary, but fortunate, act of deception? When will they discern that her distress is interfering with the scene's development? And when she crashes, as she soon must, will they be impressed by the raw energy that has been goaded out of her? Lynch knows that we are eager to seize on the prospect that we are being let in on something that others aren't privy to—that we are being given, at last, a peek at *Mulholland Dr.*'s inside story. For that reason, we find ourselves believing, almost unreservedly, the audition scene as it begins to unfold. The fact that Betty's "real" feelings are putting her into conflict with the demands of a trite scenario—and that we are catching those feelings as they erupt, ahead of other spectators who are more readily duped by movie conventions—makes it a "smart move" to surrender to Lynch's illusion. We do so because we imagine we are doing the opposite; we are entranced by our own wariness. The viewer is sold on the audition's truth, in its early stages, because we have a stake in the tension arising from an actual person's protest against being submerged in sterile make-believe.

While all of this is going on, Lynch has surreptitiously corrected, and beautifully enhanced, the scene's color scheme. Betty's sky-blue blouse mates appetizingly with the rich, patrician blues of Woody's suit. Behind this harmonized pair, the previously overstated brown on the walls and woodwork begins to soften and to acquire an elegant sheen. The wall no longer traps Betty but quietly supports the actors, lending its own burnished solidity to theirs.

The major transition in the audition scene occurs when Woody moves in to embrace Betty a second time and she registers with a different quality of awareness the fact that his hand is hovering near her ass. It is here that Betty, as actress (and character) evolves, in a matter of seconds, into a more advanced organism. We all understand, at some level that doesn't require much reflection, that good acting involves (minimally) a mixture of pretending and believing. Our initial skepticism about Betty's ability to take on the demands of another character is that she seems to have almost no faculty for living up to her own character (if that means diverging from type). She does not show any signs of having begun to consider that others may imagine her—or evaluate her actions—in a decidedly different manner than she does. The resistance of other minds to her fantasy of what she is is not a question she has reckoned with, or even formulated. We might grant her a willingness to enter into the scripted sentiments assigned to her (like a child playing with dolls), but her grasp of pretending is rudimentary. She does not see how pretending can be informed by detachment, calculation, and duplicity. Her approach to pretending is akin to a young girl's announcement after a visit to her mother's clothes closet: "Look. I'm wearing your hat and fur. Isn't that funny?" We have also seen Betty's amateur experiment with "little white lies" in her attempts to assist her new friend-in-a-jam, Rita. Nevertheless, a split of a very different kind suddenly manifests itself in the playing out of the audition scene. We behold Betty crossing over, in so many ways at once that the effect is breathtaking, from guileless pretending to majestic double-dealing.

Lynch highlights the divide by deserting, as if in secret, the playing area framed for the actors and inserting a close-up of an action below the public performing space, where urgent "under the table" business is being conducted. We observe Woody's hand grazing the rear of Betty's skirt and Betty's answering hand—with an almost autonomous sentience—making a decision about how to take charge of it: either by warding it off or inviting it closer. The hesitation of the actress about how to contend with the encroaching hand endows Betty, for the first time in the film, with a visible calculating power. She elects to control her antagonist by taking control of his hand, pressing it against herself harder than Woody had dared to. Betty's hand, still in clandestine close-up, covers his, and thereby takes possession of it. By guiding his hand to make a strong sexual claim on her, Betty makes the aptly named Woody understand that if he takes her with sufficient boldness, she will respond fully. When the audition commenced, less than a minute ago, we were chiefly concerned that Betty would be degraded by an old-hand predator in front of a group of venal L.A. buffoons who would be likely to go along with any of Woody's lewd antics. (Our conception of her as a plastic innocent briefly gave way, in the course of her suddenly real physical struggle with her fellow actor, to the thought that a convincingly vulnerable woman was being threatened. The depiction of abuse is viscerally disturbing, and the victim seemed to be in no position to defend her.) Betty's acting choice to make her own sexuality part of the "game" is a thunderbolt for the viewer because, right up to the moment of choosing, her sexual nature has lain utterly dormant, folded beneath her vulcanized naïveté, so that it seemed not even available for private acknowledgment. The release of sexual awareness is offered as a heightened form of a "let's pretend" moment. All we have time to absorb, as Betty's hand makes its move and the face of the actress seems to confer with her hand tactically (looking down at this furtive ally), is that an actress is making a spontaneous choice to give the character she is portraying a strong erotic connection to her partner.

The aptitude to unleash her libido comes from out of nowhere, but once Betty consciously seizes on the impulse, her expression conveys to us that she knows exactly what to do with it. She expertly refocuses the scene so that her excitement at Woody's proximity (or conversely, her excitement over successfully manipulating him into thinking so) is the new center of interest. The actress is becoming attuned to dimensions

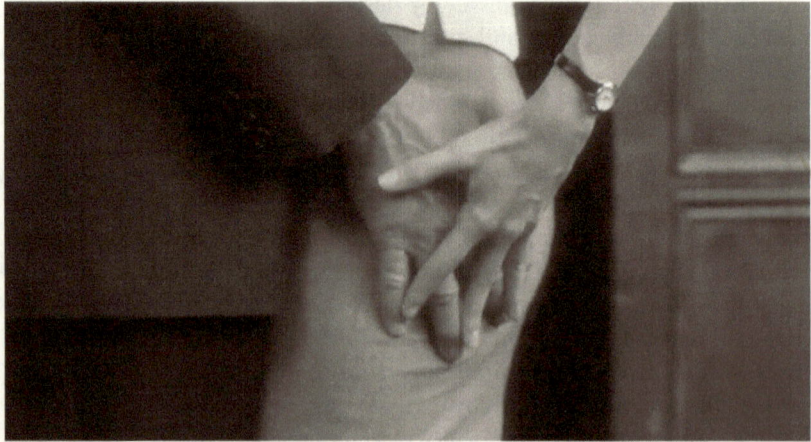

Figure 6.3. Betty makes us believe during her audition in *Mulholland Drive*.

of her role that were hitherto undreamed of—not only by her, but by the viewer. The viewer understands the well-worn convention of an anxious performer receiving sudden inspiration when "up against the wall" and then ceasing to flounder. That is the most convenient explanation to latch onto as we try to subdue our bewilderment and convert the alarming infusion of strangeness into something familiar. We may well entertain the question "Who is using whom, at this point?," but in part we are merely relieved that Betty the actress is, against all odds, up to the demands of what is taking place. "She is more talented than I had supposed" is another convention-dictated impression that gains fleeting entry into the viewer attempting to sort things out—and to find the least taxing route to restored clarity.

The delayed recognition of what is really transpiring has to do with the abruptly transformed character of the actress herself. A talented performer is indeed rising to the challenge under the most adverse circumstances, and she is making a series of magically right split-second decisions. Nevertheless, we need more time than we are given to register the fact that the woman who intuits under pressure what her role might include to enrich itself (moving well beyond the cramping straightforwardness of the scriptwriter) is not—cannot be—Betty, as we have known her. To become the cagey, experienced professional who now confronts us, she must part company completely with the "dewdrop" Nancy Drew type that she has relied on for her entire onscreen definition. Someone new is at the controls, someone whom—we dimly sense—we know nothing about. To find out who she is, or might be, we are obliged to turn our attention to the fictional character being enacted—a figure that graduates, for the balance of the scene, to the status of primary source of meaning.

Notice how the deep soundlessness of the offscreen group of witnesses, and of the room itself, creates a "just like at the movies" effect at this interval. We are following Betty into her newfound trance of involvement, with no sense of the world's competing presence, or ability to distract her from her make-believe goal. She is alone with her partner, with the camera, and with us. As Betty leaves her ingénue persona behind, who does she become for the truth-seeking camera? What is the nature of this metamorphosis? Who is auditioning for us now? The viewer is virtually commandeered into thinking about "Naomi Watts" herself—especially if we have no experience of her beyond her presentation in this film. The character that Betty is reading for, after all, has no special dramatic significance at first viewing. Prior to the audition, Watts's potential range as an actress has not been an issue that we have been given much cause to dwell on. If anything, she appears to match up almost too flawlessly with Betty's resolute blandness. Nowhere have her eyes signaled an alertness, a sensitivity, a degree of achieved inwardness greater than Betty's own. So we receive a salutary shock when we are reminded, past the halfway mark in *Mulholland Dr.*, that the aspiring actress Watts has capacities for expressiveness and allure that she has been expertly holding in reserve. One is inclined to congratulate Watts for her handling of the audition, as we gradually catch on to the fact that "Betty" has been slipped off like the gray jacket and another, far more formidable presence stands in her place. We compare "Betty's" acting with Watts's more intense, exposed impersonation of an aroused lover and conclude, however irrationally, that Watts is a better, more accomplished artist than Betty. For a short, unhinged interval we have the impression of watching Betty expand emotionally to incorporate the larger persona of the mysterious "Watts," while simultaneously considering the possibility that Betty has sneakily, shadily kept something from us.

We speedily reverse that judgment in favor of the more sensible idea of Watts emerging in triumph from a "Betty" cocoon of her own making, and applaud her for carrying off such a brazen, instantaneous transformation. We are pleasurably struck by how thoroughly the skill of this new actress has deceived us. Yet we may lingeringly also feel, albeit hazily, that Watts is betraying Betty—both by exceeding her scant powers as an insecure amateur and by cunningly violating her innocence, shredding it beyond repair. She is somehow competing against her former self, and grabbing every available advantage in order to trounce her. She is free to mock, because the audition scene allows it, every last outcropping of timorousness in her personality, including that schoolgirl variety exemplified by her bewildered rival, Betty. Lynch treats us to a sexual version of one of those speeded-up nature films in which a plant grows to full maturity and luxurious blossoming in the space of a single breath. We watch, with a prurient, volatile blend of queasiness and excitement, as an unseasoned girl, lacking every protection sophistication offers, advances by means of a solitary squeeze of the hand to the farthest reaches of sexual knowing. Watts reveals a figure who is not merely practiced and utterly confident in her ability to excite and subdue a male quarry, but one who calculates (always) from a bruised position.

Sex is no sooner established as a shared language for the acting couple than it shifts from a spur for provocative teasing to a recognition of authentic hazard. Every maneuver Betty initiates upholds the motto "break or be broken." She significantly reverses the order of one line from her previous rehearsal scene with Rita. "You're playing a dangerous game here" now begins, rather than concludes, the speech that mentions a blackmail threat (from the male) that is "not going to work." Rearranging the sentences places Watts/Betty on top of the danger. She glows with it and gains strength from it, while serving notice that the danger is real—however much sexual play intervenes. As the actress takes convincing ownership of the menace that underlies the film as a whole, in the guise of acting it out, Naomi Watts secures our allegiance to herself as the rightful star of *Mulholland Dr.* Until this scene, Laura Elena Harring's Rita has been the dominant, glamorous female presence in the narrative, in spite, or because of, her amnesiac discombobulation. She is firmly wedded to the film's principal mystery from her initial drive up the street of the film's title during the credit sequence, after which she is instantly set up for murder and saved by a gruesomely providential car crash. We assume that either she or the objects associated with her hold the key (a blue key, as it turns out—Betty's color in the audition) to the past.

In the acting out of her nameless character in the audition, Watts/Betty effectively steals the sense of danger and darkness that her friend Rita had previously embodied. These were the two known ingredients (or reference points) of Rita's otherwise vaporous identity. Watts not only appropriates Rita's "danger and darkness" (and theft is exactly the right word for it, calling to mind the old acting phrases "scene stealing" and "stealing the show"), she enhances their interest by making fully conscious use of them, as far as the audition circumstances permit. She appears to know everything that is at issue, at least for the time being, and by turning up the sexual heat while announcing her involvement in masquerade and her intention to murder, she trumps Harring's more passive possession of mystery. Watts is like a shimmering, ravenous bird bearing the truth of bloodlust out to us on its beak. (Think of the end of *Blue Velvet*, where just such a bird poses for us like a mechanical toy, proudly displaying the insect-kill in its beak.) Betty's incarnation of the bird flies near to us in close-up, where the ragged, excited breath of the lovers is as audible as beating wings. The vulnerable heart of the once faltering actress turns to animal indifference as she metamorphoses for us and then rises to her full acting height.

Woody is bound tight to this fledgling creature, and he gains a surprising amount of fresh interest as the overshadowed half of a couple. His assigned role is that of the young woman's father's best friend. We learn that he is accustomed to taking advantage of this family attachment as soon as dad leaves for work. Almost all of his lines focus attention on the absent father, either by speculating on his present whereabouts or considering the consequences of his getting wind of the friend's betrayal. The repeatedly invoked father streaks the love scene with shadows of incest. "Dad" seems to be peering over the lovers' shoulders and serving as a troubling stimulus for Betty's arousal. When Betty tells Woody twice to "stop"—unconvincingly, because her continued kissing coaxes him forward—it would appear that she is replying to his query, "What will your dad think of you?" She is lodging a faint verbal protest against Woody's repeated reminders of her father, yet at the same time "fanning her own flames" with the reminders, and using them to push herself out of control.

Near the end of the audition, when Betty brings the dialogue to a halt, places an arm with a closed fist around Woody's shoulder and initiates a lengthy, open mouth kiss, we may remember that the director had instructed Woody—as his last piece of muddled advice to the players—not to rush the line "Before what?" this time. Betty's forceful intervention to create a "motivated" pause makes Bob's acting note to her partner something else that she has taken over. The kiss masterfully prevents Woody from rushing, and fills the resulting silence to the brim with suggestiveness and anticipation. Betty's clenched fist is a pantomime carryover from her rehearsal with Rita where she brandished a harmless-looking dinner knife to make clear the extent of her vengeful rage. Now she merely pretends to hold a knife, it would seem, though there is no longer need for one. Perhaps Betty's closed palm holds a "blue key," which will later be the object designated to seal "Rita's" death warrant. Lynch ventures a second Hitchcock allusion here—to the famous Ingrid Bergman embrace of Claude Rains in *Notorious*, which is used to conceal a key hidden in the deceiving partner's hand. In that scene as well, the hidden key marked a major act of betrayal.

Woody's most noteworthy moment in the audition follows Betty's announcement, once the kiss is concluded, that she means to kill him. He takes several beats to assess the seriousness of the threat she has made, letting us see his deliberations about whether to place his trust in her convincing passion or her whispered warning. For the first time in the scene Woody actually establishes prolonged, searching eye contact with Betty. What he discovers in her look not only causes his character to draw back in fear, but the actor himself to do so. (Lynch brilliantly extends the pattern of role confusion at every possible opportunity.) Here we have a parallel to Betty responding at the outset of the audition to the actor's brusque sexual forwardness with a discomfort that appeared to issue from her. Woody's upset resembles Betty's earlier scare; if we watch him carefully we see that it is the performer's deadly resolve that panics him slightly, and obliges him to draw back. He uses his final line ("Then they'll put you in jail") as a means of recovering his acting composure.

The main purpose of Woody's momentary perturbed dislocation is to establish the idea that Betty is resorting to what actors describe as the trick or technique of "substitution." In order to play an emotionally difficult action with the requisite truthfulness, an actor may supplement the scene's fictional circumstances with an emotional memory (or substitution from another relationship) that increases the size and strength of her commitment to the fictional givens. We cannot be certain who or what Betty is envisioning, but we do have time to consider that she is looking through Woody—rather than directly at him. It is possible that we flip through our own memories of Betty to find a feasible answer to the double question: "Who is she staring at, who is the missing person?" Since nearly all of Betty's life in the film, such as it is, has been spent in Rita's company, and since we have witnessed her practice this same climax (comically) with Rita's faltering assistance only minutes ago, we may well return mentally to that rehearsal to see how Rita fits the present picture. When Betty arrived at the big emotional moment in rehearsal, she told Rita how silly it seemed to shed plausible tears for such a "lame" melodramatic confrontation, and summarized for her benefit the action she was not yet in the mood to "play for real." After the two women share a laugh, and Betty loses concentration, she explains: "Then I cry, cry, cry, and then I say, with big emotion, 'I hate you. I hate us both.'" Rita responds to Betty's embarrassment by reassuring her that whatever the limitations of the scene, Betty has enough talent to make it work. She compliments her with the unstudied admiration of the nonperformer, and with the fine-tuned judgment of an amnesiac.

If Betty is, indeed, picturing Rita when she replays the scene with Woody, she is also disregarding all of her earlier stated notions about how the end of the scene should be handled. She speaks the "hatred" lines softly, and once more she appears to be disengaged from Woody—physically as well as emotionally—when she sounds them out. Her tears, which surface with no cue for active weeping, follow rather than precede the lines, and are visible very briefly. Betty is not attempting to weep. She hardly conveys the impression of even noticing her tears. She is rather caught on the hook of an unbidden painful thought, and she closes the audition in the same trancelike condition that she assumed when entering it. She is "alone with herself," yet again ironically taking one of the director's inept preliminary notes and transmuting it into a thing of beauty.

In the logic of the scene itself, the female character may be addressing her hatred to her absent father, with whom she may have a dreadful score to settle. However, in the logic of *Mulholland Dr.* as a whole, the playacting of a projected death intersects with the already executed hired slaying of "Betty's" one-time friend and female lover. While Naomi Watts is still busy delineating, on one level, Betty's potentially life altering audition, her acting speaks to and encloses another woman's tragedy (a woman we haven't, at this point in the narrative, officially met). Given a first-time viewer's state of partial knowing during the audition, the buried tragedy and the guilt flowing from it are pretty much a blank to us, but we can feel them nonetheless taking shape in Betty's face here, long before the sordid "true history" comes to light.

As we return to an awareness of Betty's audition evaluators in the Hollywood office, we are at the very least mindful of how far we have traveled from the episode's misleadingly crude satiric setup. When Betty demurely descends to earth with her sheepish "Well, there it is" (accompanied by a dancer's hand gestures), our most honest questions for ourselves are likely to be: "How did I believe so thoroughly what that actress was doing, and what precisely did I believe?" For belief, of the most impressively various sort, was hauntingly at stake throughout. All the cynical advance preparation we were given did not provide us with any of the expected detachment from, or intellectual jurisdiction over, the Big Movie Scene's life. The skeptic in us came into the room laden with a will to expose (once again) the Hollywood charade, thereby disavowing our once-upon-a-time enthrallment to such things. What happens instead is that the skeptic is unwelcomely relieved of his superior, scoffing pose. Perhaps the skeptic is secretly pleased to have it taken away, and to be suddenly at the mercy of a sincerity hatched at the very core of artifice.

I began by describing the audition scene as a master key to star acting. Lynch sets before us, with a thoroughness that is not compromised by extreme compression, all the major barriers to identification with performers and their contrived roles that movie viewers enamored of their own reality sense commonly complain about. He also illuminates how rife with contradictions our engagement with any star performance is, yet shows how an awareness of contradictions, far from rescuing us from naive involvement, can increase the likelihood of wholesale surrender to the acting hoax. The "argument" of the scene is that both our resistance and assent to what stars reveal to the camera has little to do with what we know about the lines dividing imaginary situations from life as it is actually lived. We watch with a feeling approaching awe as a star emerges from the husk of a mildly appealing nonentity, in circumstances that are peppered with warnings against taking fakery of precisely this sort to heart. The full-throttle romantic acting of the old Hollywood school penetrates our defenses just as we are most confident that we understand the limitations of the unembarrassed obviousness of this kind of acting. Moreover, we find ourselves attending to Betty as someone involved with matters of genuine consequence as she makes her way through a script we have already judged empty, and after she expressly announces her intention to act a part for our critical evaluation.

As viewers, we are struck by the seeming disclosure of a mesmerizing Watts star persona at exactly the point where we have logical grounds for objecting that this "confusing" actress has entirely lost touch with her assigned character. Perhaps our involvement with all-star personae works in a similar fashion. The persona is never quite accounted for by the attributes of a specific character, however beguiling that character may be, and in spite of our conviction that a persona and a certain type of role naturally fuse. I would argue that the persona depends on a divided but not grating experience of someone as both emotionally accessible (thus known to us in a persuasively intimate way) and continually eluding our grasp. In the supposedly simple case of John Wayne, for example, the more intensely he appears to be known, the more he manages to preserve (or even increase) his margin of unknownness. The unknown in its seductive relation to the known is always the split that makes a star persona compelling. Betty takes us "through" the screen of appearances, while acting, to suggest a depth of misery-fueled chicanery in herself. This is a wrenching turn for the viewer because we have been so thoroughly convinced that she dwells entirely, and contentedly, on a flat surface: an ideal inhabitant of a movie screen. Betty's face suddenly opening up to us to demand an emotional response is an exemplary instance of the still inexplicable primitive rite that is cinema—as theatre. A moving picture image somehow acquires enough living dimension to swallow the credulous viewer whole. How is it that we invest these dubious framed reflections with so much embracing power? How many "real" sights and sounds get through to us with such potent immediacy? Lynch provides us with a quilt of densely interwoven recognitions to take away from his audition scene, leaving us snuggling for a glimpse of terra firma within its capacious folds.

Betty, for her part, leaves the audition encumbered with an imperious sex drive that came into being for the actress at the moment she pretended to have one. Succeeding with her audition also results in her acquiring an initiate's sense of darkness, an eagerness to manipulate others' wills, and a troubled awareness of the transformative potential lurking in previously "stable" persons and objects. She must somehow hide all these newfound discoveries from her freshly intrigued (now wary) spectators as well as from herself if she is to keep "Betty" credible. This necessary retreat inward with its demand that she now act Betty as one of many possible roles, instead of simply "being" her, serves notice that the person bearing that "see-through" name and temperament is rapidly decomposing. Her time to occupy this cohesive identity, as though it were a permanent safe refuge, has run out.

The emotional structure of this episode, which depends on an unlikely performance taking hold of spectators, onscreen and off, and generating perilous consequences for the performer who risks belief, is a repeating pattern throughout the film's narrative. Also repeated is the alternation between scenes that present riveting, disquietingly exposed performers and scenes that debunk and ridicule the tricks of performance. The latter suggest that all performance boils down to a deceiving stunt when we are let in on the secret. After Betty's audition, recall, we are briefly deceived by a doo-wop quintet of retro-1950s singers lip-synching their way through another audition piece on a briefly hidden sound stage. Once we are apprised of this simple simulation technique, we promptly appraise the next auditioner with a practiced, skeptical air ("How wooden she seems!"), as though our freshly gained knowledge of the precise strings being pulled had always been in our possession. Distance can so easily seem preferable to closeness.

Armed with an awareness refined by repeated demonstrations of the method of artificially linking voice to mimed vocals, we are nevertheless undone by belief once again as we accompany Betty and Rita to the Silencio Theater. A Fellini-esque master of ceremonies clearly (and one would think, needlessly) explains to us how sound and image lead separate lives in this illusion-saturated setting. No sooner has he completed a prolonged demonstration of the fact that everything we hear is taped (using musical instruments to demonstrate) than a performer reminiscent of Betty at her audition takes the stage, and causes us to forget instantly the elaborate counsel about sight and sound splitting. In a ravishing Spanish rendition of Roy Orbison's "Crying," the female

Figure 6.4. Rita (Laura Elena Harring) and Betty break down as they witness a performer's self-division onstage in *Mulholland Drive*.

vocalist, with a single painted tear on her face and dark hair and lipstick suggestive of Rita's recently discarded "vamp" look, carries us so far into the unsuspected depths of this overfamiliar pop song that she becomes the tragic embodiment of all lovers' weeping: scalding tears personified. At the height of her aria, she stops moving her lips and collapses on stage; while unconscious she is summarily dragged off by two stagehands. The sound of someone's voice continues singing in her absence—powerfully, mockingly. Betty, who is on the verge of her own final disappearance from the narrative, is a spellbound witness of the singer's ardor, entering unreservedly into the spirit of the performer's sorrowful self-division, and weeping (persuasively) along with Rita, who sits beside her.

Just before the Spanish song commences, the sound of an impending storm onstage, connected—like a traumatic memory—to Betty's nervous system, causes her to convulse in her seat. She attains the maximum pitch of visceral identification with a staged event, and has no capacity to separate any part of herself from what she absorbs in this charged atmosphere. On subsequent viewings, it becomes clear that the storm sounds are fused with Betty's (a.k.a. Diane Selwyn) earlier/later act of suicide by pistol shot. The death overtakes her briefly during a performance, as one of the consequences of her belief, and then grants her permission to mourn herself and the woman she herself has caused to die for a few moments before fading from view.[2]

The narrative will soon allow us to conclude that sweetly affirmative "Betty" never existed outside of another actress's fantasy and dream life. (Diane Selwyn, Betty's author, is depressive, morbidly jealous, and unsuccessful in her career, a killer, and teetering toward death-by-suicide. Her so-called real life is a melodrama as improbable as the one that Betty tries out for in Woody's office.) Strangely, Betty becomes most "real" to us when we are certain that she had no chance of living at all, and that there are no means, once she is gone, to revive her. As we consider Betty in retrospect, we may well find something terribly truthful about this girl who never imagines herself lost: a purely synthetic, but still striving image of hope, outfitted in the pathetic remnants of everyone's failed innocence. And because Naomi Watts does such a stunning job of expanding and expunging Betty in their joint audition scene, for the duration of *Mulholland Dr.* she gets to fulfill Betty's animating dream. She turns into a movie star, one (it is worth noting) whose mimicry of total failure becomes a recipe for success.

---

2. This image of a woman convulsing in the act of witnessing her own likely death scene may have its source in Agnès Varda's *Vagabond*. The corresponding moment in that film depicts a woman staring at herself in a mirror after she accidentally electrocutes herself.

Theatres Rational and Irrational in Alfred Hitchcock's *Vertigo*

> There are moods in which we court suffering, in the hope that here at least we shall find reality, sharp peaks and edges of truth. But it turns out to be scene-painting and counterfeit. . . . Well, souls never touch their objects. An innavigable sea washes with silent waves between us and the things we aim at and converse with.
>
> —Ralph Waldo Emerson, "Experience"

> The poem of the mind in the act of finding
> What will suffice. It has not always had
> To find: the scene was set; it repeated what
> Was in the script.
>   Then the theatre was changed
> To something else. Its past was a souvenir.
>
> —Wallace Stevens, "Of Modern Poetry"

THEATRE IS A LARGE, COMPARATIVELY neglected theme in Alfred Hitchcock's exhaustively analyzed *Vertigo* (1958). The reason for this neglect is likely due to the fact that issues of performance, role confusion, and directorial manipulation and control of actors to achieve questionable ends have as much to do with the medium of cinema as the stage. In addition, *Vertigo* so readily lends itself to various allegories of filmmaking practice (of an authoritarian sort) and the perils of spectator enchantment that theatre's separate claims to attention are easily blocked from view. Unlike *Stage Fright* (1950) or the expressly theatre-conscious films Hitchcock adapted from plays—most notably *Rope* (1948) and *Dial M for Murder* (1954)—there are no spaces in *Vertigo*'s world that loudly, unequivocally declare their kinship with stage drama. Theatre enters *Vertigo* early on, in Scottie's stool chair demonstration to Midge of how his illness might be overcome. It remains a powerful realm of proof and counterproof until the film's concluding scene, where Judy is forced to join Scottie in the tower to restage the killing of Elster's wife. There are many episodes in which one character functions as a director of a staged scene and assigns a role to another character as performer. Sometimes the designated actor is aware of the role, at other times not. So much of the narrative's pressuring of love and death into the realm of terrifying illusion is accomplished with the aid of theatrical devices. Theatre finally alternates continually as a testing ground for the oscillating claims of reason and irrationality.

The single setting that provides the strongest evidence of a specifically theatrical deployment of illusion as well as a proscenium frame for storytelling reenactment is the livery stable at the San Juan Bautista mission. Scottie Ferguson (James Stewart) insists on taking Madeleine Elster (Kim Novak) there after she visits his apartment in the early morning hours to recount a frightening dream she has had. When she describes the Spanish town where the dream took place, with its old mission and tower, Scottie suddenly realizes that the location is a place that he knows well. All of the physical details that Madeleine identifies correspond to actual features of this literal site. "It's all there," he exclaims, with a detective's elation at having solved a mystery. Scottie feels that he has been returned to solid ground at last. Until now, his faith in the workings and logic of ordinary reality has been severely tested by Madeleine's apparent possession by the ghost of her dead great-grandmother, Carlotta Valdes, who had been driven mad by a lover's treachery and abandonment, and by the loss of her child. Carlotta, who eventually killed herself, seems to have entered Madeleine's unconscious, and by means of obscure trances and directives, is pressing the young woman to repeat her own journey to self-destruction. Some sort of sacrificial rite is being demanded, for unfathomable reasons. Scottie, who has fallen in love with

Madeleine, feels that Madeleine's "irrational" dream will lose its power to harm her if he can show her that the materials of the dream have clear, unthreatening objective counterparts. The dream's otherworldliness will be undone if its spectral components collide with daylight fact and submit to rational inspection.

What is more unsettling and complicated than has been generally noticed is that the place designated for confirmation of real world ordinariness and solidity turns out to be a sphere steeped in make-believe. The livery stable at Mission San Juan Bautista is a tourist preservation site, whose artifacts and stage properties attempt to keep alive the atmosphere of the mid-nineteenth century. Temporal frozenness is the official goal. Scottie, therefore, is obliged to make his case for the reliability of appearances ("And it's all real") in the midst of reenactment artifice. Our visual approach to the livery stable is preceded by a dreamlike camera movement through the shadowy walkway of the mission cloister, with its row of melancholy, Giorgio de Chirico arches. There is an immediate tension established between an aura of timelessness and Scottie's forthcoming desperate appeal that Madeleine recognize the present moment. We behold the proscenium frame of the livery stable stage, in which Madeleine sits, immobile, on the passenger seat of a covered surrey. Scottie stands, when we first observe him, equally statue-like, with his back to the doorway, gazing at Madeleine. It is Scottie's curious task to get Madeleine to grasp the meaning of her current placement in real time, which is concurrently stage time. We assume that he has directed her to assume her position onstage, and to let the given circumstances of her surroundings sink in. As he moves closer to her he asks Madeleine, "Where are you now?" Her initial response, "With you," indicates that her enclosure in whatever time frame she mentally occupies does not exclude his presence or her awareness of his proximity. When Scottie presses her to think more precisely of when she was last here, the request precipitates Madeleine's swift reversion to a state of trance. (Of course, the actress, Judy Barton, who is impersonating Madeleine, has a likely sense of things quite different from the seated woman "losing control." Nevertheless, the tension within the staged appearance of Madeleine's jeopardy, whatever our level of viewer knowledge, somehow continues to prevail.)

In Madeleine's memory (suddenly joined to Carlotta's), the stable as it exists on this visit contrasts with the stable's contents in her (Carlotta's) childhood. In that faraway time, which memory brings near, the stable's claims to an immediate connection with lived reality were much stronger:

Figure 7.1. "And it's all real." Scottie (James Stewart) directs Madeleine (Kim Novak) in *Vertigo*.

"There were not so many carriages, then. And there were horses in the stalls: a bay, two black, and a gray. It was our favorite place. But we were forbidden to play here." Scottie has brought Madeleine to a stage re-creation of an earlier era to break the hold on her of certain dream images generated by this same environment. He apparently hopes that contact with the sensory furnishings of this in-between realm—a theatrical limbo—will restore her to solid ground, and a sense of her genuine identity (as Madeleine) at this very hour. And yet, oddly, what he enjoins her to acknowledge and feel is not the dominance of an authentic milieu, in the present, over a gossamer dream of the past. He has led her to a zone where even bona fide material objects appear to be standing in for themselves. The whole setting is simulated, an imitation of a vanished life. Madeleine, communing with Carlotta, intriguingly recalls that she was "forbidden to play here." But playing—involving, in this situation, a recognition of make-believe pitted against the remoteness of Carlotta's own experience and its oppressive constraints—is what Scottie is pleading for Madeleine to enter into. When he discovers the crude model of a gray horse and taps it to demonstrate to Madeleine its harmless toy status, Scottie is directing Madeleine to regard the stage she is placed on as nonsensical, laughable, a space of obvious illusion, and thus unworthy of her belief.

Yet, of course, the avowed purpose of this visit to San Juan Bautista has been to replace dream imperatives with the security of undeniable facts. The facts Scottie propose to her prove as shifty as the landscape of Madeleine's dream life. Unlike Scottie, Madeleine assents—with the belief and concentration that the art of theatre asks for—to the binding force of this artificial stage. She accepts the mélange of outward signs she is confronted with as a foundation for full immersion. She is not obliged, however, to choose between her prior dream and the physical evidence arrayed before her. She seems to grasp, and accept without strain, the continuity between them. The livery stable makes possible a deeper communion not only with Carlotta's past, but with her ghost's present requirements.

At this point, it is worth reminding ourselves again that Madeleine is no more than a role taken on by Gavin Elster's mistress, Judy, as an elaborate feat of deception: a scheme of nonstop feigning. It is remarkable how little this knowledge affects my experience of Madeleine's behavior in the narrative, however firm my possession of it. No matter how many times I view *Vertigo*, I am unable to keep steadily in mind the idea that Madeleine is being artfully controlled and embodied by Judy. The Madeleine persona, despite all the supernatural tale-spinning surrounding it, strikes me as more present, defined, self-possessed, and indeed grounded than the actress behind the mask. Judy, as we later discover, is all about anxious uncertainty, a guilty need to lessen her complicity in crimes against Elster's murdered wife and Scottie by an endless round of self-effacing appeasement. Madeleine, by contrast, seems gravely in touch with a dark destiny that drives her somnambulist self forward. During those intervals when she is not under Carlotta's spell, she possesses a poise and assurance that Judy (in our times of viewing her directly) never approximates. And when Madeleine is possessed, she pursues, like a transforming creature in Ovid, the commands of an internal female force that is itself richly seductive, and that refines Madeleine's gait and manner further. The aura in which she operates, which cannot be reasoned away, is beautifully, majestically irrational. The spectator, however conscious that Scottie is being duped, cannot simply "see through" the Madeleine performance. Judy is not available to us as a supplementary informed and monitoring presence in the way that, say, Barbara Stanwyck's Jean Harrington is always palpably there in Preston Sturges's *The Lady Eve* (1941) when she is pretending to be Eve.

Madeleine is anchored to the terms of Carlotta's vision in the livery stable scene, and if we detect a growing panic in Madeleine's sense of what awaits her in the bell tower, it is a panic that eerily belongs not to Judy, but to the Madeleine persona, whatever that consists of. Scottie, as stage director of the livery stable drama, is put in a peculiar bind when the reality of the scene that he was so intent on Madeleine recognizing and accepting becomes something that he himself must strive to discredit the moment Madeleine achieves his goal. Madeleine's sense of danger troublingly amplifies as soon as she treats her environment as entirely substantial, and surrenders to it. Her actor's belief on this makeshift stage exceeds her previous faith in her dream. Madeleine's confident fusion with the space of the livery stable and the grounds beyond it supplants the frightened bewilderment she exhibited before the trip to San Juan Bautista when she recounted her dream to Scottie. Scottie declares "There's an answer to everything" when he wants her to share his skepticism about the props on the stage set they jointly inhabit. These artificial trifles should have no power over her. In Coleridge's "Rime of the Ancient Mariner," the lines "Idle as a painted ship / Upon a painted ocean" express Scottie's sense of the stage illusion's ingenuous mildness. What complicates Scottie's appeal to rational solutions here is the incontestable fact that Scottie is as enamored with the mysterious ghost driving Madeleine to trance, memory loss, and the brink of destruction as he is with Madeleine herself.

There is a strong parallel between Scottie's insistence that his livery stable stage set is an amusing, easy to dismantle contrivance and the failed attempt of Midge (Barbara Bel Geddes) the previous night to stage the Carlotta Valdes portrait for Scottie with insouciant mockery. That scene too was planned as a theatrical event, with director Midge carefully timing the unwelcome surprise of her satiric portrait for spectator Scottie. His disastrous unreceptiveness to the joke is due to his being as caught up in a phantasmagoric obsession as Madeleine is in the livery stable. Midge appeals to Scottie's rationality when she invites him to adopt a perspective outside the magnetic field of his bewitchment.

Perhaps the most extraordinary tonal shift in all of Hitchcock occurs during the brief interval where we assume we grasp Midge's portrait burlesque in its entirety and confidently greet it with knowing laughter. Within seconds, however, after Scottie passes judgment on the joke ("No, it's not funny, Midge") our point of view may sharply realign itself with Scottie's, and we lose the sense of the joke we have just surrendered to. Scottie's overwhelmed state has grown contagious by this point in the film, and we too can experience the mockery inscribed in Midge's painting as an affront to Scottie's transcendental longing, and a profanation of the love that has, by slow immersion, enveloped him. The self-portrait that Midge unveils becomes a creation as complicated and fraught with pain as the original Carlotta portrait it imitates, with its vertiginous swirl of hair, glowing teardrop necklace, and fetishistic bouquet. We may well be startled to realize that our own investment in looking at static, charged images in an environmental dreamscape is no longer small. We may, in fact, share to some degree Scottie's baffled enchainment. As soon as Scottie refuses to contemplate Midge's portrait in a light spirit, Midge herself realizes (perhaps for the first time) that the painting was not a joke to her either. When Scottie is mortified by the portrait's brash exposure of his heart's secrets, laced with ridicule, he thrusts aside the image's concurrent plea—that he come down from the clouds, find his way back to his neglected friendship, and once again confide in Midge. He abruptly leaves Midge's apartment, and no sooner has he done so than she instantly commences defacing her painted likeness with her brush, then further repudiates her image by hurling her brush at her reflection in the window and yanking at her "unbeguiling" hair in torment. Her choice of hair as the locus of self-punishment redirects our memory attention to the enigmatic, composed coil of Carlotta's hair in the gallery portrait. Scottie will later plead with Judy to duplicate this coil, in just the way that Madeleine did, in his effort to complete Judy's physical transformation into his perished lover.

Vertigo is constantly urging us to consider what the desire to imitate means (which of course is a primary issue in theatre), and the sort of tragic potential there is in being a failed imitator, a deficient surrogate. As we take time to consider more deeply Midge's attempt to produce a demystifying, down-to-earth self-portrait that will somehow break the obsession-engendering spell of the Carlotta painting, we become aware of Midge's necessary concentration as artist on every detail of the original. Midge can scarcely avoid absorbing some of the hauntedness of Scottie and Madeleine's relation to the portrait in her effort to scale down its impact and critique it. And what sort of artistic blindness is required to regard one's own face as the element that will kill an image's mystique and reduce it to travesty? Beneath this aspiration of Midge the "deflating" director was the unacknowledged greater wish to have Scottie discover and perceptually prize the woman who has intruded herself on his bizarre, transcendent attachment: "Look at this lesser, unromantic image which I propose as the antidote to your foolish grand passion." Midge's image is constructed in such a way as not to offer an appealing substitute, but rather to make infatuation—in response to her own possible claims upon his attention—unthinkable. What she compulsively, unwittingly painted for her theatrical event was self-hatred, misconstrued as self-amusement.

Scottie similarly misconstrues his own intentions in taking Madeleine to San Juan Bautista. He seeks to take control of her vision and overcome it with a more manageable dramatic framework of his own devising. Though he may believe that dispelling Madeleine's fantasy of possession is his actual goal, he may in fact be motivated by an unacknowledged desire to create more space inside this fantasy for himself. The trip to the mission permits him to occupy palpable material ground that corresponds to the dangerous ground of Madeleine's unconscious. Watching her commune with her vision will allow him, as director, to venture close to the heart of it. One can lose sight, when viewing the livery stable scene from Scottie's "rational witness" perspective, that he harbors a spell of his own, for which the unfathomable promptings of his vertigo are the outward physical signs. As he endeavours to dismantle Madeleine's need to be held captive by what she sees in her troubled mind's eye, he fitfully reveals himself as a prisoner of a kindred sort. His spell rests on top of hers, guiding his speech and actions. Later in the film, when Judy finally agrees to transform—unreservedly—back into Madeleine, at Scottie's crazed behest, we are returned (from what we understand is Scottie's point of view) to the livery stable in the midst of Scottie's delirious first embrace of her. He is both inside the passionate consummation of his unearthly dream and watching it unfold. He but not she imagines being transplanted to the livery stable once more, and it slowly swirls around him as a necessary supplement for his "giving in" to rapture. Clearly then it is not only Madeleine who—in their previous visit—is subjected to the trance potential of Scottie's theatre scenario.

There is a death drive pull in Scottie's encounters with heights, which echoes Carlotta's inaudible death song to Madeleine. His paralysis, prior to swooning away or going into shock, includes a summons to let go. Moreover, the progression of Scottie's original vertigo experience remains disturbingly unresolved—indeed, impossible to resolve by any imaginable sequence of real events. We begin with Scottie's dreadful slide down the cobbled roof of an extremely tall building, which is interrupted by a desperate grab at a roof gutter. He somehow manages to cling to it while dangling in midair. Then a benevolent older policeman halts his pursuit of an unidentified criminal suspect to come back and rescue Scottie. His face looms large as he extends his arm—without having any visible means of support—risking everything for the sake of a possible near stranger. The policeman loses his balance in his effort to reach out to Scottie, then—screaming—drops to his death, a dream substitute or surrogate for Scottie, whose own predicament seems impossible to undo. The paternal policeman dies and Scottie, by unaccountable intervention, is spared. We are prevented, as many commentators have noted, from parsing the rescue in any fashion. All we can do is submit to the ancient logic of scapegoat sacrifice. One man perishes so that another can be granted a reprieve. But, tellingly, Hitchcock makes this ineradicable blur at the onset of Scottie's trauma the foundation of all the narrative episodes that follow. The concept of "being saved" is fully tethered to the image of frantic dangling, without end. Irony suggests that "letting go" and accepting the plunge to doom is the only action that can bring Scottie's problem to resolution. What the images of his trembling powerlessness show us is a momentary waiting: a waiting for imminent, certain catastrophe.

When Scottie, as livery stable director, presses Madeleine nearer to the risk-filled territory of Carlotta's dark commands, he is in thrall to his own vision of ungovernable, unshakable peril. Although Scottie may well not perceive the tie between his own dread (and "suspended" state) and Madeleine's, his love for her has much to do with her hazy narrative of being pursued relentlessly by death. Carlotta Valdes is the dead woman to whom Madeleine's body and mind play host, and she is attempting to release herself somehow through another desperate plunge. It is as though Carlotta's only point of full contact with the life that she has lost, and in ghostly rigidity mourns for, is in the act of falling once more. Hitchcock brilliantly attaches Scottie and Madeleine's initial dreams of falling to the experience of falling in love. The imagined, haunting, longed-for descent is somehow interrupted and replaced by a love embrace. Love is the point where two prayers of letting go and being caught cross. Scottie thinks he will find the means to cure Madeleine's sadness unto death, but the persistence of her affliction is a crucial component of his bewitchment by her.

Walter Benjamin, connoisseur of melancholy, said of mourning: "That which mourns feels itself thoroughly known by the unknowable" (quoted in Rose, 186). Scottie needs to track his own mourning and guilt to Madeleine's own place of unyielding lostness. In her apparently helpless movement on the path to disintegration, Madeleine is known by the unknowable. She seems to have something vast, immeasurable within her that Scottie is deeply drawn to. He does not really want her to be divested of the unknowable by his rational probing. He is more intent on swooning into it, making her the circling space into which his own fall can be completed. Scottie becomes certain of his love for Madeleine, and of his readiness to declare it after she leaps into San Francisco Bay at Fort Point. When Scottie dives in after her, retrieves her body, speaks to her unconscious form in his car, then takes her home to his apartment, undresses her, places her in his bed under covers and waits for her to revive, the whole elaborate process constitutes a double rescue operation. She becomes a source of all resurgent imagery for him, but also remains (incomprehensibly, elusively) in the grip of death. She appears fated to fall again, despite his efforts to forestall such an outcome, and perhaps next time further, deeper. What is it precisely that Scottie has dredged up from the watery underworld, and which opens her eyes to him? The deathly trance still clings to her, and he is both pulled into her lostness and detached from it as a savior, who has restored her—provisionally—to life. It is the tentativeness of her standing as a living being, which it is his obligation to enhance and protect, that gives Scottie's love its powerful impetus.

He does not grasp the mirroring function of Madeleine's possibly incurable ailment. (Gavin Elster [Tom Helmore], recall, has aimed all the elements of Madeleine's theatrical performance at Scottie's own malady.) It is significant that Scottie never speaks to Madeleine before her "death" of his vertigo, his own unshakable traumatic ordeal, his ongoing convalescence, and his fear of his own weakness. After he falls off the high chair and swoons into Midge's arms in her apartment, he refrains from discussing his illness, and the dread encircling it, with anyone. Madeleine is granted her first private, autonomous point-of-view shot moments before her own leap into the bay, as she clasps Carlotta's floral bouquet and gazes at it while strewing the flowers one by one into the waves beneath the Golden Gate Bridge. This point-of-view shot, in a manner that defies first-time spectator (or even informed spectator's) sorting out, fuses Carlotta's perspective, Madeleine's perspective as Carlotta's entranced victim, and the actress Judy's perspective. However we choose to consider "Madeleine"—as an actress in control of her part, or a character with mystifying claims on the woman recruited to impersonate her—the sense of what the flower strewing means to her, and how she views it, remains complicated. Is this action willed or involuntary? Judy is conscious of being watched by Scottie, and is apparently choosing her moment to feign an out of control action that threatens her with drowning. The moment that Scottie is seized by love in his determination to rescue her coincides almost exactly with the moment that Madeleine-Carlotta is born—through a point-of-view shot—into a state of discrete character consciousness. What that consciousness consists of, however (no matter how well we know the film), is extremely difficult to determine.

Madeleine does not utter a word in the narrative until after Scottie has furtively removed her clothes, beheld her nakedness, and placed her "unrevived" form in his bed. Her waking to his love, which she almost immediately seems to acknowledge and accept, like a version of Eve in the Garden, means that for her as well as for him a plunge into love is the only self-defining issue. Scottie and Madeleine have their love and their respective, twinned affliction to contend with, and, it appears, nothing else. They both present themselves as "wanderers," and where they wander is in a world emptied of social obligations, responsibilities, jobs, prior attachments, even memories of prior life. If the forces of "possession" can be dealt with and disposed of, Scottie imagines that Madeleine and he will have nothing but love to occupy them, and they will stand, free and safe, within its orbit. To put this another way, apart from the couple's intensifying conviction of mutual love, there is only death to contend with. Death-haunted consciousness (a form of possession that in both Scottie and Madeleine's case seems to link memory with drift and trance) is the sole obstacle to love's full release. We might regard this prospect of release in terms of "letting go," which is the thrust of Scottie's directorial plea to Madeleine as she performs her scene for him on the livery stable stage.

Letting go also conjures up the policeman with his extended hand on the rooftop, and Madeleine's jump into the swirling waters at Fort Point. Love and death may be the sole forces in play in the couple's relationship, but the drama arises from their deep intermingling, and the resultant difficulty in distinguishing between them. Pursuit and escape, holding tight and setting loose grow increasingly scrambled, infected with dizziness. Scottie seeks to salvage and re-create himself by creating a version of Madeleine that is safe from death, having at last shed the urge toward it that the seemingly bottomless past presses upon her. Madeleine is, in Scottie's sight, above all the death drive made animate. She is an enchantingly beautiful incarnation of inexorable drift toward nothingness. And that drift is mesmerizing. It lodges at the heart of Scottie's avid will to possess. As he desperately declares to Madeleine during their embrace in the livery stable, as she thrillingly oscillates between Carlotta trance remoteness and a concurrent awareness of him beside her: "Nothing you must do . . . No one possesses you. . . . You're safe with me . . . my love." He is replying to Madeleine's repeated phrase "too late," which seems to grasp and accept the end that Carlotta has in store for her.

We have made a lengthy detour away from the overtly theatrical aspects of the livery stable scene in which Scottie, as watching, frustrated director, beholds an actress entering into a level of performing belief that exceeds his control and understanding. My purpose in reviewing the wider terrain of their relationship dynamic is to argue that Scottie's ostensibly failed theatre experiment in his expedition to San Juan Bautista in fact achieves the result that he unknowingly requires to maintain his love at fever pitch. To succeed in making rational theatre out of her death drive would threaten his own need to remain haunted and spellbound. Scottie drives Madeleine to the mission to produce conditions of deeper danger for her, not safety. The livery stable stage becomes the place where he can replay the fierce abandon of his initial embrace of Madeleine at the Cyprus Point bluff, where the solitary twisted tree and the thunderous ocean waves serve as witness and accompaniment. Scottie is enough of a stranger to himself at this point to be unmindful of his attachment to Madeleine in her in-between states and her unresolved desperation. When he declares from behind the stable surrey, where Madeleine sits, facing away from him, "There's an answer to everything," her gaze moves her beyond the stable's theatrical frame to the mission tower grounds outside. Throughout the time that he clutches her, seeking to focus her attention on his sheltering, devoted presence, Madeleine's eyes anxiously seek out this sunlit outdoor arena, which becomes, very quickly, a second stage. In this setting, Madeleine will take over as director. She will be both the one directing her performance and enacting it, in a delirious reversal of the original staging protocol.

The drift toward a new scenario of finalized destruction ushers in Madeleine's seeming dominance by a force outside of knowledge. It is a scenario in which love secures the death that rests just beneath it, supplying so much of love's reality and power. The lovers, without exactly choosing death, take turns pressing each other toward it. Scottie has told Madeleine in the livery stable to "Try—for me." It is by no means clear what he is requesting that she try for. As they stand near the edge of the stable stage, Scottie strives equally to break Madeleine loose from her Carlotta possession and to be absorbed by it himself. Beyond this stage boundary is a blazing light. The very air in which Scottie offers his searching embraces becomes fiery. And he seeks that fire, like a thieving Prometheus, a fire that depends for its rise on the felt proximity of a fall, which Scottie will prove powerless (again) to prevent.

As Scottie grips Madeleine near the edge of his chosen theatre space, he repeatedly kisses her in an effort to be with her once again in the already lost stillness they shared in the redwood forest or the timeless reality of their first impassioned kiss by the sea. Madeleine has not yet been lost to him. But already Scottie struggles to get moments back from their brief shared past, moments that are, of course, irretrievable. He is, in effect, staging what he hopes are the right conditions for a past love scene, making Madeleine's tenacious dream memory the basis for his own compulsion to repeat what is no more. As we will discover again in his later attempts to make Judy a simulacrum of what memory has frozen, Scottie's theatre, even in the livery stable phase, when he still professes to believe in future time, is not about moving forward. Resorting to theatre always means to Scottie an exclusive concern with reenactment, recapture. Madeleine's apparent haunted state, which forces her to pull anxiously away from Scottie and retreat from their no longer shared transport, is what saves Scottie from disappointment. In his despair is his salvation.

Scottie stands outside Madeleine's timeless reality—which she now inhabits alone—and his sickness returns to plague him as he falls short of reaching her. The director feels deserted on the little stage he has prepared, and the laws governing the performance to which she assents are beyond him. There is no settled calm for him here. Deprived of his tools for rational capture and of the hope for a cleansing redemptive solution, Scottie shifts his faith to the only intensity available: the intensity of deprivation. Madeleine's ghostly absence from his directorial control excites him because it explains his own inability to reexperience his earlier transcendent release. The feel of her slipping away from him, which his embraces cannot answer for, or remedy, seems as momentous to him as his former time of having. What we see in his attempt to subdue her fear—and his own—with repeated kisses is the willed opposition to the threat of kisses wearing out, of their suddenly losing their mystical power.

Madeleine walking across the green open space leading to the cloisters and tower is the action marking her complete takeover of the role of director, however much against her will. She still continues, of course, to play her assigned part. She knows that her acting task is to lead Scottie into the tower and up the staircase. These movements must result in his paralyzing stage fright if the prearranged drama is to have the resolution and impact that Elster's script intends. Very soon, the body that Madeleine has been standing in for will be thrown from the bell tower. That prior Madeleine (Elster's actual wife), more real than the haunting Carlotta, exists inescapably in the "imitation Madeleine's" foreseeing eye. When this designated victim, scarcely known to her, is flung down in her place, the surviving actor, in many different senses, will be stranded. Her role will disappear, and all traces of what she has imparted to the role to bring Madeleine "to life" must vanish with it. The character with whom she has gradually merged will turn, in the wake of this namesake's murder, purely incriminating. Her role must die completely, the moment she arrives at the top of the bell tower, as though never inhabited at all.

When Scottie catches up with her near the cloister archway, as she intends him to, she is filled to the brim with the identity she must shortly relinquish. She does not need to feign the experience of being under threat, or of an imminent emptying out. What can Madeleine, as Scottie's director (as well as fellow actor) within what she understands is their final scene together onstage, give to him as a palliative for the suffering about to be inflicted on him—this credulous, untrained performer, and hopelessly vulnerable dupe? Initially she strives, for a few moments, to disclose herself as an actor trapped in a role that has no room for her present feelings. ("It wasn't supposed to happen this way. It shouldn't have happened.") These statements are a protest against what she has done, and has yet to do, a small bid for freedom from this dire, scripted necessity. If only Scottie could see the face behind the mask. This unpremeditated departure from Elster's play is also a despairing plea for exoneration. She is free—for the length of this brief protest—to warn Scottie. In fact, she is trying to wake Scottie out of his assured sense that he is partaking of life rather than theatre, in a pathos-laden variation on his own persuasive efforts to waken her in the livery stable. If he can be roused from the trance of love her performance has induced, he may be spared a portion of the grief and derangement that the Elster script has prepared for him. But Madeleine is too frightened to proceed further with her unmasking. And she is perhaps too possessed, at this point, by the logic of her role.

Insofar as she exists as a separate entity in this scene, Madeleine is innocent of wrongdoing. She is driven to her doom, as much as Scottie is driven to pursue her. When the one who must impersonate Madeleine (Judy Barton) regains focus as director of the events to come, she creates a space of innocence for herself apart from the manipulative trajectory of her actions. She regroups, within the Madeleine persona, and asks Scottie to confirm his faith in her love for him: "You believe that I love you. . . . If you lose me, you'll know that I loved you and wanted to go on loving you." She can speak these words without the burden of deception, since the actor is persuaded that her genuine love for Scottie—which arose in her without calculation or warning—is something separate from the plot against him, and perhaps lives independently of that plot's evil. As director, she realizes that Scottie must be sufficiently pacified by her expression of love in order to trust her to venture into the church alone. Her farewell kiss gains his temporary compliance. Yet at the same time she feels she is giving him an assurance that may stand him in good stead later, because her "innocent heart" is bound up in it. She gets him to be an immersed participant in Gavin Elster's play while giving more of herself to him (or so she believes) than either the role or the purposes of deceit demand. As performer, she dwells inside the love that, as director, she must cruelly wrest away from him.

As she walks toward the church she makes certain to execute the stage blocking that will excite Scottie's alarm. She gazes up at the tower, knowing that Scottie's gaze will follow her own, and that the mere sight and thought of this high edifice will reactivate all the endgame terrors that constitute his vertigo illness. She is a detached director and a performer willing her own possession at the same time. If she were to convince herself that Carlotta commands her deranged ascent of the stairway, it could open up a space between actor and director. The believing performer would not be in touch with the crime, or assent to it. She strictly adheres to the choreography of her assigned movements, but may invoke simultaneously the performer's blindness to mere fabrication. The actor is able to penetrate so far inside the emotional circumstances of the theatrical event that she cannot evaluate its meaning or consequences. She is not outside, but inside, the dramatic action.

Scottie, for his part, enters the church interior before discovering the stairway that Madeleine has already begun to climb. Scottie's survey of the immense church space and distant altar suddenly links his hope of rescuing Madeleine to the theatre of Catholic ritual and its sacrificial propitiations. Christian logic will inform the narrative of Madeleine's death. It is he, after all, who deliberately brought Madeleine to this arena, perhaps to undo his own sin. In order to be cleansed of his own transgression, resulting in the police officer's death, a woman, who is free of taint and who has placed herself in his care, is to be sacrificed in his place. And as a result of his own blind enchantment, he has brought this dreadful deed to fulfillment. Scottie accepts responsibility for the entire play he mistakenly believes he has directed. The events he set in motion, and supervised, all become entangled (in the miasma of thought and dream) with his need to repeat his original "crime," as he dangled over the abyss. Madeleine and the policeman are fused in a single scenario, which he has both created and guiltily willed to repeat.

The coroner's inquest scene reveals more parallels with the scenes immediately preceding it if we recognize that it too is a theatre episode, in which the coroner-director's staged speech is designed to expose all of Scottie's grounds of justified inaction in the lead up to Madeleine's death as deeply suspect, if not absurd. Scottie's professed concern for Madeleine's welfare and his benevolent motives are, in the coroner's telling of Scottie's "story," as unreal as the gray model horse in the livery stable, a structure that stands right beside the building where the inquest takes place. In a second story chamber that seems too vast for the intimate drama conducted there, the coroner adopts the language of reason, accompanied by pointed irony. Scottie, of course, had resorted to reason's claims himself with Madeleine on the livery stable stage. The coroner does not directly address his observations to Scottie, despite the fact that every skeptical word is clearly aimed at him, with the intent of shredding his credibility and competence, and piercing his conscience. An audience of male jurors is gathered to witness this crafty, quietly devastating theatrical confrontation. Scottie is technically one of the spectators in the audience gathered to hear the coroner's findings, though his seat is, by the coroner-director's fiat, made continuous with the performing space. The coroner's measured delivery of the summation proceeds inexorably, allowing no chance for interruption or protest. He assumes all the prerogatives of voice in this dramatic encounter.

Scottie, visibly stricken by the force and logic of the coroner's interpretation of events, seems entombed in silence. His first question to entranced Madeleine in the livery stable scene—"Where are you?"—now has become applicable to him. As Charles Barr has pointed out in his BFI Classics commentary on *Vertigo*, after witnessing Madeleine's fall to her death, Scottie is seemingly "struck dumb," gripped by a silence that lasts for fourteen minutes of screen time (63). For most of this period of agonized, wordless passivity, Scottie is present onscreen. It is a deathly enthrallment that Scottie has been thrust into, deeper—in our experience of it—than Madeleine's own. The coroner, whose mode of speech at the inquest suggests a menacing caress, seems to usurp Scottie's earlier directorial stance with Madeleine and to twist it into a new shape. Scottie's appeals to Madeleine were characterized by an air of composure, alternating with plaintive beseeching. In the inquest, the coroner uses reason to pillory all of Scottie's dubious motives for action and implicitly to condemn the net result of "doing nothing . . . when most needed." If Scottie were able to formulate a reply to the coroner's bruising insinuations, it must finally rest (entirely) on the same edifice of unreality that his love for Madeleine rests upon. Nothing in his pursuit and loss of her can be grounded and accounted for in the discourse of his detective profession, even though he had consistently believed, while Madeleine was under his "protection," that he was steadily guiding her in a rational direction. The coroner's speech reduces every decision that Scottie has made to delusion, artifice, and cowardice. Whatever he has done, and failed to do, is dismayingly inaccessible to the light of reason.

Scottie's listening state on the coroner's stage is paradoxically both tormented and remote. It is as though he is dropping through this barrage of words and entering his subsequent nightmare of free fall, where his silhouetted form descends endlessly, with no place to land but the darkness of an open grave or the mission roof that claimed Madeleine, a roof that is now airy rather than hard. The hole of Madeleine/Carlotta's gravesite has become the ground beneath Scottie's feet when he is awake and mobile. The coroner reports, with unconcealed scorn, Scottie's claim of blacking out after the traumatic sight of Madeleine's splayed corpse on the roof. Several hours after this shock, as if reproducing Madeleine's trance wanderings within himself, he discovers that he is back in his apartment, with no memory of his previous actions.

The inquest has required him to return to San Juan Bautista, to be seated in a building situated between the livery stable and the bell tower, and to hear his story punitively recast, until it consists of nothing but guilt and delirium. Everything that constituted his functional identity after his original rooftop tragedy seems to decompose as the coroner itemizes sane alternatives to his own egregious, impenetrable missteps. He now finds himself imprisoned in an ever-intensifying phantom realm, whose links to actual life circumstances have all snapped loose. Scottie's mode of being, from now until the end of the *Vertigo* narrative spiral, will consist entirely of return moves, circlings back, and compulsive reenactments. On the coroner's stage, Scottie sits like Madeleine, transfixed in the stable surrey, frozen in her conviction of "too lateness." The coroner's stripping away of plausible rationales and any claim to honorable intent serve to make the remnants of real-world arrangements and expectations into a confounding riddle of the real.

To stage something—as Scottie believed when he brought Madeleine to a private theatre in the mission livery stable—is to take control of it, to show what lies behind deceiving appearances. But Scottie became lost in his theatre experiment, because he was fully as enamored with being controlled as controlling Madeleine. He did not, in fact, wish for Madeleine to see through the dream that possessed her, dismiss whatever it was made of, and "let it go." Scottie instead let Madeleine go, when she requested permission to leave him, and she has seemingly perished as a result of the performance he coached her to give. The coroner's mindset—as a man presumably constrained by legally admissible evidence and professional decorum—is as split and devious in his own theatrical domain as Scottie was in the stable. The coroner knows that there is no legal basis for suggesting that Madeleine's death was caused by criminal neglect or by certifiable wrongdoing. He repeatedly stresses that his musings about Scottie's failures and his dubious motivations should not affect the jurors' verdict. He is laying the groundwork for a verdict of suicide, but one in which the acceptance of Scottie's innocence is composed completely of imputations of guilt. One might paraphrase the coroner's conclusion in the following terms: "I cannot punish you with recommendations to arrest you and put you on trial, but this death belongs to you in every particular that counts. You have no right to be released from responsibility." Every strand of Scottie's declared attachment to Madeleine, and every move he made as her appointed "protector," was instrumental in her destruction. Guilt, if we accept the coroner's logic, is without boundaries or limit. The hidden impetus for the actions that Scottie performed, and for those actions (equally damning) that he failed to perform, are culpable forever. The end of the coroner's play is a moment of unbearable seeing, as in *Oedipus Rex*, but unlike Oedipus, say, Scottie lacks the tragic stature to blind himself.

The coroner's ruthless, public paring away of Scottie's "supernatural" promptings for his conduct invites comparison with Gavin Elster's theatrical staging of his need for Scottie's assistance with ghostly matters in the lengthy shipbuilding office interview early in the film. Elster is placed in an oversized, double room office space that reminds us of the equally disproportionate environment in which the inquest is held. Behind his massive desk is a broad picture window view of shipbuilding activities under way, which his company directs. The walls of Elster's office are covered with memorabilia of an older, "freer" San Francisco, although the many maps, models, and paintings on display make a coordinated appeal not only to the romance of the past but to historical authenticity. Elster's cushioned swivel chair behind his desk, in which he is initially shown turning back and forth, establishes him as the comfortably grounded and in control executive of a thriving business but at the same time conjures up the disquieting revolve of Scottie's vertigo. Elster's office is divided into two distinct areas, one of which, on a raised floor, resembles a conference room and is dominated by a long table. When Elster moves to this upper level and begins circling behind the formidable table, he leaves Scottie in the space below him, and Scottie further accentuates the distance separating them by choosing to sit in a far corner chair.

Elster's account of his wife's wandering spells, her memory failure, her possible subjugation to the spirit of Carlotta Valdes is mostly presented from this elevated, sequestered chamber, which is equipped with its own version of a proscenium arch. Elster was initially presented in a ground level, work world space that he and Scottie share in their reunion as "old friends." But his careful staging of his fantastic tale of Madeleine's possible possession subtly disengages him from the material, practical trappings of his reassuringly staid business milieu. Elster's physical movements in conjunction with tale-spinning and his anxious appeal for help are calculated to seduce Scottie with intimations of deviant, off-kilter possibilities, linked in their strangeness to Scottie's own alienation from previously matter-of-fact job procedures. The pictorial excess of the office's San Francisco archive decoration creates a slippage between a real and a poetic history of place. Elster's admiring reference to the former glory days of "power and freedom" in San Francisco suggests not only that the past is more alluring to him than the tedious "caretaker" responsibilities of his current position, but also that the present is open to disruption. The present, as Madeleine's peculiar predicament implies, may have cracks in it, mysterious passages to undefined realms that Scottie, in his own displaced condition, may know something about.

Elster makes the pragmatic work world that he himself is aligned with sound suffocating, while the wandering sphere inhabited by his possibly demented wife is more "questionable," yet fascinating in its erasure of normal constraints. Is this not a territory particularly well suited to someone with Scottie's suddenly altered capacities, and his release from mundane tasks? The stage of Elster's office is gradually, cunningly discredited by him as a base of meaningful operations. Scottie's awkward attempt to "fit in" to this demoralizing, onerous space (he never succeeds in making himself comfortable) would fare better, Elster hints, in a space where the shipping magnate would be out of his depth. Scottie, who is bereft of fixed obligations and any professional definition, is enviably free to explore metaphysical labyrinths of all sorts. Elster acknowledges the solidity of his office surroundings, but confesses that his mechanical, daily decision-making feels like a bindingly restrictive trap. Scottie may still be wearing a literal corset from his recent ordeal, but his present opportunity to rethink everything he might wish to do with his life connects him to the "romantic openings" and explorer advantages celebrated in Elster's San Francisco art.

Elster's dramatic presentation steadily privileges dream callings over the summons of unwelcome duties in this "hemmed in" seat of power. The world he induces Scottie to reflect upon, and after Scottie's first "staged" vision of Madeleine at Ernie's restaurant immediately put his faith in, is precisely the world that the coroner will later demean as meretricious and absurd. The coroner insists that Scottie return to the rational skepticism that was his own instinctive position in his meeting with Elster. It is in the light of this rational interrogation of deed and motive that Scottie must be evaluated. And he must be held accountable to reason's charges of dereliction. What else, in all this emptiness, can serve as guide? The drift in Scottie that Elster's theatre of the irrational sanctioned, with its chance of enlarging unorthodox freedoms, is reduced to nothing in the postmortem glare of the coroner's cold theatre of reason. Scottie's discovery of transcendence, and his mission to save another being from its sacred terror, crumples into paltry stagecraft, shot through with delusion and deceit. Instead of thinking sensibly of what would truly be in another's interest, Scottie had become lost in a private, selfish, feeble, and ultimately cowardly dream. On this stage, the reverse of Elster's, Scottie cannot emerge with any honorable standing, either as a moral actor or an interpreter of reality. Scottie's sense of reality, the coroner deftly argues, is nothing but error, by turns sinister and heedless. The error that Scottie entered into, on Elster's stage of freedom and mysterious new potencies, has multiplied, by the time of Madeleine's fatal leap, into a vast, incapacitating wilderness.

In the scene immediately preceding the Gavin Elster drama of seduction, Scottie stages his first piece of theatre in the film, with Midge as audience. His purpose is to persuade her that his vertigo is a temporary, not too debilitating threat to his former "balanced" navigation of life experience. He will be able to conquer it gradually, by tackling slightly higher elevations, one cautious step at a time. He explains his theory of self-cure to Midge while lifting the cane that he has been holding since the start of the scene, and marking out his imagined progress with it, point by point in the air. Our first view of Scottie in this episode revealed him attempting to balance the cane on one finger, and failing. The effort to catch the cane as it gets away from him causes a spasm of pain, and prefigures his bodily collapse into "mothering" Midge's arms at the end of his theatrical demonstration of how he can master the child's art of climbing steps.

Midge's apartment, unlike the Elster office, with its extensive display of historical artifacts, highlights an internal conflict in Midge between fashion sketches and designs (how she makes her living) and a somewhat thwarted drive toward art that is less orderly and restrained. Midge may well crave the release of abstraction, emotional exploration, and exuberant playfulness, to judge from the paintings she has chosen for the wall behind her sofa. Her apartment is filled to bursting with pictorial stimulation of all sorts, and Midge plays a subtle, solacing piece by Bach as she contemplates a model of a strapless brassiere that she must accurately reproduce for a magazine display ad. The music has the effect of taming the otherwise jolting force of the brassiere "sculpture" when it first appears. The bra stands out in the open between Scottie and Midge, inviting a fetishistic attention. Midge halts the Bach recording, at Scottie's request, and Scottie slowly appraises the miraculous floating bra at close range, with expressions of admiration that hover between joking and prurience. The brassiere (with its sexual reverberations) and Scottie's never relinquished cane conduct an object colloquy throughout the scene: a promise of sexual unveiling teasingly alternates with reminders of wounded virility, impeded motion, a "corset" not yet removed from the male body.

Scottie's effort late in the scene to show Midge that his infirmity can be overcome, that he can "lick" it, takes place close to the taunting brassiere, stretched on a square of wire. Scottie locates a small footstool for his first trial, and manages to stand confidently on top of it, acting as though he is well on his way to dispelling the mystery and the affliction associated with "simple" height. Midge has prompted this sudden foray into theatrical improvisation with her troubling report from a doctor that Scottie's condition may be incurable. Midge has also just christened him "old man" when she turns down his offer of a date that evening, reminding out of work "Johnny-O" (her pet name for Scottie) that she has job-related demands to fulfill while he restlessly stews in enforced idleness. The stage that Scottie impulsively sets up to prove the possibility of recovery reminds the viewer that theatre evolves from childhood games and the closely connected spirit of play. Scottie's insistence that his memory can be wiped clean of its present traumatic disturbance is coupled here with a willingness to return to the young child's challenges of learning to walk and climb. He demonstrates to Midge that he is not embarrassed to reverse direction and begin again. He dramatizes the act of taking steps as fundamentally innocent, and the movement upward as also something to which innocence naturally accrues. Darkness can be purged if one reenters the world of movement with a child's light-hearted freedom and perseverance. Scottie takes visible pride in standing upright on his stool, repeating "I look up, I look down," and basks in the ease of his accomplishment. "There's nothing to it."

At this juncture, Midge enters the stage space that he has established, urging him to try a chair that is higher and, in fact, equipped with actual steps. She brings over the step stool and places it close to the apartment window, with its plunging vertical "exposure," perhaps anticipating and even delighting in the increased sense of danger for Scottie. Throughout this lengthy, superficially amicable discussion scene, Midge seems to take a measure of satisfaction in the reversal of a previous power imbalance in her not quite romantic friendship with Scottie. His increased uncertainty and dependence on her perhaps alters a previous pattern of neglect and a proclivity on his part to take her devotion to him for granted. Now she exhibits an assured command of her professional identity and her stable life circumstances. I have previously described the strapless brassiere sculpture as an undraping of sexual tension and preoccupation, in spite of its floating free of any attachment to either a living form or a manikin.

Figure 7.2. Scottie playfully proves to Midge (Barbara Bel Geddes) that he's taking steps toward convalescence in *Vertigo*.

While Midge industriously sketches a female figure to display the bra, the object itself discloses something discordant, unspoken, refused in the emotional dynamic of the Scottie-Midge relationship. The brassiere is an incitement to fantasy, but provides no "bridge" for Scottie to a heightened awareness of Midge's own presence as a sexual being. So her means of helping him with his little play later on in the scene has a component (perhaps unwitting) of bringing him down, willing his failure.

She stands near the yellow counter chair, whose forceful color echoes her blondeness and her lighter yellow sweater, and critically evaluates his attempt to ascend. When he arrives safely on the first step and is pleased he is keeping his balance, she instantly recommends that he tackle step number two. Midge's manner here is a continuation of her dismissal of his initial stool climb as inconsequential. She is subtly skeptical of his progress, and withholds positive reinforcement. As Scottie reaches step number two, after we witness his shoes in close-up carefully move the tiny distance upward, we sense a growing tension in him as he repeats his steadying mantra: "I look up, I look down." It is at this precise moment that Hitchcock plans for the spectator to feel that the simple stage has gone beyond the performer's powers of prediction and control. The "prop" chair is no longer securely contained, or a cooperative ally. It overflows its physical boundaries.

We anxiously notice a square of blue sky and the white top of a tall distant building in the window just to the left of Scottie, beneath the half-drawn blinds and out of his sightline. The camera looks up at him, adopting Midge's point of view, and Scottie is suddenly exposed at a palpable height we had not anticipated. We are more aware than he is of his augmented vulnerability as his eyes raise up toward the ceiling rather than attend, as we do, to the looming expanse of the sky in the revealed portion of the window. Scottie talks himself into a state of near calm (that we now judge as unwarranted) as he jokes to Midge about going out to buy a small stepladder. We return to a medium shot of Midge gazing up at him, the brassiere sculpture on its wire mount adding in its own dimension of strain just behind her right shoulder. Midge tells Scottie to "take it easy now" in the sort of maternal voice that breeds worry in the guise of encouragement. She wants him to take the third and final step, but she seems ambivalent about his succeeding. Scottie's shoes—once again becoming, in close-up, the key to Scottie's fragility—awkwardly and fearfully traverse the distance that separates him from the seat of the step stool. Hitchcock inserts an almost subliminal chair sound as Scottie completes his ascent, which conveys pressure from receiving his full weight. The stool imbibes Scottie's fragility, as though it might give way itself, and collapse without warning. Scottie's face and voice are in conflict with the psychological indicators of his feet in the previous shot. As so often in his films, Hitchcock divides the human agent, through editing, into segments of divergent expressiveness, and invests an object—in this case the step stool—with its own intimate access to a character's internal state.

The moment when Scottie's point of view breaks the frame of his safe theatre space, and is struck by the vertiginous drop visible within inches of the window frame, marks the spot where the stage disintegrates, swallowed up by the abyss pressing against its border. Scottie has deliberately adopted the child's position on the first stage he constructs for performance in *Vertigo*, and Midge joins him there, taking on the ambiguous role of mother. She is torn between wanting him to grow in confidence and to have his dependence on her reinstated. His topple into unconsciousness is such a disproportionately intense outcome for a performance conceived as "child's play." The shattering of a rational demonstration onstage anticipates Midge's later scene with the disastrous self-portrait and Scottie's announcement in the livery stable that "there's an answer to everything," minutes before Madeleine's rush to destruction.

An undercurrent throughout the first scene in Midge's apartment has to do with the temptation and perils of "letting go." Midge doing ad copy at her desk, Scottie's corset, the floating brassiere, Midge refraining from speaking to Scottie about why her engagement to him "broke off," all speak the language of restraint, a reining in and holding back. Equally prevalent in the scene is Midge's "looser" personal art on the facing wall, Scottie's freedom from work commitments and relationship commitments, and the possibility of "letting go" of the nightmare of hanging suspended over a chasm. The sheer density of bric-a-brac, wall decoration, and the pressing in, white cityscape beyond Midge's windows work in concert to fasten Scottie and Midge firmly to the inside of the room, as though being hemmed in were the essence of security. The apartment serves as visual antidote to the previous rooftop scene's precipitous emptiness, creating a protective shelter in this site of surplus furnishing. The work world and the domestic sphere tightly overlap in Midge's living quarters, and in their mingling seem to supply all indoor needs. But the urge to let go is subtly activated in the midst of such stifling plenty. Scottie, cane always in hand, seeks out breathing space in Midge's domain. His entire scheme of "game playing" with a chair is a protest against feeling oppressively enclosed. The little drama he enacts with the step stool is meant to simplify an obscurely dense playing field, allowing Scottie to rise into the light and air, shedding the impinging constraints of both his malady and social regimentation. The world is too much with him in Midge's well-regulated, engulfing realm, and although we have been overwhelmed just a short time ago by the dread of Scottie letting go of his precarious gutter, we swiftly shift our desire back in that "letting go" direction. Scottie appears disturbingly weighed down by fear and potential hollowness. The theatre "escape" he devises miscarries, of course. He winds up letting go of his will and control in a negative, helpless fashion. As he lies crumpled and unconscious in Midge's arms, he seems disturbingly remote from any self-definition or competence.

How readily the props in *Vertigo*'s various theatre episodes offer reassurance of an impending release from a conspicuous bind, only to betray the director-actors who put their faith in them—stools, paintings, artificial horses—plunging them back into overmastering fear, and what John Keats has termed the "Penetralium of Mystery." In his brilliant essay, "Crime and Punishment: Murder in Your Own Room," R. P. Blackmur discusses a scene in the Dostoyevski novel when Raskolnikov lies in bed after completing his double murder. His servant, Nastasya, oblivious of Raskolnikov's involvement in the killings, begins to speak to him about the second "unplanned" victim, Lizaveta, who had occasionally visited their building. Raskolnikov mumbles her name aloud, and Nastasya mentions that she used to sell old clothes: "Didn't you know her? She used to come here. She mended a shirt for you too." At this point Raskolnikov turns away from her and lets his gaze wander over his dirty wallpaper. He finds himself staring at "one clumsy, white flower with brown lines on it." It suddenly appears to him worth noting "how many petals there were in it, how many scallops in the petals and how many lines on them" (Blackmur, 320). Blackmur elucidates Raskolnikov's act of mentally transforming his unassimilated victim into this stubbornly vivid flower on his ragged wallpaper: "The blankest or the most conventional image is, Dostoevski knew, the best to hold the deepest symbol if only there is enough tension present when it is named" (320). Visually highlighting an object in film is the equivalent of naming at the propitious moment on the page. The chairs Scottie strives to mount and dominate, like the casual arrangement of white flowers on Midge's sedate windowsill, are conventional images, to be sure, eager to support illusions of security, regularity, and the existence of a familiar human ground that cooperates with our intentions. Scottie turns away from his big predicament with its dreadful impenetrability to little objects that are knowable and docile. But his shift of concentration, like Raskolnikov's, allows the big terror to sprout in the previously blank image of, say, a little flower in a wallpaper pattern, something almost beneath notice. The chairs initially have nothing to do with Scottie's paralysis, but as soon as he seeks them out as a refuge and a shield against his besetting fear, the step-stool chair summons all the images of slipping off the edge, and plunging to a death that is instantly, unbearably close at hand. Window, flowers (anticipating Madeleine and Carlotta's bouquet), and chair "open up," so to speak, disintegrating the protective atmosphere of theatre make-believe, and Scottie swoons into the adamant emptiness. Similar reversals of Blackmur's accommodating, near-blank objects occur, as we have seen, with the hollow horse model in the livery stable theatre, with Madeleine's petal-shedding floral bouquet before her plunge into the bay, and with Midge's teasing self-portrait. The contrived staging falls apart in each instance and the small fragment or emblem of ordinariness acquires a sinister power to conjure up the irrational and to sweep us toward disaster.

There remains one final piece of elaborate theatrical reenactment to contend with in *Vertigo*: Scottie's return to the mission bell tower with Judy/Madeleine after his discovery of his betrayal by her. The impetus for this last resort to staged demonstration is another small object, Madeleine's necklace, casually and unthinkingly brought out of hiding by Judy as an item of adornment for the dress that matches the one that "Madeleine" wore at Ernie's, when Scottie first beheld her. We might well conclude that Judy has unconsciously brought out the necklace in order to certify her complete capitulation to Scottie's desire that she become Madeleine for him, with no Judy Barton residue. He had asked her to alter her hair as the final obstacle to his reenchantment, and she had reluctantly done so. It seemed the only possible solution to the problem of how to preserve and resurrect the past for Scottie, so that the entire burden of tragic loss would be effaced. The spectator as well is primed for the removal of the one remaining impediment to fusion of actress and character. Once Judy has pinned up her hair for her demanding director, who "knows what he wants," she manages to rekindle his grand passion and win him over, dissolving the surreal barrier to romantic recognition and acceptance.

The necklace, which "Madeleine" had never worn in Scottie's presence, but whose image had figured prominently in the portrait of Carlotta Valdes, which Scottie has absorbed piece by piece in obsessive contemplation, is a further gift to Scottie from "Madeleine," a reward he hasn't anticipated, marking a more total convergence of Madeleine and Judy than even Scottie knew how to ask for. Scottie has demanded that

Judy painstakingly eliminate all of the irrelevant signs of her own being from view so that he can reclaim the image of Madeleine from death—perhaps more than the image. Madeleine's appearance will so decisively displace Judy's compliant, and to Scottie inconsequential, barely articulated person in a manner strangely reminiscent of Carlotta's earlier takeover of Madeleine, from within. Carlotta, as I have earlier argued, loomed large in Scottie's love for Madeleine. Her mystique had much to do with involuntary surrender to an ever-more tyrannical ghost. Accompanied at most times by Carlotta, Madeleine sleepwalked not merely through the times of Scottie's pursuit of her but also through the fresh entanglement of her professed love for Scottie. When he and Madeleine were together, both the frustration and the thrill of being with her was the oscillating, uncertain romantic focus: "Now you see me, now you don't." Scottie vows to save her from the perils of "unseeing," but I contend that the invisible rival for her devotion is what accounts for Scottie's deepest fascination. Carlotta is a forever renewable obstacle, both fiery and death-driven, seemingly beyond Madeleine's control.

Perhaps Judy's inadvertent exposure of Carlotta's necklace, her request to Scottie to fasten it for her, and her self-incriminating question "Can't you see?" as she stands in front of the mirror and waits for Scottie to complete the task are a performer's memory of the dual requirements of playing Madeleine successfully. Madeleine always presented herself as split between "struggling to return" in her own right and being under the sway of an alien force that is intent on obliterating her. Madeleine communed continually with Carlotta's directives. For Judy to bring Madeleine fully back to life, as Scottie fiercely desires, there must be an aspect of her appearance that attests to Carlotta's influence as well. Madeleine without Carlotta exceeds Judy's comprehension of the role's demands. What active concerns are there for her to express and handle? In its very bid for rationality and ease, the Madeleine persona turns indecipherable to the actress who created her. The necklace is the surplus defining detail that Scottie, as authoritarian director, did not think to include in his checklist of acquisitions. But the necklace, as a kind of dreamed exorbitancy, grants the revived Madeleine the unearthly clarity of her prior integrity. Without Carlotta, after all, Madeleine is hardly a role with an internal dynamic, or dramatic substance.

We note that Judy rather quickly sheds the vocal patterns of her true Salina, Kansas dialect, as well as Judy Barton's awkward, self-conscious gait and social manner. Judy's attributes are not only unwelcome, they are not strong enough to draw upon. Her pervasive uncertainty as Judy lacks what a director might term "acting focus," as well as vividness. The reason Midge disappears abruptly from the film is that "Judy" assumes the secondary role that had been hers, though in a sadly diminished form. As for Judy donning the necklace to complete her transformation, it had been the case for Judy as much as for Madeleine that an impending death was always preying on her thoughts. The actress floated in the hollow of a nightmare about the real Mrs. Elster and what was to become of her. The necklace then is the aura and the emblem of death that were from the outset an integral component of the performer's reality. Like the flower in the wallpaper that Raskolnikov turns to in an effort to escape the meaning of Lizaveta's voided life, the necklace is the blank insignia that is suddenly suffused with all the death and subterfuge in which Judy has been embroiled. We are given time to notice—sharing Scottie's gaze—not only the central blood red stone on the pendant, but three smaller red stones beneath it, evoking tears. Judy, in her confused image perfection as Madeleine, poignantly expresses the hope that Scottie will "muss her" a little. She has perhaps momentarily forgotten that her hair had required a sculpted exactitude for Scottie to succeed in finding his implacable image of her. As she initiates an embrace with the man who already feels betrayed and is again lost to her, she timidly allows herself a declaration of possession: "I do have you now, don't I?"

What does the necklace signify to Scottie, as he appears to reclaim the rational skeptic's ground and thus an unillusioned perspective on the whole chain of prior events? Even before Scottie has his revelation of Elster's plot against him, the height of rapture he attained in making Madeleine alive and present once more has precipitously declined. What he has managed to possess, first as vision and then as sexual completion, is the ideal, memory-consecrated image of Madeleine, but the thing itself is obviously not located there. As Scottie sits and waits for Madeleine-Judy to finish dressing for dinner, he projects an air of slightly weary and impatient complacency. The situation he now occupies is earthbound, familiar, ordinary in the disappointing sense. The turbulent excitement and desperation of his wait for the reincarnation of his beloved to appear in the green mist of his hotel room, followed by the exalted tears of beholding, and the fulfillment of his otherworldly longing have attenuated, in passion's aftermath, by the simple prospect of availability: of filling time together as a couple in an unencumbered way.

What Scottie no longer senses between himself and this exact, but demystified, unhaunting semblance of Madeleine is an obstacle. Denis de Rougemont, in his classic study *Love in the Western World*, anatomizes the passion-myth where the beloved's magnification is achieved through the persistence of obstacles, epitomized by the sword placed between the lovers Tristan and Iseult as they lie in bed, which furnishes a symbolic barrier to consummation. For Scottie, the obstacle, and perhaps the source of passion, is—as I have repeatedly argued—the hidden figure of Carlotta, who is at once a formidable rival for Madeleine's enthralled attachment and the key to all that is unknown, all that refuses rational containment. Carlotta, in life, was, according to legend, lonely, pitiful, abandoned, mad, but in death she is all concentrated purpose, one who darkly possesses the one she has chosen, toying with her unto death. The necklace is crucially an object that belonged to Carlotta—as the painting in the gallery attests. The material necklace that Madeleine-Judy brings forth in the hotel room is an imitation of a lost, painted original. For Judy-Madeleine to claim the necklace as her own is, in the logic of the Carlotta bond, an act of spiritual theft. The act of putting it on brings death swirlingly back into play, and powerfully restores the obstacle that Scottie requires.

He feels his love for Madeleine break loose and flee to an impossible distance, leaving a death image and a freshly awakened hatred in its wake. The owner of the necklace knowledge and the accumulated heap of treachery it illuminates now, in effect, dons the necklace himself as he peers at it simultaneously in mirror reflection and memory. Carlotta returns as the necessary missing third in the Scottie-Madeleine relationship, and it is now Scottie, in his vengeful silence and instant determination to stage one final theatre piece at the bell tower, who carries Carlotta inside him. It was Carlotta, after all, who led the false Madeleine (who is now in danger of vanishing completely, a mere trembling figment in Scottie's tortured psyche) to the tower, forced her up the stairs, and enjoined her to leap. Scottie, confident that his power to reason has been fully recovered, believes that another play, enacted under his forceful, unyielding supervision, will "free him from the past" for good. It will also cancel the experience of the overwhelming play he has just witnessed in the hotel room, with Judy's secret authorship. He had unreservedly believed that she had walked toward him in the eerie green light. He was once again absolutely, abjectly vulnerable to Madeleine's presence and her offer to be "his." She had managed, by a trick of light and appearance, to replenish for a brief interval his depleted self. The necklace knowledge Scottie absorbs in a rush takes him outside of love and makes him feel he has gained in its place a ghastly purchase on death-dealing manipulation. The rational playwright in him will bring the whole pernicious scheme to light and, in so doing, end its hold over him. (In a sense, he is reenacting the mock-portrait scene with Midge at an intensified pitch, this time affixing the blame to the impersonator Judy for failing to resemble a Carlotta whose image she has betrayed.)

We observe then a culminating double-sided mission in Scottie. One side involves the objective servant of the truth—the revived, clear-sighted detective—who will lead Judy around the scene of the crime, demystifying the artifice of the former, elaborate plot against him, and replacing it with a fiercely righteous redistribution of blame. This reversal will exonerate Scottie of all wrongdoing, and set him beyond the reach of vertigo. The fall of the policeman, which strangely transformed into the equally ungovernable experience of falling in love, will now give way to a sense of "rootedness" on high—a holding one's ground in detachment. With exorcism will come a return to earthly solidity. Notice how the return to the bell tower stage parallels and mimics Scottie's earlier theatrical foray with Madeleine in the livery stable, but at a hysterical pitch. In both instances the goal is demystification, the movement away from the elements of entrapping illusion. As I noted earlier, Scottie as director in the livery stable is torn between seeking an explanation and thus a cure, or preserving Madeleine's possession by Carlotta, which somehow amplifies his own possession. He is equally driven toward the healing release of love and a fated destruction.

Madeleine's spell, as she takes the stage, proved stronger than his urge to reduce the atmosphere to something familiar, commonplace, and, in its more fanciful details, harmless. In Scottie's return trip, he envisions the tower as a place where the actress will unmask and confess. The setting's prior formidableness and unapproachability in his frozen memory will at last be reduced to see-through stagecraft. The veil of captivating artifice will be systematically shredded. In spite of Scottie's determination to stage a confession scene within the tower where Judy will have no choice but to divulge her heartless masquerade and her hidden collaboration with a rival director, he largely usurps the role of speaker (the one who confesses), and in his hallucinatory bewilderment alternates between calling the ashamed, fearful figure before him "Judy" and "Madeleine." He mourns what he takes to be the previous intensity of his love ("Madeleine, I loved you so") and seems chiefly appalled not by the murder that has been committed, with the paralyzed detective as "fall guy," but at Elster's superior skill as director-manipulator: "He made you over just like I made you over. Only better." Scottie conceives of a stage that will overcome, in its illusion-eviscerating light, the stage that Elster designed and inhabited before him. What was at stake in the first production was Scottie's unquestioning, stricken spectator belief, so strong as to hollow him out, reducing him to the state of a walking dead man. The cure Scottie sought by rehearsing and remaking Judy in Madeleine's image resulted in another fit of helpless belief, which rekindled his passion, with the seeming supplementary benefit of removing the ghost, of washing death away.

The other side of Scottie's mission is to make the previously meretricious stage of mad Carlotta's punishment into a genuine stage, where her truth is reborn and her death drive is shown to be real. The earlier haunting is exposed as a mere "game," though one steeped in cruelty, whereas the haunting of Scottie as he drags Judy-Madeleine up the stairs and makes her see the ghost of Carlotta in his mind's eye, like the governess in Henry James's *The Turn of the Screw* demanding that the child Miles acknowledge her ghost, will yield the corpse that Carlotta previously demanded. A pure sacrifice—that will bring love to its appointed, sacred end.

Scottie at some level understands completely the facts of Judy's complicity. The Elster play that she enacted (under its author's meticulous guidance) was arranged to bring about the collapse of her besotted dupe. What he believes, and thinks he understands, is that he is now in control of all the elements. By walking Judy through the Elster play that was originally scripted and performed against him—with love as the blinding agent—by proceeding bit by bit through the blocking with his own commentary as a rational redescription of the till now impenetrable tragedy, he will free himself entirely from captivity. ("I have to go back into the past—once more, just once more, for the last time.") Scottie imagines that by remounting the fatal play, with himself as director, he can comprehend his seemingly endless subjection to its logic, and undo its power. He enters physically and emotionally into the dramatic mechanism that had victimized him, feeling each image and action afresh, and by being inside the structure of the staged progression, to seize control of it. The restaging alters the role he formerly played, in anguished ignorance. It is now his character who is armed with knowledge, and the actress, whom he once could not follow up to the bell tower, in this version lags behind him, in fear and trembling.

The action outwardly duplicates the path of the original script, but in spite of Judy being obliged to perform her previous actions in order, she cannot grasp either the full purpose or meaning of the new presentation. Scottie's interpretation of the reenactment unfolds only gradually. The old actions become decisively different given that "Madeleine's" actor's intention and point of view have been suppressed, nearly obliterated. Scottie trusts that his talking cure will conquer the terrors still lingering on this haunted stage, in every daunting, dire particular. Scottie has no heart left for the world, only for the small number of spaces within it that activate his memory of Madeleine—the words they exchanged, their gestures, their physical comportment. For Scottie, the disenchanting of the tower stage, the blotting out of its power to recur as memory, dream, and fantasy and swallow him up, will (he hopes) bring the reality of the world back to him, and open up the present as something other than the past revivified. If Scottie can see things clearly on a stage lit by reason, and if "Madeleine" accompanies him through each phase of the theatrical repetition, confirming his sense of what is there, his vertigo fixation will cease.

As Scottie gets closer to the tower summit and feels his control over his physical environment increase, his emotional frenzy and irrationality are simultaneously on the rise. The theatre he establishes here grants him lucidity and hysteria at once, braided together. Scottie "makes it" to the tower belfry, with Judy literally dragged in his wake, and gains assurance that his head is now clear to accomplish the work that will free him. In fact, he is no wiser than before, though he surveys the setting with hyperrational attentiveness to all the actions from the Elster play that preceded the one he is staging now. He wants Judy to acknowledge that she sees what he sees, and not only to corroborate but to identify with his vision. He tearfully addresses Elster's "apt pupil" upon the stage the two conspirators once shared, referring to the incriminating necklace that was the giveaway—the sparkling key to all duplicity. Scottie plaintively utters the word "souvenir," which has associations not only with the murder plot, but with the host of obsessive of details (including Judy's present black dress and hair arrangement) that his memory has faithfully kept—indeed, hoarded.

The hardest fact for him both to confront and let go of is that the Madeleine who stands before him—a perfect replica of his lost love—cannot play "Madeleine" again in any fashion that will elicit belief. The reason that she can't is that the figure on which a veritable world of feeling has been created never truly existed at all. It is "too late" for anything further than the disintegration of the entire edifice and history of his love. There is a crushing difference between the anguish of "no more" and that of "never was." Scottie is staging a funeral in this mission tower, and in his brain. The memory that is turning into a blank memory is agonizingly accused—in the bewildering form of Judy—of not-being and never-being. It is too late in this theatre to believe that anything that was once beheld, embraced, cherished, and preserved in memory during Scottie and Madeleine's mystifying, brief time together was real—real enough to hold on to. The blankness Scottie hysterically experiences in the immediate aftermath of his vertigo "cure" is akin to the blankness of his prior nervous breakdown. He is no longer falling, as in his old recurring nightmare, but emptiness nevertheless engulfs him.

His mad state is one of abandonment by all protectors and illusions of protection. This affliction approximates Carlotta Valdes's broken withdrawal in life after being deserted and stripped bare. Like her, Scottie's condition demands some propitiation. The only play that Scottie, in his berserk strandedness, can conjure up is the drama that belonged to Carlotta: a scenario resulting in Madeleine's entranced run up the tower stairs, with the inevitable plunge downward immediately after. Scottie does not fully grasp the script he has brought Madeleine to re-create

Figure 7.3. Scottie stares down an ever swirling, ever deepening loss in *Vertigo*.

before finally separating from her. But the logic of the play requires her death, so that loss can be reconnected to love. By completing the plot of Carlotta's ghostly claim on her, and dying a second time, Madeleine makes that mystery real again, along with the "loved one" herself, who in this staging is no longer Judy. (The real nun who appears, at a climactic moment, in the tower is wholly absorbed into the theatre space as Carlotta's stand-in.) The actor-director stands at the edge of the tower, arms extended and bent as in his nightmare, and stares down at the figure who can be his again, for real, in the endless cycle of letting go and losing.

8

Stage Deaths in Film

The *Hamlet* Factor

MANY FILM NARRATIVES INCLUDE death scenes enacted in a theatre setting. The character deaths are, in most instances, real, but their occurrence on a formal stage invariably introduces an element (or reminder) of illusion to the fact of termination. Theatre as a realm of make-believe, subterfuge, fakery, and exemption from the full weight of loss is emphasized, at least for a brief interval, so as to create a tension between a character's actual end and the machinery of drama, which calls the authenticity and irreversibility of death into question. Our casual assumptions about stage death as something excessive, artfully contrived, and instantly decipherable are played upon in order to reinforce the distinction between theatre as one sort of reality (illusion-based representation) and film as another (more linked to "the way things are," the unembellished, quotidian truth). A character dying on a stage is less bound to his untransmutable life circumstances than a character dying, say, on a battlefield, a street, at home, on a deserted beach, or in a noir hotel room.

Every death in a fictional film narrative is, obviously, a staged death, and sometimes the evidence of staging is extremely conspicuous. Nevertheless, directors customarily take great pains to remove the evidence of framed performance if they hope to elicit belief and an emotional response from a character's final moments of life. The body and voice in extremis must be cleansed of importunate artifice. The actor must not appear too mindful or fully in control of what they reveal. In contrast, a character who is "caught" onstage for his or her passage to "the other side" cannot easily escape the dilemma of overt, heightened showing. The tone for such convergences of death and theatrical display is frequently ironic, or preoccupied with the culpable consequences of masquerade. The departure from life can be diminished or mocked by the character's aura of feigning—as though a core fraudulence is exposed by a figure being bound to the stage when his consciousness and gestures "give out."

And, yet, the false theatrical aspect of these death scenes readily lends itself to swift, startling reversal. When this turnabout is accomplished, the preliminary appeal to stage artifice does not prevail unchallenged. The spectator's initial sense of a sharp reduction of death's usual grim force is followed by a recuperation of mystery. Death's double-sidedness (the theatrical pretense of dying turned real) intensifies the collision of the fantasy of life persisting with the fact of an irrevocable end. Our conviction of death's binding "thereness" is enhanced by the temporary permission to disbelieve what we are witnessing. The acknowledgment of a performer's ability to make light of the death throes, to mimic the behavioral excess or spectacle of coming to an end gives the claims and constraints of illusion their due. We are allowed to penetrate the stage illusion to which we initially believe ourselves superior, because we know what theatricality consists of, and can bring it into alignment with everything we understand about pretending. But the game of dying has yielded a corpse nonetheless, and the camera's insistence on the presence of death, in spite of all the tricks, exaggeration, and wit of stage convention, burns through the insulation that apparent make-believe has provided. We make our death faces, and play at agony and collapse, but nullity enters in just the same. Playacting our destruction stands in for all the varieties of human assurance—our sense of safety, control, the abundant continuities of consciousness and experience. Just behind these protective layers, as near as breathing is to not breathing, is the truth of mortality, and the limitless darkness of our end. A man finds a stage to perish on, and the stage briefly argues against the finality of his egregious gyrations. Suppose then that the freedom to repeat or repeal the action of pretend dying is snatched away, and the theatrical presence (a stage corpse) turns persuasively into pure absence. The film image is, of course, always in close contact with death and implacable completion. (What was photographed live is now done and fled.) Film brings its own proximity to frozenness—the still, silent frame—to bear on the "theatrical remains" of a stage corpse. The machinery of film contrasts its own death-dealing and resurrecting powers with theatrical simulation, and pulls what has appeared theatrical into film's separate territory, where every dimension of "the real" that theatre excludes can gain admittance. The line between stage illusion and film illusion is conceived in such a way that film illusion becomes allied with the viewer's sense of reality in order to counteract and transcend stage fantasy. Film allows us to flirt with theatrical artifice, extravagance, and confident repeatability before turning us, with startling abruptness, to an image of death that feels absolute and irreversible. Theatre's artful remedies for stage disasters freeze on contact with an action violently severed from dramatic motion.

In this chapter I will be examining three films—Herbert Brenon's *Laugh, Clown, Laugh* (1928), Ernst Lubitsch's *To Be or Not to Be* (1942), and Alfred Hitchcock's *Stage Fright* (1950)—in which stage deaths of a significant character are prominently featured. All three films make ample use of the stage as an alternative world. The viewer's growing sense of what theatre means as a richly textured escape route from imprisonment in a severely compromised, painful realm outside its precincts is crucial to the way in which death ultimately bores into the theatrical revels. In death's presence and aftermath the consequences of masquerade are tested, then stage life resumes on different terms. The result in each narrative will be to give sharper relief to what Henry James has termed "mysteries abysmal," and to make the spectacle of film death more potent precisely because of its profound entanglement with theatrical play.

Before beginning my commentary on the three films, I shall make my conception of stage death more layered and challenging by considering the famous swift succession of deaths that concludes Shakespeare's *Hamlet*. It so happens that each of the films I have chosen is in steady dialogue with this play, and Shakespeare's characters (their sense of themselves and their impasses) are intricately referenced and mirrored, sometimes overtly (as in the Lubitsch comedy) and more often obliquely. The death scenes on the *Hamlet* stage offer a startlingly varied perspective on theatre's ways of conceiving and representing the final curtain. To think about the closing stage picture of the tragedy, which includes four corpses of major characters, in addition to Hamlet's chief mourner, Horatio, and the newly arrived Fortinbras, flanked by a retinue of soldiers and attendants, one might initially seize upon the parodic potential in this heavy burden and "sight dismal" of Death's feast (5.2.352). Four figures—victims of an elaborate, miscarried feat of plotting—lie motionless, in close tableau proximity. This chaotic heap might strike the reluctant theatregoer as disproportionate. The felt overload of carnage, so briskly dramatized, is arguably at odds with the play's more exalted aspirations as a comprehensive probe of Hamlet's consciousness. Harold Bloom has wittily imagined Hamlet complaining to Shakespeare about imprisoning him in a rickety revenge melodrama that was unworthy of him. Yet I intend to praise the final scene's parade of retribution and recognitions as a miraculously effective theatrical resolution.

If we try to recall how the setup of the duel and the subsequent sequence of character discoveries and actions operate, from a vantage point outside the spectator's actual experience of it, we would be likely to discern something meretricious and mechanical in the precipitous settling of accounts. A play whose central character problem involves cryptic delay suddenly lunges into the imperatives of heroic demonstration. Hamlet arrives at a grace-illuminated clearing in his mind where "The readiness is all . . . Let be" (5.2.202–203). Harold Bloom characterizes the "unlimited" consciousness that Hamlet exhibits throughout the tragedy as the possession of a "god in ruins," but one who transforms, following his reckless fifth act return to the Elsinore court, into an "angel of destruction" (96). This "god in ruins" that Hamlet so movingly resembles is Prometheus. He is, in effect, chained to the rock of Elsinore, his inner life permanently ablaze with a "heat and light" comparable to the gift of fire Prometheus stole from his fellow gods. At the center of all his valiant, astonishing, and obsessive thought—ever-striving for an impossible to secure balance and order—is an incurable wound. An eagle relentlessly pecks and tears at Hamlet's ravaged memory of his once familiar, now alien world. Crimes unexpiated, the onerous commands of a forbidding, unknowable paternal ghost, and a mother who herself seems ghostly and unreachable in her betrayals remove Hamlet further and further from genuine contact with others. The only thing that quickens him in his rock captivity is additional jabs of isolating pain. All the majestic, confounding cross-currents of his unlimited consciousness make and unmake Hamlet's self by turns. The very air into which Hamlet casts his words seems on fire, and never has a dramatic character seemed more alone, even (and perhaps especially) in the company of others.

Self-transcendence and self-acceptance are equally impossible. In the words of Aeschylus's Prometheus: "Painful thoughts devour my heart as I behold myself maltreated in this way. And yet who else but I . . . assigned their prerogatives to these upstart gods?" (437–440). Hamlet cannot ever silence himself, in spite of all the prudent reasons for doing so, and like Prometheus, his tormented utterances expose every danger present in the "light of consciousness" gift. Thinking is an everlasting atonement for his benign, but guilty, theft of fire. Introspection, however capable of rising to the utmost height of expressiveness, is tinged continually by the proximity of rot and nothingness. The ceaseless biting of the eagle's beak punishes without quite completing the work of annihilation.

Until act 5, Hamlet finds no persuasive refuge or safety. He is immersed in theatricality throughout the play, but the various powers and stratagems of stage feigning and illusion do not provide a place where he has license to be free. A visiting troupe of players may find freedom in their ability to inhabit fictional characters' emotions, but not Hamlet. ("What's Hecuba to him, or he to Hecuba, that he should weep for her?") Hamlet's madness may partake of theatrical dissembling, but he is caught up in it in a manner that summons the Furies, deprives him still further of equilibrium and control, and exacerbates an already thorough estrangement.

What then is the effect of the arrival of multiple violent deaths on the *Hamlet* stage, as the play draws to a close? The deaths display extraordinary lucidity in their fitting, carefully interlocked succession. For all the haste of the exterminations, the clarifying power of these culminating character actions and disclosures is immense, and the dramatic "gathering in" of retributive thrust-and-counterthrust does not feel rushed. The duel between Hamlet and Laertes replaces the whirlpool of incessant self-scrutiny with a breathtaking public exhibition of courage, physical prowess, and readiness. However complex the reasoning leading up to the duel, however deranged the fight at Ophelia's grave that prompted the duel challenge, when the swordplay commences the stage atmosphere seems charged with a different quality of light and a composed momentum. The spectator is privy to all the scheming precautions taken at Claudius's behest to ensure Laertes's victory. Not only has Laertes's fencing foil's tip been poisoned, but a goblet of wine containing still further poison has been prepared for Hamlet in the event that the fencing plan miscarries. Hamlet has requested Laertes's pardon for his "mad acts" in advance of the duel, and Laertes's personal feelings are satisfied, though he still opts for the judgment of a rigged trial of honor. These moves toward reconciliation seem to expand the outward freedom of the two duelists, though the spectator is simultaneously mindful of the snares and obstructions surrounding them. Claudius's distrust of an "open," undevious stage in many respects mirrors Hamlet's earlier staging of the Mousetrap, in which an incriminating dumb show cunningly usurps the place of an unthreatening entertainment. Instead of the Mousetrap's intent to rip open the King's internal defenses, the poison of the duel is meant to replace honor's claims with an underhanded death "by scratching." It is a mouse bite's route to extermination, in which the tiniest skin puncture will yield disproportionately total ruin of the noble prince. The projected killing echoes as well Hamlet's heedless manner of stabbing Polonius through the arras in act 3, scene 4. Death will be achieved again through the crude annulment of ceremony, stature, and agreed upon ritual. The faint brush with poison will instantly undo all that Hamlet accomplishes by fair means on the stage proving ground. And yet Claudius taking extra measures to guarantee his safety unwittingly lays the groundwork for his shameful and spectacular defeat. The stealth that has been his accustomed method of protecting himself and concealing enormities will double back on him. All that is craven and emptily self-serving in Claudius will spill out into the open, for public witnessing.

I earlier referred to the sequence of stage deaths in *Hamlet*'s concluding scene as arrestingly lucid. It feels as though everything enclosed in the play is striving to reach the plane of outward representation. The temporal gaps between the four deaths are small, but there is sufficient dramatic breathing room in these intervals for the last acts, gestures, blindnesses, and realizations to achieve a powerful crystallization. Claudius has time to be dismayed that Gertrude has unwittingly drunk from the fatal goblet, but after futilely attempting to warn her, he also has time to attempt yet again to conceal his wretched plot ("She swoons to see them bleed"), to reveal no sense of grief at the loss of her, and to turn his thoughts compulsively to his own welfare ("O, yet defend me, friends"), as he too is stabbed by the rapier tip he has poisoned (5.2.293, 309). Following hard upon this mortal wound, excess crowns his dying, as Hamlet forces him to drink (as if from a bridal cup) the same liquid that has consumed his wife.

So many motives that have hitherto remained agonizingly hidden from Hamlet's sight and whose varied, murky ramifications Hamlet has inwardly debated at fever pitch now seem to be attaining unmistakable shape and plain statement for the first time. Queen Gertrude, ensphered in blind trust, raises a toast to her son and then perishes of a poison linked to that poured in King Hamlet's ear. Until this seizure, her eyes and ears have been ceded to Claudius, but she grasps in her final utterance that she has been poisoned, and through the thrust of a glance, by whom. Gertrude emerges at last from a mental darkness that has been impenetrable since her hasty remarriage. She addresses her lament about being poisoned to her son, countering Claudius's claim that she "swoons" at the sight of blood, and through the simple movement of her concluding gaze, discovers the identity of her executioner.

Hamlet's death in the duel is anticipated and known by the spectator, but not by him. It is a rare instance of our being permitted to think and see beyond his powers. Claudius's abortive prayer is the most salient prior example. Hamlet has continually demonstrated, dauntingly, that no thread of suspicion is too fine for him to grasp. He divines all that is cankered and miasmic in his outer world, yet he is also capable of majestic inner leaps to surviving shreds of beauty and imaginative creation. Hamlet complains often that he cannot attain certainty or a stabilizing clear-mindedness, but he persuades the spectator that he is in fact utterly at home in doubt, and that he resists the comforts of clinching assertion. He acquires a desirable and surprising expansiveness of mood and prowess once he commences swordplay. Perhaps because taking revenge on Laertes means nothing to him, he is free to pursue victory in a duel single-mindedly. After all, the duel seemingly does not demand death as its outcome. This theatrical public display of an acquired skill intensifies his hold on life. He acquiesces to the rules of the contest, but of course the rules have secretly been abrogated, and the sham that replaces them dispenses with order and meaning.

Our involvement in the duel would be less complete if it were not so ambiguous a clash. It is strange and heartening to watch Hamlet function so capably in an arena where his usual promptings of doubt about the forces conspiring against him have been silenced. No bewitching, conflicted metaphysical claims arise to stymie him, or provide a competing focus. The outer dark (a rigged competition) displaces Hamlet's customary, specter-haunted inner dark, but within that outer dark the spectator encounters, with thrilling definiteness, Hamlet released into a luminous sphere of enactment. In the course of the duel, the opponents' foils are accidentally exchanged (*Hamlet* is a play in which messages, deaths, skulls, and theatre performances are propitiously and unpropitiously substituted). Timed with this exchange is a sudden restoration of clarity to Laertes's mind and heart, and the simultaneous dissolving of his burden of hatred. He asks "noble Hamlet" for a further "exchange of forgiveness" before death gathers him in (5.2.314). He casts no blame in his passing, either for his own destruction or that of his father, Polonius. The lifting of acrimony seems to confer absolution on Hamlet's spirit, so long bent on raging and grieving. I should also mention how, in preparation for this unknotting of malignity, having to do with accursed misunderstandings in Hamlet's dealings with Laertes, Ophelia, and Polonius, the duel's commencement shows Hamlet in an ebullient mood. This vivacity is notably different from the overwound playacting of Hamlet's theatrical madness, which swung back and forth between feigning and real possession. An easeful blitheness is somehow accessible to him now, removed from previous false accommodations. The ritual of combat in a firmly bounded arena seems to restore to Hamlet a forgotten affection for codes, boundaries, and propriety.

Many commentators on *Hamlet* find persisting evidence of a suicidal urge in Hamlet's final wager, and the fated mischief with the poisoned foils. I see rather that death finds its opening with Hamlet when he at last surrenders his preoccupation with it. Hamlet is no longer terrifying to those around him in his usual way. G. Wilson Knight has characterized his "mysterious force [of causing others to feel tormented by his mere presence in their midst] which derives largely from his having seen through them all" ("An Essay on Hamlet," 41). Until his mother's cry of having been poisoned and Laertes's revelation, right on its heels, that Hamlet and he are equally "envenomed," doomed by Claudius's plot, Hamlet seems for once to be in a frame of mind that is unconcerned with seeing through anything. His liberty is due in a way to an inexplicable retrieval of innocence. He carries so little of his past deeds, past obsessions, and past striving to know into the dueling arena. And once he is fatally wounded, he is granted no more time to recover his presence of mind and tell what he understands about the play's final sequence of events. He is, of course, conscious that his time is spent, extinguished, and that only Horatio remains clear from the world known to him, and preserves any sense of who he is. When Horatio rashly offers to do away with himself, in a sacrificial gesture of kinship, by drinking the poisoned wine, Hamlet opposes the impulse. He is anxious to have his story carried forward and told by someone who is not a stranger. This is not quite the same thing, of course, as active concern for his friend's well-being.

From the play's outset, Horatio lives in a state of purity set apart from malignant machinations. No awareness of rot or iniquity can corrode his integrity. His friendship with Hamlet necessitates no sordid compromises or devious, crippling entanglements. At play's end, as he attends to Hamlet's concluding words, he is a human embodiment of the schemeless place that Elsinore has now become. The version of Hamlet's story that he will be capable of imparting to others is not Shakespeare's play. It will instead be a tale of moral cleansing and victory attained by rational means. For Horatio, Hamlet achieves something like perfect transparency in his dying, and the "heart that cracks" is unambiguously noble. "The rest is silence," Hamlet says with his last breath (5.2.343), and the implication is that whatever part of the story lies beyond generous Horatio's imaginative reach and capacity for moral interrogation will vanish with Hamlet into that silence.

Yet Shakespeare gives no obvious sign of treating Horatio's reception of Hamlet's story and his requests ironically. Horatio is a fit container and spokesman for the meaning of Hamlet's end and the surrounding death spectacle if the tragedy is to secure balance in its conclusion. Hamlet predicts that Fortinbras will be elected his successor, and when Fortinbras, moments later, enters with his retinue, there is a sober rush toward "fulfilled" aims and reclaimed order. Fortinbras's arrival is hardly a cause for spectator rejoicing, or even of emotional interest. The instructions he delivers feel continuous with Horatio's spoken pledge to inform the "Unknowing world / How these things came about" (5.2.387–388). Norms are reestablished and what can be clarified is valued for its swift dispersal of elements vast, tendentious, and mystifying. Call these the remnants of Hamlet himself.

The narrow light rendered dramatically admissible by Fortinbras's timely but also "too late for saving" intervention is in striking contrast to the fiery illuminations of Hamlet's consciousness "unlimited" that came before him. Hamlet's endless outpourings and wrestling with tormented thought offered no containment or harmonious arrangement. In the prince's absence, actions and their interpretation can attain sensible proportions once more. The loss of Hamlet seems at once massive and something that spectators may find relief in. We mourn but do not necessarily wish that the outcome could be reversed. Hamlet is finally too much to wish back into being, and the heaped corpses in his vicinity speak in a violent whisper of the excess that at all times propelled and engulfed him. Nonetheless, it is strange to witness alien forces, to which we have no attachment, almost entirely displace the social world with which we have been concerned, and to sanction—however mechanically—these forces' decisions for the survival of the state. Fortinbras so efficiently declares procedures that will work in the interests of whatever "common good" can still be envisioned. Horatio does not recoil from this invasion and supplanting. He can and will be assimilated. Yet his temporarily bereft aloneness, visibly pitted against the solidarity of the new conquerors, certainly revives our memory of the isolation of Hamlet throughout his long ordeal. He was a figure singled out in so many plaguing respects for unbreakable apartness.

The first film death on stage that I will examine—Tito the clown's in Herbert Brenon's *Laugh, Clown, Laugh* (1928)—is, in many respects, deliberately reminiscent of Hamlet's. Tito/Flik (Lon Chaney) expires in the arms of his long-term stage partner, Simon (Bernard Siegel), after failing to complete, in a maddened-by-grief state, a dangerous theatrical stunt that under normal circumstances he could perform without difficulty. Tito/Flik, clad in full clown regalia and with his face a painted mask, is cradled by Simon, his head resting in his lap, while he delivers a last, affecting speech. Simon obviously functions here as a Horatio figure, an honorable, wholly sympathetic friend who is only dimly attuned to Tito's emotional torment and to the complexity of his character and predicament. Simon's benediction, when Tito fades away, is presented in a tableau meant to echo Horatio's epitaph for Hamlet: "Now cracks a noble heart. Good night, sweet prince; / And flights of angels sing thee to thy rest" (5.2.367–368). The death scene takes place on a large, mostly bare proscenium stage. We see curtains and the backstage area plainly. There are no remnants of a stage set. In addition to Simon, six young children, who do not understand the gravity of what is transpiring, are also present as witnesses. They have snuck into the theatre hoping to catch a glimpse of the beloved, famous clown rehearsing his routine.

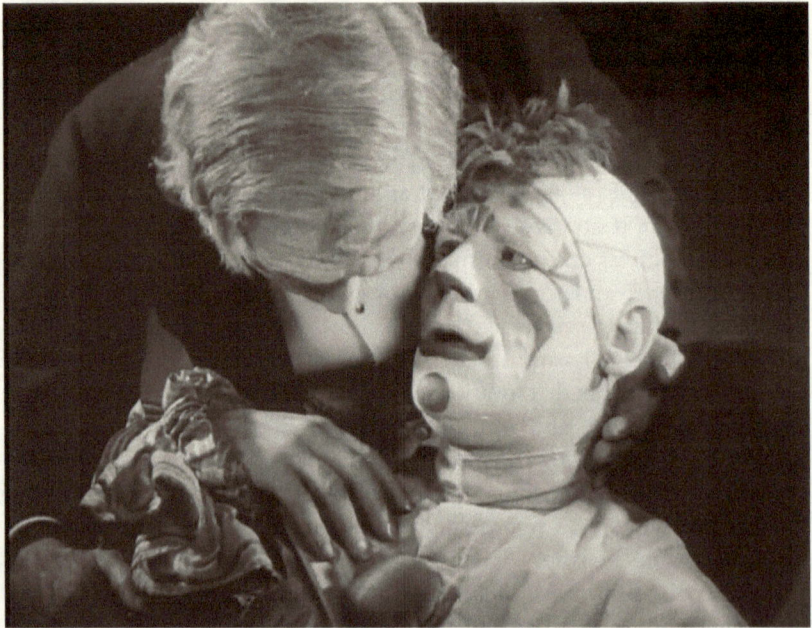

Figure 8.1. Simon (Bernard Siegel) bestows a final good night upon Tito in *Laugh, Clown, Laugh*.

I shall elucidate the separate contributions of the stage milieu and the film reality that borders it in providing the sense of Tito's ending. A double space is created for our contemplation of the clown's death, in which we oscillate between a cinematic and theatrical mode of beholding. The tension among the many elements of the *Laugh, Clown, Laugh* finale—the repetition of the clown's death-defying act, the artifice of the rehearsal, Tito's delusion about what is actually happening in his performance, the confused children's witnessing, Simon's helpless collaboration in his partner's self-destruction, and the enigma of perishing within a formal theatrical scene—yield a complexly layered effect. The children's limited perspective on Tito's death scene is, significantly, the spectator's concluding vantage point for witnessing the event. As they stand in the wings and observe Simon holding the body of the clown on an otherwise bare stage, one of the young boys in the group raises a finger to his lips, and, as if acknowledging the conditions of the silent film medium, advises the others to be quiet. Having figured out that it is Tito/Flik "lying on the floor," he informs his uncertain friends that the clown is "playing that he's dead."

Figure 8.2. A group of curious, captivated children unwittingly watch the swan song of Tito from the wings in *Laugh, Clown, Laugh*.

This seemingly naive declaration paradoxically gets to the heart of the matter. On the one hand, the boy seems to lack the capacity to make grown-up distinctions between playing at death, sleeping, and death itself. He regards himself as a spectator with the sophisticated power to see through illusion, though he is unable to detect, in this instance, the boundary between clever feigning and authentic tragedy. On the other hand, he makes an accurate assessment (however unwittingly) of the nature of the scene that he, and the film spectator, have jointly witnessed. Lon Chaney the actor has indeed, with Tito/Flik as his chosen vessel, been performing a theatrical farewell for the camera. He has, with enormous skill and commitment, been playing at dying and then at being dead. Contemporary viewers possess the additional knowledge that Lon Chaney is an actor long dead. The surviving prints of the film available to us are markedly faded as well as incomplete. Even the duration of the film's last shot has been noticeably "jumped" in the middle, a casualty of lost footage. Thus, Lon Chaney is both performing an end and anticipating the death that claims him not long after this fiction is completed, in 1930. The film's scratch-laden closing shots supply another curtain, partially covering, like streaks of time rain, Chaney's masked, ghostly finish. The stage ambience in this film seems overlaid with extra hauntedness, and is suffused with intimations of mortality.

The mysterious emergence of the six child spectator spies, who believe in the clown's godly theatrical powers, including resurrection, returns us to the narrative's beginning, and the tragic crux of Tito's narrative fate. Tito/Flik's life as an innocent clown, touring the forest and countryside and performing for audiences as simple and unworldly as he is, is interrupted by his discovery of an abandoned female toddler, lying next to the river, with her feet bound by a rope. The various uses of ropes, for tightrope balance, binding, and romantic attachment, will be intricately developed throughout the narrative. Tito/Flik, having decided to adopt the foundling, names her Simonetta, in order to appease his cantankerous partner, Simon, who opposes any additional bonds of family (especially female ones) beyond the already established union of the two clown partners. As Simonetta (Loretta Young) grows older, Tito trains her in his own art of tightrope walking. And tightrope walking becomes his own internal dilemma, as he becomes conscious that he has fallen in love with the girl that he has rescued.

His clown costume becomes increasingly a mask for him, a hiding place, sundered from the spontaneous, performer joy he used to draw upon effortlessly. His paralysis is akin to that of Hamlet, in that he must conceal all that he has previously been in the face of an impossible disorder that infects his world. In Hamlet and Pagliacci tradition, the man whom the antic clown persona conceals is morose and agonized, hemmed in by perplexities that cannot be untangled. Tito/Flik's comic act becomes progressively tinged with hysteria, and ultimately madness. In the conflation of derangement with a comedy that is bursting at its seams, we find further parallels with Hamlet. Familial and romantic love, both for Tito and the stricken prince of Elsinore, can find no unpoisoned channel through which to flow.

Director Brenon brings additional pressure to the internal split besetting his clown protagonist by creating a doppelganger for him in Simonetta's other suitor, the young and wealthy Count Luigi (Nils Asther). Before he falls authentically in love with Simonetta, Luigi is a decadent aristocrat who laughs compulsively at everything, because he feels nothing and believes in nothing. He goes to the same physician that Tito/Flik seeks out in an effort to regain contact with his lost capacity to be inside his life. Luigi's affliction is akin to the deep-rooted sadness that encases Tito/Flik in depression. The two men, both aspiring to win Simonetta's love, form a friendship meant to ease their painful isolation and restore psychic balance. Luigi longs for cathartic tears, and Tito for the release of genuine laughter. Together they create an emotional equivalent of Tito's tightrope act, with melancholy and levity achieving the right delicate equilibrium.

The culminating feat of Tito's act is the "death-defying slide" that ultimately results in the clown's fatal tumble. The "trick" involves Flik ascending a rope ladder to a point adjoining the highest theatre balcony. He then turns himself upside down, and rides a head mount with a grooved wheel attachment down the tightrope leading to the stage, far below him. It is clear that this spectacle is an objective correlative for the once innocent parental love that has somehow "turned upside down" and become an incurable, scorching desire. Simonetta, bound to Tito/Flik by a profound, unshakable devotion, is also in love with Count Luigi. The count's first meeting with her occurs when she is caught on a barbed wire fence that protects his property. The barbed wire is another manifestation of the tightrope, as Simonetta seeks (childishly) to sneak over it and obtain a rose she covets to adorn her hair. When Simonetta returns to Tito/Flik's traveling wagon, it is the sight of Simonetta wearing the rose that unleashes Tito's previously unrecognized passion for her.

In the scene immediately prior to the sequence in the theatre that climaxes with his death, Tito has received an unambiguous assurance from Simonetta that his romantic love for her is reciprocated. She discovers the nature of his attachment to her as she witnesses, unobserved, her "father" communing fervently with the objects associated with her childhood that he has resurrected from an old theatre trunk. The trunk bears an unsettling resemblance to a coffin. Simonetta tells him, with no outward hint of struggle, that she will break her engagement with Count Luigi and marry Tito instead. The offer is not accompanied by any "private" shots that convey Simonetta's conflicted state of mind or the expected signs of regret or resignation. Nonetheless, once Simonetta bids him a tender goodbye and leaves the room, Tito instantly shows his disbelief in the sincerity of her avowal. He is persuaded that Simonetta is motivated by pity, gratitude, and long-standing filial affection rather than passion. We see him lost in thought, pondering his quandary and hers as we cut to a view of him in his stage dressing room, awaiting Simon's arrival. A rehearsal has been scheduled, but Tito has absentmindedly put on his entire Flik clown costume and makeup, as though preparing for an actual performance. Simon, after going through the motions of the pair's first onstage greetings of one another, complains that Tito is worlds removed from the spirit of his character, and that he is too listless to lead an audience to laughter. Simon, whose clown name is Flak, is formally attired in evening clothes, providing the sharpest possible contrast to his partner's clown garb. He leads Tito to a standing mirror to demonstrate more forcefully the distance at which he stands from his persona and the artful truth of humor. Simon performs Flik gestures himself, which he encourages Tito/Flik to imitate.

The cavernous empty stage surrounds the suddenly cinematic mirror, which yields an identity image that transcends—indeed demolishes—the lower level guise of theatre illusion. Flik's attempt to duplicate an amusing physical embrace of himself that Simon suggests turns into a fit of writhing—a near literalization of Hamlet's "mortal coil" being painfully "shuffled off." As he stares at his alien clown double in mirror reflection, Tito reveals to Simon that Simonetta loves him. Simon promptly assumes that his partner's long-standing problems have been magically resolved. But as his mirror confrontation continues, Tito beholds an impasse that becomes an abyss. He stands paralyzed between aching need and impossibility. Tennessee Williams once told his biographer James Grissom that "the most frightening of all places is . . . the intersection of desire and aptitude" (*Follies of God*, 382). Simonetta has unreservedly offered him her heart, but he believes that if he takes her from Luigi, her heart will be consumed by his own poisonous possessiveness. The clown that grimaces at him images back the fact that he can neither move forward nor backward in the order of his emotions.

At this point, the agonized soul hidden beneath the clown's jovial makeup becomes an unbearable dwelling place. In a flash eruption of insanity Tito disappears entirely into the capering clown and the act that defines him completely for his audiences. Tito begins to hallucinate that the empty theatre is presently full to overflowing with expectant, applauding spectators. Director Brenon devises an expressionist heightening of the theatre vehicle in order to deliver the tenor of the clown's deranged consciousness.

It is worth noting that Tito's delirious vision of a crowded theatre matches the cinematic conditions of *Laugh, Clown, Laugh*'s screening. The dramatic stage—empty and isolating—magically acquires the vital hubbub of a 1920s movie palace. It is as though the expressionist device of "going behind" Tito's face into his mad fantasy/memory of crowd endorsement and rapture sanctions a concurrent "going behind" the barren stage setting to release a counter-reality of film. Tito also hears an orchestra playing in the pit, whose instruments (playing themselves in ghostly fashion) and conductor we discover through his perceptual delirium. Tito usurps the conductor's role and perhaps infects the pianist or other accompanying musicians in the theatre presenting *Laugh, Clown, Laugh* with his own wild rhythm and gesticulations. Shortly after imagining the orchestra backing his movements, Tito makes rejuvenating contact with a phantom theatre crowd that materializes in front of him. He catches sight of the ladder and tightrope that are literally present in the auditorium amid all the delusory elements, and they appear to be summoning him to perform the climax of his act. It is worth repeating that the "death-defying slide" is not an action that is played out within the demarcated bounds of the stage. The tightrope stretches out above the audience, and the clown's rapid descent begins near a high spectator balcony and involves risk for the audience members directly beneath the path of the tightrope. Tito's destination is the stage itself once his rapid descent downward, balancing on his head, is completed. If the trick is successful he will arrive onstage safely and then stand upright (feet returned to the stage ground) to take his bow.

In a number of respects, then, stage space, film space, and overlapping audience space have their customary boundaries blurred. The clown's perilous balancing act—once he is flipped over on his head and commences to ride the grooved wheel—echoes the simultaneous balancing act of the powers belonging to complementary but conflicting media.

Theatre and film likewise feel inverted, turned on their heads, with film the sphere of greater illusion. Theatre and film both offer representations of Tito/Flik as he embarks on his fatal downward motion toward death. His upside-downness, which we behold at closer range than that available to any witness but the camera, powerfully conflates the clown's madness, the helplessly muddled, enslaving nature of his passion for Simonetta, and the refuge of life-reviving comedy that Tito/Flik seeks out in his despair. Far below the clown, occupying what appears to be a minuscule spot on stage, stands Simon. From our vantage point at the top of the ladder Tito has climbed, Simon feels as far away from us as the supports ordinarily provided by the entrancing dreams of theatre performance. Flik cries out to Simon to announce the impending finale of both his stage show and the encircling film narrative of *Laugh, Clown, Laugh*.

Simon is a Horatio figure, as I previously noted, an utterly loyal friend, cantankerous in a manner that separates him from Horatio, but utterly ruled by his friend's will and needs. Like Hamlet's devoted companion, Simon can only dimly comprehend the magnitude and dimensions of the ordeal that the tragic protagonist is going through. In this concluding episode, Simon observes the events that transpire, and no doubt fears a bad outcome, but he is denied access to the frenzy, delirium, and contradictions of Tito's "inside life" and thus of the inside life of the film that illuminates the clown's plight. The physical distance separating the tortured clown and his stage-bound partner approximates the emotional distance suddenly revealed between cinematic and theatrical surfaces. When Flik takes his last plunge and loses contact with the tightrope, the fatal fall occurs before he reaches the stage. His form is splayed out on what we might designate the boundary line between audience space and the proscenium stage. Simon and a night watchman carry the broken body of the clown back to the stage, and once he has been placed there Tito acquires the actor's dispensation to die a noble and composed theatrical death. The split in him has somehow been healed by his collapse and by the certainty of his fast-approaching end.

As with *Hamlet*, the theatrical atmosphere has turned restorative and benevolent. Lucidity prevails in a space so recently overrun with madness and incessant heartache. As Simon holds him and leans close to listen, the clown's grinning mask, in a subtle supernatural conversion, seems to merge with the face of the sufferer hidden beneath it. The painted eyes and smile are no longer a barrier to full seeing. Tito reflects with bewilderment on his inability to complete a "trick" that had always been easy and natural for him before. He graciously blesses the union of Count Luigi and Simonetta, and tells Simon to remind Luigi to "be good to her," thus achieving in his own mind a meld between his original parental role and that of the coveted part of lover—husband. He begins his speech lamenting the fact that he is an old man, with no right to spoil Simonetta's youth with his tears. As the speech proceeds, however, the burden of years lifts, and his face becomes imbued not only with a spiritual light but with an attendant lightness, as though the clown's youthful, buoyant temperament were, flickeringly, returned to him. His closing pronouncement is "The comedy is ended," and as he beckons Simon with outstretched finger to draw even nearer to him, he points to his painted smile to indicate that it has absorbed and surmounted melancholy. His statement about life's comedy is cleansed of bitterness. The clown mask is sufficient to face death's swift approach with no diminishment of human force or stature. The artificial smile conveys not unresolved inner strife, but an unartificial acceptance. Tito touchingly affirms a regained unity with his persona—the prodigious identity as entertainer that the audience recognizes and believes in.

The close-up intimacy of Chaney's subtle shifts of expression (a combination of willed giving and a "giving off" of an atmosphere that is beyond his control) fuses theatricality with a dimension of privacy, hiddenness, and grace. The camera and the privileged spectator are attuned to this death in a fuller sense than Simon-Horatio. The stage frame allows for gestural extravagance and a self-conscious summing up, but the camera probes Chaney's visage for deeper secrets and a mortal ebbing away that leaves theatre behind in the very act of coalescing with it. As death lays hold of him, Tito/Flik loses his power to assert and accept. His face presses inward against his partner's coat, and he kisses his hand in farewell. For all we know, the hand may have transformed for Tito into Simonetta's face, or the gathering point for all earthly love.

The shot that returns us to the knot of child spectators is taken from behind them, and the camera briefly advances as they press forward, acknowledging both their desire to see more and to solve the riddle of what they have just witnessed. The boy who mirrors Tito/Flik's employment of a single upraised finger brings it to his lips, urging the silence of this silent film scene to become even more pronounced. His conviction that Tito/Flik is "playing that he's dead" recognizes the stage setting and the protection that it customarily affords from real calamity. He stands at a certain distance (a stage distance) from the event that the camera has delved into in a different manner. The boy's perception and declaration confuses sleep, pretending, and death, and all of these inform our last glimpse of immobile Tito/Flik, viewed from the privileged wings of cinema, rather than the seats reserved for theatre spectators. Hamlet dies this time as a Fortinbras "army" of children advance to recast the stage in their own likeness, with their own innocent, merciful vision. It is an innocence as pure as the bond that first led Tito to rescue the toddler Simonetta from abandonment, and drew her in turn to trust in him, with wonder and laughter, as he showed her his performer's tricks.

Ernst Lubitsch's 1942 comedy, *To Be or Not to Be*, about a Polish theatrical troupe resisting the more deadly theatre of Nazi occupation, makes an obvious allusion to *Hamlet* in its title. One of the film's major recurring gags, coinciding with the only segment of *Hamlet* that we are shown being performed, commences (each time) with Joseph Tura (Jack Benny) solemnly strolling onstage in a fussily ornate Hamlet costume, preparing himself to deliver the "To be or not to be" soliloquy. As he intones, after a protracted dramatic pause, the soliloquy's opening line, a young, uniformed air force lieutenant (Robert Stack)—following instructions given to him by Tura's actor wife, Maria (Carole Lombard)—rises from his seat in the audience and, excusing himself, crosses conspicuously in front of a row of spectators, then exits the theatre. The interruption is immediately noticed by Tura on each recurrence. His concentration broken, a visible rift appears between a vain actor and a role whose demands vastly exceed his skills. The fragmentary use of the soliloquy transpires on a divided space. The stage action and the audience—who belong to the film's implied real world—are given equal prominence and emphasis. The man who interrupts the speech, Lieutenant Sobinsky, is, of course, involved in theatrical behavior himself. He is a plant in the audience, though Tura is unaware of the fact, and "To be or not to be" is the cue line for his scene-stealing departure. The lieutenant's unexpected movement down the row of seats sabotages the onstage illusion of the melancholy Dane "alone with his thoughts," and, intriguingly, allows the reality of Tura's consternation to displace and scuttle an unpersuasive depiction of character agony. Joseph Tura's fear of acting failure is unmistakably authentic, and the truth of that response emerges for us through the cracks, as it were, in the Shakespearean stage picture.

The title, *To Be or Not to Be*, proves to be almost inexhaustibly layered in the Lubitsch film. It links the most frequently invoked line in Shakespeare to a narrative that is never far from wild buffoonery and an unnerving callousness. Defeated Poland is struggling "to be" more than a fictional entity in the face of conquest and endless tragedies, while the "not to be" of Nazism refuses Poland's identity claims and tears them to tatters. But Lubitsch persistently questions whether any aspect of this ongoing catastrophe is beyond the reach of theatre, and more audaciously, comic theatre. The foundational phrase "To be," in its basic alignment with life energy, suggests, when Tura delivers it, how stage performance can approach tragedy through the wrong door ("I, Joseph Tura, am a ham actor tackling Hamlet") and in the process confound the linkage between "being" and tragic perception—that is, by making tragedy's most disquieting recognitions and effects only available in comic guises. Death forces invading life are opposed in Lubitsch's film by vainglorious ineptitude and makeshift improvisation. The improvisation is never polished, always rough and slipshod, and ready to expose its flimsiness. Nazism is treated by Lubitsch as a mode of performance belief undone by another performance style that is unbeholden to it. This counterperformance repeatedly breaks loose from order and rigid forms. "Being" in the atmosphere of Nazism is almost entirely fear-based. The Nazi stage world relies on utterly mechanized theatrical behavior, wholly inhospitable to spontaneity, deviations from assigned text, or expressions of weakness and doubt concerning the general masquerade.

Writing about what Hamlet's own sense of what "to be" encompasses, G. Wilson Knight, in his essay "Hamlet Reconsidered," suggests that the goal is "not merely to live, to act, to exist, but really to be; to be, as an integrated and whole person . . . a lived poetry blending consciousness and unconsciousness like Keats' 'might half slumbering on its own right arm' . . . Hamlet defines his major problem and proceeds, from a height or depth [To be or not to be], half enjoying in a dreamlike confusion the state he aspires to, to survey those different approaches through time and eternity that are open to him" (*Wheel of Fire*, 308–309). Knight goes on to remind us that Hamlet does not succeed in finding his way, since the state "devoutly to be wished" is an "impossible integration" (309). Hamlet's antic madness—half-feigned, half-real—is the strategy of one who has become, unwittingly, a death force himself, hemmed in on all sides by theatricality. Lubitsch rethinks Hamlet's nonsuccess, his failure to integrate. If we think of the film as an adaptation of the soliloquy and its impasses, the characters in the theatre troupe are all colored by the enjoyable "dreamlike confusion" that Knight describes. The approaches open to them, like Hamlet's twists and turns of thought, are marked by continuous interruptions, the inability to sustain any mood or bring any speculative thrust to conclusion. Their best chance at salvation is to preserve their aptitude for disorganized flexibility.

Like Hamlet, the actors in *To Be or Not to Be* feel trapped in a regime system beyond their competence to destroy or fully expose. They must become adepts at mirroring the Nazi style of theatre (a major weakness of the Nazi occupiers is that they cannot see their own complete dependence on theatrical forms). But the Polish actors must not attain too much expertise, which would reduce the qualities distinguishing them from their system-enslaved foes. They must stay as lost as Hamlet himself, but wandering in the lower echelons of comedy—farce, burlesque—which becomes their most secure contact with "being," and the theatre equivalent of Hamlet's mad feigning. Comedy offers them a fragile haven from death-consciousness and death, of a sort that Hamlet's tragic elevation denies him, except in fugitive glimpses.

There is but a single depicted serious death in *To Be or Not to Be*, that of the initially disguised Nazi spy, Professor Siletsky (Stanley Ridges). His dying takes place on the Polish theatre company's stage, in the same setting earlier employed by Joseph Tura for his mangled and interrupted Hamlet soliloquy. The sound of a gun repeatedly fired is a bravura piece of attention-getting fanfare that precedes the raising of the theatre curtain. Lieutenant Sobinsky, the culprit spectator who had previously been instructed by Maria to play a prank on her husband, Joseph Tura, by harmlessly walking out on his big speech, is now revealed as an onstage player, covered in shadow but clearly holding the gun that has fired, unseen, behind the curtain and executed the trapped Siletsky. Siletsky himself is fully illuminated by a stationary spotlight, as though he were a star about to perform a musical number or audience-addressing speech. The camera is placed—as it has been during Tura's earlier soliloquy—at a distance from the stage and once again includes the audience's vantage point. We view from behind a number of the Polish actors who have become frozen with apprehension after the gunshots. They are standing spectators, incongruously outfitted in Nazi uniforms. By the time the curtain is fully raised, the decisive action (the shooting of Siletsky) has already happened, and both the executioner and the victim are perfectly motionless, as in a theatre tableau. The tableau effect is reinforced by an equivalent "stock stillness" in the actor witnesses in the audience. Lubitsch places enormous emphasis on the lengthy pause preceding Siletsky's collapse onstage: the confirmation that a nontheatrical, irreversible death has indeed occurred. We are given time to notice a sizable, persuasive bloodstain on the professor's business suit before we see the figure briefly reanimate, attempting to complete a Nazi arm salute and declaim "Heil Hitler." His intention is only half-realized, as he crumples to the stage, lifeless. Lubitsch places us completely on the stage for his framing of the death fall, and we view it at close range. When Siletsky tumbles down, we are aware of our placement above him. The shot dissolves into a close-up of Siletsky's steamer trunk back in his hotel room, before the killing has had time to be fully contemplated and absorbed by the viewer.

Figure 8.3. Professor Siletsky (Stanley Ridges)—midsalute—bends toward death in *To Be or Not to Be*.

The Siletsky pause—an unconscious imitation of an actor "milking" the suspense in a climactic death scene—is designed to echo Tura's extended pause before his first attempt at the "'To be or not to be" soliloquy. (Tura's wait is so histrionically prolonged that the prompter hidden in his box beneath the stage believes that Tura has forgotten how the speech begins, and stage whispers the celebrated line to jog his memory.) But the death pause is also a highlighted interruption of the natural dramatic flow, and interruptions are perhaps the most important structural device for tone management and shifts of register in Lubitsch's narrative. Before we examine the ramifications of Siletsky's stage death more fully, I will supply a larger context for this singular, fearsome interruption by a death that cannot be comically evaded.

To Be or Not to Be begins with a wistful narrated evocation of Warsaw in August 1939. The setting initially seems to be offered as a plausibly real (in studio terms) rendering of a Warsaw city street scene. The male narrator's voice establishes a tone of fond reminiscence in his opening observations, as he accompanies the visual presentation of shop signs with a crooning poetic listing of the owners' names: "Lubinski, Kubinski, Lominski, Kozanski, and Poznanski." As the narrator surreptitiously moves toward the sudden comic break with his introductory serene tone, he assures us that "at the moment" we are dropping into the story "Europe is still at peace, and life in Warsaw is going on as normally as ever." "Normally" alludes to a state of unhurried ordinariness, which is pointed in neither a comic nor a tragic direction. Sentiment feels here like a reasonably secure wrapping for this visit to a cozily traditional way of life, carrying on in a lamentably vanished, unruffled tempo. The raising of an alarm by the narrator comes with surprising speed, and in such a manner that not merely the opening mood but the stable reference points of the movie world—its method of documenting appearances, of differentiating film setting from theatre—are stridently disrupted.

When the narrator loudly shifts gears to announce the panic of the local populace over "something" that "seems to have happened," he is still not indicating whether a comic or somber viewer response is warranted. The excited voice might remind us of the newscaster too stunned to compose himself while witnessing the *Hindenberg* disaster. The horrifyingly swift conquest of Poland was certainly a disaster that was well known to 1942 spectators. And yet the images accompanying the melodramatic heightening of the narrator's delivery do not properly synchronize with his loss of control. Instead of presenting "invasion" terror realistically, Lubitsch resorts to a series of increasingly theatrical reaction shots of drivers and pedestrians. What they are observing is hidden from us, but the narration exaggerates the level of fright that the gawking, bewildered passersby convey, as citizens are singled out for close-up inspection. Their frozen poses, akin to Siletsky's later death scene, might be part of a silent film montage sequence, with German expressionist or Odessa Steps faces in exclamatory mode. The faces have been coached to overreact, but not so much that a satiric intention is clearly signaled. As the narrator follows his description of the "frightened" and "terrified" looks with the emphatically less ominous term "flabbergasted," we are led to understand that the Warsaw bombing and takeover are not what is at issue here. Yet we are swiftly knocked off balance again with the visual and oral revelation of Adolph Hitler, in full-dress uniform, standing "unconcernedly" outside Maslowski's delicatessen, and peering at the goods on display in its shop window.

The narrator begins to joke disparagingly about "the little man with the mustache, all by himself" on the city streets, and a version of a theatre curtain is rolled down over the shop window by the apprehensive delicatessen proprietor. Hitler has been set before us to contemplate, but the atmosphere and attitudes seem wrong for an acknowledgment of his malignancy and dire purpose. He is too incongruously mingling with the signs of ordinary life that preceded his appearance. Neither the crowd nor the film world that contains them feel persuasively menaced by Hitler's presence. What happens in this interruption—a melodramatic buildup and pause in *To Be or Not to Be*'s exposition scene—is that film reality is decisively undermined (briefly) and everything we behold turns troublingly theatrical. Theatre is not yet plainly identified as the realm that is taking "film reality's" place. We are temporarily cast adrift between two modes of being—film and theatre—in a mildly disconcerting limbo. The Warsaw film set becomes more and more affiliated with stage apparatus, and we are prodded toward an uneasy disbelief, and a resultant severing of our ties with a story that has scarcely begun. "Hitler" refuses to align himself with the conventions that belong to him. He is bizarrely divested of a fittingly odious stature, but he is not yet small enough to be lampoon-worthy. He is stranded from the meanings that would permit him to enter the dramatic action as fear-engendering foe.

Intriguingly, the failure of Hitler to command sufficient belief is coupled with our simultaneous loss of belief in beleaguered Warsaw. We are planted in some sort of perhaps unintentional stage reality where the two conflicting forces are confronting each other without adequate tension or grounding definition. The mysterious encounter, in spite of the narrator's disproportionate insistence on urgency, feels hollow, stymied, and incomplete. The narrator raises the question of how Hitler managed to arrive here, and—relying on the well-established rules of third person storyteller reliability—tells us that the answer to this perplexing state of affairs can be found if we go backward in story time to the Gestapo headquarters in Berlin.

When that setting is revealed to us, we are initially prepared to see it as reestablishing film reality. Nothing in the narrator's reference to "Gestapo headquarters in Berlin" can readily be heard as an extension of the prologue's bewildering comic gambit. The Warsaw thoroughfare, however shifty its appearances, is at least largely in possession of a benign, not yet brutalized, assemblage of Polish citizens. Only Hitler seems peculiarly and unnervingly out of place. The narrator's wavering, unsettled tone can be accounted for in terms of the difficulty of assimilating the story fact of Hitler's unlikely alighting on the scene. Gestapo headquarters, as an unequivocally dark concept, would seem to promise a reworking of the opening scene's fanciful tone—for at least a short while—into something solemn, and stable, in its acknowledgment of evil. Our desire for situational clarity, however, is promptly denied by our astonished discovery that Jack Benny is the apparent ranking officer. He is dressed in a Gestapo uniform, and sits behind a large desk, backed by a large formal portrait of Hitler, with swastika-bearing Nazi flags nearby. Benny as a plausible orchestrator of Nazi torture and execution is as immediately far-fetched as his subsequent appearance in a foppish Hamlet costume. We anticipate that the film will quickly resolve this new muddle.

Benny's first character action is to yawn while repeating "Heil Hitler" to the officer entering with news about an impending interrogation. The yawn is a signal that Benny is only impersonating a Nazi, and that the ruse (whatever it means) will soon be uncovered. But Benny's Gestapo officer instantly catches himself, corrects his yawned salutation with one that is crisply convincing, and efficiently conducts business with an apparently authentic fellow Nazi. The entrance of a preadolescent Hitler youth as the interrogation prospect partially revives an atmosphere of absurdity, but working against that tendency to full-on farce is the continuing employment of Benny as a figure attempting, however maladroitly, to further Nazi aims. The persona does not promote viewer comfort, nor is it something that the putative film reality can absorb. And we are denied the security of being informed in advance that the Gestapo scene is part of a play rehearsal. Theatre, in other words, is not allowed to settle the jostling contradictions without some mystifying delay. Lubitsch wants us to believe that we are still contemplating a film space with an in-between status. There is a border or limbo realm delineated where theatre and film reality secretly contest for dominance. What is perhaps most surprising as the provisional Gestapo episode proceeds is an increasing overlap of Benny's Nazi officer with the familiar foibles of the exceedingly well-known Jack Benny radio character. Like Benny's standard comic character persona, the officer is vain, petty, foolish in his handling of his own authority, self-congratulatory, and willing to take advantage of others' weaknesses. He endeavours to be sly, but his maneuvers are transparent. He is prone to cowardice, and his grandstanding usually results in humiliation. What we witness happening then is the seemingly preposterous mismatch of Benny and the Gestapo officer becoming a smoother fit. At the very least, we recognize the Benny character we think we know playing—with alarming gusto—a role we need to disbelieve in, to hold at a distance from him: in effect, to protect our investment in Benny's harmless comic being. To be this with no reprieve is not to be Jack

Benny. It is an annulment of our audience contract with the comedian, a shredding of our dependable relationship with him.

When "Hitler" once again makes an entrance onscreen in the headquarters setting and speaks the improvised line "Heil myself," Lubitsch finally breaks the illusion of a film world narrative unfolding and returns us decisively to the stage. A director, Dobosh (Charles Halton), rises from his chair next to the footlights in an empty theatre auditorium and halts the rehearsal due to Bronski-Hitler's (Tom Dugan) attempt to insert a line that would get a laugh. Dobosh feels that a laugh on Hitler's entrance is a blunder—that it would establish the wrong tone. As this interruption and dissolution of film space occur, a squabble within the theatre troupe manages to defuse the spectator's anxious uncertainty concerning Hitler's whereabouts and reality status. At the same time, the declaration of theatre's presence thrusts genuine political menace into the background. The Nazi presence quite literally disappears in the pause during which everything visible transforms into stage material. Theatre is presented as the welcomely artificial antidote to looming destruction and terror.

The comedy-basted realm of backstage and onstage antics (including the conversion of *Hamlet* into a burlesque—both calculated and unwitting) gains ground steadily as the dependable milieu of this film—its cohesive and reasonably stable reality. But eventually another interruption takes place that temporarily ravages the designated theatre spaces and deprives the actors (and film spectators) of free access to them. A siren sounds during a *Hamlet* performance, and both the visible assembled theatre audience and the performers on the other side of the proscenium respond with panic to the first bombing raids on Warsaw. Soon we are granted a return to the film's prologue setting for a tragic reenactment of the opening sequence's successively sentimental, slyly amusing, and fake emergency survey of the Warsaw streets. On this second scrutiny, the shop signs are broken or fallen, separated from the bombed storefronts they once identified. The male narrator's voice reemerges, adopting a convincingly grave tone, supported by a string-dominated orchestral lament from the film's score.

The major tonal contrast between these parallel episodes has been frequently pointed out by other commentators. Perhaps not as readily noticeable is the revived confusion of film and theatrical components in the depiction of the fallen city. Lubitsch conspicuously mingles overtly stage-bound elements with flashes of newsreel footage (mostly rear-screen background) throughout this extended comparison with the film's opening. His determination to make the two segments a series of poetic visual rhymes necessitates a degree of undisguised artifice, and Lubitsch boldly underscores the linkages. I am fascinated by the revived tug-of-war between theatre and film "reality frames" in the chronicle of dislocation. Instead of being vanquished by the austere documentation of a city in ruins, theatre framing strangely maintains its own ground. The film reality of Nazi soldiers marching through the city streets is juxtaposed with observers in deliberately statue-like theatrical poses. They are stage tableaux of citizens miming attitudes of grief and despair. The images are affecting, but operate as though they were part of an ongoing theatre spectacle—a powerful Romantic melodrama. The shots feel like composites of broken stage settings with cracks and tears in them through which scraps of war in a different medium can be glimpsed. The film backgrounds establish a partial claim to the framed space, and the theatre performers are both aware of these reference points and emotionally in touch with the real-world consequences of Poland's surrender. The consequences are, to some extent, inescapable. Even so, theatre manages to absorb the war footage into its separate perspective, and keeps the forcefully distinct larger reality from usurping its "surface" prerogatives. The narrator pointedly reinforces the connection between the sense of war from a theatre vantage point when he ruefully concludes: "A curtain had fallen on the Polish drama. A tragedy with no relief in sight." Greenberg (Felix Bressart), one of the actors in Joseph Tura's company, adds a coda to the narrator's speech when he is shown standing in the bombed street, surveying the poster for the cancelled Nazi satire with the older advertisement for *Hamlet* still visible beneath it. "There was no censor to stop them," Greenberg remarks to his fellow actor Bronski, who is now shorn of his Hitler mustache and costume, and attracting no one's attention.

As we move ahead to the scenes that supply the setup for Professor Siletsky's death onstage, we may be struck, as William Paul points out in his fine reading of the film, by Siletsky's behavioral resemblance to the suave protagonists of earlier Lubitsch comedies, perhaps most notably Herbert Marshall's Gaston in *Trouble in Paradise* (1932). In the cases of both Siletsky and Gaston, Paul argues, "impeccable manners [as well as an impressively invulnerable, dryly urbane style] may be seen as a sign of quiet ruthlessness in that Gaston manipulates those around him as much for his own selfish ends as Siletsky" (252). Attempting to distinguish between a nearly amoral, smiling opportunist like the jewel thief, Gaston, and the slightly colder, more sternly judged Siletsky, Paul claims that Siletsky is a soulless "company man, inured to the horrors of the regime" he serves (253). But Paul less convincingly suggests that Siletsky, as a company man, is all of a piece, and "in his wholeness is finally beyond the ironies of the actors with their understanding of a split reality" (253). Siletsky is as much a split character as his comic forebear, Gaston. As a spy, he proves as adept at role-playing as Gaston is, who cloaks his thievish ways behind gentlemanly aplomb.

Perhaps the primary reason for *To Be or Not to Be*'s ongoing ability to confound and discompose is that it provides no firm boundary line between its Nazi characters and their adversaries in the Polish resistance. Lubitsch knows that it would take only minor adjustments and internal finessing for his elegant comic rogues in evening attire—the stock-in-trade of so many of his earlier film comedies—to choose the wrong role (or side) and become Nazi opportunists. Siletsky is, finally, to paraphrase Hamlet's first private statement about comfortably insidious Claudius, a little more than emotional kin and "less than kind" in his connection with the theatre troupe. He performs his spy mission of name gathering (for roundup and extermination of relatives of airmen) with a smoothness and captivating openness that makes him at least equal, if not superior, in theatrical proficiency to the actors in Tura's company. When he courts Maria Tura, Siletsky is not alert to all her verbal ironies at his expense or her indisposedness to his advances, but he nonetheless adroitly matches her skill in wordplay, powers of argument, and silken sophistication. Although he is strongly attracted to her, he never relaxes his guard or loses his self-possession. He combines pleasure with the business of recruiting her to his cause (if possible), but is never so caught up in ideological rhetoric that he can't function as a committed hedonist, one who finds delight and excitement in his game-playing and provocative banter. Like the other "actors" in the film, he is split among rival commitments and roles. The impression of a unified character—what William Paul terms "wholeness"—is largely due to his efficient navigation of transitions.

Smoothness is often an honorable attribute and aspiration in Lubitsch's world. In stage performance rules of conduct, it is the element that must be pitted against the chaos-breeding force of missed cues, accidents, and unplanned interruptions from "beyond the theatre frame." Actors who can retain their poise and smoothness when the unexpected occurs can subdue these threats. Siletsky knows how to play a love scene and then calmly redirect his elegant style and assurance when he receives a surprising summons to go immediately to Gestapo headquarters. The language of romantic ardor is not disquietingly at odds with the language of obedience, even if the latter demands a docile submission to higher authority. Authority, in turn, like a potential lover, can be flattered and manipulated to strengthen one's own position. At one point, Siletsky asks Maria, "Do I look like a monster?" He correctly assumes that he neither looks, acts, nor sounds like one. He is sometimes obliged to play what some would see as a monstrous part in order to advance the grisly war agenda of his chosen side—what he describes as the "winning" side. He has no trouble believing that one can dexterously, almost without effort, shift from monstrous deeds to the "happy world" that Nazism endeavors to build—not a devouring world with jagged teeth, but one replete with dance, singing, fine dinners, and artful flirtation.

Lubitsch deems it necessary, in the subtle moral division of this film's narrative terrain, to choose theatrical brokenness—interruptions and repeated mistakes that sabotage the orderly stage picture—over the smoothness of expertise. The solidarity among the players must not run efficiently or it will become a suspect mechanism. Theatre fellowship in *To Be or Not to Be* is a medley of rough-and-tumble, disorderly impulses, in this respect having some affinity to Hamlet's thought process, which rarely moves on a clear, straight path. Lubitsch keeps egos inflated, arguments unresolved, tactics foolish and panicky, stalling and the needless repetition of prior errors continuous. A pure, sustained actor's belief in unified performance and reproducible effects is likely to push one nearer to Nazi theatre, with its insistence on rigidly consistent role dynamics within the system and unwavering allegiance to a Master script. The once delightful Lubitschean pleasures of harmonious comportment—the style appropriate for the uniform of a "Smiling Lieutenant," for example—have been overtaken by mechanization, a stiffly compulsive "Heil Hitler" decorum. Broken theatre, by contrast, is compatible with broken windows, streets, hearts, impending assaults, and eviction from formal theatre spaces. The superimposition of theatre on an incoherent, interruption-bombarded film world supplies it with a metaphysical grounding—a place "to be" and make patchwork meaning as opposed to an always encroaching Nazi "not to be."

The killing of Siletsky onstage is performed by an entirely earnest, humorless nonactor, Lieutenant Sobinsky, who—like Siletsky—is entirely and smoothly sealed within his military commitments. Sobinsky lacks the cracked or broken "double vision" of the theatre company. Killing and dying here are, on the one hand, a staged event with an audience wholly composed of seasoned actors (performers in Nazi costume watching a naturalist master class, which in quick succession makes them envious, bewildered, and shocked). On the other hand, the killing and dying are "unperformed" (that is to say, removed from theatre) by a pair resistant to playful pretending and hyperbolic self-display.

Siletsky jokes to Maria Tura during their tête-à-tête in his suite at the Nazi compound: "I am willing to die for the Fuhrer at any moment, except for the next few hours." With this pronouncement he exhibits his ability to compartmentalize, and sneak a brief reprieve from Nazi self-sacrifice in order to complete a romantic assignation. The hours in which he slips away from single-mindedness will not be missed. He assumes that on the margins of sacrificial duty, he can bring the nonmonstrous "happy world" Nazism envisions into being by dancing, feasting, and indulging his carnal appetite. It is within this brief span of intended truancy, however, that he will be interrupted, required to perform a brisk errand for a theatre simulacrum of the Gestapo, and, in the course of this "straightforward" mission, crudely put to death.

The Gestapo headquarters he visits immediately before his onstage execution is a disguised and relocated set from the company's cancelled Nazi satire. The concealed audience from the theatre troupe is directly adjacent to the auditorium and stage proper, and linked to it by a Lubitsch door, through which Joseph Tura (playing Gestapo Colonel Ehrhardt) makes exits to receive further instructions from his fellow actors (who are now novice Resistance fighters as well). Siletsky begins to recognize that the entire Gestapo milieu he has entered is fraudulent—stagecraft hocus-pocus—when Tura helplessly allows jealousy of his wife to overwhelm his more consequential political commitment to his assigned role. His repeated failure to stay in character—though many lives depend on his ability to do so—establishes yet again the brokenness of theatrical intention. The film spectator is obliged to dwell on the spreading cracks in the façade of stage illusion. We are compelled, as we have been since the film's outset, to hold theatre and film world imperatives in perplexing double focus. As Siletsky attempts to escape from the Gestapo stage set we hear an offstage shot (paralleling the offscreen sound of the shot that will soon kill Siletsky). Tura regards the shot as real, and moreover successfully discharged at him within the stage set he still occupies. Imagining that the bullet has pierced his own body, he instinctively draws on theatre performer memory, finding a fit pose to strike and a touching backward stagger (which he milks) so that his approaching end will appear theatrically worthy of his supreme sacrifice. It is only after further inspection of his person that he halts the trajectory of his momentarily "believed in" death. Siletsky's related attempt to escape the stage space he has been lured into proves as impossible as Tura's efforts to perish nobly, without cheap theatrics. The door Siletsky passes through leads only to a more uncompromising theatre space, decked out with rows of spectator seats and a majestic curtain. Siletsky scans all the available aspects of his expanded stage environment for successful hiding places. It is no doubt growing clear to him that he is being hunted down in earnest by actors in Gestapo costumes.

The spaces between rows of seats through which Siletsky fearfully crawls become, with no need for literal conversion, identical in their oppressively narrow confines to alleyways and desperate escape routes used by the human quarries of Gestapo pursuers. The spotlight probing the various areas of the auditorium for the marked victim is precisely not distinguishable from scanning searchlights in real-world prison towers. The frenzied emotions of pursuer and pursued are not theatrically heightened or compromised by their reliance on a stage domain. The apparatus of stage spectacle, illusion, and witnessing engender an unconditional film reality effect. If anything the theatre follow spot's transformation into a military or prison searchlight compounds our belief in its "being" and meaning because the raking light has been defamiliarized. We grasp the light as active revelation rather than a familiar melodramatic convention. Nothing that surrounds Siletsky in his frantic search for a way out displays the leniency or protectiveness of stage fabrication. When he at last arrives at the stage proper and attempts to elude the searchlight by disappearing behind the curtain, director Dobosh exhorts one of his cohorts to go backstage and raise it.

In the interim—before the curtain lifts—Sobinsky's fatal shots have been fired, and Siletsky's course is set. All that remains for him to do is to realize that he is "no more" and accept it. I must stress again that the nearly bare stage, containing residue from the *Hamlet* set, on which Siletsky appears, in a lengthy frozen pose, hovering perhaps between realization and incredulity, does not serve to reduce the scale, authenticity, or impact of his dying. In fact, the region of make-believe seems transferred to the costumed group of "Nazi" spectators who match Siletsky's immobility and silence on the other side of the footlights. Death on the bare stage (finally the botched Tura "not to be" receives a credible parsing) seems to locate this absolute severing where it belongs, beyond the reach and consolation of the fictitious appearances in which we customarily enfold ourselves. It is the trappings that the "play actor" survivors cling to and count on that feel—by contrast with Siletsky's death throes—counterfeit, the stuff of artifice. The stage seems to endow Siletsky's fall with a purity and clarity that pierces the heart of theatre in such a way that the stage becomes a kind of ultimate, unassailable film space. Siletsky, cognizant that his last moment approaches, attempts to give some parting sign of who and where he is. His arm raises (voluntarily or mechanically, it is hard to be sure) in a Nazi salute that breaks off before it is completed. Once more brokenness confronts us, as Siletsky struggles to remember his line ("Sieg Heil") and strives as the dark curtain pulls away his world to validate something that is real to him.

This is the sovereign tragic moment that the comedy of *To Be or Not to Be* brushes against, and like everything in the film it is turned upon its head through a later return and reversal. Siletsky's actual corpse reappears as a "Yorick skull" stage prop used to intimidate and expose Joseph Tura, who has been assigned the task of impersonating Siletsky in meetings with actual Nazis. Tura confronts his more imposing, perished double, set up in a chair like the ghost of Hamlet's father. Taking advantage of his concealment behind another Lubitsch door, Tura outwits the Nazis (and perhaps the viewer as well, who is placed with the Nazis on the other side of this door and given time to wonder about his pending unmasking). The Nazis have arranged their own version of Hamlet's Mousetrap, whose purpose is to terrorize Tura into confession. Tura decides to make the incriminating corpse theatrically suspect by shaving off the dead Siletsky's real beard and reapplying it to the corpse's face as a bit of stage makeup. In the process of "bringing off" this masquerade, Tura transforms the formerly authentic death of Siletsky onstage into an event that is neither here nor there, and that now belongs, worrisomely, to no one. As Siletsky is reduced to an untrustworthy stage dummy, his previously unmistakable extermination becomes a curious case of postmortem hamming and pretense, and no longer warrants the serious faith of his former confederates. The death we earlier beheld possessed startling gravitas in its presentation. The corpse's power to return to the stage renders Siletsky's death, in retrospect, lightly theatrical. The truth of being vs. not being, whatever we have made of it in Siletsky's case, has fled, irretrievably.

In Alfred Hitchcock's *Stage Fright* (1950), the stage death is reserved for the film's false protagonist, Jonathan Cooper (Richard Todd), who claims to be the director's guiltless, on-the-run "wrong man" at the outset of the narrative, and is eventually shown to have concocted a fictitious account of his own victimization by circumstances. *Hamlet* is less directly addressed in this film than in Lubitsch's, but *Stage Fright* strikes me as full of *Hamlet* analogies and echoes. Hitchcock had been in discussion with Cary Grant since 1945 about the possibility of filming a "modern dress" version of Shakespeare's play as soon as Hitchcock's contract with producer David O. Selznick had expired. The chief obstacle to the film going forward (Grant was surprisingly willing) was a lawsuit by playwright Irving Fiske, which claimed that Hitchcock and Grant had stolen the idea from his play "Hamlet in Modern English." The suit had still not been settled when Laurence Olivier directed and starred in his own highly successful film of *Hamlet* in 1948. There is abundant evidence then that Hamlet was very much on Hitchcock's mind in the late 1940s (Eyman, 218).

Stage Fright opens with the raising of what is identified in bold lettering as a theatrical safety curtain. An emphasized correlation between theatre and safety thus ushers us into the film's world. But almost instantly, in a striking parallel with *To Be or Not to Be*, a jousting between theatrical safety and disconcerting real world elements takes place. On the other side of the curtain is an establishing shot of post–World War II East Side London, in which a surviving St. Paul's Cathedral (perhaps extending the promise of safety further) coexists with bombsite ruins, still unrepaired five years after the war's end. A relentless preoccupation with every conceivable aspect of theatrical masking, decorum, impersonation, onstage performance, and sleight of hand marks the narrative that follows the opening curtain lift. Very close to the film's end, Jonathan Cooper, having tripped and fallen in his effort to escape a literal stage, is cut in two by a rapidly descending theatre fire curtain, this one made of iron. The safety of the initial curtain, in the course of Hitchcock's sinuous story, steadily acquires greater density, weight, and menace as our entanglement with stagecraft maneuvering and duplicity is stretched to the breaking point.

Immediately after a still dazed and damaged London cityscape is revealed to us, we are invited to concentrate on a fast-moving vehicle, in apparent flight. The sports car convertible, driven by Eve Gill (Jane Wyman) and with Jonathan sitting beside her as a passenger, is initially headed straight toward the camera and the viewer. The visual attack on the viewer's safe position is reminiscent of the dawn of film history, camera-crowding train approach presented to audiences by the Lumière brothers. Legend has it that many spectators of the train image bearing down on them experienced panic because they did not yet understand the limits of the cinematic frame and the nature of their own spectator security. Hitchcock deliberately evokes one of silent cinema's first distressing illusions to set beside the guileful slipperiness of the rising theatre curtain. Less conspicuous, no doubt, to 1950 viewers than to moviegoers of the present is the abrupt departure from the actual London streets and substitution for them of studio shots with rear screen projection.

It is at this juncture of film world "opening up" that the couple in the car (our perspective on what has just happened) is introduced to us. The female driver of the car speaks the first line: "It looks like we got away with it." We are led to suppose that she and the male passenger are equally involved in some sort of criminal activity. Soon we will learn that only Jonathan is on the run and that Eve—his potential romantic interest—is merely assisting a man whose "innocence" she believes in before he explains any of his actions. By film's end, Eve's initially blameless position has been replaced by something considerably darker, and she will make her final exit from *Stage Fright*'s world having "gotten away with something" less than honorable. But at the start, our confusion about events, roles, and behavior is combined with a shift from authentic London to an artfully concealed studio sleight of hand and rear screen projection. Such trickery commonly functions in studio era filmmaking as "real enough" rendering of depicted events. But in *Stage Fright*, the insertion of film artifice precisely here—with Hitchcock's sly, unstressed shift from street to sound stage—coincides with the commencement of Jonathan's thirteen-minute flashback account of a murder in which he was a reluctant accomplice. This flashback is revealed, near film's end, to be largely fabricated by its guilty teller. Jonathan's narrating voice is heard only at the beginning and end of his tale. Hitchcock creates an elaborate visual narration to stand in for the unheard vocal outpouring of Jonathan's memories. The incidents he relates have transpired so recently that they have hardly had time to settle into what is demonstrably past. Hitchcock makes every possible effort to persuade us that the story Jonathan presents to Eve is as accurate and reliable as any other movie flashback we have encountered. Its arrival so close to our own entry into the movie's sense of things, and its offering of intimate access to secrets that no one but the teller and listener, Eve, are privy to, enhance its apparent truthfulness and the solidity of its specification. It also, of course, does the work of narrative exposition.

Jonathan owns up to his culpable involvement in Charlotte Inwood's (Marlene Dietrich) crime, and does not conceal the ruthlessness and poor judgment that he has consistently exhibited from the moment that Charlotte arrived at his door. Hitchcock's introduction of Charlotte, as well as the revelation of her romantic relationship with Jonathan, occurs in the flashback. In the latter stages of Jonathan's recollections, Eve Gill—the person to whom the story is told—takes part in the action, in a manner that she would recall and easily manage to verify. If the flashback proves ultimately to be a sieve (with respect to truth claims), it is a sieve constructed with the same dazzling camera rhetoric that Hitchcock employs in his depiction of trustworthy film world events. It matches the "meshes" of what later counts as legitimately captured character life. We are encouraged to forget the theatre curtain that masked and then rose to provide our initial view of the film's world. The establishing shot of contemporary London creates a powerful disjunction between theatre conventions and a spacious, deep cinematic representation of the reality we supposedly occupy. The flashback reinforces our sense of how to divide the treacherous and make-believe components of theatre from the anxious "real life" circumstances surrounding them.

Charlotte Inwood is concerned, from the moment we meet her, with how to cover up the just completed killing of her husband. But she soon seems almost equally preoccupied with her ability to arrive at the theatre on time for her evening performance and to summon the composure necessary to play successfully. Eve Gill, when she appears in the flashback, is rehearsing a scene onstage at the Royal Academy of Dramatic Art just before Jonathan contacts her. He boldly joins her scene in progress in order to escape detection by the police officers who are pursuing him. Jonathan whispers a secret to Eve while they are both onstage that we cannot hear. We do, however, instantly recognize the secret as communication distinct from the "period piece" dialogue of the scene being presented for Eve's teacher. These examples demonstrate how Hitchcock places us in contact throughout the flashback with seemingly reliable boundaries of spaces designated for "acting" in order to distinguish them from the more chaotic and diverse milieu belonging to the world beyond the stage. Although events unfold with great speed and urgency in the flashback, we seem to know where we are located in it from start to finish. Our primary orientation is supplied by Jonathan's point of view, but as in so many Hitchcock sequences the anchoring perspective subtly widens out at various junctures to include supplementary vantage points—Charlotte, the police detectives, Nelly (the dresser who discovers Mr. Inwood's body), Eve's mother, Eve, and the drama teacher at the Royal Academy. We are also given a brief segment of Jonathan imagining actions that are likely to happen, and these are subsequently confirmed within the flashback. Hitchcock incorporates much bravura camerawork, including crane shots and sequence shots with a mobile camera, to place us securely inside his constructed story world, using his trademark methods for heightening viewer emotional participation and belief.

As eventually becomes clear, however, all of the flashback's nontheatrical moments are, in fact, disguised extensions of theatre masquerade. Our faith that we are inside a reliably documented series of linked episodes proves to be groundless. Neither are we genuinely connected to a narrator's perspective. A second viewing of the film leads us to consider that we have been positioned somewhere between Jonathan's improvised revision of the sequence and substance of his murder-related activity and the collaborative listening/imagining of Eve. As he speaks to her, she envisions the events he describes to her. Jonathan no doubt attempts to picture the tale he tells while he moves through it, in order to strengthen his own belief in it and render it crystalline and cohesive enough for Eve to be drawn into the narrative—as a movie viewer might be—and assent to its logic. Her seeing, like our own, endows Jonathan's implied narration with weight and value.

One of the most remarkable moments in the flashback arrives when Jonathan is making his getaway from his detective pursuers outside his apartment, where they have come to question him. He quickly enters his sports car and tries to start the engine, but it sputters without immediately engaging. Jonathan locks the car doors to prevent capture. The policemen hammer against the windows of his vehicle, in response to which Jonathan curiously points out to them that the windows carry a "safety glass" label. The glass almost instantly cracks after Jonathan's silent gesture, yielding a spider web pattern. Nevertheless, the window continues to hold together, in spite of the violent fracture, and Jonathan successfully drives off. The safety glass serves to direct our memory back to the safety curtain (prominently marked as such) whose raising opened the film. An attempt is made in this struggle to enter Jonathan's vehicle (and by implication, the vehicle of his story). It is not merely the glass that is shattered here but the seemingly transparent film rhetoric that seals Jonathan into his own self-exonerating account. Hitchcock signals a "shattering" of cinema's illusion-generating power, and links film's powers of enchantment to theatricality. A further reference to film-theatre crossover is found in Charlotte's demand that Jonathan draw the cord that will close the ample window curtains in his apartment as she makes her entrance. The action has the effect of transforming Jonathan's apartment into a private stage for the pair. Everything that passes between the two of them depends on intimate secrecy, screened off from the light of day. Neither the filmic nor theatrical dimensions of this episode are dependable. There is no authentic ground of being to be found here. Both media are intent on generating "false" gestures.

The language of film reality is being sabotaged along with the theatre devices placed within it.

We seem to be reaping the advantages of film viewers when we partake of Charlotte's private confession to Jonathan. After all, whatever the film image shows us, be it an action designed for public or sequestered scrutiny, belongs to us. The film image is predicated on the fact that the viewer is never excluded from what it displays. But the film world's apparent openness—its generous and receptive visibility—is a function of what remains hidden. Part of that hiddenness belongs inevitably to staging and the "disguised" theatrical frame. In Hitchcock's 1948 film, *Rope*, Hitchcock adapted what was manifestly a work originating in theatre. Nevertheless, the intricacy of its visual treatment was an effort to inconspicuously invade the realm of theatre and put all its elements in the service of a daunting mirror language of film. We need only note in passing *Rope*'s strict fidelity to actual time, its ever-prowling camera opening up and closing down segments of the restricted setting and handing off point-of-view authority in a constant subtle relay, its severely curtailed use of editing, and its elaborate miniature cityscape on view beyond a large curving picture window, whose appearances undergo a multitude of small changes as the evening advances. Theatre remains a prominent stressed element throughout *Rope*, but film shadows it at every point, quietly asserting its control of the stage and its superior powers of revelation.

In *Stage Fright*, made two years later, a different kind of explication is at work. The terrain that counts as film reality gradually loses its capacity to stand separate from stage reality. Theatre infects every aspect and gesture of film expression, and it is equally the arena in which heroism, delusion, and treachery find their definition, and seek refuge. Theatre is both a liberating force and a nightmare where, in Vladimir Nabokov's haunting words about Gogol's fiction, "shadows of other worlds pass like the shadows of nameless and soundless ships" (149). "All reality is a mask" (148), Nabokov declares, describing Gogol's short story "The Overcoat," and that seems to be the case in *Stage Fright*, where theatre and film continually confront each other, exposing their respective masks. Settings, actions, memory, and the process of individuation all seem to be presented to us as a phantasmagoria of "whirling masks."

Hamlet resembles *Stage Fright* most closely in its depiction of the inescapability of theatre in the world of Elsinore. Hamlet, Claudius, Gertrude, Ophelia, and Polonius are all caught in the coils of seeming rather than being. Being—that is to say, a condition distinct from performance disguise—is one of the most blighting losses in the aftermath of King Hamlet's death. The court, filled with spies and counterspies, demands feigning and withholding as the only acceptable currency of human exchange. Whatever possibilities for direct, unselfconscious, unmanipulative affection between, say, Hamlet and Ophelia have entirely been replaced by fanciful, desperate, and often coerced role-playing. Within this widening orbit of deceit, there is for both Hamlet and Ophelia a frenzy of alienation from trustful, vulnerable expression. Ophelia, the weaker of the pair, succumbs entirely to madness and finally suicide. Hamlet, of course, assumes madness "gingerly" as a disruptive guise, a protection of his own deep-seated torment and his elusiveness, but he remains throughout most of the play, as G. Wilson Knight puts it, "on the knife edge" (300) between sanity and inward collapse.

At the center of *Hamlet*'s action rests the Mousetrap, a theatrical sneak attack designed to catch and expose to the glare of court inspection "the conscience of a king." Hamlet's ghost is a storyteller who enlists his stricken and harrowed son with every cue and motive for revenge. But the dead spirit is a baffling surrogate for the no longer "living" father and son relationship. He is himself a Player-King from beyond the grave, impersonating the man from whose earthly concerns and attachments he has been cut off. His account of his death at Claudius's hands is in all likelihood tethered to fact, but the poison he describes being poured into his ear by scheming Claudius eerily mirrors the figurative ear-poisoning that he inflicts on his son, thus doubling the stakes of vindictive malignity.

Hamlet's encounter with the ghost is of necessity a veiled encounter. The father seems death-cleansed of his former capacity to recognize his child as a being with needs of his own and immense vulnerability. He can make no allowances for human confusion or limitation. The tormented spirit hollowly paces in the circle of his aborted hopes and anxious, unappeasable grievances. There is only vanquished power and an ego stripped of resources left to issue commands. This performing phantom seeks out a submissive instrument, whose will can become an extension of his once full, now empty sovereignty. When Hamlet is alone and free to pursue his own thoughts, observed only by the theatre spectators, whose existence as a listening force he somehow apprehends and, however faintly, acknowledges, he regularly excoriates his performing self for its insufficiency or perfidy. The advice Hamlet offers to the players about how to present his own "masked" play persuasively argues for a controlled repose in their behavior, a self-possession that none of his own assumed roles seem to allow for.

Hamlet's creative groping within the vast fields of his intellect is so often, as he is keenly aware, overstrained, and at a bewildering distance from the grace, balance, and undisturbed readiness that he prizes. Repose is the key to integration. The performing players, in their exquisitely managed artifice, and later the gravedigger in his sportive, easygoing execution of his grim task, present enviable theatrical models for authenticity. Theatre never loses its incessant shaping influence for Hamlet as a reality determinant. And Hamlet's final, life-concluding duel is Claudius's theatrical act of reprisal for the prince's Mousetrap, mimicking the pantomime plot of secret poisoning, and making pointedly literal the poison's no longer feigned presence.

In *Stage Fright*, we are given two versions of Hamlet's Mousetrap. The first involves Eve's father, Commodore Gill (Alastair Sim), who interrupts Charlotte Inwood's musical performance by having a young Boy Scout carry a doll garbed in a bloodstained dress to the stage and presenting it to her. The second, nearing the film's climax, is engineered by Eve Gill and the police. It requires Eve, who has been playing the role of a stage-dresser assistant to Charlotte, to extract a confession from Charlotte about the slaying of her husband, which is to be secretly recorded, and later broadcast, in a reverberating, empty theatre. Jonathan Cooper, *Stage Fright*'s gradually displaced, faux-protagonist, provides a curious amalgamation of Hamlet's situation (tormented and victimized, it would appear, through his enmeshment in a murder that demands his cover-up assistance after the fact) and that of Claudius (who, like Jonathan, has in fact secretly committed the murder that ignites the film's plot, through a mixture of ambition and passion). Jonathan's lengthy confession to Eve at the beginning of the film could be characterized as a visual soliloquy, in which he lays claim to be caught up in an immense sacrificial effort on Charlotte's behalf. He wishes to rescue her and preserve both her reputation and his romantic relationship with her . . . ("The time is out of joint / O cursed spite, that ever I was born to set it right"). He elaborately insists in this visual "telling" of his current woes on his "cursed" participation in Charlotte's sordid deeds, and on his alienation from all potential allies other than Eve. In so doing he reveals himself to the spectator as the inevitable central figure in this rapidly unfolding drama.

At the end of the film, as he hides out in a theatre storage room with Eve, we see Jonathan seated with her in another vehicle, this time a static stage prop resembling an old-fashioned carriage in a period play. Shorn of his opening scene sports car, which kept pace with his dizzying, tumultuous narration, Jonathan is now literally encased in artifice. Within the carriage frame he drastically revises the content of the first visual soliloquy, unraveling all of his preliminary identity and story assertions. In their place, wearing now the constricted, helpless demeanor of a madman, he offers a self-diminishing retelling of his first tale. It seems that he only barely grasps, confusedly and with a measure of astonishment, that he has killed two people, and may be driven to kill one more.

Eve, his believing listener at the beginning and at story's end, is an Ophelia figure to Jonathan's hollowed-out Hamlet. She has surreptitiously stolen his protagonist status by steady amplification of her own feats of role-playing and an undeclared (to Jonathan) shift in romantic loyalty. Unlike Ophelia, then, she avoids a breakdown of her own and self-destruction in the aftermath of Hamlet's rejection of her. Her gradual mastery of theatre makes her so proficient a role player that not only Jonathan but the ever-suspicious Charlotte and Eve's replacement love, the detective Ordinary Smith (Michael Wilding), are taken in by her performances. Without quite recognizing the extent of her immersion in deceptive, duplicitous conduct, Eve approaches all of her dealings with others—whether sincere or manipulative—as theatrically instrumental. It is her will to perform vividly and successfully that brings reality into focus for Eve, and keeps it sharp and accessible. When she is deprived of a risky role to inhabit or a double game to be caught up in, Eve feels exposed and pitiably small, as though she were dwindling away to nothing. As she painfully declares to Jonathan after being the sole audience of his initial, flashback confession—a confession that includes the revelation of Jonathan's continued, consuming passion for Charlotte—she must grow accustomed to being "second fiddle."

Eve's eventual, cold triumph in the film comes from securing power and incriminating knowledge in the unthreatening guise of "second fiddle" roles. Although successively overshadowed by the theatrical ostentation of Jonathan, Charlotte, and even her own father, the Commodore, Eve's calculated hiddenness and sweet dissembling give her ample scope for maneuvering through the film's many stage settings, and a final, understated revenge on her oppressors. She manages, for example, to attend to her once beloved Hamlet's final confession and lure him to exposure and a violent theatrical death without being divested of her meek Ophelia persona. She becomes the embodiment of that undependable "safety curtain" that rises in *Stage Fright*'s opening moments.

It is worth noting, as still another complicating factor, that Eve is also adrift from the outset of the narrative, Hamlet-fashion, within her own family, where her parents' relationship (living more apart than together, and making a game of their nonintimacy) is an impenetrable theatrical act. The Commodore's seaside home and retreat is misty and ghost-like, starkly differentiating it from Mrs. Gill's genteel London quarters. Eve can query the two of them as insistently as Hamlet queries Gertrude about her true attachments to Hamlet Sr. and Claudius, but the answers she receives are slippery and mystifying. There is no home for Eve to return to that reduces the omnipresent sense of staginess, artifice, and double-dealing. (Patrick McGilligan's Hitchcock biography intriguingly documents Alma Reville's brief affair with Whitfield Cook, her co-screenwriter for *Stage Fright*. The Hitchcocks' daughter, Pat, made her screen debut in this film as the cruelly named Chubby Bannister, a friend of Eve's. More to the point, her resemblance to Jane Wyman was strong enough that she doubled for Eve in a number of scenes.) Jonathan—the unexposed killer who oscillates between the roles of anxious Hamlet and perfidious Claudius—finds safe haven in both of Eve's family dwellings.

I will now consider the scenes immediately preceding *Stage Fright*'s ending, where Eve counters Jonathan's second confession and homicidal threat to her with a final performance as his trustworthy friend, which instantly leads to her last act of deception and his death onstage. Eve's betrayal is intimately tied to Jonathan's being stranded onstage and the ensuing cutting in half of his stumbling body by the plummeting steel curtain. We begin with Eve's last appearance in her mother's house. Eve is standing beside her replacement suitor, Detective "Ordinary" Smith, who feels disappointed and duped by the extent of her "performance" dishonesty with him in the first stages of their courtship. Eve's mother, oblivious to the tensions flowing in the windowless study, enters in the company of her half-estranged husband, offering Smith a drink before innocently divulging to Smith the information that there is another houseguest upstairs. She believes that he is a "Mr. Robinson," but Smith's look—upon hearing the name spoken—makes us understand that he has figured out that the "lodger" guest is, in fact, Jonathan Cooper, whom the police have been fruitlessly searching for since the beginning of the narrative. As Commodore Gill pours himself a drink, he settles down to business, confident that his own alliance with Eve, strengthened by the savory theatrical plot they are engaged in, outweighs any loyalty or romantic feeling she may hold for Detective Smith. His wife, having let the Jonathan Cooper "cat" out of the bag, leaves the room at this juncture, carrying no knowledge and having no theatrical role of her own to advance further. It is a casual exit, but it marks her disappearance from the film. Knowledge and theatrical engagement have become inseparable at this point, and her exclusion from the game of artful withholding and from any awareness of the masquerade being conducted all around her make her a dramatically weightless figure. Only those characters who recognize the stage's ineradicable presence in every human exchange remain consequential in the closing scenes of *Stage Fright*, and are granted by Hitchcock some stake in the ending.

Mrs. Gill's parting observation is that she has changed her mind about the previously disconcerting "Mr. Robinson": "He seems like a nice young man after all." She takes a glass of sherry with her, which she plans to give him as a peace offering. Mrs. Gill's change of attitude proves to be a perfectly wrong intuition, but both the Commodore and Eve presently agree with her assessment. They merely regret that her lack of knowledge about Detective Smith's suspicion cause her needlessly, garrulously to announce the whereabouts of "Mr. Robinson," and to give away his actual identity. The Commodore does what he can to speed his wife's departure ("wife" in a manner of speaking) before her naive blurting does even more damage, then closes the door after her.

When he returns to have a more candid discussion with Detective Smith and his daughter, Eve informs him that her attempt to explain to Smith their efforts thus far (to adopt theatre strategies to save Jonathan and expose Charlotte's guilt) have failed to sway—much less please—the detective, and that he is urging them to stop. As I noted above, the Commodore brushes aside Smith's concerns. To him they are signs that Smith (like Mrs. Gill) is an incompetent theatrical practitioner. Because of the detective's seemingly entrenched opposition to the inspired scenarios that Gill and his daughter have conceived and enacted, he will be hard-pressed to find the truth on his own and set things to rights. Smith in turn accuses Gill of being an irresponsible fool in his attempts to encourage Eve's dangerous role-playing. When he asks Gill what sort of father he is, Gill with calm smugness replies "unique," and then, with scarcely a moment's pause, proposes a fresh blackmail scheme in which Eve will deepen and darken the role of "Doris Goode" (Charlotte's replacement dresser) that she has been playing. And "Ordinary" Smith will be a hidden theatre spectator. Smith inquires whether there is, in fact, a genuine bloodstained dress that would implicate Charlotte in her husband's murder. (It is a garment that will function crucially in Commodore Gill's proposed blackmail ruse.) Gill sheepishly admits that it once existed, but was accidentally destroyed. In an abrupt, surprising turnaround, Smith, somewhat surprisingly, accedes to Gill's idea, and recommends that Eve return to Charlotte at the theatre and resume her role-playing. His behavior here is strangely split, however. At the same time that he agrees he coldly suggests that Eve's ability to act so persuasively calls all of her previous declarations of love for him into question. Smith holds on to his scorn while tacitly encouraging Eve's intensified commitment to theatrical duplicity. Eve shifts back and forth between a pose of chastened repentance in her close-up responses to Smith and a visible pride and hunger for further performing opportunities. A tacit consensus that no effective alternative to stage masquerade and calculating falsehood exists in the plan to expose Charlotte is arrived at by the three initially at odds players in this discussion. It is fitting then that, apart from a brief phone call that Smith makes from a booth—requesting support for Eve's blackmail performance—all the remaining scenes in *Stage Fright* take place in the theatre proper.

Theatre now openly lays claim to what was implicit in the film's "curtain raising" credits. It powerfully subsumes the entire film world being presented to us. As we move into the stage realm "for keeps," we are given high angle views of the exterior and interior of Charlotte's theatre home. The view of the inside shows us the auditorium darkening as the last spectators have departed and the cleaning staff prepares to remove "evidence" of audience presence. An elderly man ushers a much younger one, who is carrying a standing microphone, into a dressing room not far from the stage, explaining to him that a little experiment is being conducted. He points to a white dress hanging on a hook as a suitable place of concealment for the broadcasting device. The white dress reminds us of the bloodstained dress that Jonathan had presented to Eve as proof of his innocence, but also as a sign of his accomplice role in Mr. Inwood's murder. Jonathan subsequently burned the dress, which now seems to have rematerialized as a costume, minus the incriminating stain. This simulacrum of the primary material evidence of Charlotte's guilt metaphorically suggests Eve's unshaken belief in Jonathan's "clean hands" relation to the bloody crime. It also carries the additional suggestion of Eve's equally strong faith in her own virtue as she launches (with the aid of these male assistants) her final offensive against Charlotte. Nevertheless, the combination of the covering white dress and the shrouded microphone behind it—which will violate the confidentiality that Eve will falsely offer Charlotte and "bare her secrets" to an audience of cold adversaries—creates a memorable image of treachery in the "white" guise of rectitude.

When we see Charlotte and Eve together in Charlotte's upstairs dressing room shortly afterward, we are not immediately sure whether this is the location where the microphone has been planted. Hitchcock introduces his Ophelia version of the Mousetrap with a two shot of the actresses. Charlotte is adjusting her hat while inspecting her appearance in a bulb-lined makeup mirror in the right of the frame. Eve is simultaneously closing a wardrobe door, which contains another mirror (full-length), and as her hand guides the door a complete reflection of Eve is startlingly disclosed to us. The mirror image that Charlotte consults is visible only to her, while the doorway mirror image of Eve is beheld only by the *Stage Fright* spectator. Hitchcock employs the conspicuous doubling of Eve to emphasize the split between the dresser role of Doris, whom Charlotte believes she is addressing, and the conniving Eve, who is adroitly laying the conversational groundwork for a final act of betrayal. For perhaps the first time in the film, Charlotte has relaxed her guard sufficiently to divest herself of her carefully maintained theatre persona. She confides to Eve that she has never had a day she is more eager to see the end of. Almost immediately after this declaration. she expresses an unprecedented level of concern for another's well-being. She acknowledges that Eve's tiredness may equal her own, and extends her empathetic awareness further by recognizing the difficulty of being a dresser when one has had no prior experience. She then ventures a compliment—revising her evaluation of Eve's job performance from "quite good" to "very good indeed." We are unprepared for the degree of Charlotte's warmth, sharing, and vulnerability. She becomes more intimately confiding as she talks to "Doris" about how "rainy funerals" distress her, and how troubled she had been when confronted with "the doll in the bloodstained dress" that had been presented to her onstage. "What vermin some people are," Charlotte concludes. She has, for this brief interval, relinquished all connection to acting and its safeguards. And she appears to be testing the waters for a possible friendship with "Doris," even possibly a romantic one. It could be the case, of course, that Charlotte indulges in these open, kindly gestures precisely because she knows the time of "Doris" with her as dresser is nearing an end. She invokes the image of "two ships passing in the night," which to her is linked with the intense, fleeting communion experienced with fellow actors onstage: the compressed life expectancy of character relationships in drama. Charlotte further confesses that she likes Eve, appreciates her sweetness and patience in dealing with someone as demanding as herself, offers her extra money as a parting gesture of appreciation, as well as a "lift" to wherever she may be going.

Hitchcock presents this entire exchange in a sustained medium two shot—a setup in which both women are facing the camera. Charlotte, wearing a white fur, a veil, pearls, and elaborate makeup, seems to be breaking out of the carapace of her magisterial, artificial style. When Eve declares to her how much she loves the theatre, Charlotte retorts that she doesn't know why. "It's an awful life, really," she says. The actress who temporarily separates herself from the demands of role-playing and the strain of keeping up illusions gains emotional stature in doing so, yet at the same time loses power to the dissembling actress, docilely accommodating, who stands beside her. Eve manifests mild discomfort as Charlotte creates a space for genuine affection, but as her subsequent actions demonstrate, Eve grasps that Charlotte's sudden lack of theatrical armor will make her easier to ambush and manipulate.

Notice how Eve's steadfast commitment to her goal and her assumed role in this elaborate charade leaves no room for adjustment in the face of

Figure 8.4. Eve (Jane Wyman) shows us both sides of herself in the dressing room of Charlotte (Marlene Dietrich) in *Stage Fright*.

Charlotte's almost penitent unmasking. Eve's strength within the Mousetrap she and her father have devised is maintained through a continual diminishment of empathy. Her responsiveness to Charlotte's "bids" for a closer attachment is wholly performed. All the power that accrues to theatre in this scene exacerbates coldness and detachment. Whoever is not protected by a conscious role has no safety. Eve's situation here resembles Hamlet's when he is faced with an unexpectedly vulnerable Claudius, in the act of praying. Hamlet persuades himself that Claudius cannot be attacked while kneeling and perhaps (through a determination to repent) making his peace with God. Eve, unlike Hamlet, does not hesitate when Charlotte shifts course, emotionally and even (to a degree) ethically. Charlotte's obliviousness to her danger, in fact, heightens Eve's dedication to her role and the joy in her own proficiency.

The pair leave Charlotte's dressing room, and descend a stairway together as Eve chooses her moment to insist on a private conversation. She asks that Charlotte accompany her to a room where "no one can hear us," in effect answering Charlotte's unveiled warmth and bid for greater closeness with a false invitation to protective seclusion. Eve insists that Charlotte follow her through what seems a dark maze to a space where Charlotte will be utterly deceived and thrown to the wolves (every word of hers broadcast in the immense adjoining theatre) without her having the slightest awareness of Eve's double-pronged betrayal. When Eve locates the right door for her prepared blackmail scene, she secretly peers out before shutting it to take in the nearby stage, where she has time to observe a curtain going up. It is the cue for a new character entrance in the drama. After being confronted with a demand from "Doris" for a confidential discussion of the "bloodstained doll," Charlotte is revealed emerging from a shadow into a close-up. What is caught in her expression is a touching convergence of surprise and vulnerability. Her walk speeds up as she tries to catch up with Eve, who has already taken command of the prearranged stage space in which their talk will play out. Charlotte's way of moving behind Eve gives her the appearance of one taking part in a "Follow the Leader" exercise.

Eve, relishing her role of cunning, pitiless blackmailer, tells Charlotte—with no internal struggle and with no suggestion of truth telling—that she "hates all this." She claims, staying in character, to be "nervous, and . . . so afraid of doing the wrong thing." As she elaborates on her simulated state of fearfulness, we witness Charlotte, in another two shot, recoiling at the sudden realization that "meek" Doris is completely unknown to her. In a blink of time, she sees in the person standing before her a chilling, grasping stranger whose "human attributes" were perhaps all put on. The intent on Doris's part to blackmail is clear, but it is coming to Charlotte as a jolting reply to her decision to open herself to another, with a rare kindness and trust. The theatre space in which she finds herself, as she registers the shock, itself rebukes her for her assumption that she could blithely ignore what the stage demands: a constant recognition of its deceptive power. The hard, level, American voice Eve adopts after dropping her "Doris" persona as she demands money to "hide what she knows" is not a tone she has employed in any of her earlier scenes. Her preferred mode of self-presentation until now has emphasized softness and docility. Eve would like to be regarded, and perhaps regards herself, as a beleaguered helper of those in need, persevering, dutiful, at times out of her depth but capable in a crisis. The abrupt shift to a chilly voice and ruthless demeanor is not only a jolt to Charlotte but also to the spectator. And Hitchcock intends that effect. On the one hand, Eve is playing yet another role, permissibly at some distance from the self she and others recognize. She is, of course, fully aware that she is the enterprising heroine whose every word is being attended to by the police audience in the adjacent theatre. On the other hand, as her remaining encounters in the film—each involving betrayal—suggest, perhaps the Eve who revels in her sudden power to intimidate Charlotte and do harm to her (a larger harm than Charlotte can take in, in spite of her immense, alert intelligence) may indeed be revealing an identity to the audience more authentic than that we have until now relied on.

It is my sense of the narrative that not only Jonathan (the film's false protagonist) is shown to be someone other than he seems to be in his first confession and subsequent fugitive hiding. Eve, too, his partner in eluding capture as the film opens, is unmasked for us during our approach to the film's climax, as we study her quietly self-serving usurpation of the protagonist role that Jonathan has vacated. It is likely that we are too concerned with Eve's adroit handling of the blackmail confrontation to consider whether Charlotte's question to her ("Who are you?") should be ours as well. We seem to be watching Charlotte being forced back into a slippery, specious theatrical mode in the face of Eve's threats and accusations. What is, in fact, actually transpiring is that Charlotte reassumes her grand stage manner to present a large portion of the truth about Jonathan's primary role in the murder of her husband. We are led to believe that we have arrived at the film's climax in this dressing room, but crucially (and misleadingly) it is the first of two confession climaxes that mirror each other. Eve accuses Charlotte of lying in her account of the murder she committed, losing sight of the fact that her own present performance as blackmailer and the covert broadcasting of the pair's "confidential" talk are the major demonstrable falsehoods in evidence. Charlotte avows in response to Eve's disbelief that she is telling the "sacred truth": "I swear to you it is." Addressing Eve here as "Whoever you are," Charlotte expresses her willingness to give this dangerous stranger her jewelry and anything else of value she possesses to keep her name (and professional reputation) separate from the crime.

Their ensuing dialogue is not shown to us. We only hear it echoing, disembodied, in the theatre auditorium while we watch Eve's father and Detective Smith reacting to the melodramatically pitched voices. Commodore Gill, tellingly, is the hypnotically absorbed listener. His rapacious hunger for the incriminating, dramatically charged particulars is designed to match his daughter's "transport" in playing her grand part "to the end." Charlotte's question to Eve, "Why have you been pretending all this time?," is comparable in ethical force to Lars Thorwald's question to Jeffries in *Rear Window* when he finally confronts him face to face: "What is it you want from me?" Eve's answer, disingenuous, attempts to ally her efforts with the interests of a police investigation, a justice-seeking enterprise much larger than herself: "Let's say we needed more evidence." But in fact Eve's motives have entirely been determined by her passion to perform—or, more precisely, to masquerade for many hours in the presence of a great actress without being found out. In Charlotte's shadow she has quietly operated, biding her time for the ultimate recognition scene, proving herself the stronger player in the domain reserved for real life concerns, and even securing sympathy and a bid for friendship from a self-absorbed diva. What is the traction of Eve's disgust at Charlotte's lying, when not a moment of their time together has been anything but deceptive, on her side?

When Eve issues her final warning to Charlotte about not persisting with her evasion and fabrication, the police—offscreen voices—intervene to end the two women's now heated discussion. We see Eve emerge through the dressing room door, advancing toward the camera as though weighed down by an emotional burden, perhaps a ripening regret at her participation in this variation of Hamlet's Mousetrap. Her detective suitor, Smith, comes up behind her and briefly places his hands on her shoulders. She catches the viewer off-guard again by recoiling from his touch. At first it appears that she is attempting to come to terms with whatever was shameful and underhanded in her protracted "false position" as Charlotte's dresser. It is as though her immersion in acting finally pierces her awareness as a form of culpability, and she is, for the first time, inwardly shaken through her no longer "safe" involvement with the stage. In her attempt to "catch the conscience of the Queen," she has not quite succeeded in her backstage melodrama. Instead, it is perhaps her own conscience, Hamlet-fashion, that has been snagged. As she walks closer to the camera, unaccompanied, her tearstained face registers more forcibly, and as she leans against an ornate wall divider, it would appear that she has broken her tie with playacting, and is haunted by her just completed, cruel indulgence of her appetite for it. At precisely this moment, however, Hitchcock cuts to Commodore Gill in the audience area below her. As he moves to intercept her look—which shifts from a shielded privacy to something reserved for a privileged spectator—Gill applauds her for what she has brought off, and though he claps quietly, his rapt approval and standing position make it an ovation. When we return to Eve, she covers her face to reestablish contact with authentic sorrow, but the fact that her father acknowledges her soul-searching and contrition as the capping strokes in the performance he has witnessed lets us feel the theatrical net drawing tight around Eve once again.

Hitchcock cuts from the revelation of Eve's double self-presentation—straddling the divide between authentic and imitated action—to Charlotte, who is being held in custody. She has resumed her imperious persona and composure with "Ordinary" Smith, as she attempts to ward off further police scrutiny. At this juncture, prior to Charlotte learning of the covert broadcast of her conversation with Eve, Jonathan reappears, also with a police escort, but in the crowded confusion makes a break for it, precisely mirroring his attempt to escape police capture in *Stage Fright*'s opening sequence. After racing down the backstage stairs and successfully concealing himself, we watch Eve in pursuit of him. She too is recapitulating her first character action in the film—siding with Jonathan against his law enforcement antagonists, and driving (leading) him to safety. The initial flight by car ("I think we've lost them") is replaced in their prop storage room hideaway by an eighteenth-century carriage set piece, inside which they take refuge.

Before Jonathan launches into his second, revised confession to Eve, we return to Charlotte, who is in the presence of another, older police officer, Sergeant Mellish (Ballard Berkeley). He has been ordered to "keep an eye on her," which provides Charlotte with an opportunity to captivate him with another display of her onstage power. She quickly persuades him to bring her a chair, light her cigarette, and listen to an artfully composed speech. She has not quite decided how to "get around him" when she discovers that every word she spoke to Eve has been overheard by Mellish and transcribed by him in the book he carries. The shorthand record has become the script of her impromptu play with Eve. In one of the most remarkable passages in *Stage Fright*, Charlotte impulsively makes Mellish her confidante, and everything becomes still. Stillness of this sort seems to me the very center of cinema. It reminds me of the moment in *Shadow of a Doubt* (1943) when Uncle Charlie (Joseph Cotten) discovers, while running up the stairs of his sister's home, relieved at his escape from further investigation for murder, when he recalls that his niece (Teresa Wright) knows the truth about him. He turns around and looks down to discover that she is standing in the front doorway below, looking directly at him, a small figure who exudes immense power in the fact of knowing. Or in *Psycho* (1960) when we emerge from the bathtub drain into Marion Crane's (Janet Leigh) dead eye, and survey her face and body in the immobility of death, while the water emitted by the shower head continues its own oblivious music above her. Charlotte tells Mellish, with a detachment and irony that characterize both her own theatrical persona and Marlene Dietrich's, a story with no obvious applicability to her current plight. It concerns the one dog she had as a pet that would not love her and finally showed its aversion by biting her. She had the dog shot, she informs Mellish, which she regards as a just return for "treachery and hatred" when she herself has given "all her love" futilely. She disconcertingly concludes her memory with an analogy linking the dog not to her dead husband or the duplicitous Eve, but to her mother. She refers in close-up to an occasion where her mother struck her across the face, and in the act of alluding to it relives the shock. It is a controlled theatrical presentation of her reason for guarding herself against betrayal in all her relationships. Everyone she knows, we suddenly intuit, is categorized as either an ungrateful dog or an unreadably vindictive parent. Her face visibly tightens as she speaks, and her final expression makes her appear lost somewhere inside her performance, more persuasively than Eve. Silence blossoms deeply all around her.

Charlotte's mother reverie may put us in mind of the erratic, flighty mother of Eve, who seems too distracted to recognize her daughter's needs and provide love, or possibly of Eve's maternal nurturing of Jonathan, which will soon end in a disturbing act of abandonment. Our last view of Charlotte is an extreme close-up as she repeats Mellish's politely puzzled statement about dogs biting their caregivers: "It takes some of them that way." Charlotte leaves us while still caught in a state of surprise over what her performance for Mellish has released emotionally. She speaks her line about dogs seized by an impulse without quite knowing how to take its meaning in, and where it might lead her.

The return to Eve and Jonathan lying side by side in the carriage in the theatre's basement storeroom begins with a stealthy camera approach that makes both of them appear like small children, playing a game that involves not being found by grown-ups. Before their final conversation gets under way we have already been alerted to Jonathan's guilt (of not one but two murders) in an upstairs exchange between a persuasively informed Detective Smith and Eve's abashed, at a loss father. Eve's mental collision with both her own mistaken judgment of Jonathan and of her perilous plight as they rest in their stage prop hiding place lags behind the spectator's. Our viewing knowledge is still not securely held, however. To believe in Jonathan's homicidal exploits we are first obliged to revoke our firmly established conviction of the opening flashback's truth. We know more than Eve at this point, but our knowledge is in disarray. As Eve begins to speak to Jonathan about the near-confession she extracted from Charlotte, she informs him without a trace of apprehension of how Charlotte insisted that he was, in fact, her husband's killer. Eve believes that her time of "enforced" yet exhilarating role-playing has come to an end. With Jonathan she can be the protector and friend she had merely pretended to be with Charlotte, to the latter's shock when the performer's mask was lifted. At last she can unburden her heart without misgiving or barrier.

As soon as Eve arrives at the dangerous phrase "She said you killed him," Hitchcock cuts to a profile two-shot close-up of Eve facing Jonathan. Her eyes and his eyes are both emphasized to a marked degree by a band of light that separates the upper portion of their faces from a lower half kept in shadow. The gaze of each is forcefully probed by this concentration on the isolated stare as the sole discernible feature of the visage landscape. Jonathan concocts an explanation for his apparent arrest that satisfies Eve, briefly. She still rejoices in her mission to make Jonathan's narrative of innocence her primary orientation in the ethical morass around her. Saving him from ill-treatment by others and from the collective assumption that he has performed monstrous deeds has been the main justification for all of her own dubious immersion in theatrical masquerade. Suddenly both of them hear Commodore Gill's disembodied voice—an enveloping force like the ghost of Hamlet's father—breaking into their hiding place with an anxious warning for Eve. "Wherever you are, come away from him. Come away from him. He's dangerous. He's a killer." Jonathan's head has turned away from her when Commodore

Gill's voice floats toward them. He seems to be seeking to ascertain the ghost's whereabouts.

With Jonathan severing eye contact, Eve's eyes—still banded with illumination—respond with palpable horror and confusion to the ghostly command to leave Jonathan and the sense of reality he carries with him. Jonathan makes no attempt to dispute the father's claims. As he attends to the words privately, he nods and turns back to confront Eve again in extreme close-up. "He's right, you know. Charlotte was telling the truth." He divests himself, with apparent relief, of the mask that he has worn with Eve since their first encounter in the film. He endeavors to clear a space for nontheatrical self-declaration in their new vehicle—the immobile, artificial carriage. He seeks to divide the blame for his actions between himself and Charlotte, declaring that he was deliberately goaded into murder by her, and her assurances of love for him proved to be false. Another lover, Freddie Williams, had captured her imagination, and he waited in the wings for her, so to speak, while Jonathan became her expedient tool.

It is worth noting that a similar romantic configuration has developed in Jonathan's and Eve's narrative. Jonathan has been gradually displaced in her affection by the cagily "Ordinary" Detective Smith. She has kept this new attachment a secret from Jonathan. The "hidden," and, in this instance, unsuspected rival is determined to incriminate Jonathan and eradicate his claims to Eve's loyalty and devotion. From the moment that Jonathan (at the ghostly prompting of Eve's father) makes his second and real confession to her, Eve begins to collaborate with Smith (who, like Freddie Williams, is waiting in the wings) to betray Jonathan. It must, of course, be conceded on her behalf that she is now convinced of Jonathan's flagrant previous deception of her and his present complete lack of control. These discoveries, from her perspective, demand increased measures of self-protection and warrant her abandonment of both her lover's role and its maternal supplement.

Jonathan appears unable, on this new confined stage he shares with Eve, to engage in further role-playing or to devise new stratagems for concealing or reconfiguring his guilt. Whatever thoughts arise in him, whatever dark intentions he harbors, he now helplessly utters. His child-like need to reveal all to Eve, whether he trusts her or not, resembles a descent into madness. His madness becomes a kind of transparency, and an unexpected route to authenticity, unlike Hamlet's madness in which calculation and feigning conspire with all the urges in him that he can neither restrain nor fathom. Hamlet's control of the game coexists with a dismantling of his identity in his radical isolation. His soliloquies are efforts to reassemble himself in relation to bidding and purpose. He can no longer fully believe in either of these—doing another's bidding or his sense of purpose—but he cannot forsake them. Jonathan's madness is much simpler, and clear in a childlike way. He unburdens himself entirely to his Ophelia, in the hope of being pardoned, granted absolution, even if his present course of action demands that he eliminate her.

What fascinates in Jonathan's declarations is the air of intimacy he preserves with Eve at all points, whether he is noting Charlotte's manipulation and rejection of him, his susceptibility to rage, or his disbelief in Eve's profession of concern for him. He keeps alive the sense that she is the only person capable of hearing whatever he divulges with the proper recognition and understanding. She is, in a Hamlet-inflected way, both Ophelia and a more powerful Gertrude, the mother who can cleanse and set things to rights, simply by being receptive to his outpourings. In the film that he made just before *Stage Fright*, *Under Capricorn* (1949), Hitchcock also made use of the double confession, where the later retelling alters our awareness of the crime committed, the perpetrator's motives, and the appropriate redistribution of penitence and shame. In *Under Capricorn*, the dramatic question has to do with who is entitled to make the final sacrifice, Lady Henrietta (Ingrid Bergman) or her husband, Sam Flusky (Joseph Cotten). The sacrifice turns on the shame of concealment of a crime versus the shame of status, the latter having to do with Sam's permanent sense of class unworthiness: the former groom who presumed to marry an aristocrat. In *Stage Fright*, the question turns on the reassignment of guilt. Sacrifice and the weight of shame play no part in the transformation of circumstances brought about by the second confession. The exchange of roles transpires in a more heartless atmosphere. Ed Gallafent's essay, "The Dandy and the Magdalen: Interpreting the Long Take in Hitchcock's *Under Capricorn*" (1949), does a brilliant job of elucidating the shame theme in that film, and in separating the dynamic of shame from that of guilt. Gallafent invokes Eve Kosofsky Sedgwick's explanation of what most crucially distinguishes the two behaviors: "shame attaches to and sharpens the sense of what one is, while guilt attaches to what one does" (71). The role Eve adopts with the newly exposed Jonathan is one that, in her view, does not require her to do anything that affixes guilt to her.

In the most remarkable moment of Eve and Jonathan's reversal-filled dialogue, Jonathan asserts, while the camera scrutinizes, in extreme close-up, Eve's eyes and tearstained cheeks: "I'm telling you the truth now." We are permitted to assess her response to this avowal, with no cutaway. Hitchcock's visual presentation of her reaction seems to validate her continuing emotional attachment to him and a reciprocal silent truth-telling on her part. It may well be the case, however, that—without her full awareness—it is precisely here that Eve shifts back into role-playing. Choosing her words carefully, lest she do anything to distress him, she whispers: "Jonathan, I feel desperately sorry for you." The unwavering camera gaze locked on her concentrated, open expression cannot unearth the slightest hint of deception. And yet when the camera returns to Jonathan's listening face (at equally close range) as she attempts to convince him further of her sympathy by saying—in repetition—"Really, I do," his head turns directly toward her and he issues an unsettling refusal of her claim: "No, you don't. You're not sorry at all. You don't care what happens to me." At first the spectator is led to infer that he misconstrues her words and expression and that it is his madness that blinds him to her genuine fellow-feeling. We also detect in his voice the petulant child's demand for reassurance, which, if provided, he would, even if doubtful, inwardly accept. When Hitchcock cuts back to her look as she silently processes his accusation, we have grounds for believing that it is the self-protective actress who is now confronting him. Jonathan's instincts were certainly quicker and possibly sounder than ours in noticing her emotional withdrawal. He now, retroactively, seems right in sharply pointing it out.

Eve's revised tactic, instigated by his announced suspicion, is a whispered suggestion that he could "give himself up." She adds that the authorities he entrusted himself to would "take care of him." They would know that he couldn't have perpetrated such deeds were he not "sick." She deftly tiptoes around the word "madness," which we see her considering briefly before setting it aside in favor of a more ambiguous substitute. Jonathan again disagrees with her formulaic counsel. He has no reason to believe that he will be dealt with leniently. He observes, astutely, that both he and Charlotte are likely to be hanged—he for executing the crime, Charlotte for planning it. Then, taking up Eve's reference to his "sickness," he seems to find, under the auspices of madness, a solution that derives from Eve's logic. Were he to murder Eve, for no ascertainable reason, there might indeed be grounds for him to be dealt with as one deranged, rather than rationally accountable. Hitchcock cuts to a close-up of Jonathan's and Eve's hands, resting beside each other, at waist level. Jonathan's hands seem to be responding to the mental signal to strangle. They express a tension of indecision. Eve's hands reach out to his kindly and cover them supportively. They are the hands of an actress here, and assume the directive power of a mother who will lead her bewildered son to safety.

By this stage of the scene, we have been apprised not only of Jonathan's capacity for forgetting his close connection to Eve and irrationally attacking her, but also of Jonathan's involvement in a second act of murder. Another victim, a female, preceded Jonathan's slaying of Charlotte's husband. For this earlier crime, Jonathan had been exonerated for acting in "self-defense." The revelation of a second murder is curious. The victim plays no part in *Stage Fright*'s story world. She seems to have been brought in as a surplus sign of Jonathan's guilt, as though Charlotte's husband's death did not establish his ingrained and incurable destructive nature with sufficient clarity and force. The corpse of Mr. Inwood, revealed to us in the false flashback, perhaps still does not "belong" to Jonathan sufficiently. The flashback images we have beheld and believed in earlier still linger as a countertruth to Jonathan's revised account. And for Jonathan to be tilted in the direction of madness, a darker pattern needs to be drawn. I regard this hovering specter of a tenuous "other death" as a floating signifier introduced into Jonathan and Eve's last encounter. From the beginning of the film, Eve has been a secret sharer of Jonathan's hazy guilt in the killing of Charlotte's husband. The nature of her involvement and her culpability as a "shield" for her would-be lover rather closely resembles Charlotte's own. And murder is once again straining to happen, to be made visible and solid. Eve is justified in plotting Jonathan's death now to save herself if the weight of Jonathan's monstrous acts, his utter lostness, has been decisively communicated to the viewer. And I would argue that this phantom earlier crime and victim suddenly imposed on Jonathan, then acknowledged by him, doesn't quite attain this weight. He and Eve seem equals in self-division, and his confused torment is not more troubling than her expert manipulation of him. The death image that floats in the air indefinitely seems uncertain of whether to fasten itself to Jonathan or Eve.

As Eve covers the hands of a potential strangler with the strong clasp of an intervening mother surrogate, we may recall Charlotte's final reference to her mother striking her across the face. Are Eve's hands (separated for now, in close-up, from the face of their owner) gentle, or are they brutality in disguise, awaiting their moment? They manage, in any event, to win Jonathan's trust and compliance to a degree that her words thus far have not. As he relinquishes his hostile urge, she renews her effort to reach him verbally, using the power of sustained touch to give her language credibility. The hands speak of her intention to protect him as she leads him out of their shared darkness to safety. "Jonathan, I don't hear a sound now. I think we can go now. We'll go out through the orchestra pit, and then I'll take you [back] to my father's boat. Come along." Throughout this whispered speech, we view the two figures' heads in close proximity. Jonathan accepts the promise that the hands convey to him, and finds poignant further confirmation in her gaze and gentle tone. Eve opens the door of the prop carriage, steps free of it, and waits for him to follow, which he does, like a child steered back to grateful submission to his parent's will. She alone can make sure that the two of them avoid the traps that the world has laid. "She has led me to her father's boat once before" is the subtextual prompting for Jonathan's following her, "and I found refuge there."

Eve continues to walk ahead of him, through a jumble of props, which are shorn of any identifying or cohesive narrative context. This field of mixed up objects seem linked to Jonathan's revised confession. The elements of self-presentation that once endowed his speech and person with enchanting power have fallen to pieces. After the pair arrive at the door leading to the theatre orchestra pit, they pause and look at each other, a look meant to confirm the truth of their bond. Eve stands beside the open door, inviting Jonathan's trust in confronting the risks ahead. If he simply makes the choice to pass through it, they will somehow succeed in "finding their way back" to a lost realm of belief and security. Contemplating her features for what will be the last time, Jonathan places his faith in the image of the person she offers to him; he is persuaded that she has not given up on him, that she still means to protect him. We are reminded here that she first entered his story when he barged onto the stage she occupied during a scene rehearsal at the drama academy and brought his crisis to her. His own urgent plot interrupted the role she was performing for her drama teacher, and it immediately absorbed her, as a more heroic, worthy script than the one she had been assigned, whose memorized lines she was delivering. Now, with a single, repudiating gesture, she ends her involvement in his play. No sooner does Jonathan go through the door Eve has led him to than she swiftly shuts and locks it, preventing his return. She then cries out "Here he is" for the benefit of the police who are no doubt searching for him.

The locking of a door to sever connection with a former romantic partner is reminiscent of Devlin (Cary Grant) in the final scene of Hitchcock's *Notorious* (1946) locking the car door against Alexander

Sebastian (Claude Rains), thus ensuring his destruction. Sebastian's wife, Alicia (Ingrid Bergman), sits groggily beside Devlin as he makes the decision: "No room, Sebastian." Devlin's action implies that the vehicle the restored couple escapes in neatly divides the innocent from the guilty, a false assumption that brings to an ironic conclusion the pervasive masquerade that has dominated the entire narrative. Eve's shout to the police through the sealed door culminates her grandest feat of role-playing. She rekindled the lost, mad Jonathan's faith in their emotional connection and what it still meant to her, then abruptly disavows the attachment, turning it into an expedient "act" that entailed no lingering moral claims. Like Charlotte, Jonathan is punished in *Stage Fright* for his belief that he can somehow transcend or forsake theatre, by exchanging captivity in artifice for something more authentic, open, humanly anchored. Our next view of Jonathan, on the other side of the door, incorporates the theatre space he has reentered, shown from a vast height. He is reduced to a tiny, disoriented, scurrying presence, below the stage. Hitchcock's bird's-eye, surveillance perspective declares that the theatre space defines a world, the only world we have access to. Having futilely pounded against the door once Eve abandons him (a spectacle we hear rather than see from Eve's side of the door, which she leans against in relief, expressing her newfound freedom of detachment), Jonathan appears dwarfed by the theatre maze that opens before him. A voice answering Eve's shout directs Jonathan's pursuers to look for him in the orchestra, where he is indeed visible. The disembodied voice crying out sharply focuses our own searching gaze—Look there! Our sighting is instantly implicated in the task of capturing.

The following shot is a close-up of Jonathan's desperately exposed, frightened face. He is pitifully adrift and infirm of purpose, unable to regain command of the theatre that was once his "home." It will no longer serve his needs. It seems that the theatre, like Eve, is repudiating him. His anxiety-filled weakness causes us to repudiate him as well, breaking whatever threads of identification that may have lingered after he boldly disowned the "spent" truth of his flashback story. We are now in league with the footsteps audibly approaching Jonathan and the shadowy figures closing in on him. Jonathan, in blind panic, climbs onto the stage itself. Another voice calls out "He was in the theatre after all." The stage is immense and not quite bare. A prop trellis stands near the backstage wall. Jonathan slips as he attempts to vacate the stage again, where adversaries enter through doors to the left and right of him. His clumsiness at the edge of the stage results in his being crushed by a plunging fire curtain, made of iron, that a stagehand has released. The curtain's descent carries with it the implied force of a blade that slices through him. We imbibe the horror of this execution through a reaction shot of Eve, who makes her own stage entrance—accompanied by Detective Smith—at precisely the moment when Jonathan is destroyed. He goes to his death on that ambiguous edge of the proscenium, which divides the realm of performance from that of "life elsewhere" in the audience space beyond.

Detective Smith turns Eve's head so that it is pressed against his chest. She is spared the sight of what her victorious last trick of role-playing has brought about. When she strives to look back, just once, he turns her face away again with his hands, and prevents her from doing so. He does not tarry at this bloody scene, out of concern for Eve's well-being. He efficiently leads her through doors that afford distance and possible release from the dire spectacle. Smith's wordless action of taking her away, with the prominent highlighting of his hand gestures, subtly reenacts the movement of Eve guiding Jonathan to what she had identified as his doorway of rescue. As Smith and Eve walk away from the camera, their backs turned to emphasize their remoteness, Hitchcock allows us to see that the floor they cross consists of a series of spotlight circles, separated by shadow. Eve, we may presume, both feels stricken by the death scene she has beheld and intuitively commences a performance of grief, which echoes the performance she gave after breaking her ties with Charlotte. A soft piano theme accompanies the couple's departure, a departure that we observe from a fixed distance, as we discern the various circles of stage light that emerge in Eve's wake.

Audible and left behind in this ending are the voices of policemen endeavoring to make sense of the grisly mess onstage. They are like Fortinbras arriving to impose order on the tableau of corpses in *Hamlet*, but Hitchcock grants them only the feeble force of perplexed murmuring, one more spectral volley of echoes from the cavernous stage. In the course of *Stage Fright*, the theatre curtain that lightly raised in the opening credits, proclaiming safety, has turned to lethal iron. Perhaps the film's first establishing shot of a visibly unrepaired London, laid low in the stunned aftermath of the war, supplies a clue as to why theatre accumulates such oppressive weight as *Stage Fright* proceeds. The entire effort to regroup and collectively start afresh in the years following war trauma—the prolonged Blitz, the ravenous, devastating conflict in Europe, and the mandated separation of so many English children from their parents for "safety's sake"—has resulted in a seemingly endless postwar rationing of material goods and pinched pleasures. The resumption of normal life, the sense that things are moving forward again in peacetime clemency is perhaps—from the film's perspective—a general charade. Instead of loss and horror being given their due (in massive ceremonies of grief) a national self-hypnosis has taken place. The entire panorama of so-called ordinary life has been overlaid with theatre. We create a theatre of heightened, stylized gestures to cover up the multitude of common activities, ways of engaging, from which we have become estranged.

Jonathan is a representative, diminished Hamlet for a kingdom steeped in decay and repressive, survivor posturing. Italo Calvino wrote in his late novel, *The Castle of Crossed Destinies*, of a Hamlet sealed off from the reflective grandeur of his language. He is exposed as someone not ineffective in the least where vengeful murder is concerned. Far from being incapable of killing, "it is the only thing he succeeds in doing" (94). Hamlet, in his balked struggle to kill the right man, mercilessly dispatches many wrong, mistaken substitutes: Polonius, Rosencrantz, Guildenstern, Laertes, and, as the last in the series, Claudius. He might also be held accountable for Ophelia's death, if not literally guilty of it. In a recent rethinking of the play, *Hamlet and the Vision of Darkness*, Rhodri Lewis writes: "Whatever an individual [in Hamlet] might strive to believe, he always and only exists as a participant in a form of hunting—one in which he, like everyone else, is both hunter and prey."

Jonathan's angry, arguably mad embroilment in two foggy murders suggests a figure groping for definition in a realm where all the available criteria are seductively theatrical. He decides to dwell entirely in this alienated theatrical mode. His doom comes about when his theatre resources fail him, and he loses the protection and sharable meaning of his cover story. Hamlet's cover story, in contrast, is not broken and lost in the same fashion. He remains a supremely effective hunter disguised by his language, by the imposing range and adeptness of his thought. Horatio—the unwaveringly loyal friend—preserves his story on stage, and pledges to carry it unsullied into the future. Fortinbras, with all his military order and new authority, cannot compete with it or supplant it.

Jonathan and Charlotte, the two characters initially designated as larger than life performers in *Stage Fright*, eventually exhibit the strain and constriction of lives entirely performed. They crave a reprieve (somehow, from some untainted human source) from theatrical saturation, and turn to Eve to be succored, because she seems to stand outside the sphere of compulsive playacting. In their decision to cast role-playing aside for exposure to something better, more substantial, higher on the plane of real-world feeling, they forfeit their grounding on the stage and their ornately crafted identity. Jonathan, who entrusts himself more completely than Charlotte does to Eve (his Ophelia guide and rescuer, the defender of his innocence) loses his life. He is cut in two for his temerity in assuming that there is a real life, a life beyond theatre, awaiting him, to which he can return. The shock of the ending of *Stage Fright* is that the gradually revealed protagonist and ethical arbiter, Eve, is herself a purely theatrical personage. Through her ministrations, the forces of unconditional theatricality triumph. She is remarkably dangerous in her maneuvering as an innocent, unmindful of her actual loyalties. She marries herself to the stage, and releases its darkness, in the unselfconscious guise of restraint and conventional decency. With Eve's final entrance, following the Mousetrap play she has improvised for Jonathan's belief and capture, she experiences a moment of harrowing stage fright at the sight of Jonathan's stage death, cruelly demarcating the border between theatre and whatever lies beyond.

Works Cited

Aeschylus. *Prometheus Bound.* Translated by Herbert Weir Smyth in two volumes. Cambridge: Harvard University Press, 1926.
Affron, Charles. *Cinema and Sentiment.* Chicago: University of Chicago Press, 1982.
Anderegg, Michael A. *William Wyler.* Boston: Twayne Publishers, 1979.
Auiler, Dan. *Vertigo: The Making of a Hitchcock Classic.* New York: St. Martin's Griffin, 2000.
Balázs, Béla. *Béla Balázs: Early Film Theory.* Visible Man *and* The Spirit of Film. Translated by Rodney Livingstone, edited by Erica Carter. New York: Berghahn Books, 2011.
Barr, Charles. *Vertigo.* London: BFI Publishing, 2004.
Bazin, André. *What Is Cinema?, volume 1.* Translated by Hugh Gray. Berkeley: University of California Press, 2005.
———. *What Is Cinema?, volume 2.* Translated by Hugh Gray. Berkeley: University of California Press, 2005.
Belknap, Robert L. *Plots.* New York: Columbia University Press, 2016.
Benjamin, Walter. "Berlin Childhood around 1900." In *Selected Writings, Volume 3: 1935–38.* Cambridge, Mass.: Belknap Press of Harvard University Press, 2002.
Blackmur, R. P. *Selected Essays of R. P. Blackmur.* Edited with an introduction by Denis Donoghue. New York: Ecco Press, 1986.
Bloom, Harold. *Hamlet: Poem Unlimited.* New York: Riverhead Books, 2004.
Bossuet, Jacques-Bénigne, and Collier, Jeremy. *Maxims and Reflections on Plays.* London: Printed for R. Sare, at Grays-Inn Gate, in Holborne, 1699.
Bowman, Barbara. *Master Space: Film Images of Capra, Lubitsch, Sternberg, and Wyler.* Westport, Conn.: Greenwood Press, 1992.
Bresson, Robert. *Notes on the Cinematographer.* Translated by Jonathan Griffin. Copenhagen: Green Integer 2, 1997.
Brook, Peter. *The Empty Space.* New York: Touchstone, 1996.
Calvino, Italo. *The Castle of the Crossed Destinies.* Translated by William Weaver. New York: Mariner Books, 1979.
Cavell, Stanley. *Pursuits of Happiness: The Hollywood Comedy of Remarriage.* Cambridge: Harvard University Press, 1981.

———. "The World as Things: Collecting Thoughts on Collecting." In *Cavell on Film*, edited by William Rothman. Albany: State University of New York Press, 2005.

———. *The World Viewed: Enlarged Edition*. Cambridge: Harvard University Press, 1979.

Chion, Michel. *Film, a Sound Art*. Translated by Claudia Gorbman. New York: Columbia University Press, 2009.

———. *The Voice in Cinema*. Translated by Claudia Gorbman. New York: Columbia University Press, 1999.

Coleridge, Samuel Taylor. *The Complete Poems*. London: Penguin Classics, 2004.

Cukor, George. *Interviews*. Edited by Robert Emmet Long. Jackson: University Press of Mississippi, 2001.

Deleuze, Gilles. *Cinema 2: The Time Image*. Translated by Hugh Tomlinson and Robert Galeta. Minneapolis: University of Minnesota Press, 1989.

de Rougemont, Denis. *Love in the Western World*. Translated by Montgomery Belgion. Princeton: Princeton University Press, 1983.

Dreiser, Theodore. *An American Tragedy*. New York: Signet, 1964.

———. *Jennie Gerhardt*. New York: Penguin, 1994.

Eyman, Scott. *Cary Grant: A Brilliant Disguise*. New York: Simon & Schuster, 2020.

Fisher, Philip. "Acting, Reading, Fortune's Wheel: Sister Carrie and the Life History of Objects." In *American Realism: New Essays*, edited by Eric J. Sundquist. Baltimore: Johns Hopkins University Press, 1982.

Fowler, Gene. *Good Night, Sweet Prince: The Life and Times of John Barrymore*. New York: Viking Press, 1944.

Fujiwara, Chris. *Jacques Tourneur: The Cinema of Nightfall*. Baltimore: Johns Hopkins University Press, 1998.

Gallafent, Ed. "The Dandy and the Magdalen: Interpreting the Long Take in Hitchcock's *Under Capricorn*." In *Style and Meaning: Studies in the Detailed Analysis of Film*, edited by John Gibbs and Douglas Pye. New York: Manchester University Press, 2005.

Grissom, James. *Follies of God: Tennessee Williams and the Women of the Fog*. New York: Alfred A. Knopf, 2015.

Gross, Daniel M. *The Secret History of Emotion: From Aristotle's* Rhetoric *to Modern Brain Science*. Chicago: University of Chicago Press, 2006.

Jackson, Russell. *Theatres on Film: How the Cinema Imagines the Stage*. Manchester: Manchester University Press, 2013.

Jacobs, Lea. *Film Rhythm after Sound: Technology, Music, and Performance*. Berkeley: University of California Press, 2015.

Keating, Patrick. *Hollywood Lighting from the Silent Era to Film Noir*. New York: Columbia University Press, 2010.

Kerrigan, William. *Hamlet's Perfection*. Baltimore: Johns Hopkins University Press, 1994.

Klevan, Andrew. *Aesthetic Evaluation and Film*. Manchester: Manchester University Press, 2018.

———. *Disclosure of the Everyday: Undramatic Achievement in Narrative Film*. Trowbridge, Wiltshire, UK: Flicks Books, 1999.
Knapf, Robert, ed. *Theatre and Film: A Comparative Anthology*. New Haven: Yale University Press, 2004.
Knight, G. Wilson. *The Wheel of Fire*. Rev. ed. London: Routledge, Kegan and Paul, 1998.
Kouvaros, George. *Where Does It Happen? John Cassavetes and Cinema at the Breaking Point*. Minneapolis: University of Minnesota Press, 2004.
Kozloff, Sarah. *The Best Years of Our Lives*. London: Palgrave Macmillan (BFI Books), 2011.
Kracauer, Siegfried. *Theory of Film: The Redemption of Physical Reality*. Introduction by Miriam Bratu Hansen. Princeton: Princeton University Press, 1997.
Lash, Dominic. *The Cinema of Disorientation: Inviting Confusion*. New Brunswick, N.J.: Rutgers University Press, 2020.
Lewis, Rhodri. *Hamlet and the Vision of Darkness*. Princeton: Princeton University Press, 2017.
MacDowell, James. *Irony in Film*. London: Palgrave Macmillan, 2016.
Miller, Gabriel. *William Wyler: The Life and Films of Hollywood's Most Celebrated Director*. Lexington: University Press of Kentucky, 2013.
Moretti, Franco. *The Way of the World: The Bildungsroman in European Culture*. Translated by Albert Sbragia. New York: Verso, 2000.
Morrison, Michael. *John Barrymore, Shakespearean Actor*. New York: Cambridge University Press, 1997.
Mulvey, Laura. *Death 24x a Second: Stillness and the Moving Image*. London: Reaktion Books, 2015.
Munro, Alice. "Chance." In *Runaway*. New York: Alfred Knopf, 2004.
Nabokov, Vladimir. *Nikolai Gogol*. New York: New Directions, 1981.
Naremore, James. *Acting in the Cinema*. Berkeley: University of California Press, 1988.
Olivier, Laurence. *On Acting*. London: Sceptre, 1987.
Paul, William. *Ernst Lubitsch's American Comedy*. New York: Columbia University Press, 1983.
Perez, Gilberto. *The Eloquent Screen: A Rhetoric of Film*. Minneapolis: University of Minnesota Press, 2019.
Pippin, Robert B. *Filmed Thought: Cinema as Reflective Form*. Chicago: University of Chicago Press, 2020.
———. *The Philosophical Hitchcock: "Vertigo" and the Anxieties of Unknowingness*. Chicago: University of Chicago Press, 2017.
Pomerance, Murray. *Alfred Hitchcock's America*. Cambridge: Polity Press, 2013.
———. *The Horse Who Drank the Sky: Film Experience beyond Narrative and Theory*. New Brunswick, N.J.: Rutgers University Press, 2008.
Pomerance, Murray, and Steve Rybin, eds. *Hamlet Lives in Hollywood: John Barrymore and the Acting Tradition Onscreen*. Edinburgh: Edinburgh University Press, 2019.

Rilke, Rainer Maria. "Sunset." Translated by Robert Bly. In *Risking Everything*, edited by Roger Housden. New York: Harmony Books, 2003.

Rivette, Jacques. *Rivette: Texts and Interviews*. Edited and with an introduction by Jonathan Rosenbaum, translated by Amy Gateff and Tom Milne. London: BFI, 1977.

Rose, Gillian. *Judaism and Modernity: Philosophical Essays*. London: Verso, 2017.

Ruefle, Mary. *My Private Property*. Seattle: Wave Books, 2016.

Rybin, Steve. *Gestures of Love: Romancing Performance in Classical Hollywood Cinema*. Albany: State University of New York Press, 2017.

Sedgwick, Eve Kosofsky. *The Weather in Proust*. Edited by Jonathan Goldberg. Durham: Duke University Press, 2011.

Sesonske, Alexander. *Jean Renoir: The French Films 1924–1939*. Cambridge: Harvard University Press, 1980.

Shakespeare, William. *Hamlet*. Edited by Cyrus Hoy. New York: W. W. Norton, 1963.

Sikov, Ed. *On Sunset Boulevard: The Life and Times of Billy Wilder*. New York: Hyperion, 1998.

Snow, Edward. *A Study of Vermeer. Revised and Enlarged Edition*. Berkeley: University of California Press, 1994.

Steimatsky, Noa. *The Face of Film*. New York: Oxford University Press, 2017.

Taylor, Aaron, ed. *Theorizing Film Acting*. New York: Routledge, 2012.

Thompson, Kristin. *Breaking the Glass Armor: Neoformalist Film Analysis*. Princeton: Princeton University Press, 1988.

Trahair, Lisa. *The Comedy of Philosophy: Sense and Nonsense in Early Cinematic Slapstick*. Albany: State University of New York Press, 2007.

Trotter, David. "Hiatus at 4 a.m." *London Review of Books*, June 4, 2015, 19–22.

Index

accidents, theatrical, 10, 60, 63, 221, 241
actor-directors in *Vertigo*, 6, 182–214
Aeschylus, 218–19
Agee, James, 48
aloneness, 98, 104–5, 176; in *Carrie*, 86–94; in *The Crowd*, 76–81; in *The Eddy Duchin Story*, 27–28; in *Hamlet*, 218, 223, 232, 251; in *In the Bedroom*, 94–97, 98–104; John Barrymore, figure of, 145, 153, 155; in *True Heart Susie*, 81–82; in *Umberto D*, 69–76, 97–98; in *Way Down East*, 82–86; in *Woman in Blue Reading a Letter*, 73
American Tragedy, An (Dreiser), 110–14
Apartment, The (Wilder), 65
Arnheim, Rudolf, 34, 35
artifice, theatrical, 121, 217; in *Dinner at Eight*, 151; in *The Eddy Duchin Story*, 1–2, 16, 24, 31; in *Hamlet*, 252; in *Laugh, Clown, Laugh*, 231; in *The Lost Weekend*, 58, 59, 63; in *Lust, Caution*, 13; in *Mulholland Drive*, 164, 176; in *Stage Fright*, 252, 254, 258, 270; in *To Be or Not to Be*, 239, 240, 244; in *Vertigo*, 183, 185–86, 197, 205, 210. See also illusion
authenticity: of film, 35–36; in *Hamlet*, 252, 265; historical, 184, 198; of setting, 36, 43, 47, 58, 247;

in *Stage Fright*, 265, 270. See also "reality"

Balázs, Béla, 34
Barr, Charles, 196
Barrymore, John, 141–57; in *Counsellor at Law*, 148; in *Dinner at Eight*, 142, 144, 145–47, 149–57; in *Dr. Jekyll and Mr. Hyde*, 152; as François Villon, 142, 143–44; in *Grand Hotel*, 141, 145; as Hamlet, 144, 151; in *Midnight*, 147–48; as Richard III, 140, 150, 152; in *Twentieth Century*, 142–43
Bazin, André, 3, 44–45, 69–70
Beckett, Samuel, 45
Beloved Rogue, The (Crosland), 142. See also Villon, François
Benjamin, Walter, 159, 166, 189
Benny, Jack, 232, 238–39
Berkeley, Bishop, 39
Berkeley, Busby, 38–43
Berry, Wendell, 38
Bicycle Thieves (De Sica), 44
Blackmur, R.P., "Crime and Punishment," 205–6
Blue Velvet (Lynch), 173
Bossuet, Jacques-Bénigne, 69
Brenon, Herbert, *Laugh, Clown, Laugh*, 217, 223–32
Bresson, Robert, 34, 35, 74
broken theatre, 242, 243, 245
Brook, Peter, 45

Calvino, Italo, *The Castle of Crossed Destinies*, 272
camera-life, 33–37
camera-truth, 33–37
Carrie (Wyler), 86–94, 98, 101, 108
Carrington, Margaret, 150
Casablanca (Curtiz), 11
Castle of Crossed Destinies, The (Calvino), 272
Cavell, Stanley, 37–38, 109
champagne song (Verdi), 49–52
Chaney, Lon, 223, 226, 231
Chaplin, Charlie, 45–46, 98; *The Circus*, 45–46
characters as directors. *See* actor-directors
child, 99, 182, 271; and childhood, 9, 18–20, 183–84, 201, 228; Peter in *The Eddy Duchin Story*, 1–2, 16–31; spectators in *Laugh, Clown, Laugh*, 224–26, 231–32. *See also* play
Chopin, Frédéric, 25–30
Chopin's Nocturne in E flat major, 25–30
Circus, The (Chaplin), 45–46
Coleridge, Samuel Taylor, "The Rime of the Ancient Mariner," 186
comedy, 12; in *Double Indemnity*, 61–62; in *Laugh, Clown, Laugh*, 227, 230, 231; in *The Lost Weekend*, 46, 54, 56, 58–60, 61, 63, 66; *The Royal Family of Broadway*, 146; *To Be or Not to Be*, 232–33, 234, 235, 236, 237, 238–39, 241, 245. *See also* romantic comedy
Cook, Whitfield, 254
Counsellor at Law (Wyler), 148
Crime and Punishment (Dostoyevski), 205–6, 208
Crosland, Alan, *The Beloved Rogue*, 142
Crowd, The (Vidor), 76–81, 98
"Crying" (Orbison), 178–79

Cukor, George, *Dinner at Eight*, 142, 144, 145–47, 149–57

danse macabre, 7, 36–37, 52
"Danse Macabre" (Saint-Saëns), 36
death, 215–73; in *Dinner at Eight*, 145, 151, 152, 153–57; in *Dr. Jekyll and Mr. Hyde*, 152; in *The Eddy Duchin Story*, 1–2, 7, 16–31; in *Hamlet*, 215–73; in *The Heiress*, 120; in *In the Bedroom*, 94–97, 98–104; in *La Règle du Jeu* (Renoir), 36–37; in *Lust, Caution*, 16; in *Mulholland Drive*, 165n1, 174, 176, 179–80; in *Stage Fright*, 217, 245, 246, 247–48, 252, 253, 254, 264, 268–73; in *To Be or Not to Be*, 217, 233, 234–35, 242–45; in *Vagabond*, 180n2; in *Vertigo*, 165n1, 182, 188–92, 195–96, 198, 206, 207–11, 214; Violetta's, 50
Debord, Guy, 7
de Lisle, Claude Joseph Rouget, "La Marseillaise," 11–12
de Rougemont, Denis, 208–9
De Sica, Vittorio, 45; *Bicycle Thieves*, 44; *Miracle in Milan*, 44; *Umberto D*, 69–78, 97–98
Dial M for Murder (Hitchcock), 182
Dickens, Charles, *A Tale of Two Cities*, 149
Dinner at Eight (Cukor), 142, 144, 145–47, 149–57
Dinner at Eight (Ferber-Kaufman), 145
Dostoyevski, Fyodor, *Crime and Punishment*, 205–6, 208
Double Indemnity (Wilder), 61–62
Dreiser, Theodore, 108–9; *An American Tragedy*, 110–14; *Jennie Gerhardt*, 107, 109; *Sister Carrie*, 86, 108
Dr. Jekyll and Mr. Hyde (Robertson) (film), 152

Dubus, Andre, "Killings," 94

Easy Living (Leisen), 60
Eddy Duchin Story, The (Sidney), 1–2, 7, 16–31
Emerson, Ralph Waldo, "Experience," 181
enchantment, 4, 161; object, 117; in *Stage Fright*, 249, 269; in *Vertigo*, 182, 195, 206, 212
Eurydice, 165n1

fantasy, 13, 19, 21, 48, 216–17; film, 37–38, 55; in *The Lost Weekend*, 52, 54, 55, 57, 60, 62, 64, 65, 66; in *Mulholland Drive*, 160, 169, 180; in *Vertigo*, 188, 203, 212
fathers and father-figures: Commodore Gill, 252, 253–55, 259, 261, 262, 264–65; Dr. Sloper, 114–17, 119–40; Eddy Duchin, 1–2, 7, 16–31; George Hurstwood, 86–94, 101; Hamlet's, 251, 264; Matt Fowler, 94–97; in *Mulholland Drive*, 173–74, 176; Tito/Flik, 223–30; Wang Chia-Chih's, 13
Fellini, Federico: *La Strada*, 98; *Nights of Cabiria*, 98
Ferber, Edna and George Kaufman: *Dinner at Eight*, 145; *The Royal Family of Broadway*, 146
Field, Todd, *In the Bedroom*, 94–97, 98–104
film reality. *See* reality
Fisher, Philip, 108
Fiske, Irving, 246
Freud, Sigmund, 143
Fujiwara, Chris, 3–4

Gallafent, Ed, 266
Gibran, Kahlil, *The Prophet*, 96–97
gifts in *An American Tragedy*, 110–14
Gish, Lillian, 81–84

Gogol, Nikolai, "The Overcoat," 250
Goulding, Edmund, *Grand Hotel*, 141, 145
Grand Hotel (Goulding), 141, 145
Griffith, D. W., 104: *True Heart Susie*, 81–82; *Way Down East*, 82–86
Grissom, James, 228

Hamlet (Shakespeare), 49, 144, 151, 215–73
Hansen, Miriam, 34
Harring, Laura Elena, 161, 173
Hawks, Howard, *Twentieth Century*, 142–43
Heiress, The (Wyler), 107–8, 114–17, 118–40
hiddenness, 57, 73, 153, 231, 250, 253; hidden objects, 57, 63, 64, 66, 174; hidden theatrical components, 5, 20, 38, 105
Hitchcock, Alfred, 166; *Dial M for Murder*, 182; *North by Northwest*, 6; *Notorious*, 53–54, 174, 269–70; *Psycho*, 263; *Rear Window*, 261; *Rope*, 182, 250; *Shadow of a Doubt*, 263; *Stage Fright*, 182, 217, 245–50, 252–73; *Under Capricorn*, 266; *Vertigo*, 6, 165, 181–214
Hitchcock, Pat, 254
Hitler, Adolph, 236–39
Hopkins, Arthur, *Richard III*, 150
Horatio, 217, 222–24, 230, 231, 272

illusion, 5, 7, 23, 46, 216–17, 219; in Busby Berkley musicals, 39; in *Laugh, Clown, Laugh*, 226, 228, 230; in *The Lost Weekend*, 52, 56, 64; in *Lust, Caution*, 14, 15, 16; in *Mulholland Drive*, 168, 178; in *Out of the Past*, 3–4; of privacy, 71, 104; in *Stage Fright*, 246, 249, 258; in *To Be or Not to Be*, 232, 239, 243, 244;

illusion *(continued)*
  in *Vertigo*, 182, 184, 186, 205, 210, 211, 213
In the Bedroom (Field), 94–97, 98–104
Intermezzo (Ratoff), 13
Invasion of the Body Snatchers (Siegel), 8
irrationality, 41, 182–83, 185, 200, 206, 212

James, Henry, 217; *The Turn of the Screw*, 211; *Washington Square*, 108, 117
Jennie Gerhardt (Dreiser), 107, 109

Kafka, Franz, 33–34
Kazan, Elia, *On the Waterfront*, 7–8
Keats, John, 205, 233
"Killings" (Dubus), 94. See also *In the Bedroom* (Field)
Knight, G. Wilson, 222, 233, 251
Kracauer, Siegfried, 33–34, 35, 37–41, 44, 66

La Grande Illusion (Renoir), 9–13, 16
"La Marseillaise" (de Lisle), 11–12
La Règle du Jeu (Renoir), 7, 36–37, 52
La Strada (Fellini), 98
La Traviata (Verdi), 46–63, 66
Lady Eve, The (Sturges), 185
Lang, Fritz, *You Only Live Once*, 4–5
Lash, Dominic, 8
Laugh, Clown, Laugh (Brenon), 217, 223–32
Leave Her to Heaven (Stahl), 166
Lee, Ang, *Lust, Caution*, 13–16
Leisen, Mitchell: *Easy Living*, 60; *Midnight*, 147–48
Letter from an Unknown Woman (Ophüls), 45
Lewis, Rhodri, 272
"Libiamo ne' lieti calici" (Verdi), 49–52
Little Foxes, The (Wyler), 139

Long Day's Journey into Night (O'Neill), 151
Lost Weekend, The (Wilder), 35, 46–47, 48–53, 54–61, 62–67
Love in the Afternoon (Wilder), 55
Love Me Tonight (Mamoulian), 43–45
Lubitsch, Ernst, 64, 66; *To Be or Not to Be*, 7, 217, 232–45, 246; *Trouble in Paradise*, 240
Lust, Caution (Lee), 13–16
Lynch, David: *Blue Velvet*, 173; *Mulholland Drive*, 159–80

Mamoulian, Rouben, *Love Me Tonight*, 43–45
Man with a Movie Camera (Vertov), 40
Marcus, Millicent, 70–71
Masina, Giulietta, 98
Maxwell, William, 159
Midnight (Leisen), 147–48
Milland, Ray, 46, 57–61, 63–64, 66
Miracle in Milan (De Sica), 44
mothers and mother figures:
  Catherine's, 115, 116, 120, 134; Charlotte's, 263; Chiquita, 1, 21–30; Eve, 268, 269; Mrs. Gill, 254–55; Maria, 69–78, 97–98; Marjorie, 19, 26, 28–29, 30; Mary, 76, 78, 80; Midge, 200, 203, 204; Mother Chao, 14; Ruth Fowler, 94–100, 103
Mousetrap, the, 219–20, 245, 251, 252, 257–62, 273
Mulholland Dr. (Lynch). See *Mulholland Drive*
Mulholland Drive (Lynch), 159–80
Munro, Alice, 139
Murray, James, 76, 79

Nabokov, Vladimir, 250
Naremore, James, 81
Nights of Cabiria (Fellini), 98
Nocturne in E flat major (Chopin), 25–30

North by Northwest (Hitchcock), 6
Notorious (Hitchcock), 53–54, 174, 269–70

objects, hidden. *See under* hiddenness
objects, significant: bloodstained dress, 252, 255, 256, 257; blue key, 173, 174; bra, 201–3; Carlotta's necklace, 187, 206–9, 212; Carrie's hairpin, 94, 98, 101; coats, 49, 56–57, 59–66, 67; in Frank's bedroom, 100–3; gifts in *An American Tragedy*, 110–14; in *The Heiress*, 107–8, 114–17, 118–40; key, 53–54, 174; ring, 83; whiskey bottle, 49, 53, 56–57, 63, 65–66
Oedipus Rex (Sophocles), 198
Olivier, Laurence, 86, 151, 246
O'Neill, Eugene: *Long Day's Journey into Night*, 151; *Strange Interlude*, 83
On the Waterfront (Kazan), 7–8
Ophelia, 219, 221, 250–51, 272; Eve as 253, 257, 266, 273
Ophüls, Max, *Letter from an Unknown Woman*, 45
Orbison, Roy, "Crying," 178–79
Orpheus, 165n1
Out of the Past (Tourneur), 3–4
"Overcoat, The" (Gogol), 250

Paul, William, 240–41
performance, 5, 11, 35–36, 42, 55; in *Carrie*, 88; in *Double Indemnity*, 61; in *The Eddy Duchin Story*, 1–2, 7, 16–31; in *Hamlet*, 221; in *The Heiress*, 120; John Barrymore's, 141–57; in *Laugh, Clown, Laugh*, 224–32; in *The Lost Weekend*, 46–47, 48–61, 62–64; in *Love in the Afternoon*, 55; in *Lust, Caution*, 13–16; in silent film and the sound era, 42–43; of stage deaths (*see* death); in *Stage Fright*, 246, 248–50, 252–73; in *Mulholland Drive*, 159–80; in *To Be or Not to Be*, 233, 239, 241–42; in *Vertigo*, 78, 181, 185, 190, 192, 193–94, 198, 204. *See also* star acting
play, 23, 55, 76, 118, 128; in *Mulholland Drive*, 164–66, 169, 173; playground, 17–20, 24; in *Vertigo*, 184, 200–5
playacting, 7, 47, 216; in *Dinner at Eight*, 145, 151; in *Hamlet*, 222; in *The Heiress*, 120; in *Midnight*, 148; in *Mulholland Drive*, 176; in *North by Northwest*, 6; in *Stage Fright*, 262, 272
political critique, 7–8
political theatre, 9–16
privacy. *See* aloneness
Prometheus, 218–19, 192
Prometheus Bound (Aeschylus), 218–19
Prophet, The (Gibran), 96–97
Psycho (Hitchcock), 263

rationality: 182, 186, 188, 192, 196–97, 200, 208, 209
reality, 8, 33–38, 215–17, 225; in D. W. Griffith's films, 81, 85, 104; in *The Eddy Duchin Story*, 1–2, 17–19, 23–24, 25, 26, 31; in *Hamlet*, 252; and John Barrymore, 141, 151, 156; in *Laugh, Clown, Laugh*, 225, 229; in *The Lost Weekend*, 64, 66, 69; in *Lust, Caution*, 13, 15, 16; in *Midnight*, 148; in *Mulholland Drive*, 159–80; in *Out of the Past*, 3–4; political, 9; in *Stage Fright*, 248, 250, 253, 265; of suffering, 143, 145; in *To Be or Not to Be*, 232, 235–41, 243, 244; in *Vertigo*, 6, 165, 181–214; in *You Only Live Once*, 5
realism. See *reality*
Rear Window (Hitchcock), 261
reenactment, 58, 71, 165; in *To Be or Not to Be*, 239; in *Vertigo*, 182–84, 193, 197, 206, 210, 212

Renoir, Jean: *La Grande Illusion*, 9–13, 16; *La Règle du Jeu*, 7, 36, 52
Reville, Alma, 254
Richard III (character), 144, 152
Richard III (Shakespeare) (play), 150
Rilke, Maria Rainer, "Sunset," 101–2
"Rime of the Ancient Mariner, The" (Coleridge), 186
Rivette, Jacques, 2
Robertson, John S., *Dr. Jekyll and Mr. Hyde*, 152
Rodgers and Hammerstein, *State Fair*, 161
roles and role-play, 45; in *The Eddy Duchin Story*, 18, 23, 25, 26; in *Hamlet*, 251; in *The Heiress*, 120; in *La Grande Illusion*, 11; in *Laugh, Clown, Laugh*, 229, 231; in *The Lost Weekend*, 59, 60, 66; in *Lust, Caution*, 16; in *Mulholland Drive*, 164, 171, 174, 176, 177, 178; in *North by Northwest*, 6; John Barrymore's, 141–43, 145, 152, 155; in *Stage Fright*, 252–60, 264, 265–67, 269–72; in *To Be or Not to Be*, 232, 238, 241, 242, 243, 247; in *Vertigo*, 181–82, 185, 193–95, 204, 207–8, 210, 211; in *You Only Live Once*, 5
romantic comedy, 57, 60, 63
Rope (Hitchcock), 182, 250
Row, Arthur, 150
Royal Family of Broadway, The (Ferber-Kaufman), 146
Ruefle, Mary, 104

Saint-Saëns, Camille, "Danse Macabre," 36
Sedgwick, Eve Kosofsky, 266
Selznick, David O., 246
Sesonske, Alexander, 11
Shadow of a Doubt (Hitchcock), 263
Shakespeare, William: *Hamlet*, 49, 144, 151, 215–73; *Richard III*, 150

Sidney, George, *The Eddy Duchin Story*, 1–2, 7, 16–31
Siegel, Don, *Invasion of the Body Snatchers*, 8
Sister Carrie (Dreiser), 86, 108
skepticism. *See* rationality
Snow, Edward, 71–72, 73
solitude. *See* aloneness
Sophocles, *Oedipus Rex*, 198
stage deaths. *See* death
Stage Fright (Hitchcock), 182, 217, 245–50, 252–73
stage illusion. *See* illusion
Stahl, John M., *Leave Her to Heaven*, 166
star acting, in *Mulholland Drive*, 159–60, 162, 171–73, 176–77, 180. *See also* Barrymore, John
State Fair (Rodgers and Hammerstein), 161
Stevens, Wallace, "Of Modern Poetry," 181
stillness, 71, 72, 92, 116, 154, 193, 234, 263
Strange Interlude (O'Neill), 83
Strange, Michael, 143
Sturges, Preston, *The Lady Eve*, 185
"Sunset" (Rilke), 101–2

Tale of Two Cities, A (Dickens), 149
theatre. *See* accidents, theatrical; artifice; authenticity; broken theatre; death; illusion; performance; playacting; political theatre; reality; roles and role-play; transformation, theatrical
Thin Man, The series (Van Dyke, Thorpe, and Buzzell), 58
timelessness, 73, 183, 193
To Be or Not to Be (Lubitsch), 7, 217, 232–45, 246
Tourneur, Jacques, *Out of the Past*, 3–4
transformation, theatrical, 5, 9, 41, 45, 98, 119, 231; in *Crime and*

Punishment, 205; in *The Eddy Duchin Story*, 16–17, 20; of John Barrymore, 141–57; in *La Grande Illusion*, 12; in *Mulholland Drive*, 171, 172, 178; of objects, 65, 67, 102, 113, 136; in *Stage Fright*, 266; in *To Be or Not to Be*, 239, 244, 245; in *Vertigo*, 185, 187, 188, 208, 210

Tristan and Iseult in *Love in the Western World*, 209

Tristan und Isolde (Wagner), 55

Trotter, David, 40

Trouble in Paradise (Lubitsch), 240

True Heart Susie (Griffith), 81–82

Turn of the Screw, The (James), 211

Twentieth Century (Hawks), 142–43

Umberto D (De Sica), 69–78, 97–98

Under Capricorn (Hitchcock), 266

Vagabond (Varda), 180n2

Varda, Agnès, *Vagabond*, 180n2

Verdi, Giuseppe, *La Traviata*, 46–63, 66

Vermeer, Johannes, 71–72; *Woman in Blue Reading a Letter*, 73

Vertigo (Hitchcock), 6, 165, 181–214

Vertov, Dziga, *Man with a Movie Camera*, 40

Vidor, King, *The Crowd*, 76–81, 98

Villon, François, 142, 143–44

Washington Square (James), 108, 117

Watts, Naomi, 159, 162, 171–73, 177, 180

Way Down East (Griffith), 82–86

Wayne, John, 177

Wilder, Billy: *The Apartment*, 65; *Double Indemnity*, 61–62; *The Lost Weekend*, 35, 46–47, 48–53, 54–61, 62–67; *Love in the Afternoon*, 55

Woman in Blue Reading a Letter (Vermeer), 73

Wyler, William: *Carrie*, 86–94, 98, 101, 108; *Counsellor at Law*, 148; *The Heiress*, 107–8, 114–17, 118–40; *The Little Foxes*, 139

You Only Live Once (Lang), 4–5

Also in the series

William Rothman, editor, *Cavell on Film*

J. David Slocum, editor, *Rebel Without a Cause*

Joe McElhaney, *The Death of Classical Cinema*

Kirsten Moana Thompson, *Apocalyptic Dread*

Frances Gateward, editor, *Seoul Searching*

Michael Atkinson, editor, *Exile Cinema*

Paul S. Moore, *Now Playing*

Robin L. Murray and Joseph K. Heumann, *Ecology and Popular Film*

William Rothman, editor, *Three Documentary Filmmakers*

Sean Griffin, editor, *Hetero*

Jean-Michel Frodon, editor, *Cinema and the Shoah*

Carolyn Jess-Cooke and Constantine Verevis, editors, *Second Takes*

Matthew Solomon, editor, *Fantastic Voyages of the Cinematic Imagination*

R. Barton Palmer and David Boyd, editors, *Hitchcock at the Source*

William Rothman, *Hitchcock: The Murderous Gaze, Second Edition*

Joanna Hearne, *Native Recognition*

Marc Raymond, *Hollywood's New Yorker*

Steven Rybin and Will Scheibel, editors, *Lonely Places, Dangerous Ground*

Claire Perkins and Constantine Verevis, editors, *B Is for Bad Cinema*

Dominic Lennard, *Bad Seeds and Holy Terrors*

Rosie Thomas, *Bombay before Bollywood*

Scott M. MacDonald, *Binghamton Babylon*

Sudhir Mahadevan, *A Very Old Machine*

David Greven, *Ghost Faces*

James S. Williams, *Encounters with Godard*

William H. Epstein and R. Barton Palmer, editors, *Invented Lives, Imagined Communities*

Lee Carruthers, *Doing Time*

Rebecca Meyers, William Rothman, and Charles Warren, editors, *Looking with Robert Gardner*

Belinda Smaill, *Regarding Life*

Douglas McFarland and Wesley King, editors, *John Huston as Adaptor*
R. Barton Palmer, Homer B. Pettey, and Steven M. Sanders, editors, *Hitchcock's Moral Gaze*
Nenad Jovanovic, *Brechtian Cinemas*
Will Scheibel, *American Stranger*
Amy Rust, *Passionate Detachments*
Steven Rybin, *Gestures of Love*
Seth Friedman, *Are You Watching Closely?*
Roger Rawlings, *Ripping England!*
Michael DeAngelis, *Rx Hollywood*
Ricardo E. Zulueta, *Queer Art Camp Superstar*
John Caruana and Mark Cauchi, editors, *Immanent Frames*
Nathan Holmes, *Welcome to Fear City*
Homer B. Pettey and R. Barton Palmer, editors, *Rule, Britannia!*
Milo Sweedler, *Rumble and Crash*
Ken Windrum, *From El Dorado to Lost Horizons*
Matthew Lau, *Sounds Like Helicopters*
Dominic Lennard, *Brute Force*
William Rothman, *Tuitions and Intuitions*
Michael Hammond, *The Great War in Hollywood Memory, 1918–1939*
Burke Hilsabeck, *The Slapstick Camera*
Niels Niessen, *Miraculous Realism*
Alex Clayton, *Funny How?*
Bill Krohn, *Letters from Hollywood*
Alexia Kannas, *Giallo!*
Homer B. Pettey, editor, *Mind Reeling*
Matthew Leggatt, editor, *Was It Yesterday?*
Merrill Schleier, *Race and the Suburbs in American Film*
Neil Badmington, *Perpetual Movement*

www.ingramcontent.com/pod-product-compliance
Lightning Source LLC
Chambersburg PA
CBHW032044230426
43672CB00009B/1471